The Ethics of Marginality

The Ethics of Marginality

A New Approach to Gay Studies

John Champagne

Foreword by Donald E. Pease

University of Minnesota Press
Minneapolis
London

Published by the University of Minnesota Press
111 Third Avenue South, Suite 290, Minneapolis, MN 55401-2520
Printed in the United States of America on acid-free paper

Library of Congress Cataloging-in-Publication Data

Champagne, John.
    The ethics of marginality / John Champagne ; foreword by Donald
Pease.
        p.   cm.
    Includes bibliographical references and index.
    ISBN 0-8166-2532-8 (hc : alk. paper)
    ISBN 0-8166-2533-6 (pb : alk. paper)
    1. Homosexuality—Philosophy.   2. Marginality, Social.
    3. Homosexuality and art.   4. Homosexuality and literature.
    I. Title.
    HQ76.25.C43   1995
    305.9'0664—dc20   94-33607

The University of Minnesota is an
equal-opportunity educator and employer.

Contents

Foreword

Donald E. Pease

As its title indicates, John Champagne's project entails the deployment of a critical genealogy to dislodge the problematic of marginality from two sites—the carceral society and the field of academic disciplinary formations—wherein, as he argues, it concealed the bankruptcy of the "universalizing" discourse of liberal humanism (including its latest ascetic alibis on both sides of the political correctness controversy). By way of this displacement Champagne successfully realigns the problematic of marginality with poststructuralist themes—Derrida's critique of the subject, Foucault's critique of the carceral society, Spivak's account of textuality—as well as the historically specific dilemmas of the culturally marginalized. Crucial to Champagne's ethical project is his persistent restaging of the contradictions between and among liberalism's multiple subject positions designed to call into crisis liberal humanism as well as its disciplinary legitimations. The discursive practices Champagne calls an "ethics of marginality" should consequently be understood as transgressive of all known modalities of modern subject formation in the name of an impossible freedom from subjectivity as such. By way of this transgressive inflection of his ethics, Champagne rigorously scrutinizes representative uses to which both disciplinary society and academic disciplines have already put the socially marginal (gays, Blacks, subalterns, the underclass), particularly at those junctures wherein what Derrida called a counterlogic of the supplement enables the tactical redeployment of the marginal against the normalizing practices of a disciplinary society as well as otherwise (in)corrigible academic disciplines.

In naming his post-Foucauldian project an "ethics of marginality," Champagne depends strategically on a criticism frequently directed against

Foucault's critical genealogies, namely, that in their implicit appeal to the Enlightenment norms of liberty and social justice whose truth value they discredit, these genealogies are in the service of a performative contradiction.[1] But Champagne's ethics do not entail adherence to any of the remedies Foucault's critics have recommended. In place of a coherent normative framework Champagne refers to supplementarity as the normative agency for his genealogical analyses. As a lack in the norm, this logic "reasons," the marginal other is not simply denied subjectivity, it is structurally necessary for the production of the norm. Holding the place of the lack originally missing from the norm, this supplemental figure at once supplies what was originally missing yet adds something to the dominant term. Foucault's counter to the transcendental subject in the Western philosophical tradition entailed his patient genealogical exposition of the "technologies of self" instituted through industrial, educational, military, juridical, and medical regimens and productive overall of a function of ongoing subjugation. Foucault's account implicates the disciplinary mappings of all the human sciences with programs of governmental rule. Champagne focuses more narrowly on the marginal sites where the subjugation is incomplete. Because Foucault's analytics extend to the discursive as well as nondiscursive practices of subjection, exploitation, and oppression, they have been faulted for the refusal to differentiate behavioral from hermeneutic and critical modes of governmentality. Champagne narrows the dimensions of Foucault's project and practices his ethics at the shifting intersections between social movements and academic disciplines, instituting there a critical practice that explicitly turns the relative excess of the subject position into the opportunity to interrogate academic and social norms:

> What would it mean to work as a critic to understand and counter one's having been produced as a certain kind of (academically privileged) marginalized subject—marginalized in the discontinuous but interwoven registers of sexuality/gender but having a certain (relative) privileged entrée into the discursive practices of the liberal academy, all the same? How might one deploy one's having been produced "socially" as a "transgressive" (marginalized) subject in the service of a transgressive criticism located primarily (although clearly not exclusively) in the university?

Champagne, that is to say, would strategically deploy the position of cultural marginality as an ongoing resistance against the processes of subject formation active in the university's academic disciplines as well as in society's universalist ideologies. Such a positioning of marginality supplants the academy's understanding of matters of race, gender, ethnicity, and locale as homogeneous categories with a shifting dynamic whereby the marginalized articulate for themselves a negotiatory context of power relations.

In his often brilliant stagings of their resistance to all modes of subjection, Champagne depends on a theoretical apparatus supplementally interlinking Foucault's critical genealogies with Spivak's theories of postcoloniality and Gramsci's of hegemony as related problems of subject formation. As each theorist leaves the process of subject transformation she or he initiates open to the threat of recuperation by one of the power/knowledge systems that structure the carceral society, the others, by way of a complex textual interweaving, supply the discursive materials able to resist that outcome. The most significant transactions recur at those nodal points where objects constructed within academic disciplines intersect with the social forces at work within social movements. In negotiating between the conflicting needs of figures within these distinct fields, Champagne focuses on objects—gay male pornography, drag balls, "avant-garde" representations of interracial sexuality—of interest to both constituencies. Since the negotiations at a crossroads between an emergent academic field and highly conflicted social movements would "normally" serve immediately calculable interests, no matter whether disciplinary or political, Champagne establishes a wedge between these artifacts and those uses by describing the outcome as "antiproductive expenditures," constituting losses that cannot accumulate symbolic gains. "Transgressive" in Georges Bataille's sense, this postsocial category includes the filthy, the impoverished, the abject, and all other matters that cannot be reconfigured within an economic system designed to maximize profits.

In thus describing the artifacts under consideration as examples of nonproductive expenditure, a waste of profitable surplus, Champagne intends a terminological defense against their inclusion within either a conceptual system or a program affirmative of identity politics. Subsisting within the domain of "impure" objects heterogeneous to the interests of the culturally dominant, these "transgressive objects" become weirdly appropriate for the attention of marginals who would resist either privilege or subjugation.

But as with the image of the crucifixion, even the most abject of transgressive objects is susceptible to redefinitions in the service of normative interests. To secure his project against such a transfiguration, Champagne provisionally aligns his practice with the rituals and practices of s/m subcultures for ethical exemplars:

> One of the most interesting characteristics of s/m scenes is in fact their deployment of such nonproductive forms of expenditure as ritual and

spectacle. The emphasis on costuming, role playing, and theatricality all attest to the high degree of affect unleashed by s/m. The emphasis on a strict set of rules, as well as Foucault's casting of s/m as a "game," suggests Bataille's contention that what characterizes nonproductive expenditure is its insistence on the possibility of loss. For Bataille, this loss must be as great as possible for the activity to take on its fullest meaning.

Each of the figures involved in intense sadomasochistic transactions opens himself to the limitations activated in the other. By way of this technology, no coherent subject emerges as separable from the related processes of subjection and desubjugation. Insofar as they reveal the interdependency of subjection and subjugation with more inclusive processes of subject formation, s/m technologies become for Champagne (as for Foucault) exemplary ethical practices. As theoretical simulacra of an s/m subculture, Champagne's marginals become transgressive when their ethical practices threaten to become academic norms.

In place of the self-assured academic's disciplinary practices, Champagne struggles to disclose the limits of the literary critic as a knowing subject, but without disavowing thereby his political agency. Although marginal critics, in Champagne's representations of the matter, can never be certain of the grounds for their judgments, their ethics nevertheless require that they ceaselessly replace the desire for a stable normative identity into technologies for endless self-transformation. In deploying the marginal other against the recuperative practices of disciplinary society, Champagne is not intent on "freeing" subjects from their marginality but in specifying a cultural site wherein it might become possible to "liberate" the subject from subjectivity altogether.

By way of this remarkable goal, Champagne associates his ethics of marginality with the sociocultural projects Foucault shared with Maurice Blanchot and Georges Bataille, who understood transgression not merely as the contentious violation of socially constructed and reproducible norms of thought but more radically as an encounter with the point where power ceases, altogether. Although such a dimension would normally be declared radically out of reach, Foucault designates death as one example of this surpassing that cannot be surpassed:

> We should not restrict meaning to the cognitive core that lies at the heart of a knowable object; rather, we should allow it to establish its flux at the limit of words and things, as what is said of a thing (not its attribute or the thing itself) and as something that happens (not its process or state). Death supplies the best example, being both the event of events and meaning in its purest state. Its domain is the anonymous flow of speech; it is that of

which we speak as always past or about to happen and yet it occurs at the extreme point of singularity.[2]

Because Champagne aligns his critical practice with what Foucault has called a technique of "impossible liberty," his project traffics in an untotalizable subject position whose artful incompletion resists interpellation within a range of ideological apparatuses—liberal humanism, literary disciplinarity, academic Marxism—that would have been otherwise accommodating. In contrast to these established practices Champagne's project as a whole should be understood as the elaboration into a technology of the self of the following two statements drawn, respectively, from Foucault's "Final Interview" and "The Subject and Power": "I will call subjectivization the procedure by which one obtains the constitution of a subject, or more precisely of a subjectivity, which is, of course, only one of the given possibilities of organization of self-consciousness"; and, "The political, ethical, social, philosophical problem of our days is not to try to liberate the individual from the state and from the state's institutions but to liberate us both from the state and from the type of individualization which is linked to the state."[3] In constructing this technology, Champagne focuses on academic disciplinary formations as privileged social spaces wherein forms of subjection associated with state power are linked with liberal humanist assumptions and thereafter reproduce state governance as if it were an "exercise of individual freedom," and he proposes ethical transgression as an overdetermined contradiction to these various forms of subjecting.

I have called Champagne's ethical practice "overdetermined" to specify an insistent feature in its otherwise contingent resistances and to indicate the rationale for a project that moves from an (ideological) supplementation of Foucault's refusal of ideology to an affirmation of ideology as a category crucial to his genealogical project. Through a series of "transgressive" readings of the elevation of culturally marginal (gay and lesbian, feminist, African American) critics to the status of privileged "marginals" whose inclusion within the (liberal humanist) academy has only resulted in a reaffirmation of liberalism's power to (re)construct exemplary individuals out of the culturally marginalized, Champagne's eminently readable yet rigorously theorized critiques of the assumptions informing the works of Richard Dyer, bell hooks, Lee Edelman, Thomas Yingling, and Kaja Silverman will as a consequence be readily (if inappropriately) assimilated by the emergent field of gay studies as an enrichment of the dialogical surface on which its discourse exfoliates the logic of disciplinarity. Moreover, Champagne's quite original counterexplanation of gay pornography in general (as a mimic literalization of the phallic lack that reproductive sexuality suppresses), and Marlon Riggs's *Tongues Untied*, Jennie Livingston's *Paris Is*

Burning, and John Greyson's *Urinal* in particular, will result in the (uncritical) addition of these artifacts to that field's canonical objects.

I say inappropriately and uncritically because Champagne has turned to these critics and cultural artifacts not to corroborate an academic field's disciplinary logic, but to expose its complicity with the social logic of liberal inclusion and to activate by way of this remarking of their common boundary an ethics resistant to inscription in either regime and non(re)productive of their norms and practices. In place of associating himself either with these academic fields or with the liberal individualism whose ethics they validate, Champagne critically addresses their latent functions as related processes of subject formation in the service of commodity logic and critically negates both regimes.

Champagne's project, as well as some of the tensions informing it, has been cogently described by Jonathan Dollimore, who is one of Champagne's precursors in the emergent academic field of gay studies that would aspire to appropriate their ethics to its imperatives:

> We know that the centre remains vulnerable to marginality because its identity is partly created and partly defined in opposition (and therefore also at) the margins. But the concept of reverse discourse suggests another dialectic sense that the outsider may be said to be always already inside: a return from demonized other to challenging presence via containment, and one involving a simultaneous, contradictory, yet equally necessary appropriation and negation of those dominant notions of sexual identity and human nature by which it was initially excluded and defined.[4]

I do not cite Dollimore's remarkably similar account of an ethics of marginality simply to indicate its solidarity with Champagne's project but rather as an occasion to consider Champagne's stance on the possibility of a coalition politics. Because Dollimore shares Champagne's ethical attitude, his work raises the question whether resistance at the level of subjectivity can be sutured into resistant, that is, material political practices. In encountering Dollimore's project, however, Champagne does not explicitly address the political prospect of affiliating his project with Dollimore's but chooses instead to criticize the inadequacy of Dollimore's understanding of ideology that is at work in the following passage Champagne quotes from *Sexual Dissidence*:

> Thus the view that homosexuals are naturally inferior to heterosexuals is (in my sense) ideological; the view that homosexuals are equal with heterosexuals, and deserving of equal rights in law is not [ideological],

resting rather on an openly admitted ethical commitment to equality (from which the practice of a materialist/political criticism arises).[5]

Dollimore's ethics of marginality requires that he align his critical practice tactically with the natural discourse of equal rights and because he believes in its political efficacy rather than its truth. That Champagne's ethics requires him to separate from Dollimore's project at this juncture deserves reflection. In his critique of the discourse of equal rights as it pertains to homosexual practices, Dollimore has carefully discriminated his political appropriation of that discourse from an uncritical belief in the ideology of liberal humanism underwriting it. But Champagne ignores Dollimore's strategic distinction. In his reading, Dollimore's ideology enables the return of an undivided subject "capable of knowing his interest adequately and aligning his desires with that interest." In thus disaffiliating his project from a precursor's at the moment when their political interests might productively coalesce into a political demonstration in favor of gays' equal rights, Champagne instead demonstrates his superior knowledge of the ideological as an instance of an unknowable factor rather than (as the term is more usually understood) as a problem of false consciousness.[6] But Champagne does so only after having registered in an aside not nonknowledge but what he definitively does know: "Leaving aside an interrogation of the limits of a liberal humanist discourse of rights," he would still find in Dollimore "a move exactly opposite to the one I suggest throughout this study."

Champagne's resistance to Dollimore intensifies at the site wherein Dollimore's otherwise strictly political agenda endorses a specific academic practice of marginality. In the passage Champagne cites Dollimore has expressed his ethical commitment to altering existing conditions of power, and he has aligned his academic practice with that initiative. In his restaging of this site as an occasion to instruct Dollimore in the correct understanding of ideology, Champagne has not "deployed the other to resist the normalizing practices of disciplinary society" but to assert the superior disciplinary power his knowledge of Foucault, Spivak, and Gramsci secures for him within the emergent field of gay studies.

In spite of his reiteration of the impossibility of normalizing the ethics of marginality, Champagne's critical encounters with other marginal academics nevertheless disclose the presence of a normative code whose ethical mandate was given the name "critical negation" by Paul A. Bové, Champagne's dissertation director and perhaps the academy's most astute reader of Foucault. "Criticism must be negative," Bové observes, "and its negation should be of two sorts: invested with knowledge and the skills to produce more, it should destroy the local discursive and institutional formations of the 'regime of truth.' " In his critical refusal of Dollimore's understanding of ideology, Champagne constructs his ethical practice out of his mentor's imperative but he thereby fails to follow Bové's instructive addendum: "But the negation must have a positive content, it must carry out its destruction with newly produced knowledge directed not only against the centers of the anthropological attitude but with an eye to its utility, to others in one's own locale and elsewhere."[7]

In his efforts to positivize his critical negations, Champagne turns a blind eye to their political utility. His blindness depends on a theoretical apparatus that oscillates between two asymmetrical practices, the ethics of marginality and what he calls transgressive criticism. The second of these practices intervenes at those precise moments at which the first practice threatens to turn the "impure marginal" into a disciplinary exemplar. Champagne names the outcome of this unwanted transformation a "privileged marginal." Unlike the "impure" marginal, this figure does not resist cultural norms, but rearticulates the antiproductive expenditures of the culturally marginalized into a supplemental corroboration of the three operative components of the dominant culture, namely, liberal humanism, universalist ideology, and identity politics. By "wasting" the work of a fellow marginal at the moment it acquires cultural dominance, Champagne intends the substitution of an antiproductive for a utilitarian use. Champagne's ethics of marginality become transgressive, that is to say, when the marginal acquires academic or political privilege.

But this use of the nonuse of what Bataille calls nonproductive expenditure only repeats what Foucault's critics have labeled his performative contradiction at another level of theoretical abstraction. In constructing a theoretical apparatus out of the lack of normative guarantees for his ethics, Champagne successfully refuses subjection within, respectively, the dominant culture, established academic fields, and the realm of identity politics. Champagne's resistance to these interpellations, however, results from the capacity of his theoretical apparatus for the (re)production of a nonproductive expenditure. Champagne discloses the usefulness of this theoretically produced nonuse in his accounts of the liberal humanists' efforts to associate such transgressive objects as gay male pornography, s/m paraphernalia, drag balls, and avant-garde performances, with the ideology of individualism. But in rendering these artifacts unavailable to such efforts at recuperation, Champagne has himself trafficked in the exchange of antiproductive for theoretically and academically productive forces.

A more significant contradiction informs Champagne's identification of gay s/m as an exemplary transgressive practice. When Champagne provisionally situates himself within an s/m gay subculture that he elsewhere refers to as among the most transgressive in the gay movement, he authorizes practices that indirectly reaffirm the violence directed against women in straight male pornography and nonconsensual sex. Champagne's analysis of transgressive practices within the s/m gay subculture focuses on their close entwinement of power and sexuality. As was the case with Foucault, Champagne's understanding of the functional operations of power and sexuality is profoundly genderless. Confining his inquiry to the problematic of subjectivization, Champagne interrogates whether power/sexuality's conjoined transgression of the limits of subjection can free the subject from subjectivity as such. But a troubling political consequence attends Champagne's and Foucault's correlation of this genderless, functional description of s/m practices with their highly gendered concept of the subject, who bears close resemblance to the same adult male that the rape culture presupposes as normative agent.

Champagne struggles to ameliorate this deficiency when he makes explicit reference to Foucault's androcentric refusal to account for female subjects, but then he inexplicably rationalizes this exclusion by arguing for its strategic positioning in Foucault's overall project, namely, cognitively to disturb Western notions of a transcendental, transhistorical consciousness. In providing Foucault's practice of marginalizing women with an epistemological rationale, however, Champagne does not complicate but rather enforces the gender hierarchy at work in the dominant culture.

Given this intermingling of ethical with epistemological operations, Champagne might also fairly be asked why he presupposes the immanence of other marginal figures to his theoretical acts of knowing. In his theoretical introduction, Champagne states flatly his refusal of the epistemological temptation to produce a new categorization of alterity:

> If an oppositional cultural criticism on the order of Cornel West's "new cultural politics of difference" is going to do more than simply replace the bourgeois white male heterosexual sovereign subject with his female, colored, working-class, and/or homosexual counterpart, the epistemological projects of feminism, Black studies, and gay and lesbian studies, for example, must be to contest the terrain on which "truthful" statements might be made and recognized as such.

Insofar as Champagne's choice of adversaries for his oppositional practices always refers him to other marginal academic critics, his ethics of marginality do not disturb but instead reaffirm the power structure discriminating the center from the periphery. He does not deploy the marginal as a resistance against the normal; he reads his fellow marginals as susceptible to the very work of cultural recuperation his project alone can resist. In his determinate negations of their social ontology, Champagne redoubles the marginalization of his academic rivals, and deprives them of their alterity by totally encompassing it within his theoretical apparatus.

As he resistively inhabits the power/knowledge mappings of academics the dominant culture has already marginalized, Champagne only reinforces the disciplinary norms circumscribing the academic field. Moreover, as we have seen, the technology of reading enabled by Champagne's highly sophisticated theoretical apparatus inexorably advances to the detriment of Champagne's competitors in an emergent academic field—Essex Hemphill, bell hooks, Richard Dyer, John Stoltenberg. Champagne's critical interventions reveal in painstaking detail how these critics have rendered the transgressive artifacts whose nonproductivity Champagne values so highly, available to the uses to which liberal humanists would put them: Dyer's effort to read gay male pornography as if it were compatible with the bourgeois values of heterosexual romance; Essex Hemphill's reactionary condemnation of Robert Mapplethorpe's photography as collusive with white racists' representations of Black male bodies; bell hooks's criticism of *Paris Is Burning* as bearing witness to the recapture of Blacks' embodiment within a white cultural imaginary. According to Champagne, each of these projects can be read as having fallen prey to one or another of the epistemological traps he designed his ethical practices to evade.

In recharacterizing their projects as if they were indistinguishable from native informants' reports to literary anthropologists, Champagne effectively denies these critics either of the key social resources—the intertwined capacity to be interpellated ambivalently across multiple subject positions without thereby confirming any single hierarchical order, and the ability to become the subject of the process of critical transformation rather than subjected to any one of the (provisional) knowledges strategically empowering critique—that he had earlier associated with his ethics of marginality. If the repeated outcome of his ethical practices only (re)authorizes the marginality of his fellow critics, it does not oppose but strengthens what Foucault described as the central hegemonic practice of carceral society, namely, its deployment of marginals to supplement the centrality of its (his) own (supramarginal) position.

Given Champagne's use of ethical terms to describe his adaptation of Foucault's critical genealogy, is he not obligated to respond to critics who would understand those terms and Foucault's practices as dependent on sex categories that would position women outside its masculinist autoerotic economy? Such androcentrism is also evident in Champagne's selection of transgressive artifacts to analyze, of Foucault as a precursor, of gay male subcultures as the representative instance of cultural marginality. In aggressively contrasting the exorbitant inutility of his interventions against other proposed categories for resistance, Champagne inadvertently corroborates a superordinate cultural binarism discriminating masculinist from effeminate knowledge/power constellations. As he supplements their projects with the theoretical resources necessary to render their by now useful abjection useless once again, Champagne adequates their incomplete critical negation to the academic site where resistance is totalized. If that site is likewise inhabited by other Others, however, why does Champagne not, as it were, refind the limit of his transgressive criticism in the limits of their transgressions? Why, given his notion of marginality, does he not understand his own ethical practices as already inhabited by the marginality of Others rather than refinding the extensibility of his own practice by way of a circumscription of theirs?

In what is perhaps the most telling scenario of a troubling ethical response, Champagne frames his criticism of bell hooks's critique of *Paris Is Burning* by way of an autobiographical account of a departmental chair's mistaking him for a woman at a departmental meeting. Champagne's representation of this scene of professional misrecognition constitutes the third occasion—the two others concerned his participation in a hiring interview and in a gay studies conference—wherein he inscribed himself within existing academic sites. But neither of the other scenes elicited from Champagne a comparably intense reaction. "Of course," Champagne explains apropos this misidentification of his gender, "I reassure myself that it is highly unlikely that this man could have mistaken someone my age, with my thinning hair, my razor stubble, and my recently gym-tailored swimmer's build for a woman." Following this careful semiotic differentiation of the gender markings inscribed on his body from those culturally understood to encode the category "woman," however, Champagne does not understand himself as being obligated (as he had when preoccupied with the social categories of class and race) to propose a critical genealogy of the category "woman." Instead of inquiring what relations of domination and exclusion were inadvertently sustained by the chair's inappropriate attribution of this category to his identity, Champagne simply records as his affective response to this misidentification the following testimony to his internalization of the culture's misogyny: "But a small enough doubt remains to act as a reminder of how absolutely terrifying and shameful it is in this culture to be a man mistaken for a woman." When he reinscribes this autobiographical narrative into the terms of his disagreement with bell hooks over the culture significance of *Paris Is Burning*, Champagne reaffirms the racism and misogyny hooks reads as everywhere evident in the film:

> In its conflation of effeminacy and drag, it assumes that gay men willfully assume the feminine; it ignores the way gay men often find themselves positioned within the feminine against their will and even in spite of their

own expressed wishes, and it can't account for the feelings of shame I
described at the beginning of this chapter that occur when one is, against
all acts of agency, still mistaken for, or positioned as, feminine. For many
gay men, being called effeminate is a drag, and effeminacy is not something
one might court comfortably.

The transgressive practice informing this quotation turns on Champagne's disagreement with bell hooks, a Black feminist critic who had
argued that Jennie Livingston's representation of gay Black males' exaggerated and spectacular efforts to impersonate displays of white femininity sub-
tly enforced the cultural power of the white woman who directed the film.
The drag balls comprising the film's subject demonstrated, according to
hooks, a masculinist power to exchange femininity as a masculine privilege
and showed further that such an expropriation, insofar as it was compelled
to pass through Black males' impersonation of the "white" feminine, doubly confirmed "whiteness" as an unmarked cultural universal. In his critical
reaction to this reading, Champagne accuses hooks of a failure to recognize
the "ambivalence" in drag—how it traffics all at once in the degradation as
well as the celebration of woman. But the "celebration" of woman registered in Champagne's account of the drag ball does not square either with
Champagne's earlier admission that he found misrepresentation as a woman
"absolutely terrifying" or with his sense that in general gay men found "being called effeminate a drag" (rather than a ball). The absence of any ambivalence in Champagne's reaction to effeminization casts doubt on his
claim that a male drag queen's extravagant acting out of culturally permit-
ted cross-gender displays of femininity draws on emotional resources that
are different from the shame and terror to which Champagne already at-
tested. Whether the male drag ball instantiates a transgressive object
whereby Champagne would work through the limitations of hooks's
"monolithic" subject position or whether it more tellingly reactivates the
abjection he had experienced after being named a woman does perhaps re-
instate an ambivalence, but in a register other than the epistemological.

Having all too briefly indicated what I take to be Champagne's remarkable critical accomplishment and expressed a very few reservations, I
shall conclude with a brief critical survey of the specific modes of critical
resistance Champagne recommends. In arguing that the "logic of the supplement" inherent to the socially marginalized represents a space (that he proceeds to occupy) wherein one might "free the subject from subjection,"
Champagne might himself be accused not of transgressing but of uncritically reenacting disciplinary society's modus operandi. In the use to which it
puts this logic, disciplinary society turns its "other" into a lack in the normal, thereby (as Derrida has persuasively demonstrated) both adding some-

thing to and supplying what was (originally) missing from its dominant norm. Because the culturally marginalized unsettle the self-givenness of cultural norms and make visible the otherwise invisible (its coercive[ly] ideological) forces instantiating them, Champagne construes their anormativity as constitutive of ethically transgressive spaces, and he deploys the culturally marginal as if evocative of the (ethical) imperativity of (critical) resistance. Having defined the cultural marginalized as a (socio)logical alternative to the (liberal) desire to universalize, Champagne simply confuses their asymmetry to the liberal humanist project with the critical resistance out of which he has constructed a technology of self. As a result of this conflation of critical resistance and (as) cultural marginality, Champagne turns his critiques of the reading practices (and horizon of expectations) out of which he has constructed his academic identity into (at another register of density) the equivalent of the (socially) Other. At this critical juncture, however, the culturally marginalized tend to disappear into the critical resistance whereby Champagne (self-consciously) refuses interpellation (or suturing) within any academic disciplinary formation. His ethical project becomes more or less interchangeable with the imperatives of a disciplinary society.

A strategic slippage from (social) resistance by way of the (cultural) Other to critical resistance as the (socially inappropriable) Other induces an identification between the ethics of transgression and an ethics of deconstructive reading that Champagne everywhere else disavows. In order to discriminate his ethics of transgression from academic deconstruction, Champagne is obligated to elaborate on the distinction between the culturally marginalized and the (already academically privileged) marginal critics (Dyer, hooks, Edelman, Silverman) he has subjected to his ethics of marginality. It is not enough simply to assert that each of these critics has already disavowed cultural marginality by misrecognizing it either as universal humanism or as an already read disciplinary code. The differences in the subject positions of these critics who (like Champagne in his self-representation) are at once culturally marginal and empowered (by liberalism) to put that alterity to use against liberal humanist assumptions should be more carefully discriminated than Champagne's somewhat impatient reading (that renders each one all too legible either as a good liberal humanist or as already fully sutured in an academic discipline) permits. If Champagne wants to be "true" to his transgressive project of turning the "other" into a force of resistance able to free the subject from subjection, he should have construed Silverman, Edelman, Dyer, and Dollimore either as marginal to or as *incompletely* interpellated within an academic discipline. These practitioners of gay studies cannot in fact be described accurately as serving a reading code that is separable from their ongoing contestation of humanist assumptions. If he desired political rather than academic efficacy for his transgressive practice, why did Champagne not deploy already articulated critiques of Yingling, Edelman, and others to effect a redoubled resistance to already established disciplinary subject positions as well as to what remains insufficiently resistant in this emergent field?

Had Champagne read "queer theorists" against the grain of both their critics and their criticisms, he could have retrieved as a transgressive self-division, the culturally marginal figure who resists the *social logic of the supplement* at work in the discursive formation of the academic field. Had he then discriminated the difference between the (socially marginal) "queer" and the (privileged marginal) academic queer theorist, he could have activated a marginal figure from within his own discourse who resisted both (neither) social normalization and queer theorization.

Finally, without (and perhaps even with) such a counterlogic of the supplement, Champagne's argument (as did Foucault's) invites confusion with the "negative freedom" underwriting certain versions of liberalism. To differentiate this version of the sovereign subject from what he means by resistance without a subject, it is not enough for Champagne to assert that "the name ideology might in fact hold the place of those materials factors that even the ethical critic cannot know, given the limits of subjectivity." In such a deployment, "ideology" does not, as Champagne would have it, name nonknowledge as the exorbitant release from epistemic constraints, but performs the ideological disavowal of critical negation's power as a disciplinary formation for the emergent academic field of Foucault studies. This unworked-through ideology of disciplinary formation instantiates a critical difference between transgressive ethics as a social and transgressive ethics as an academic practice, and it thereby demarcates the impossible limit between social subjugation and (academically) subjugated knowledges. Champagne might take up this transgressive figure within his text, discriminate it from what Foucault means by transgression,[8] and deploy it as a lever for subsequent refigurations of his ethics of marginality.

Acknowledgments

This book could not have been written without the aid of a number of people; space constraints allow me to thank only some of them by name. The manuscript began as a doctoral dissertation at the University of Pittsburgh. My committee members offered extensive and welcomely contentious commentary on the project throughout the various stages of its writing. My director, Paul Bové, provided extremely detailed written feedback on the first draft, and was always available for both intellectual guidance and moral support. I thank him for being my teacher. Throughout the past five years of our friendship, Marcia Landy has offered me important ways of reconsidering my thinking. The other members of my committee—Danae Clark, Lucy Fischer, and Dana Polan—all proved to be careful and generous readers. Several of my former colleagues at the University of Pittsburgh, including Richard E. Miller, Jan Beatty, Rashmi Bhatnagar, Elayne Tobin, Eric O. Clarke, and Donald Freeman, contributed in a variety of ways to this project, discussing some of the ideas presented in these chapters, and offering both friendship and candid criticism. Roberta Salper at Penn State, The Behrend College, offered intelligent and spirited comments on a final draft of the manuscript.

The University of Minnesota Press provided generous and engaged readers' reports from two anonymous readers and Donald Pease. I thank all three for the seriousness with which they treated the initial manuscript, and I am grateful to Pease for writing the foreword. The readers' comments have shaped the final project in important ways. Throughout the revision of the manuscript for publication, I have greatly appreciated the intelligence, wit, and patience of my editor, Janaki Bakhle.

Acknowledgments

For the past six years, Barbara McCarthy has remained an astute critic and fiercely loyal friend. My parents, Jack and Marguerite, and my brothers and sisters, Salvatore, Christopher, Maria, Jacquelyn, and Rosanne, offered much love and unqualified support. Finally, throughout these past two years of preparation in particular, Conrad Carioto responded to my many travails with patience, love, and a sense of humor. I thank him for trying to ensure that I never took myself too seriously.

Introduction

We are never trapped by power: we can always modify its grip in determinate conditions and according to a precise strategy.

Michel Foucault[1]

In the months immediately following the April 1993 March on Washington, local and national media—gay and straight—featured a flurry of stories on the question of increased political rights for sexual/gender minorities. Over two days in June, two separate editorials in the *Pittsburgh Post Gazette* by avowed conservatives called for gay rights. James P. Pinkerton, in "Gays on the Right: Proposing a Marriage between Unlikely Allies," urges conservatives to support the cause of gay marriages. He suggests that in light of a recent ruling by the Hawaii Supreme Court that marriage is a right for same-sex couples, too, conservatives have a choice: "Having fought the leftist politics of gay liberation, do they now fight the conservative instinct to form families? The Right may choose to act as if all gays belong to Queer Nation. But if they do, they will alienate the vast majority of gays who seek to join the mainstream."[2]

Apparently assuming that the will of the "vast majority" of gays is self-evident (or at least as self-evident as the "instinct" to form families), Pinkerton approvingly cites (gay) conservative editor Andrew Sullivan's view that gay marriages would "foster social cohesion, emotional security, and economic prudence," as well as George Gilder's contention that men require the civilizing influence of marriage. In terms reminiscent of the nineteenth century, Gilder argues that marriage (assisted, no doubt, by the "nesting instincts" of women) serves to tame the male, "converting barbarians into useful citizens." Although Pinkerton admits that Gilder is talking about heterosexuals, "the same logic applies to everyone."

To support his conclusion, Pinkerton marshals the familiar biology-is-destiny argument (again, a legacy of the nineteenth century), an argument recently revitalized by many gays and lesbians themselves. Pinkerton suggests that since "homosexuals are born that way" it is "counterproductive to make them fugitives inside the legal system."[3] Ultimately, however, it is a kind of pragmatism that leads Pinkerton to call for gay marriages. Claiming to follow the example of Abraham Lincoln, Pinkerton suggests that "You conquer your political opponents by making them your friends."

The very next day, the *Post Gazette* ran an editorial by former Senator Barry Goldwater opposing the Pentagon's ban on gays in the military. According to Goldwater, "No American able to serve should be allowed, much less given an excuse, not to serve his or her country."[4] Goldwater appears here to be following the lead of *The Advocate*, a national gay magazine, whose cover stories have recently been taken over by the theme of gays in the military. Rarely, if ever, does any position questioning the continued investment by queer activists in the gays-in-the-military agenda appear in the pages of *The Advocate*. In fact, Goldwater himself showed up prominently in a recent issue. What are we to make of a political moment in which conservatives benevolently extend to gays/lesbians/bisexuals/queers/et al., in the newspaper editorials of middle America, no less, the "benefits" of a normalized subjectivity characterized by its fitness for military duty and its eagerness to embrace the "conservative" institution of marriage?

Just a few weeks after Goldwater's editorial appeared in the Pittsburgh newspaper, queer activists in Chicago distributed, at the 1993 Chicago Gay, Lesbian, and Bisexual Rights Parade, a broadside entitled "Why I Hated the March on Washington." According to the broadside, published by QUASH (Queers United Against Straight-acting Homosexuals), the march was virtually taken over by gays-in-the-military concerns, so that "the overwhelming sentiment of the day was that we are like everyone else." In several brief articles, the broadside provides a scathing critique of what it terms "assimilationist" tendencies in the contemporary queer activist movement. "Why does the fucking establishment *New York Times* challenge the desire to assimilate but our so-called gay leadership doesn't?" the broadside angrily questions. "Fuck the military," it advocates. "Fight for queer teachers and child care workers. Fight AIDS. Fuck the heterosexual, nuclear family." QUASH thus proposes a response to the "problem" of cultural marginality that is opposed, point by point, to the one offered by the likes of Pinkerton and Goldwater. Embracing the anormativity of "queer" sexuality, QUASH rejects the "conservative" effort to bring the culturally abnormal into the mainstream. How are we to understand the enabling epistemological con-

ditions of these conflicting arguments? If the efforts of Goldwater and Pinkerton and those of QUASH represent two opposing kinds of "practice" vis-
à-vis the problem of cultural marginality, what "theory" might render such
practices intelligible?

This study situates itself at the intersection of English, cultural studies,
film studies, and gay and lesbian studies. Reading the work of a number of
scholars as well as several recent films, I will argue that a text-based criticism interested in questions of marginality must continue to be animated by
theory. At a moment in the history of the discipline of English when the field
is fraught with both celebrations and lamentations concerning the "death"
of theory, I will suggest the continuing importance of such poststructuralist
themes as the critique of the subject, Michel Foucault's critique of disciplinarity and disciplinary society, and deconstructive understandings of textuality and causality. I will be particularly concerned with arguing the importance of these poststructuralist themes for a criticism aligned and affiliated
with the culturally marginalized. This claim will be argued tactically
through a series of "essays," or attempts to think through the usefulness of
theory for the Other. I am thus less interested in arguing generally for the
efficacy of theory, and more concerned with testing out what kind of work
theory can do when brought into strategic contact with a criticism affiliated
with the Other.[5]

Criticism here will loosely designate the production of "oppositional"
explanations of texts. The contours of that opposition can be defined only
in the specific instances of analysis; in broad and general terms, however,
this criticism will seek to oppose the fixing, or nonreversibility, of relations
of power. I will employ the term *explanations* rather than *interpretations* as
a way of emphasizing, among other things, the ways in which every critical
exegesis is necessarily made possible by a desire to make a text mean in particular ways and for specific, if often largely unspecified, ends. Before I begin this project, however, I would like to sketch broadly some of the concerns that animate it. Specifically, I want to locate this study in terms of
questions of marginality, subjectivity, and criticism.

I assume that in the modern period, in the West, culturally marginalized peoples are not simply denied subjectivity. They are, rather, granted a
certain (limited) and specific subjectivity that renders them useful by giving
them a position in relation to a dominant culture. Specifically, in ways that
I shall show, the Other functions as an oppositional term for the formation
of a normalized subjectivity. The relationship between normal and Other
cannot, however, be one of *absolute* opposition, for such an opposition
would render the Other "beyond" use, as it were: too abject, too radically
heterogeneous to be set in a relation—even a relation of opposition—to the
normal. My assumption here is that no relation whatsoever would be pos-

sible between margin and center if the margin did not hold something of the center, and vice versa. In other words, in order to function as its opposite, the Other must represent what is lacking in the normal, a lack that, paradoxically, must have been present, at the outset, in the normal. Deconstruction has referred to this paradox as the logic of the supplement, a logic that insists that in any relation of hierarchical opposition the inferior term supplies a lack that supplements—both adds something to, and supplies what was "originally" missing from—the dominant term.[6]

A number of different critical vocabularies have attempted to describe this situation in which the Other is posited in a certain limited and contained relationship of opposition to the dominant, center, or normal. For example, Georges Bataille has suggested that what he terms homogeneous capitalist culture does not simply banish heterogeneous, "filthy" elements but attempts to make a contained use of such elements in their "elevated" forms, such as the (sacred) body of the crucified Christ. Similarly, a psychoanalytically inflected feminist scholarship has emphasized the way that patriarchal phallocentric culture necessarily *depends* on the figure of the "castrated" woman, the figuration of the female body as lack coming to re-present the absence that signification attempts to fill. Foucault's account of transgression requires us to be attentive to the ways in which transgression is always necessarily a testing as well as a reinscription of the limit as limit. Finally, Immanuel Wallerstein has suggested that racism as an ideology does not merely banish people of color from the flow of goods, capital, and labor power that characterizes historical capitalism, but rather seeks to socialize certain peoples into their "proper" (inferior) and useful place within the work force. All of these theoretical formulations suggest that the Other is not posited in a relation of absolute alterity to the center but rather is usefully maintained in a certain place of opposition on which the dominant depends.

Recent text-based criticism affiliated with the Other has pursued at least two different paths, paths that, as the logic of the supplement might suggest, are not absolutely opposed, but are necessarily contingent upon one another. One strand of cultural criticism has attempted to grant the Other a fuller subjectivity through the deployment of what Wallerstein has characterized as the ideology of universalism. Such an ideology attempts to remake the Other in the image of the dominant or center through an appeal to a shared humanity, shored up through such fictions as scientific progress and the family of man. Throughout this study, I will characterize this as the liberal humanist response to the problem of cultural marginality. Such examples of this liberal critical response might include recent attempts to expand the humanist canon to include works by women, people of color, and gays and lesbians; and criticism that sometimes privileges recent political struggles around questions of identity and at other times privileges notions of globality and multiculturalism that celebrate cultural diversity by suggesting the intrinsic value of all human cultural production.

Alongside this response, however, another has occurred, a certain other critical response to the Other. This response might broadly be described as a valorization or privileging of the marginality of the Other, a valorization that does not seek to extend a greater subjectivity to the Other, but attempts to make a resistant and transgressive use of the very lack in and through which the Other is constituted. Bataille, for example, writing of the value of the filthy, suggests that historical forms of heterogeneity might act as models for present-day forms of expenditure that attempt to thwart the modesty of constrained capitalist consumption.[7] Feminism, in its Lacanian guise, has attempted to deploy the concept of castration "positively," suggesting, for example, that meaning is a fiction and identity impossible. These two critical interventions do not focus on the value of a (homogeneous) (patriarchal-phallocentric) subjectivity, but instead stress its constraints and failures.

The project of Michel Foucault, particularly the work from *Discipline and Punish* on, is of particular significance here. Foucault's work has argued that the production of modern subjects has involved a certain disciplining of the body, an attempt by institutions such as the church, the military, and the school to render the body "docile," cooperative, useful for, among other things, a continued investment of the body by power. In other words, Foucault has often emphasized that the production of modern disciplinary subjects has historically required practices of subjection and subjugation. Through such anonymous practices as the pedagogical examination, and through the mechanisms of continued surveillance on which such practices depend, disciplinary society deploys power "economically," that is, with reference to a normalized subjectivity to which the subject "naturally" accedes. Foucault's understanding of power, however, also stresses the possibilities of resisting such disciplining, and of saying no to the forms of power allied with the production of subjectivity. According to the implications of Foucault's theory, then, one cannot *not* be a subject. One can, however, given the play of power and resistance, resist the continuing practices of subject formation and attempt to discover ways of being that might thwart and transgress such practices.[8] Concerning the question of cultural marginality in particular, Foucault's project thus suggests not that the Other ought to be "freed" as subjects from its marginalized place, but that the Other represents a location from which it might be possible to work strategically towards a "freeing" of the subject from subjectivity.

This present study is a continuation and intervention in this second response to the problem of cultural marginality. It will argue that the Other embodies a certain resistance to the normal, and that criticism affiliated with the Other might work to render such a resistance ethically and politically useful. To this end, I will call for what I will provisionally and strategically name an ethical criticism, a criticism ethically committed to altering the existing relations of power so that they might become more fluid, more easily reversible. Broadly speaking, such an ethical criticism would attempt to make use of the "impure" position of the culturally marginalized, deploying the Other "against" the normalizing practices of disciplinary society. This criticism is "transgressive" in that it works towards a rendering of new reciprocal relations within power, while simultaneously attempting to disclose some of the limits of such a project. Thus, the emphasis throughout is on questions of strategy and tactics. I will largely be concerned here with those forms of power that subject and subjugate through the practices of subject formation, but I will also at times take up the question of other forms of power, if only to insist, after Foucault, that power pursues a variety of strategies and makes possible a number of resistances.

Some readers may be surprised at my deployment of "ethics," given its current cultural currency among certain figures on the Right such as Allan Bloom and E. D. Hirsch. Of course, the Right does not have a monopoly on the use of the term. Gramsci used it in his *Prison Notebooks*, as do a number of leftist critics working in cultural studies today.[9] Because "ethical criticism" is chiefly a provisional naming of the critical practice that this study essays to elaborate in its unfolding, I will not linger extensively on the history of the term. I would, however, initially differentiate my deployment of ethics from at least one on the Right. Hirsch has offered the following understanding of the ethics of the critic:

> Let me state what I consider to be a fundamental ethical maxim for
> interpretation, a maxim that claims no privileged sanction from
> metaphysics or analysis, but only from general ethical tenets, generally
> shared. *Unless there is a powerful overriding value in disregarding an
> author's intentions (i.e., original meaning), we who interpret as a vocation
> should not disregard it.* . . . When we simply use an author's words for our
> own purposes without respecting his intention, we transgress what Charles
> Stevenson in another context called "the ethics of language," just as we
> transgress ethical norms when we use another person merely for our own
> ends.[10]

A commitment to the poststructuralist critique of the intending author as subject renders Hirsch's formulation highly problematic. One need not be a full-fledged deconstructionist—if in fact there is such a thing—to wonder how the author's intentions manage to override what we might inadequately name as the rhetorical or figurative qualities of language.[11] We might also note how easily Hirsch equates authorial intention with "original meaning," parenthetically substituting one for the other. Such a sleight of hand alerts us, paradoxically, to the possibility that the two phrases might in fact not be commensurable. Hirsch's analysis thus "exposes" the very conditions of possibility it presumably seeks to hold in abeyance. Like the figure of the hysteric, it confesses what it goes to great pains to deny. This gesture is repeated in Hirsch's attempt to affix the meaning of "meaning" by qualifying it with the term "original": such an attempt necessarily suggests that there might be some meaning that is not original. What most concerns me here, however, is Hirsch's worry that we not use either language or a person *merely* for our own ends. Such a formulation depends on an account of power that I explicitly reject here, one that posits the possibility of an irreversible situation in which one person "holds," in some absolute sense, the power that another necessarily lacks. As I will suggest in the following chapter, such an account of power might be considered more fruitfully as either slavery or a state of domination. In the context of Hirsch's argument, this formulation of power assumes, among other things, that the interpreter has absolute control over both his own critical language and the language of the author whose text his task it is to explicate.[12] What Hirsch considers to be "unethical" I would instead assert to be virtually impossible—thus suggesting that an ethical criticism must necessarily involve something other than a humanist commitment not to use a person or text merely for the critic's own ends.[13]

Raziel Abelson, in *The Encyclopedia of Philosophy*, states that the term *ethics* is used throughout the history of philosophy in three different, though not unrelated, ways: it signifies "(1) a general pattern or 'way of life,' (2) a set of rules of conduct or 'moral code,' and (3) inquiry *about* ways of life and rules of conduct."[14] Throughout this study, I will be most concerned with the first definition of ethics. My use of the term *ethics* is inspired by the later work of Foucault, particularly the work following the first volume of *The History of Sexuality*. For Foucault, *ethics* refers not to morality but to "the care of the self."[15] This care of the self, a theme throughout Foucault's later work, represents the attempt by the (subjugated) subject to work within cultural forms of subject production, countering the practices of modern disciplinary subject formation through what Foucault terms practices of self. These practices of self are not invented by the subject. Rather, "They are patterns that he finds in his culture and which are proposed, suggested and imposed on him by his culture, his society and his social group."[16] Foucault suggests that such practices ought to move toward freedom, which Foucault suggests, after the Greeks, is an ethical practice of self-government. (We might, in Bataille's terms, cast this freedom as the ethical attempt by the self to preserve that small amount of productive expenditure required for the continued maintenance of human culture.)

The ethical represents for Foucault "the labor of self on self," the work that one does on the self to attain a certain measure of freedom—freedom from one's self and one's appetites.[17] According to Foucault, *ethics* designates "the elaboration of a form of relation to self that enables an individual to fashion himself into a subject of ethical conduct."[18] But such an ethos also implies a certain relationship to others, to the extent that care of the self necessitates behaving correctly towards others and occupying a place in a community. It suggests the need to elaborate and inhabit a means of right conduct that might hold a check on the desire to exercise an unreasonable power over others.

An ethical criticism would thus be a practice of criticism that attempted to resist, among other things, the ongoing processes of subject formation in order to court what we might term, after Foucault and Bataille, the radical heterogeneity of nonproductive expenditure in the name of an ethical commitment to freedom, a freedom that worked toward the forging of new reciprocal relations within power. This ethical criticism would concurrently attempt to resist what we might term, after Wallerstein, capitalism's deployment of a universalist subject in the service of a global homogeneity. Such a criticism would attempt to make use of the "impure" position of the culturally marginalized, deploying the Other against both the normalizing practices of modern disciplinary society and the ideology of a universalism that renders subjects useful for capitalist production and consumption.

In this study, this ethical criticism will be characterized by a number of different critical practices. As someone trained in the disciplines of English and film studies, I will attempt to use my (disciplinary) training as a reader of texts in order to argue for the Other as transgressive. This will lead me not only to read and valorize a number of "marginalized" cultural practices such as pornography and avant-garde film, but also to critique what I will characterize as certain liberal responses to such practices. I will thus be taking issue with a number of critics such as Richard Dyer, bell hooks, and Jeffrey Weeks, for example, critics sympathetic to questions of cultural difference whom I am obliged to read as perhaps inattentive to some of the perils of the liberal desire to grant to the Other a sovereign subjectivity. I will go to some lengths to demonstrate that a certain unwillingness to think through some of the limits of the liberal position necessarily produces in these critics' work certain effects that seem at odds with their stated political interests.

I would unsystematically name my critique as a kind of close reading that takes as its object both a handful of films and a variety of other close readings, while simultaneously working to disclose some of the conditions of possibility of its own critical operations. In other words, I am attempting to use close reading "against" itself, to offer up close readings while continuing to draw attention to their limits. My critique is perhaps "deconstructive" in the sense of attempting to interrupt not only the critical explanations it interrogates but its own production of explanations as well. To state that this interruption of my own critical production is necessarily inadequate is not to apologize but to insist on, and draw attention to, the limits of my own subjectivity and disciplinary situatedness. It is to remind the reader of the necessary congruence of transgression to its limit. It is to signal to the reader the limits of my posited explanation, while still continuing to explain.[19]

How might such a strategy of critical reading operate? Crucial to an articulation of one's own positionings as a reader is an interrogation of the disciplinary interests that move through one's posited explanations of a text. As Foucault has suggested, disciplines organize rules for the formation of statements. They act as a kind of repository for such rules. One of the functions of the discipline is thus to make possible a permanent reactivation of the rules, so that statements might be formulated ad infinitum.[20] This is especially the case with academic disciplines, which seek to police the boundaries of what constitute legitimate and illegitimate readings of texts by instantiating and transmitting "proper" methods of reading. Vital, then, to an understanding of one's own (academic) disciplinary practices is an interrogation of the rules and procedures whereby textual meaning is produced.

The historical positioning of the reader as a subject effect in excess of an academic discipline must also be investigated. This study might involve utilizing the determinants necessarily inadequately named as race, ethnicity, class, gender, and sexuality, not merely in an effort to specify historically and culturally one's practices of reading but also to bring to crisis the unitary status granted to these determinants. For example, it is possible to argue how something like "homosexuality" as a discursive practice might make possible particular readings of a text, while at the same time arguing the limits of such a determinant, in terms both of what it makes available in a text and of what it might designate.[21] It is possible to begin to articulate how a culturally contested weave of discourses named "homosexuality" might position a subject-effect of such discourses to weave itself into a text through something like a "homosexual" reading. But such an articulation does not require that we insist that something called "homosexuality" adequately names the heterogeneous and historically contingent weavings of subject-effects in any particular historical instantiation of what appears to operate as a subject, nor does it require that we have recourse to something like a "real" homosexual, nor that we argue that the significance of a text is exhausted in and through this "homosexual" reading.

Throughout what follows, I will be attempting to move in these two directions at once, exploring questions of both academic disciplinarity and modern subject formation as I read a variety of critical and filmic texts. To call such a practice of criticism ethical is to argue that this criticism will allow me to elaborate a practice of critical self-conduct moving in the direction of a transgressive freedom.[22] As Foucault suggests, "Ethos was the deportment and the way to behave. It was the subject's mode of being and a certain manner of acting visible to others."[23] My hope here is that, given poststructuralism's insistent warning concerning the status of the subject, the constraints of disciplinary society, and the perils of causal thinking, ethical criticism might suggest how Foucault's theme of the care of the self might operate in a criticism that specifically takes up questions of cultural marginalization and othering. What would it mean to work as a critic to understand and counter one's having been produced as a certain kind of (academically privileged) marginalized subject—marginalized in the discontinuous but interwoven registers of sexuality/gender, but having a certain (relative) privileged entrée into the discursive practices of the liberal academy, all the same? How might one deploy one's having been produced "socially" as a "transgressive" (marginalized) subject in the service of a transgressive criticism located primarily (although clearly not exclusively) in the university? For the purposes of this present argument, I will name that critical work the ethics of marginality. Such work, while acknowledging the impossible limit between social subjugation and (academically) subjugated knowledges, still attempts to use the former as a critical lever into the latter. It construes the anormativity of the culturally marginalized as suggesting the epistemological conditions of possibility for the forging of certain (critically) transgressive technologies of the self. Throughout this book, I will thus attempt to use my own (subjected and subjugated) subject-position as critic, while simultaneously insisting that such a use is always necessarily provisional, tentative, and likely to produce certain effects beyond the knowledge and control of the critic as subject—but is equally also inescapable. My intentions in offering such an insistence, so far as I am capable of knowing them, are not to disavow my offered textual explanations, but to attempt to disclose as adequately as I am able some of their founding fictions.

Additionally, this ethical criticism will gesture toward questions of the political. Throughout this study, I stress my reluctance to theorize the political, given both the limits of my own training as primarily a reader of literary and filmic texts, as well as the widespread tendency in academic criticism today to equate political action with the production of new and improved "resistant" readings of canonical texts, be those readings queer, feminist, whatever.[24] I do this not to (re)establish a binary division between criticism and the political, but to defer strategically to engage in a certain kind of academic posturing that allows one to draw too simple an equation between criticism and political action. By focusing on the perhaps modest question of the practice of the critic, I am also attempting to hold in check the desire to privilege my own craft as the most politically efficacious and effective.[25]

At the same time, however, the texts I will be discussing will force me to begin to think through some of the relationships between subjectivity and politics. Specifically, I will take issue with those theorizations of the political that assume, often with recourse to the concept of identity, that resistance on the level of subjectivity transfers seamlessly to political resistance. In other words, I will suggest that, in theorizing the relationship between individual acts of resistance on the level of subjectivity and acts of political resistance, identity politics has often posited the category of identity as the means whereby the "resisting" subject is sutured into "resistant" material political practices. Noting (admittedly, only briefly) the recent "failure" of identity in certain incarnations of gay and lesbian politics, I tentatively suggest that ethics provides a more efficacious means whereby to think the link between resistance to the forms of power that produce the subject and resistance to forms of political domination. This move leads me to examine the work of Antonio Gramsci around the question of "common sense" and to theorize the ways in which "common sense" might provide the starting point for an elaboration of a politics rooted in ethics.

What I have referred to above as the logic of the supplement reminds us that the two strains of cultural criticism engaged in this study—the "liberal" criticism that seeks to extend to the Other a greater subjectivity, and the "ethical" criticism that attempts to deploy the Other towards a resistance to subjectivity—are necessarily contaminated by one another. My own attempts to forge here a transgressive criticism that resists liberal inclusiveness is thus dependent on, and implicated in, that very inclusiveness that such a criticism attempts to contest. This is, after all, an "academic" study of otherness that is necessarily made possible by recent attempts by the liberal academy to cope with questions of cultural marginality. To put this another way, Bataille has suggested that the line between a "useless" and "useful" heterogeneity is easily crossed, so that formerly "filthy" cultural forms might be "elevated" in the service of homogeneous capitalist culture. This proposition in turn suggests that an ethical criticism affiliated with the Other must be aware of how, in valorizing the culturally marginalized at all, it perhaps renders the Other capable of recuperation by a liberal humanist criticism. As Foucault might have it, the effects and countereffects of power and resistance necessitate that a transgressive critical resistance to subjectivity in the form of an ethical criticism will (necessarily) produce certain conditions of resistance to that resistance. Power will meet resistance with resistance. In order to remind the reader of some of the limits of this ethical criticism, I will thus at times throughout this study have recourse to, among others, the term *ideology*. *Ideology* will name the material effects that the critic is not capable of knowing, and it will indicate a certain strategic refusal on my part to engage in an extended discussion of political economy from my local position as someone trained in English and film studies. *Ideology* thus interrupts the ethical, flagging the ways in which the economic text might complicate our understanding of ethics in ways we cannot adequately know, given our placement in that text, as well as the limits of that textual mapping we name the economic. In other words, in pointing toward the economic, I am not reverting to a mechanistic account of causality that understands the material as the base that produces all superstructural phenomena, but am instead using the term *ideology* to hold the place specifically of the effects of the economic, with the understanding that even such a limited account of causality must insist on the economic itself as a mapping, an attempt to name inadequately a series of forces that, given the limits of knowledge, can never be adequately named or known.

Chapter 1 will investigate Foucault's critique of the subject, Gayatri Spivak's critique of that critique around the question of ideology, Foucault's stated objections to the concept of ideology as Althusser deploys it, and a number of possible responses to those objections. This chapter demonstrates the efficacy of both Foucault's critique of the subject and a (perhaps non-Althusserian) theory of ideology for a cultural criticism affiliated with the marginalized. It will also begin a discussion of Foucault's crucial rejection of a model of power as emanating from the state. Chapter 2 is an exploration of gay pornography as an instance of what Bataille has termed "nonproductive expenditure." Such an exploration treats pornography as a text that might "resist" the ongoing practices of disciplinary subject formation. Chapter 3 is an examination of race, class, and sexuality in Marlon Riggs's video *Tongues Untied*. I argue that the video seems unable to elaborate some of the numerous contradictions in which it is necessarily embroiled. This inability in turn requires the video to deploy what I characterize, after Laura Kipnis, as a white, middle-class feminist position against pornography, a position I question for its efforts to shore up the Other as subject. Chapter 4 begins to think through the relation between resistance on the level of subjectivity and resistance on the level of the political through a discussion of Gramsci's notion of "common sense" and an application of this notion to a reading of Jennie Livingston's film *Paris Is Burning*. This chapter also critiques bell hooks's reading of the film around questions of gender. Chapter 5 offers a reading of Nietzsche's "On the Uses and Disadvantages of History for Life," examining the implications of Nietzsche's critique of historiography for a history of the Other. The analysis then turns to

John Greyson's film *Urinal*, examining the film as an attempt to mobilize and deploy a critical history of the Other. This analysis of *Urinal* brings us full circle, as it were, for it concludes with an exploration of the ways in which the film uncritically conflates resistance on the level of subjectivity with political resistance by mobilizing a notion of state power that I think I will have shown to be indefensible and beset by undesirable consequences.

I want to reemphasize here that what I have been naming as the two distinct strands of cultural criticism with which this study engages are necessarily interwoven, and often, in the work of a single critic. For example, bell hooks not only seeks to extend a fuller subjectivity to the Other through her continuing emphasis on the need for marginalized peoples to develop stronger senses of themselves as humanist agents, but also writes of the need for oppressed, exploited, and colonized people to understand marginality as "position and place of resistance."[26] This double effort suggests, among other things, how an ethical criticism aligned with the Other must be both vigilant and scrupulous in its attempts to trace out the ways in which its own claims to be transgressive are necessarily contingent upon its contradiction-laden place within a benevolent liberal academy.[27] Although such a criticism works to understand and critique the limits of the liberal academy, it necessarily depends on that academy's benevolence for its continued sustenance. We might instead imagine a situation in which, rather than attempting to contain, through an appeal to a shared subjectivity, the threat of difference evidenced by a transgressive criticism on the side of the Other, the academy might simply not "entertain" critics of difference at all. Such a refusal would, however, necessarily be opposed to the "liberal," inclusive, universalist pretensions on which the academy depends. Although recent battles over canon reform have sometimes implied that in previous historical periods the academy refused to treat with any seriousness whatsoever the cultural productions of marginalized peoples, my assumption here is that the modern liberal academy has throughout its history made a limited and contained use of "foreign" cultural material. A critical historical study such as Edward W. Said's *Orientalism*, in fact, documents the ways in which liberal scholarship does not simply ignore, but rather makes a contained use of, the Other of the white West. All of this suggests, among other things, that an ethical transgressive criticism must be willing to abandon previous critical positions and strategies should they prove to be too easily assimilable by the liberal academy, as well as to attempt to catch a glimpse of the ways in which all claims to alterity are necessarily contingent upon a certain proximity to the center.

My citation of bell hooks, however, also brings up one of the difficulties I have had to face throughout the writing of this project. In staking out this "transgressive" critical deployment of the Other, I have, in positioning such a criticism "against" certain liberal inclusive tendencies, necessarily had to take issue with those critics with whom I often feel the greatest sense of political sympathy. In other words, much of my critique throughout this study is directed towards the work of gay and lesbian critics, African American critics, and feminist critics (with the understanding, of course, that these are not mutually exclusive or reified categories). In doing so, I largely leave behind, for strategic reasons, any consideration of the "illiberal" academy, the members of which would likely find it impossible to enter into any sort of conversation with my stated concerns.

Although I will discuss this omission at some length in chapter 4, I would offer here a number of explanations. First, the fact that the (stereotypically) heterosexual, white, male, middle-class, academic critic seems largely to continue to be (interestedly) uninterested in questions of criticism and marginality necessitates that I direct my critique toward, for example, gay critics, African American critics, and so on, since we seem to be the ones still largely concerned with these issues. This is not to lay the blame exclusively at the feet of those stereotypical critics (though it is not to deny that certain heterosexist, racist, phallocentric, and class presumptions still significantly guide the "choice" of one's field of scholarship and study). Our own problematic and necessary reliance on identity politics has sometimes produced a situation in which attempts by mainstream critics to enter into, say, feminist debates are met with a series of critical responses ranging from serious demands that one think through the limits of one's historical position as investigating subject to trivializing critiques that simply bad-mouth any attempts by mainstream critics to "play" in the margins. Of course, we must insist that our own sometimes knee-jerk responses to, for example, straight white men "in" feminism are necessarily inflected by a job market that still largely privileges white, male, (apparently) heterosexual bodies. Overhearing my discomfort at certain (feminist) grumblings concerning men in feminism, a friend of mine once reminded me that one of the legacies of the men-in-feminism movement might be the staffing of positions in such fields as women's studies with white men, thus denying to women one of the token places reserved for them in the university. My friend (not coincidentally, a woman, although, as I will suggest in chapter 3, a woman "produced" "discursively") reminded me of the necessarily complicated and contaminated place from which we attempt to articulate a critique of the relation between, say, the limits of academic disciplinarity and our own continuing work within academic disciplines.

Secondly, our inevitable contamination by the historical legacies of racism, classism, phallocentrism, and homophobia means that any critical response situated within this history will itself necessarily be structured by it. In other words, there are perils in both critiquing and not critiquing other critics affiliated with the culturally marginalized, critics with whom I am largely interested in forming political alliances. There are, however, different ways of giving in to this history, all of which are not of equal pertinence. My "choice" throughout this study, inasmuch as one is capable of speaking of choice here, is to engage seriously with gay and lesbian critics, feminists, and critics of color by treating their work seriously—as worthy of careful and extended analysis. I prefer this approach to either empty critical celebrations of cultural diversity that necessarily deploy universalist ideologies, or silent refusals to take up at any length the challenges posed by such critics as bell hooks.

Finally, concerning my lack of interest in engaging with certain right-wing critics, I would want to second here Paul Bové's insistence that certain debates with the "illiberal" academy are simply not worth having. Their positions demand not response, but silence. As Bové argues in a commentary on the "unreadability" of Allan Bloom's *The Closing of the American Mind*, "the one thing hegemony requires is to set the terms of debate. In the face of the likes of Bloom and his confreres, every effort must be made precisely not to join the conversation."[28] This refusal to allow the Right to set the terms of discussion of an ethical criticism necessitates that I leave behind the likes of, for example, Bloom, Hirsch, and the Reagan-Bush National Endowment for the Humanities gang, and focus instead on the terms set by those with whom I am interested in having a critical conversation.

Some will perhaps read my engagement with the work of other critics of difference as relentless and perhaps even accusatory. They might fear that such a critique of the normalizing tendencies of liberal humanist criticism may be recuperated by the Right and for right-wing polemics and purposes. It is difficult to know exactly how to respond to this fear, as I am hard pressed to imagine, for example, how someone like William Bennett might second my valorization of gay pornography. Perhaps I should offer a few remarks on what I mean by a strategic argument, as well as how I envision criticism.

Theorists of strategy remind us that, in a strategic situation, two forces are posed adversarially. In this study, I have named the discursive forces that my arguments oppose as the "universalizing" discourses of liberal humanism. In a strategic situation, "each participant can bring some influence to bear upon the outcome. . . . No single participant by himself nor chance alone can determine the outcome completely." The problem thus becomes to devise "an optimal course of action which takes into account the possible actions of the participants and the chance events."[29] In the game of writing, one can choose such a course of action only by inhabiting the adversarial argument as fully—perhaps as relentlessly—as possible. Because "everything done in strategy is an action that meets a reaction,"[30] it is necessarily the adversarial argument that sets the terms of the strategy. My polemic thus must be "inside" what it opposes. As a (counter)logic of the supplement, it necessarily courts what it seeks to displace. Such a closeness perhaps requires or demands an especially pointed and accusatory tone, given the necessary proximity of margin to center. It might also be argued that the worthiest adversaries are those with whom one shares a certain commonality of ideas. Only such adversaries can help one to dis-cover those places where one's thinking runs up against itself.

Concerning the Right's reappropriation of my argument, we may note that the strategist Edward N. Luttwak argues, "In strategy you can never know 'exactly what you are getting in to' " (74). It is not possible for me to predict how certain right-wing forces might respond to, counter, and make use of my argument. Yes, my quarrels are primarily with scholars associated with the Left—as vague as this term might be—for reasons I have already mentioned. I have, however, attempted to take up in this study subjects that the Right is reluctant to embrace and affirm—subjects like pornography, interracial gay s/m sex, transvestitism, and public sex. Now, in his account of strategy, Luttwak insists that, in a strategic situation, "*the logic of strategy is not linear but paradoxical. If you want to succeed in it, you should do the wrong thing, not the right thing*" (69; emphasis in original). A successful strategy is one that the adversary cannot anticipate. As Luttwak suggests, "If you have an enemy who is watching your every move, paradoxical action is the best action" (70). Perhaps the problem, then, with liberal (academic) responses to the Right is that they are not strategic. Perhaps our continued and necessary dependence on the benevolence of the liberal academy prevents us from doing the unexpected when we are confronted by the Right. Rather than respond paradoxically to the Right's shrillest accusations, we attempt to counter its claims by appealing to the tenets of liberal humanism—the discourse of rights, for example, or appeals to a universal humanity under the guise of a "weak" multiculturalism, or with reassertions of scholarly disinterest. Perhaps the legacy of the political-correctness debates will be an attempt by the Left to respond strategically, rather than "reasonably," to the Right's accusations.

All of this said, I would also want to acknowledge that the overwhelming intellectual commitment of this study is not to right- or left-wing politics but to the poststructuralist critique of the subject. As Robert Young reminds us, poststructuralism challenges "not just the politics and institutions of the right but also the politics and theoretical systems of the left. Disturbing conventional assumptions about what constitutes 'the political,' poststructuralism is correspondingly difficult to place itself."[31] Because this is primarily a strategic argument mounted in response to recent attacks on theory—attacks that, for reasons I have already indicated, I will not take up at any length—I will largely leave behind a discussion of those terms "Left" and "Right," terms that in the contemporary United States are in any case increasingly difficult to define.[32]

To this account of strategy, I would add just a few brief words concerning how I imagine the role of the "oppositional" critic. A very generous and careful reader responded to an earlier draft of this study with the suggestion that I modify the tone of some of the more polemical passages. The reader feared that I tended to sound "more like an attacker than a critic, a sort of Zola of the contemporary academic left. (I accuse, I accuse!)" In response to this concern, I feel I can do no better than to second Bové's contention that one must see an oppositional critical act as "a relentless even if sometimes admiring but implacable agonism, as an indecorous enemy if you will."[33] Given the ease with which the liberal academy manages to accommodate a variety of "oppositional" stances (isn't everybody oppositional these days?), perhaps Zola is not such a terrible role model after all. In any case, I hope readers will not find it too indecorous if I admit that I wish that I had written the line with which Bové closes the discussion of oppositional criticism from which the above citation is drawn: "Critics should never be good company."[34]

Some readers will also note, however, that, in an effort to engage with certain critics of difference, another body of work, work not issuing from the political or academic Right, will also be left behind. In order to explain and account for this apparent silence, I must take a bit of a detour through the "origins" of this project.

This study began as a series of independent essays, each of which would constitute a chapter. These essays, traversing a variety of disciplines and fields, would often refer to, illustrate, and bear upon one another. Because I did not see the individual chapters as easily locatable within the purview of any one discipline, I did not feel it necessary, nor humanly possible, to provide surveys of the various fields discussed. This made it possible for me to avoid what I would characterize as the "cut and paste" method of scholarship, in which the critic wrenches a wide variety of critical and theoretical propositions from the contexts in which they initially circulated and strings them together as a demonstration of an alleged breadth of knowledge. Rather, I was interested in these chapters in carefully working through a limited number of texts, texts that I found either challenging or illuminating or particularly pertinent to my argument, or significantly underread or misread. As a result, this study is perhaps open to the charge that it necessarily contains certain "gaps" in its scholarship.

Concerning this charge, I would insist initially that my choice of texts was dictated by a desire to work through a number of problems simultaneously. For example, I was not particularly interested in examining either critical works or films that centered on one particular discursive modality such as gender, race, sexuality, or class, but rather sought out texts that drew attention to the interweavings of these discursive practices. The particular elisions in scholarship that most concern me here, and for reasons that might rapidly be summarized as personal/political/ethical, are those resulting from what some might read as a too brief engagement with recent work in feminism and gay and lesbian studies. In order to account for this book's apparent lack of immediate interest in certain feminist projects, I must refer briefly to Teresa de Lauretis's essay "The Technology of Gender" as a symptomatic, if not quite representative, example.

De Lauretis argues for a feminist revision of the concept of gender. She sees the familiar account of gender as sexual difference as a limitation, and argues for the reconceptualization of gender as "the product and the process of a number of social technologies, of techno-social or bio-medical apparati."[35] Although de Lauretis draws her vocabulary from Foucault's account of sexuality in the first volume of *The History of Sexuality*, she insists that Foucault's theories, as well as those of a number of other poststructuralist thinkers, are marred by the fact that they deny gender, and are consequently male centered (15). Though such theories often deploy the figure of woman, such a deployment invariably effaces the historicity of gender difference, one of the consequences of which is the continual definition of women exclusively *in relation* to men. According to de Lauretis, one of the projects of feminism thus becomes to "(re)construct" gender "in terms other than those dictated by the patriarchal contract" (17)—poststructuralist theory representing one instance of that contract. To do so requires that the theorist "walk out of the male-centered frame of reference in which gender and sexuality are (re)produced by the discourse of male sexuality."

My own commitment in this study to the poststructuralist critique of the subject demands that I pose the question here of how such a "walking out of" is possible. Throughout this study, I will be suggesting a position different from that of de Lauretis, even though I acknowledge the importance of de Lauretis's critique of poststructuralism—that it sometimes addresses inadequately questions of gender. In order to define a bit more precisely some of the contours of our different positions vis-à-vis poststructuralist theory, I will need to return to de Lauretis's account of a feminist theoretical practice.

In her discussion of the limitations of Foucault's theories of sexuality for feminism, de Lauretis argues that "in the patriarchal or male-centered frame of mind" (we might wonder about the force of such a construction here: is the problem of patriarchy primarily a problem of a male-centered mindset?), the female form of sexuality is "a projection of the male's, its complementary opposite, its extrapolation" (14). As I have already indicated, I will be borrowing from deconstruction the term *supplementarity* to describe this positioning of the marginalized in relation to the dominant. For de Lauretis, the terms of a different, non-male-centered account of gender do exist, even though such a view of gender "is nowhere to be seen, not given in a single text, not recognizable as a representation" (25). De Lauretis suggests that the reason for this unrecognizability is not that "feminists, women" (note the equating of the two terms) have not succeeded in producing female narratives of gender, but that such narratives reside in what she terms

> the elsewhere of discourse here and now, the blind spots, or the space-off, of its representations. I think of it as spaces in the margins of hegemonic discourses, social spaces carved in the interstices of institutions and in the chinks and cracks of the power-knowledge apparati. And it is there that the terms of a different construction of gender can be posed—terms that do have effect and take hold at the level of subjectivity and self-representation: in the micropolitical practices of daily life and daily resistances that afford both agency and sources of power or empowering investments; and in the cultural productions of women, feminists, which inscribe that movement in and out of ideology, that crossing back and forth of the boundaries—and of the limits—of sexual difference(s). (25)

What strikes me initially about this passage is the way that it invokes a vocabulary reminiscent of Foucault, a vocabulary on which I will draw throughout this study. "Micropolitical practices of daily life and daily resistances" that "take hold at the level of subjectivity," affording "both agency and sources of power"—these are themes that will be taken up at some length in subsequent chapters. There is also, however, at least one crucial difference between de Lauretis's formulation here and the position I will argue in this study. In earlier passages of this same essay, de Lauretis counters Foucault's notion of power as "productive"—a notion that will be elaborated throughout this study—with the assertion that "we have to make distinctions between the positive effects and the oppressive effects of such production" (18). According to de Lauretis, Foucault makes no such distinctions. What is interesting to me about de Lauretis's account of "where" this non-male-centered account of narrative exists is that the positing of such a space requires an implicit rejection of Foucault's model of power, for, in Foucault's now oft-cited formulation, there is no place "outside" of power. The implication of Foucault's theory for feminism is that in a patriarchal culture there cannot be a space "outside" of patriarchy. Admittedly, de Lauretis rejects this aspect of Foucault's theory, and poststructuralism in general. This rejection necessarily marks one of the differences between my project in this study and a feminist project along the lines recounted by de Lauretis. I will be arguing that marginalized cultural practices are necessarily inscribed within—although not simply contained by—the dominant. I will maintain that only within this space of marginality is resistance to the normative possible.[36]

In describing this place "elsewhere" where non-male-centered narratives of gender circulate, de Lauretis is careful to insist that such feminist spaces are not "outside" what she terms the ideology of gender.[37] Rather, for de Lauretis, a feminist movement "across the boundaries of sexual difference," a movement into and out of the "blind spots" of contemporary (nonfeminist) discourse, is not simply a movement "outside" the strictures of patriarchy. De Lauretis describes this movement as a movement "from the space represented by/in a representation, by/in a discourse, by/in a sex-gender system, to the space not yet represented yet implied (unseen) in them."[38] Although I appreciate the care of de Lauretis's formulation (and can't help noting, given her critique of deconstruction and other poststructuralist theories, the irony of her deployment of the deconstructive gesture of the "by/in"), I also can't help wondering, given my own commitment to poststructuralism: How do these spaces manage to escape a male-centered frame of reference—let alone representation? Given the logic of the supplement, isn't this implied but not yet represented space *necessarily* conditioned by the dominant? For myself, the answer would clearly be yes. As I understand it, power is the precondition for the production of resistance. There is no space "in the interstices" of discourse where power would not operate, no "chinks and cracks of the power-knowledge apparati." If there is such a thing as patriarchal power—and it is currently difficult to imagine a feminism that would do away with this concept—it must (theoretically) be everywhere.

For de Lauretis, the answer to this same question is apparently no. In her formulation, there are spaces—however far outside of the frame—in which patriarchal power does not function. But how does de Lauretis account for this? Apparently, the activity of female agents is what allows for the creation of such spaces. (Of significance here is de Lauretis's approving citation of Tania Modleski: "A *feminist* criticism, she [Modleski] concludes, should reject 'the *hypothesis* of a woman reader' and instead promote the 'actual female reader.' ")[39] De Lauretis's analysis of gender in fact depends on a recuperation of "agency and self-determination at the subjective and even individual level of micropolitical and everyday practices."[40] What about these actual female agents makes possible this movement in and out of non-male-centered discursive spaces? Apparently, it is the "historical" fact of their womanness (symptomatic here is the slippage noted above between "feminists" and "women") linked with what de Lauretis terms "the *practice* of self consciousness" (20; emphasis in original). De Lauretis defines this practice as "the analytical and critical method of feminism."

Here again, some readers may hear de Lauretis's language, with its emphasis on feminism as a practice, resonate with Foucault's notion of practices or technologies of the self. What seems strikingly dissimilar in Foucault's and de Lauretis's accounts of agency is Foucault's emphasis on a certain *relation* with the self rather than self-consciousness, as well as an emphasis in Foucault on the need to *work* at becoming a "transgressive" subject. These may seem to be minor points; actually, they are quite significant. When de Lauretis proposes a homology between Foucault's understanding of sexuality and her own theorization of gender, what is lost in de Lauretis's account is a notion of the (gendered) *subject*. Clearly, Foucault and de Lauretis are working with and from different understandings of the subject, evidenced in, for example, her account of the subject as "a concrete individual or person" (9). As I will discuss at some length in the following chapter, Foucault specifically complicates this understanding of the subject. Additionally, the invocation by de Lauretis of "self-consciousness" necessarily calls up the humanist subject explicitly rejected by poststructuralism: consciousness supplies to the subject a certain depth that Foucault's account of the subject, in its emphasis on such terms as, for example, "technologies," would disallow. Emblematic of this difference is de Lauretis's argument that technologies of gender are "absorbed subjectively" (13), as well as her positing of something "outside" discourse (3). As I will argue in subsequent chapters, a poststructuralist understanding of technologies of the self would insist that subjects are positioned in discourse regardless of whether or not such technologies are "absorbed" (notice again the reliance on a model of depth) "subjectively."

The consequences of these differing understandings of the subject are substantial. For example, in contrast to Foucault's account of subjectivity and homosexuality, these real (female) subjects in de Lauretis's account apparently do not have to work at *becoming* women, so that de Lauretis is open to the charge that her essay depends on a kind of essentialism. It appears at times in de Lauretis's account that being an "actual" woman is itself tantamount to resisting patriarchy.

Additionally, we might ask what exactly de Lauretis's female agents are resisting when they create non-male-centered narratives of gender difference. Presumably, one of the things the resistant feminist theorist is resisting is being defined in relation to man. Such a resistance must necessarily take what *is* as its starting point: male-centeredness. The logic of the supplement insists that no other place is available.

My point here is that despite the necessity of considering questions of gender, despite the necessity of affirming and valorizing the feminist political project, a commitment to the critique of the subject obliges (binds, compels) me to question the return in de Lauretis's work of such figures as the actual (in de Lauretis's formulation, "historical") woman.[41] In the current moment, at a time when theory is all too readily dismissed in the name of a "return" to unproblematized accounts of agency (though I would insist that de Lauretis's analysis does *not* represent one such account), I strategically place the emphasis in this study on the critique of the subject, rather than on questions of a certain vision of political agency. This is perhaps for some readers an overly tortuous way of explaining why a certain feminism is not a greater presence in this study.

I fear that de Lauretis and some other feminists will read this long explanation as yet another instance of a male theorist whose work does not "support or valorize within the academy the feminist project per se" but rather draws on certain positions within academic feminism that will "accommodate either or both the critic's personal interests and male-centered theoretical concerns."[42] Throughout the writing of this text, I have had to struggle with my relationship to feminism. The current state of affairs in the academy dictates that any position I take up here will be highly unsatisfactory. If I ignore or neglect feminist criticism, I will be accused of continuing to work within (patriarchal) sexist structures. If I discuss feminist theory in any detail only to critique it, I will be accused of being a kind of (male-centered) academic tourist. All of this is complicated by the considerable indebtedness of this present study to the work of a critic who names herself / is named both as and not as a feminist, a feminist who is and is not locatable in the "third world."[43] I fear, however, that even these qualifications will necessarily be read by some as the kind of male whining common in an age often all too readily named as "postfeminist."

Concerning the relationship between this book and "established" work in the "emerging" field of gay and lesbian or queer studies: although I will take up this topic at some length in all of the subsequent chapters, I feel it is necessary to make the reader aware initially of a few of this book's points of departure. First, the "origin" of this study was a long paper that provided an extended critique of the refusal by certain gay male theorists to treat with enough rigor and seriousness the poststructuralist critique of the subject. My goal in that paper was to read as symptomatic the return of the sovereign subject in the work of certain gay male critics who claimed the particular importance of Foucault to their project. Though that paper appears in the present study only in bits and pieces, the impulse behind it animates this book in its entirety.

Secondly, my own work in gay and lesbian studies is increasingly propelled by my frustration with a number of recent attempts to "rescue" (canonical) gay male authors for the canon. The recent past has given rise to studies of such "marginalized" canonical figures as Hart Crane, Frank O'Hara, Henry James, and Marcel Proust. A virtual industry has sprung up in gay and lesbian studies around the figure of Oscar Wilde. Although many of these studies offer significant and important rereadings of these writers, I can't help being suspicious of the ease with which the academy has taken up such rereadings. What troubles me most about these efforts is a certain refusal to interrogate the category of the literary in any depth and detail. Tony Bennett has recently argued that Marxists in particular have been culpable in the continued maintenance of the category of the literary, refusing to interrogate certain unspoken interests within the academy, and forsaking a discussion of why intellectuals continue to promulgate such "literary" values as individualism and the opposition of high and low culture.[44]

Both of these critiques of gay and lesbian studies arise directly from a certain hesitancy to embrace the field as an "emerging" academic discipline. Academic disciplines are group identities that move to stabilize their objects of knowledge so as to make possible an infinite formulation of statements. They thus necessarily attempt to institute a certain normalization of the Other. Academic disciplines in the humanities in particular, with their emphasis on "man" as object of study, thus (necessarily) work in tandem with the practices of disciplinary society (although, given the account of power I work with here, this is not all that they do). My fear is that gay and lesbian studies might inadvertently privilege, through a recourse to the concept of identity, the very sovereign subject that I believe is in its (political) interest to critique. Faced with the historical necessity of forging an academic discipline around an unstable collectivity of sexual behaviors knotted, disciplined, into a (fictive) personage, gay studies must, in an effort to maintain some relationship to its own historical "emergence" in, and in relation to, "real" liberationist identity politics, defer the critique of the sovereign subject—and often while simultaneously acknowledging its debt to poststructuralist thinkers. My assumption throughout this study clearly will not be that this is all that this "emerging" discipline accomplishes, or that this is even its primary point of intervention in the academy. Such a formulation could be made only through an active forgetting of the caveat with which I began this introduction. I will, however, be arguing at times that an inattentiveness to the ways in which academic disciplines work to normalize their objects of study—to state this in terms of the academic critic's practice, a certain refusal to elaborate the multiple and contradictory conditions of possibility of one's disciplinary practice—might render one's analysis at odds with its stated political sympathies, and unable to chart the competing interests that might inadvertently move through one's produced explanation. Such an inattentiveness is particularly debilitating to a criticism in the name of the Other. I am not suggesting here that programs in, for example,

gay and lesbian studies ought not to exist—though I would argue that because of the ways in which the liberal academy is increasingly skilled at
managing and commodifying difference, such a suggestion ought always to
be *seriously* entertained, particularly by those scholars working "within"
such fields. Rather, I am suggesting that if one is to have some kind of causal
understanding of one's own having been produced as an intellectual, even a
"subaltern" one, one must engage in a scrupulous and protracted articulation of the conditions of possibility of one's own intellectual production.

I hope readers will note that I am making here a theoretical argument
concerning knowledge production within structures of disciplinarity, and
not offering either an institutional history of gay and lesbian / queer studies
or an empirical argument concerning the "real" presence (or lack thereof) of
sexuality studies within the contemporary liberal academy. My hesitancies
regarding gay and lesbian studies and/or "queer theory" stand whether or
not they represent a hot publishing trend, a fad for conference and journal
papers, a rapidly emerging and soon to be entrenched discipline along the
lines of women's/gender studies or Black studies, or some combination of
the above. My hope is that this study, though necessarily a moment in the
"emerging" discipline of gay and lesbian studies (or the more trendy "queer
theory"), will also act as a kind of critique of the discipline on the eve of its
future.

All of this said, I still struggle to theorize my own interest in critiquing
the work of other critics of difference. A commitment to a critique of ideology necessitates that one can never know adequately the multiple and conflicting interests that move through one's produced explanations of cultural
texts, and so I must insist that my focusing largely on the work of critics of
difference must be read as symptomatic of larger cultural forces, only some
of which I am capable of articulating here. I hope such a warning will mark
this text as one that attempts to make a provisional, tentative, and strategic
use of my necessarily subjected and subjugated position as critic.

Chapter 1

The Subject and/in Ideology

*Men believe themselves to be free simply because they are
conscious of their own actions, knowing nothing of the causes by
which they are determined.*

Spinoza, *The Ethics*[1]

The critique of the subject has a history often associated with the names of
Nietzsche, Marx, and Freud, among others, all of whom attempted, in different ways, to interrupt a historical narrative of people's sovereignty over
their own intentions and desires, as well as the behaviors thought to follow
necessarily from them.[2] For Freud and his followers, "the unconscious"
names the force that undoes the apparently seamless fit between the subject's expressed desires and consequent behaviors. This structure irreducibly
divides the subject, rendering impossible all claims to sovereignty by insisting that what we call consciousness is always itself subject to the law of the
return of the repressed, so that unspeakable, presymbolic desires return to
interrupt the subject's workings. Psychoanalysis is thus, among other things,
the attempt to chart the interruptions of daily life by the repressed material
of the unconscious, as well as an interrogation of the subject's denial of the
force of such interruptions.[3] This critique of the subject necessarily grants
the psyche a certain primacy.[4]

For Marxists, "ideology critique" is an attempt to account for how the
subject might desire against his or her (economic) interests. Covering over
the gulf between the subject's "real" material circumstances and articulated
interests, ideology as a critical concept describes how subjects might be led
to (mis)read the relationships between material forces and "lived" experi-

1

ence. Ideology critique necessarily grants the material relations of production a certain primacy as a causal mechanism. In a celebrated passage from the preface to *A Contribution to the Critique of Political Economy*, Marx argues that a change in the economic foundation of a society is accompanied by a rapid transformation of the superstructure. "In considering such transformations the distinction should always be made," Marx suggests, "between the material transformation of the economic conditions of production, which can be determined with the precision of natural science, and the legal, political, religious, aesthetic, or philosophic—in short, ideological—forms in which men become conscious of this conflict and fight it out."[5] In Althusser's oft-cited formulation of the problem, ideology helps to secure the reproduction of the relations of production, specifically, what Althusser characterizes as "capitalist relations of exploitation."[6] According to Althusser, these relations are reproduced "by the exercise of State power in the State Apparatuses, on the one hand the (Repressive) State Apparatus, on the other the Ideological State Apparatuses."[7] For Althusser, ideology, like myth in Lévi-Strauss's understanding of the term, expresses an imaginary relationship to the real. "All ideology," he suggests, "represents in its necessarily imaginary distortion not the existing relations of production (and the other relations that derive from them), but above all the (imaginary) relationship of individuals to the relations of production and the relations that derive from them."[8]

These two critiques of the sovereign subject are themselves discontinuous, as is shown by, among other things, their significantly different accounts of why the subject is divided and yet appears to function as sovereign. According to psychoanalysis, the material evidence of the male body is (mis)read (the familiar conflation of phallus and penis) so that a repression of the division of the subject by desire is made possible. According to a Marxist ideology critique, the material relations of production are (mis)read through ideology so that the subject's (divided) desires and (economic) interests appear to coincide, making possible the reproduction of inequitable social relations.

The (non)coincidence of these two critiques is a hindrance only to those who cling to the idealist dream of accurately de-scribing, "beyond" textuality, the workings of the real. Once the rush to diagnose "the last instance" is left behind, different problematics appear. This is not to imply that one may simply "choose" one critique of the subject over the other, depending on one's desired intervention. Rather, a textualized account of these critiques would insist that an attempt must be made to work through the effects of the deployment of a particular critique of the subject in a specific discursive instance. It is our (textual) predicament that such attempts are both always necessary, and always necessarily inadequate. In other words, a commitment to an exploration of the limits of our own theoretical practice requires that we acknowledge that all knowledge is a necessarily fictive and uneven mapping of what we for lack of a more precise term might characterize as either a world or the real. Such mappings are both constituted by and constitutive of a set of historical circumstances that are beyond the knowledge of any subject claiming to know, because such a subject is himself/herself similarly constituted by and constitutive of such mappings.[9] What remains in the face of such a predicament is not "relativism" but the impossible and necessary attempt to trace out what "effects of truth" might be produced through the deployment of a particular critique, as well as the effects of such effects, the politics they might engage, the ethics they might invoke, the ideology they might embody, with the provision that all of these terms—effects, politics, ethics, ideology—must themselves be subject to a rigorous critical interrogation. We might characterize such theoretical practice, after Gayatri Spivak, as a daily act of life sustenance similar to, say, brushing one's teeth or cleaning one's house.[10] Such an activity is never complete, never "adequate" in any absolute sense of the term (in that one has to continue to perform such acts regardless of the skill with which they might initially have been accomplished), and never enough.

In the recent scramble to diagnose the supposed failure of poststructuralist theory, one of the most frequently invoked names is that of Michel Foucault, whose critique of the subject is credited with undermining the possibility of collective political action. Neither a psychoanalytic nor "properly" Marxist critique, Foucault's charting of the subject is often read as one of the most debilitating legacies of poststructuralist theory in that it suggests to some the impossibility of agency.[11] Leaving aside, at least temporarily, an interrogation of the (disciplinary) conditions of possibility whereby one might credit the name of Foucault with effectively dismantling the basis of political agency, I would like to explore in a bit more detail Foucault's critique of the subject, how it might assist in the figuration of an oppositional critical theory/practice, and where it might need to be re-thought. In this first chapter, I linger a bit over this critique, and for a number of reasons. First, as I will argue at different points throughout this study, Foucault's critique of the subject is significantly underread or misread (a curious and symptomatic fact, given the recent tendency by some academics to lament the [alleged] omnipresence of Foucauldian studies in the humanities today). Second, this critique, helpfully, goes to some lengths to specify precisely what it means by *subject*—a term that, as I have already suggested, is deployed differently in different disciplinary and theoretical contexts, and that, as a result, is sometimes used in a somewhat less than rigorous manner. Finally, Foucault's critique will inform the remainder of this study in its entirety.

3

Foucault's critique of the subject is first and foremost an intervention in a philosophical tradition that takes for granted the presence of a transcendental subject.[12] In the face of this tradition, in which the problems of thought and truth have been referred continually to a universal, founding consciousness, Foucault counters this transcendental subject with a subject "not one but split, not sovereign but dependent, not an absolute origin but a function ceaselessly modified."[13] According to Foucault, this (nontranscendental) subject is produced through historically specific processes of normalization and disciplinarity, in which power produces the individual body as an object of knowledge.[14] During the classical age, a "meticulous control of the operations of the body" (137) was instituted through military, medical, educational, and industrial institutions, as well as practices of colonization, slavery, and child rearing (314), an "uninterrupted, constant coercion" that produced what Foucault terms "docile bodies" (135-69). These docile bodies are produced through what Foucault terms a specific technique or form of power that produces the (subjugated) subject. According to Foucault, this form of power

> applies itself to immediate everyday life which categorizes the individual, marks him by his own individuality, attaches him to his own identity, imposes a law of truth on him which he must recognize and which others have to recognize in him. It is a form of power which makes individuals subjects. There are two meanings of the word *subject*: subject to someone else by control and dependence, and tied to his own identity by a conscience or self-knowledge. Both meanings suggest a form of power which subjugates and makes subject to.[15]

In order to understand both the continuing formation of this subject today, and the conditions of possibility for any kind of resistance to this form of power and its accompanying processes of normalization, we therefore must investigate

> how things work at the level of on-going subjugation, at the level of those continuous and uninterrupted processes which subject our bodies, govern our gestures, dictate our behaviors, etc. In other words, . . . we should try to discover how it is that subjects are gradually, progressively, really and materially constituted through a multiplicity of organisms, forces, energies, materials, desires, thoughts, etc. We should try to grasp subjection in its material instance as a constitution of subjects.[16]

Some critics have been led to read this account of the formation of the subject as necessarily foreclosing possibilities of resistance. For example,

Jeffrey Weeks has argued, "It is difficult to resist the conclusion—which Foucault actually denies—that the techniques of discipline and surveillance, of individuation, and the strategies of power-knowledge that subject us, leave us always trapped."[17] However, Foucault defines power, on a kind of "micro-physical" level, as a strategic relation characterized by its reversibility; hence, wherever there is power, there is, necessarily, resistance. According to Foucault, power is not inherently bad. It is not equivalent to "a system of domination which controls everything and which leaves no room for freedom."[18] Rather, it is defined on perhaps its most microcosmic level as "the relationships in which one wishes to direct the behavior of another" (11). If the conditions of possibility for the direction of the behavior of another are everywhere, at least theoretically, so are possibilities for resistance. Unless we are dealing with a situation in which no hope of altering the form of the existing strategic relations is possible—what Foucault would characterize as slavery—there must necessarily be resistance. As Foucault argues,

> If one or the other [in a strategic relation] were completely at the disposition of the other and became his thing, an object on which he can exercise an infinite and unlimited violence, there would not be relations of power. In order to exercise a relation of power, there must be on both sides at least a certain form of liberty. Even though the relation of power may be completely unbalanced or when one can truly say he has "all power" over the other, a power can only be exercised over another to the extent that the latter still has the possibility of committing suicide, of jumping out of the window or of killing the other. That means that in the relations of power, there is necessarily the possibility of resistance, for if there were no possibility of resistance—of violent resistance, of escape, of ruse, of strategies that reverse the situation—there would be no relations of power. (12)

Similarly, if the subject is "produced" through ongoing practices of subjugation, the conditions of possibility must exist for an ongoing resistance to these practices—indeed, they are the practices of subjugation themselves. Unless we are dealing with what Foucault characterizes as a state of domination—a situation in which a reversal of strategic relations is not possible, in which "relations of power are fixed in such a way that they are perpetually asymmetrical and the margin of liberty is extremely limited" (12)— then resistance is always a possibility. Thus, while power "produces" the subject, it also produces the conditions of possibility for resistance.

As I will argue in a variety of ways throughout this study, Foucault does not define resistance as "outside" of power. It is not something foreign to power that encroaches upon it, but is rather produced "within" power, as it were. As Foucault insists, "There is not, on the one side, a discourse of power, and opposite it, another discourse that runs counter to it."[19] In Foucault's formulation, power must be understood as productive rather than merely repressive, engendering resistances at every point of its articulation, and making possible "reverse" discourses: "Relations of power are not in superstructural positions, with merely a role of prohibition or accompaniment; they have a directly productive role, wherever they come into play" (94).

There appears to be a glaring problem with this account, however. In a historical period in which we have witnessed renewed attempts by the United States to pursue its interests overseas through both violent and "humanitarian" means, such as the war with Iraq and the intervention in Somalia, Foucault's account of the subject and power seems unable to deal with questions of, for example, global domination and imperialism. Foucault's "micro-physics" of power does enable microanalyses that attempt to articulate, in very specific fashion, how strategic relations might fluctuate in particular "local" situations, such as, say, the sexual, where relations are perhaps somewhat fluid (at least according to Foucault). But the category of states of domination remains relatively untheorized, so that the conditions of possibility for the overcoming of such states is largely unarticulated, leaving Foucault open to the charge of inadvertently advocating a political quietism.[20]

Foucault's reticence on global power relations is, however, in some sense required by his historical position and disciplinary predicament. Throughout his career, Foucault argued against the figure of "the universal intellectual," the figure who stood in the position of "speaking in the capacity of master of truth and justice," offering up large-scale solutions for the redirecting of global politics.[21] Over and against this model of the intellectual, Foucault proposed the figure of the "specific" intellectual, whose goal is not to mold the political will of others, but rather, "to re-examine evidence and assumptions, to shake up habitual ways of working and thinking, to dissipate conventional familiarities, to re-evaluate rules and institutions, starting from this re-problematization (where he occupies his specific profession as an intellectual) to participate in the formation of a political will (where he has his role as citizen to play)."[22] Suspicious of the disciplinary presumptions and privileges that led intellectuals historically to diagnose the problems of the world, serving as emancipators of some kind of transcendent "truth,"[23] Foucault often limited his intellectual interventions to the specific disciplines in which his work was located, those being primarily philosophy and history (though, as I will suggest in a subsequent chapter, it is perhaps erroneous to cast Foucault as a historian).

The subject is thus for Foucault a function ceaselessly modified, a form not always identical to itself,[24] produced through a historically specific set of practices of subjection and subjugation. That is, there is no subject "prior" to these practices. The discontinuity of these practices, their failure, for example, to be unified as a strategy under the will or agency of some sovereign power or logic, makes it in fact impossible to speak of "the subject" except as a position that might provisionally be occupied, a place "momentarily" assigned by a particular statement. This critique of the subject does not automatically undermine agency in general, and political agency in particular, unless that agency is imagined as producing results that the agent might adequately control. Foucault takes up the question of agency in some detail in the work following the first volume of *The History of Sexuality* through the problematic of ethics and the subject, arguing that subjects must "work" at developing an "ethical" stylistics of life from within those historical patterns "proposed, suggested and imposed" by culture.[25]

The value of Foucault's critique of the subject is that it in fact insists on the subject as a historically specific, nontranscendental figure, while simultaneously refusing to foreclose the possibilities of a subject who acts, collectively or otherwise. Unlike psychoanalysis, which often, though claiming to be historically and culturally specific, employs ahistorical notions of "the unconscious," "castration," and "difference" in order to make its claims, Foucault's critique insists that what we know as the subject is a particularly modern phenomenon—so much so that such a critique renders impossible the project of projecting back into history current understandings of subjectivity. The charge that Foucault's later work fails to take up the question of the female subject ignores Foucault's contention that there was no subject as we know it in antiquity, male or female. According to Foucault, subjects in antiquity were constituted not through practices of subjection but through practices of liberation and freedom.[26] In this specific cultural situation, in which women are not constituted as free, it thus makes no sense to speak of female subjects. Foucault's "refusal" to account for female subjects in antiquity is necessitated by his commitment to disturb Western notions of a transcendental, transhistorical consciousness that would allow the positing of something like female subjectivity across the bounds of history. While such a gesture strategically leaves women aside in an effort to unsettle Western notions of subjectivity, such a leaving aside still makes possible a continued exploration of the question "What is woman?"—a question that has animated a significant body of recent feminist theory.[27]

Critiques of Foucault's account of the subject in/and power range from the trivial and trivializing reading of his later work offered by David Greenberg, in which it is suggested that Foucault "seemed to believe that ideas about sex are altogether unconstrained by the objective conditions of the society that produces them or the body, so that emancipatory ideas could simply be substituted for repressive ones,"[28] to the more substantial and interesting critique offered by Edward Said, in which it is suggested that Foucault's account of power paralyzes the possibility of political action by denying the role of class.[29] But one of the most compelling interrogations of Foucault's critique of the subject is offered by Spivak in her essay "Can the Subaltern Speak?"[30] Reading a conversation between Foucault and Gilles Deleuze, Spivak argues that a rejection of the concept of ideology by both Foucault and Deleuze makes possible in their discourse the return of the very sovereign subject Foucault claims to disavow, this time in the guise of an oppressed subject who is capable of knowing and speaking for himself. She refers to such passages in Foucault as this:

> The masses no longer need him [the intellectual] to gain knowledge: they *know* perfectly well, without illusion; they know far better than he and they are certainly capable of expressing themselves. But there exists a system of power which blocks, prohibits, and invalidates this discourse and this knowledge, a power not only found in the manifest authority of censorship, but one that profoundly and subtly penetrates an entire societal network. Intellectuals are themselves agents of this system of power—the idea of their responsibility for "consciousness" and discourse forms part of the system.[31]

Foucault is extending here his critique of the universal intellectual by appealing to what he has termed elsewhere "subjugated knowledges," "a whole set of knowledges that have been disqualified as inadequate to their task or insufficiently elaborated: naive knowledges, located low down on the hierarchy, beneath the required level of cognition or scientificity."[32] These "low-ranking knowledges" constitute a popular knowledge (*le savoir des gens*), a "particular, local, regional knowledge, a differential knowledge incapable of unanimity" (82) that opposes the "inhibiting effect of global, *totalitarian theories*" (80), theories that historically have belonged to "universal intellectuals." It has in fact been the historical task of universal intellectuals to disqualify and disallow as "nonscientific" such subjugated knowledges (85). Foucault gives the term "genealogy" to the task of recovering these local, subjugated knowledges that provide "a *historical knowledge of struggles*" so that they might assist in the bringing about of social change (83). It is the job of the "specific" intellectual to elaborate these genealogies so that "the subjected knowledges which are thus released would be brought into play" in current "local" struggles of power (85).

I am in complete agreement with Foucault's insistence on the necessity of recovering these local disqualified knowledges, especially as they might serve to detach "the power of truth from the forms of hegemony, social, economic and cultural, within which it operates at the present time."[33] If an oppositional cultural criticism on the order of Cornel West's "new cultural politics of difference"[34] is going to do more than simply replace the bourgeois white male heterosexual sovereign subject with his female, colored, working-class and/or homosexual counterpart, the epistemological projects of feminism, Black studies, and gay and lesbian studies, for example, must be to contest the terrain on which "truthful" statements might be made and recognized as such. As Luce Irigaray has argued, "the issue is not one of elaborating a new theory of which woman would be the *subject* or the *object*, but of jamming the theoretical machinery itself, of suspending its pretension to the production of a truth and of a meaning that are excessively univocal."[35] But I am uncomfortable with the suggestion in Foucault's exchange with Deleuze that formerly "disqualified" knowledges are perfectly self-evident and available to "the masses," in need of no e-labor-ation. Without something like a Gramscian theory of the necessity of organic intellectuals, and a corollary account of how "common sense" might be transformed into theoretical knowledge,[36] Foucault's analysis runs the risk of conjuring up a kind of savvy subaltern "beyond" ideology, for whom a knowledge of the relationship between economic interests and desire is available simply by virtue of his or her status as subaltern. In an intellectual climate in which, despite an ongoing and persistent critique of essentialism, being and knowledge are often equated via reference to untheorized notions of identity, it is imperative that Foucault's position not be deployed in order to suggest that the production of knowledge is free from constraints—a very un-Foucauldian position, indeed.[37]

Although I would not want to posit any kind of isomorphic analogy between Foucault's "subjugated knowledges" and Gramsci's "common sense," it is perhaps worth noting briefly some of the similarities between Gramsci's and Foucault's projects. Both Foucault and Gramsci are interested in theorizing the question of the intellectual, the forms of knowledge that have been historically disqualified or obscured by the ruling epistemology, and how we might gain access to these previously disqualified forms of knowledge so that struggles might occur. Foucault's figure of the specific intellectual uses the "local" knowledge that this figure's particular (disciplinary) positioning affords him or her in order both "to isolate, in their power of constraint but also in the contingency of their historical formation, the systems of thought that have now become familiar to us" as well as "to work in common with practitioners, not only to modify institutions and practices but to elaborate forms of thought."[38]

According to Gramsci, all human activity necessarily engages the intellect; thus, it is impossible to speak of nonintellectuals.[39] Nevertheless, it is necessary for different social groups to form and nurture intellectuals, "organisers and leaders"[40] who might assist in the bringing about of a collective action. The problem for the intellectual in and of "the masses" (to use a phrase invoked by both Foucault and Gramsci) becomes, according to Gramsci, the working out and making coherent "the principles and problems raised by the masses in their practical activity," so that they might constitute "a cultural and social bloc" (330). This involves the "renovating and making 'critical' an already existing activity" (331), that of the "everyday" philosophical activity Gramsci calls "common sense." Common sense is neither "false consciousness" nor simply "erroneous" thinking. Rather, it is the intellectual activity that precedes critical elaboration, a conception of the world that is disjointed and episodic rather than critical and coherent (324), a conception that one "inherits" historically as a result of one's placement within a social and economic history. As Gramsci insists, this common sense is itself heterogeneous, a product of a weave of historical processes (325-26). "Common sense is not something rigid and immobile, but is continually transforming itself, enriching itself with scientific ideas and with philosophical opinions which have entered ordinary life" (326n). The intellectual labor involved in transforming this (para)theoretical form of knowledge into theory requires elaborating what Gramsci characterizes as the "healthy nucleus" that exists in common sense, making it the basis for the construction of "an intellectual-moral bloc which can make politically possible the intellectual progress of the mass and not only of small intellectual groups" (332-33).

At subsequent points in this study, I will have recourse to Gramsci's work in order to respond to Foucault's critique of ideology while still attempting to keep alive questions of the economic and the political, as well as the role of the subaltern in particular in effecting social change, "local" or otherwise. In other words, I will be attempting to bring Foucault and Gramsci together, perhaps uneasily, in such a way as to retain what I find most compelling in the work of both.[41] What is particularly significant here in Gramsci's account of common sense is his insistence on both the value of this (para)theoretical knowledge and the need to elaborate such knowledge so that it might become useful in particular historical struggles. Although, in his interchange with Deleuze, Foucault similarly values the "local" knowledges of "the masses," his refusal of a theory of ideology—a theory that might account for what Gramsci characterizes as "the 'spontaneous' consent given by the great masses of the population to the general direction imposed on social life by the dominant fundamental group"[42]—leaves Foucault unable to explain how the oppressed might in fact be led to desire against their (economic) interests.

Additionally, although I find Foucault's category of the specific intellectual valuable for making possible a variety of vitally important "local" struggles,[43] I would want to echo here Spivak's warning (in "Can the Subaltern Speak?") that Foucault's desire to distance himself from the historical figure of the universal intellectual does not automatically undo the interests that might move inadvertently through his intellectual project. It is not enough for intellectuals in power to refuse to adopt the role of, in Foucault's phrase, "referee, judge, and universal witness."[44] As Spivak suggests, "One responsibility of the critic might be to read and write so that the impossibility of such interested individualistic refusals of the institutional privileges of power bestowed on the subject is taken seriously."[45]

Spivak in fact argues in "Can the Subaltern Speak?" that it is specifically a rejection of the concept of ideology that necessitates in Foucault this conflation of desire and interest, so that a more rigorous critique of the sovereign subject is mitigated by such claims as "We never desire against our interests, because interest always follows and finds itself where desire has placed it."[46] Thus, one of the most persistent critics of the sovereign subject inadvertently ushers in a subject who is capable, without much theoretical/intellectual reflection, of knowing very well the sources of his oppression. At a time in history when the difficulties of forging any kind of collective political action make possible an anti-intellectualism—flourishing both within and "outside" the academy—mobilized in the service of a "return" to a pretheoretical understanding of political and social reality, it is absolutely imperative to explore in particular the claims of the subaltern who knows.[47]

Although I am extremely uneasy with Spivak's polemical equating of Foucault's and Deleuze's positions here—especially in light of Foucault's explicit rejection of both the question of desire in general[48] and an affinity to Deleuze's understanding of desire in particular[49]—I want to take seriously the charge that a refusal in Foucault of an understanding of ideology's role in reproducing existing relations of production seriously undermines Foucault's critique of the subject. Another passage from Foucault's interchange with Deleuze, one not cited by Spivak, highlights some of the dangers of this perhaps interested refusal of ideology. Here, Foucault is speaking of "all those on whom power is exercised to their detriment" who "struggle on their own terrain":

> In engaging in a struggle that concerns their own interests, whose objectives they clearly understand and whose methods only they can determine, they enter into revolutionary process. They naturally enter as allies of the proletariat, because power is exercised the way it is in order to maintain capitalist exploitation. They genuinely serve the cause of the proletariat by

fighting in those places where they find themselves oppressed. Women, prisoners, conscripted soldiers, hospital patients, and homosexuals have now begun a specific struggle against the particularized power, the constraints and controls, that are exerted over them.[50]

Without a theory of ideology, Foucault's words are left open to the reading that, for example, homosexuals would "clearly understand" that it is in their own best interests to join with women and people of color to fight against the system of power that oppresses them. (I realize that the terms "homosexual," "women," and "people of color" are not mutually exclusive or reified, and use them primarily in order to respond to Foucault.) Such a reading cannot possibly account in our present context, for example, for a phenomenon like the artificial scarcity of medical resources that is maintained and deployed by the U.S. government in order to play off the interests of gay men, people of color, and women against one another in the face of HIV disease. Symptomatic of this manipulation is the recent failure of a number of various "local" chapters of ACT-UP, the AIDS Coalition to Unleash Power, to integrate the concerns of women, people of color, and working-class people into their political projects. The U.S. government's continued refusal to be sufficiently attentive to the needs of people with AIDS has produced a situation in which, faced with the desperateness of the situation, a number of members of ACT-UP have called for a kind of splitting of the coalition into two groups: a (largely) white, middle-class coalition of gay men concerned primarily with alleviating the suffering caused by HIV disease, and a coalition of those people—women, people of color, and working-class people, often also gay—for whom the government's response to the disease represents something like just another moment in a long history of neglect and oppression.[51]

Similarly, Cindy Patton has recently analyzed the ways in which community-based responses to the AIDS epidemic are necessarily structured by prevailing "social relations based in shared norms and styles of organizational behavior institutionalized through patterned power relations."[52] According to Patton, these prevailing social relations, necessarily crossed by homophobia, racism, sexism, and classism, have prevented "natural allies from forming coalitions in order to address problems raised by the HIV epidemic" (6). Specifically, Patton has noted the way "the formation of a largely white, covertly gay-community based service industry" (17), an industry that continues to marginalize the concerns of, for example, people of color with HIV disease, was made possible in part by "the relative economic stability of middle-class gay men" (16), whose economic privilege made possible a response to the AIDS crisis that privileged "community self-determination in the face of government inaction" (16). As Patton notes, such

12

responses, with their emphasis on self-empowerment, "were considerably at odds with the ethos in the African American community, which generally viewed social and economic problems to result from government policies (and to a lesser extent, from government inaction) which disenfranchised African Americans" (16). According to Patton,

> African Americans were much more inclined to view access to public health and control of its agencies as critical to the community's overall empowerment strategy. Thus, African American, Native American, and some ethnic groups would view AIDS services as something the government and society owed their communities as a result of systematic discrimination: AIDS service programs were only part of the solution to a "full plate" of systematic social problems. (16)

Foucault's formulation in "Intellectuals and Power" seems not able to examine the ways in which "those on whom power is exercised to their detriment"—a group that would presumably include white gay men—might in fact be crossed by competing interests that would lead them precisely *not* to form alliances with others who struggle against power—in the case of the historical formation of AIDS service organizations, African Americans, Native Americans, and other ethnic groups. His contention that "all those on whom power is exercised to their detriment" "naturally enter as allies of the proletariat" "in a struggle that concerns their own interests"[53] seems uncharacteristically non-Foucauldian in its perhaps utopian account of power and struggle. Such a utopianism is made possible through Foucault's refusal of ideology, for it is arguably a concept of ideology that might allow Foucault to explore at some length his own contention in this same passage that "power is exercised the way it is in order to maintain capitalist exploitation."[54]

I want to turn now to an exploration of Foucault's stated reasons for rejecting the concept of ideology, in the hopes that by both responding to and taking into account Foucault's objections to ideology critique we might work toward a utilization of Foucault's critique of the subject that can still take up the question of the economic. Such a utilization will admittedly require that, with Foucault, we reject Althusser's account of ideology and attempt to think through the problem of ideology through other sources. I would argue that such an attempt to preserve the economic in discussions of power is itself Foucauldian, given Foucault's insistence, above, that power plays a role in the maintenance of capitalist exploitation, as well as his contention that power is not independent of, nor can be made sense outside of, economic processes and the relations of production.[55]

In "Truth and Power" Foucault gives three reasons why the notion of ideology is difficult to use. First, "like it or not, it [ideology] always stands in virtual opposition to something else which is supposed to count as truth."[56] Because Foucault understands truth as produced through historically specific discursive practices, he must reject as a residue of transcendental philosophy any notion of "truth" as existing outside of discourse. This requires in particular the rejection of the opposition between a "true" science and a "false" ideology.

Foucault is obviously not alone in rejecting this opposition between science and ideology. Although Althusser makes use of this distinction,[57] a number of theorists of ideology do not.[58] My own attempt to call into crisis the opposition between ideology and science leads me to use the term *ideology* as a shorthand for the system of unexamined beliefs produced out of the conflicts induced by the uneven material conditions of production. It is a way of naming provisionally that impossible-to-chart relationship between the economic and other signifying systems, a naming that works to acknowledge the predicament of attempting to describe something that necessarily escapes description. The critical concept of ideology holds the place of the material forces activated in, and activating, historical struggles over intelligibility and meaning. It makes possible a strategic insistence on the necessity of considering how the material might be woven into the text we call the real.

Foucault's second objection to ideology is that the concept refers, "I think necessarily, to something of the order of a subject."[59] Presumably, Foucault is speaking here of a transcendental subject, or at least a notion of the subject as preexisting discourse. In defining ideology, Althusser refers to notions of "consciousness." According to Althusser, ideology prescribes material practices that "exist in the material actions of a subject acting in all consciousness according to his belief."[60] Foucault explicitly rejects this notion.[61] As he argues, "The problem is not changing people's consciousnesses—or what's in their heads—but the political, economic, institutional regime of the production of truth."[62]

Additionally, Foucault and Althusser employ different understandings of the category of the subject. According to Althusser, the category of the subject "may function under other names: e.g., as the soul in Plato, as God, etc."[63] Such a subject by many other names "is the constitutive category of all ideology, whatever its determination (regional or class) and whatever its historical date—since ideology has no history." As I have already suggested, Foucault explicitly rejects, in the case of the Greeks, this projecting of the category of the subject backward into history. Additionally, as I will discuss in a subsequent chapter, the Foucault of "The Discourse on Language" insists that discourse does not merely name some kind of pregiven, prediscursive reality. We might infer that, in Foucault's formulation, a subject by any other name might not be a subject.

V. N. Volosinov presents us with an account of ideology that does not rely on the notion of a transcendental subject. According to Volosinov, idealistic philosophies erroneously locate ideology in consciousness.[64] These philosophies overlook the fact that "consciousness itself can arise and become a viable fact only in the material embodiment of signs." Because consciousness itself is produced through processes of social interaction, in which ideological (semiotic) material is necessarily exchanged, there can be no consciousness outside of ideology. If ideology is equivalent to semiotic material (which, it is important to note, is not the case in Althusser's formulation), it is not required that ideology refer to a subject whose consciousness has been constituted presemiotically, outside historically specific discursive practices. Volosinov's understanding of ideology as semiotically constituted would argue that it is in fact impossible to separate cleanly "what is in people's heads" from "the political, economic, institutional regime of the production of truth," in that they are both constituted of and by the same material.

Foucault's contention, however, is not that the two are cleanly separated, but that critique ought to be directed toward the latter rather than the former. Foucault's critique of the subject in fact insists that because the subject does not preexist "the political, economic, institutional regime of the production of truth" but is in fact constituted via that regime, a critique directed toward consciousness necessarily reinstantiates the notion of a subject prior to truth and power. In other words, a critique directed toward consciousness assumes that there is a subject in advance of the regime of truth. Such a subject can allegedly transform that regime only through a transformation of consciousness, the assumption being that consciousness precedes action. (Recall Althusser's contention that ideology and the subject, like the Freudian unconscious, have no history.) Foucault's account of the subject argues something like the opposite: the transformation of the regime of truth will necessarily produce a new kind of subject. Given that Volosinov does not take up the problem of the subject at any length in his account of ideology and consciousness, it is difficult to answer Foucault's objection here to ideology with Volosinov's attack on those who posit consciousness outside of ideology.

Foucault's final objection to ideology in the passage cited above is that it "stands in a secondary position relative to something which functions as its infrastructure, as its material, economic determinant, etc."[65] This is perhaps the most difficult objection to counter, at least as I have employed the term *ideology* thus far, especially given Marx's account of the relationship between base and superstructure in the already cited passage from *A Con-*

tribution to the Critique of Political Economy. Here again, we might turn to Volosinov, who attempts to call into crisis any simple, mechanistic understanding of how (what he terms) the basis determines ideology. According to Volosinov, historical materialism renders notions of mechanical causality "simply out of the question."[66] Rather, a careful attempt must be made to chart the interrelationship of the basis to the superstructure. To do so would require a specification of, for example, the way changes in the economic state of affairs have shaped the larger semiotic/discursive milieu in which any isolated ideological phenomenon occurs.

This specification is itself complicated by the fact that although all ideological phenomena are conditioned by their social arena, this arena is itself in a continued state of flux, characterized by struggle and contest. The sign is thus rendered one of the most sensitive indexes of social and material struggle. As Volosinov insists, "Sign becomes an arena of the class struggle" (23), not merely "reflecting" accomplished changes in the economic base but acting as a vital and dynamic indicator of changes still in progress. Volosinov's notion of the sign as an arena of the class struggle suggests not only that it acts as an indicator of change but also that it is the very realm in which struggles to accomplish such change occur. Ideology must be recognized not merely as constituted by the economic base but also as playing a constitutive role. It is thus too simple to assume a purely mechanical causal relation between changes in the (economic) base and changes in its (ideological) superstructure.

Gramsci does not seem to use the term *ideology* with any systematicity or regularity.[67] Instead, Gramsci sometimes uses the term *hegemony* to account for how classes are led to desire against their economic interests. Linked to civil society rather than the state,[68] *hegemony* describes the apparatus or field of relations exercised in order to secure the consent of the majority of the population to the general direction imposed on social life by the dominant class. Though the securing of hegemony involves a struggle, hegemony is opposed to the state in that it achieves this goal through consent rather than "direct domination."[69] Hegemony is sometimes figured in Gramsci as the means by which dominant ideologies are consolidated;[70] if ideologies " 'organise' human masses, and create the terrain on which men move, acquire consciousness of their position, struggle, etc.,"[71] hegemony works to shape that terrain in the interests of the ruling class. Like ideology, hegemony is linked to the economic base: "though hegemony is ethical-political, it must also be economic, must necessarily be based on the decisive function exercised by the leading group in the decisive nucleus of economic activity."[72]

Concerning the relation between the economic base and (ideological) superstructure, Gramsci characterizes as "primitive infantilism" the belief that "every fluctuation of politics and ideology can be presented and expounded as an immediate expression of the structure."[73] Arguing that Marx's own political and historical works warn against the establishment of a simple causal relationship between the economy and ideology, Gramsci enumerates some of the precautions offered by Marx in his "concrete researches." The precaution most relevant here is what Gramsci characterizes as the difficulty of identifying a structure "at any given time, statically (like an instantaneous photographic image)" (408). Like Volosinov, Gramsci warns of the dangers of establishing a mechanical causal relationship between base and superstructure by noting that social relations are dynamic, characterized by struggles and flux, so that it is extremely difficult to establish specific causal connections between base and superstructure. As Gramsci points out, "Politics in fact is at any given time the reflection of the tendencies of development in the structure, but it is not necessarily the case that these tendencies must be realised. A structural phase can be concretely studied and analysed only after it has gone through its whole process of development, and not during the process itself, except hypothetically and with the explicit proviso that one is dealing with hypotheses" (408). Gramsci and Volosinov, though not denying a relationship between the economic base and ideological superstructure,[74] want to take seriously a (Marxist) critique of mechanical causality.

I am not certain that either Volosinov's or Gramsci's attempts to reimagine the relationship between base and superstructure would satisfy Foucault's final objection to ideology in this passage. However, both theorists provide us with a way of beginning to think through the question of the economic with less danger of embroiling such a discussion in questions of "the last instance." Also pertinent here is Robert Young's reading of Althusser, which suggests that even (perhaps especially) for Althusser, the economic "is never a simple causal function that operates alone."[75] Noting the allusion to Freud in Althusser's insistence, in *For Marx*, that "the lonely hour of the 'last instance' never comes,"[76] Young argues that in Althusser the economic "never operates in isolation separate from all the other instances of the social totality."[77] According to Young, Althusser is suggesting in *For Marx* that the superstructure "is the more fundamental determining force, or at the very least that they [base and superstructure] are equally overdetermined."

In his *White Mythologies*, Young argues that poststructuralist theory finds at least one of its conditions of possibility in French postwar Marxism's critique of Stalin, a critique articulated most powerfully by Sartre. According to Young, "Today when the primacy of history above all else—the economic, even class conflict—is asserted within a Marxist discourse, together with an accompanying defence of humanism, it can usually be traced back to a Marxism of a Sartrean existentialist form" (25). Poststructural-ism's supposed "assault" on history is, in Young's reading, an attempt to bring an antiempiricist and antipositivist French intellectual tradition to bear on Sartre's Marxism and its accompanying debt to Hegelian histori-cism. According to Young, Althusser and Foucault share an interest in at-tacking the humanist Hegelian tradition of Western Marxism and its accom-panying understanding of history (53). As Young has it, "The accusation that poststructuralism neglects history undoubtedly harks back above all to the work of Althusser who, more than anyone else, appears to have at-tempted to eliminate [a certain Hegelian conception of] history."[78]

The implications for this present argument are that poststructuralism's critique of causality, in its attempts to undermine a Hegelian historicism, risks leaving behind an account of the economic. In its negative relation to Sartre, it risks repeating his emphasis on history rather than economics or class conflict. Spivak has been extremely attentive to the poststructuralist critique of causality as it might inflect questions of the economic. As she ex-plained in an interview in 1984,

> We can't throw away thinking causally. But if I can introduce a word that is often used within post-structuralism—it's a rhetorical term but Nietzsche used it in this way—the term "metalepsis," that one quite often substitutes an effect for a cause when one is thinking causally. That is a way of being aware that causal thinking has its own limits. One can't judge without causal thinking. But then to ground the cause that one has established for the analysis into a certainty is what the post-structuralist would question.[79]

If we return briefly to the discussion of Volosinov's account of the sign, and the relationship between base and superstructure, we can see that the term *metalepsis* reminds us of the difficulty of identifying changes in the (ideological) superstructure as being caused by changes in the (economic) base. Owing to the sign's status as the arena of social struggle, a change in the base might be an effect of ideological contest within the superstructure, which might itself be an effect of ideological contest at the level of the base.

Spivak additionally complicates mechanistic accounts of causality through the notion of textuality. For Spivak, a theory of textuality does not consist of equating everything with the linguistic text. Rather, textuality re-fers to "the worlding of a world on a supposedly uninscribed territory," a "texting, textualising, a making into art, a making into an object to be un-derstood."[80] Textuality thus refers to the weave of forces we might term economic, psychosexual, social, political—all of these names being under-stood as themselves heterogeneous, discontinuous determinants always in-adequately named, and always "produced" themselves by a weave extremely difficult to chart.[81] This concept of textuality makes possible, among other things, an understanding of something like a "world" as being produced through a highly competing and contested series of historical discursive practices, the "ends" of which are always necessarily beyond the ability of any individual to manipulate or know. This knowledge does not, however, require an abandonment of work toward "positive" cultural change (although revolution, if revolution is imagined as an overthrowing of state power, is perhaps called into question by both Spivak's critique of causality and Foucault's account of power; I will have more to say about this shortly). Rather, it suggests that reading the world is itself an act that must be vigilantly theorized. Said's contention that poststructuralism's concern with textuality represents the desire to turn away from anything that is "worldly, circumstantial, or socially contaminated" obviously understands textuality in terms quite different from the ones offered by Spivak, and is in all likelihood directed toward what has come to be known as a certain American appropriation of deconstruction.[82] Such an appropriation seems most concerned with producing elegant, playful readings of canonical texts that do not take up questions of "the world" in any significant way.

Spivak's charting of textuality makes possible an account of the subject that retains Foucault's insistence on the subject as something historically produced while also making possible a utilization of a theory of ideology to take up questions of the economic. According to Spivak,

> That which seems to operate as a subject may be part of an immense
> discontinuous network ("text" in the general sense) of strands that may be
> termed politics, ideology, economics, history, sexuality, language, and so on.
> (Each of these strands, if they are isolated, can also be seen as woven of
> many strands.) Different knottings and configurations of these strands,
> determined by heterogeneous determinations which are themselves
> dependent upon myriad circumstances, produce the effect of an operating
> subject. Yet the continuist and homogenist deliberative consciousness
> symptomatically requires a continuous and homogeneous cause for this
> effect and thus posits a sovereign and determining subject.[83]

Spivak's language is extremely deliberate here—to the degree that such a statement is possible from within a deconstructive morphology. A commitment to a critique of the sovereign subject similar to that argued by Foucault makes possible the charting of a "subject-effect" rather than a transcendental subject of consciousness. This phrase "subject-effect" suggests something of the "dispersed" quality of the subject also present in Foucault's account, a dispersal that is, among other things, a condition of possibility for resistance. Unlike either "subject" or even "subject position," the phrase emphasizes the historically contingent qualities of what we call a subject, and also suggests the multiplicity of effects that might be activated specifically in the processes of the production of explanations. (In other words, it avoids unifying the positionalities from which, for example, acts of reading and writing occur.) The emphasis on such terms as "network," "knottings," "configurations," and "strands" emphasizes the subject as produced textually, and thus avoids Foucault's positing of something "outside" of discourse that might affect the production of subjects.[84] The emphasis on "knottings" also makes possible a discussion of something like, for example, a "female" subject-effect or a "homosexual" subject-effect, without requiring that these knottings be understood as themselves anything but provisional, historically contingent, and nonexhaustive in their description of a multiplicity of subject-effects that might cross any posited instance of what appears to operate as a subject.[85]

A commitment to a critique of causality evidenced in the work of poststructuralist thinkers such as Foucault and Derrida requires the deployment in Spivak's account of such apparent hesitancies as "may be," while also requiring that no single determinant be posited as the "cause" of the subject-effect. Attempting to push the "cause" of the myriad effects into infinity, this characterizing of the subject-effect allows for a discussion of ideology and the economic without positing a mechanical causal relationship between base and superstructure. In other words, the economic is not erased as a determinant, but is instead problematized. It is treated as a mapping that, like all other mappings, is necessarily inadequate, uneven, and in need of constant interruption. The advantage of this casting of the problem of the subject over Foucault's is that it makes possible a discussion of such things as class, itself always understood textually (that is, as a catachresis that makes possible a certain weave of discursive effects).

Finally, a critique of agency here makes possible an insistence that subjects are not "free" to "weave" themselves at will in and out of the network of textuality, but are rather produced and positioned through a series of forces beyond their control, so that phrases like "I choose to be gay," "I choose to read this text from my position as a woman," or "I choose to write as a Black man" are rendered highly problematic.

Returning, then, to Foucault's problematization of ideology: Foucault offers at least one additional objection to Althusser's formulation of ideology, an objection perhaps even more fundamental than those I have already cited. In his account of ideology, Althusser explicitly locates ideology in the state, and, in particular, in the Ideological State Apparatuses. As I have already suggested, ideology in Althusser is an instrument for the exercise of state power. According to Althusser, the Ideological State Apparatuses "largely secure the reproduction specifically of the relations of production, behind a 'shield' provided by the repressive State apparatus. It is here that the role of the ruling ideology is heavily concentrated, the ideology of the ruling class, which holds State power."[86] The assumption here is that power emanates from the state and is wielded in the interests of the ruling class, the primary difference between the Repressive and Ideological State Apparatuses being not that they have a different relationship to state power but that the "relative autonomy" of the latter allows "the resistance of the exploited classes" to find expression in the Ideological State Apparatuses. As I have already suggested, Foucault went to some lengths to problematize this understanding of power. The insistence on power as a series of strategic relations suggests that power cannot be said to be "held" exclusively by either the state, the ruling class, or any other body. Such an insistence suggests, contrary to Althusser, that the disciplinary power enacted in such institutions as the church, the school, and the military neither emanates in some top-down fashion from the state, nor that so-called (Repressive) State Apparatuses, such as the military, might not themselves give rise to resistances.[87] In a passage that seems to be a direct response to Althusser's "Notes" on ideology, Foucault offers the following:

> There is a sort of schematism that needs to be avoided here—and which incidentally is not to be found in Marx—that consists of locating power in the State apparatus, making this into the major, privileged, capital and almost unique instrument of the power of one class over another. In reality, power in its exercise goes much further, passes through much finer channels, and is much more ambiguous, since each individual has at his disposal a certain power, and for that very reason can also act as the vehicle for transmitting a wider power. The reproduction of the relations of production is not the only function served by power. The systems of domination and the circuits of exploitation certainly interact, intersect and support each other, but they do not coincide.[88]

Foucault's argument is not that the state is irrelevant, nor that it plays no role in the maintenance of unequal class relations. As he suggests in "Truth and Power," analyses of both power and resistance must extend, however, beyond the state, "because the State, for all the omnipotence of its apparatuses, is far from being able to occupy the whole field of actual power relations, and further because the State can only operate on the basis of other, already existing power relations. The State is superstructural in relation to a whole series of power networks that invest the body, sexuality, the family, kinship, knowledge, technology and so forth."[89]

Immanuel Wallerstein's *Historical Capitalism* is a Marxist analysis of the relationship between state power and capitalism that might satisfy some of Foucault's objections to the casting of the state as the privileged instrument of the power of one class over another—although Wallerstein begins his analysis with the caveat that one must take seriously Marx's contention that he himself was not a Marxist.[90] In his account of capitalism as a historical system, Wallerstein analyzes the importance of state power for capitalist economic processes without equating all power with state power. According to Wallerstein, "the structure of historical capitalism has been such that the most effective levers of political adjustment were the state-structures, whose very construction was itself . . . one of the central institutional achievements of historical capitalism."[91] In other words, Wallerstein is arguing that historically the state has acted as what he terms "the most effective levers of political adjustment"—not that the capturing of state power is required if significant social change is to occur, nor that the state represents the primary locus of power. In Wallerstein's analysis, state power does not merely serve economic processes, but rather the reverse is often true, and in ways that are sometimes extremely contradictory. For example, Wallerstein argues that historically

> accumulators of capital in any given state utilized their own state structures to assist them in the accumulation of capital, but they also needed some lever of control *against* their own state-structures. For if their state-machinery became too strong, it might, for reasons of internal political equilibrium, feel free to respond to internal egalitarian pressures. Against this threat, accumulators of capital needed the threat of circumventing their own state-machinery by making alliances with other state-machineries. This threat was only possible as long as no one state dominated the whole.[92]

The play of power and resistance described by Wallerstein here in his account of the relationship between the state and accumulators of capital is perhaps close to Foucault's casting of power in the interviews cited above, whereby the two are in a strategic relation that shifts so that it becomes impossible both to locate power unambiguously in the state, and to cast the state as exercising its power in tandem with accumulators of capital against the working class.

Concerning questions of resistance to capitalist exploitation and domination, Wallerstein questions the wisdom of the attempts of what he terms antisystemic movements—historical movements against capitalism such as labor-socialist movements and nationalist movements—to make the seizure of state power their pivotal goal.[93] He notes two fundamental consequences of the strategy of antisystemic movements to attempt to seize state power. On the one hand, such a strategy forced the antisystemic movement into "tactical alliances with groups that were in no way 'anti-systemic' in order to reach its strategic objective." These alliances significantly altered the structure of the antisystemic movement, blocking its goals of a more egalitarian distribution of resources.[94] On the other hand, once the antisystemic movement actually achieved state power, it was then "confronted with the realities of the limitations of state power within the capitalist world-economy," and forced to deal with the interstate system, which held in check its ability to institute change. Such a confrontation similarly "muted the 'anti-systemic' objectives" that initially gave rise to the antisystemic movement. Wallerstein thus concludes that such attempts historically to seize state power could lead ultimately only to a reform of the capitalist system that necessarily also strengthened it. His account of the relation between state power and resistance to capitalism thus severely calls into question, as Foucault does, the assumptions that the state occupies "the whole field of actual power relations"[95] and that a seizure of the state apparatus would necessarily alter the power relations between classes.

Whether or not Foucault, whose relationship to Marxism was ambiguous and complicated (as is perhaps shown by his attempt, in one of the interviews cited above, to "correct" an Althusserian reading of Marx that would locate power primarily in the state apparatus), would be satisfied by Wallerstein's efforts to complicate questions of the relationship between state power and the economic is of course a matter for speculation.[96] But one of the things a Foucauldian analysis might find troubling in Wallerstein's account is his refusal of a more radical critique of causality that might productively interrupt even Wallerstein's analysis, which, while extremely compelling, seems at times to want to secure for itself a kind of transcendental authority. Like Foucault, Wallerstein is interested in interrupting the concept of "truth."[97] But whereas Foucault understood his own project as the forging of a certain number of "fictions" that might "induce effects of truth,"[98] there is a certain "scientificity" in Wallerstein's analysis that threatens to replicate the very instrumental rationality he critiques. In the wake of poststructuralism, it is impossible to read style simply as the external trappings of a discourse, the gilded and superficial paper that hides the valuable present, the costume that disguises the true discourse in all its authenticity. A commitment to poststructuralist theory requires that we insist that there is nothing "outside" of style, that no "true" discourse lies beneath the "form" of the utterance. Thus, analyses like Wallerstein's, if they are to interrupt the (in Wallerstein's terms) "scientific culture" they take as their object of critique, must approach the analysis of the economic on the level of discourse. If, as Wallerstein argues, scientific culture "became the fraternal code of the world's accumulators of capital,"[99] and if such a culture displaced "supposedly culturally-narrow religious bases of knowledge in favour of supposedly trans-cultural scientific bases" that "served as the self-justification of a particularly pernicious form of cultural imperialism,"[100] then some attempt must be made at the level of Wallerstein's own discourse to account for how that scientific culture inflects and moves through, despite his own best efforts, the production of Wallerstein's account of the rise of historical capitalism.

Although the term *ideology* will be largely—although not exclusively—absent from this study, I will at times provisionally take up questions of the economic, the political, and the transformation of culture toward more egalitarian ends. In particular, I will be interested in focusing these questions through my reading of such figures as Georges Bataille, Wallerstein, Spivak, and Gramsci. Because my concern will be primarily with questions of disciplinary power and the subject, I will not take up questions of the ideological at any length. I am committed here to using my current disciplinary training as a lever into a certain number of texts. That training is as a critical reader of texts educated in the disciplines of English and film studies, and not as a sociologist, political philosopher, or economist. This is concurrently my attempt to intervene polemically in discussions of ideology that erase the question of the material,[101] as well as to interrupt, productively, economic analyses such as Wallerstein's, compelling though they might be. This resistance to deploying the term *ideology* is my way of naming the effects of the economic while at the same time attempting to acknowledge the challenge of the radical critique of causality posed by such writers as Foucault, a critique that necessarily calls into question the place assigned ideology by Althusser.

My use of Gramsci will perhaps be seen by some as idiosyncratic, given my hesitations regarding questions of political economy. What perhaps makes Gramsci rather than Althusser available for use in this study is in fact the ambiguity surrounding the location of the struggle for hegemony and political transformation—specifically, is hegemony to be achieved in state or civil society? Must the attaining of political transformation involve first and foremost the seizure of state power, or might transformation occur through other means? Althusser's account of ideology answers these questions with reference to a model of power that I explicitly reject here, one that, as I have already suggested through a reading of Foucault, appears to cast the state as the place from which all power emanates and at which all resistance should be directed. Gramsci, in contrast, suggests that political struggle need not exclusively take the form of a struggle against the state.

Interestingly, Althusser's own reading of Gramsci works to elide this crucial difference. For example, in his "Notes" on ideology, Althusser pays what is perhaps a backhanded compliment to Gramsci, insisting in a footnote that he is the only one who went any distance in the road I am taking. He had the "remarkable" idea that the State could not be reduced to the (Repressive) State Apparatus, but included, as he put it, a certain number of institutions from "civil society": the Church, the Schools, the trade unions, etc. Unfortunately, Gramsci did not systematize his institutions, which remained in the state of acute but fragmentary notes.[102]

Notice that, in this particular reading of Gramsci, civil society is *included* in the state—as if the distinction between them was of little consequence. When Althusser takes up, in a subsequent passage, the question of by what right he regards as Ideological *State* Apparatuses "institutions which for the most part do not possess public status, but are quite simply *private* institutions"[103]—that is, institutions that Gramsci often locates in "civil society"—Althusser answers with a further reference to Gramsci, attributing to him the position that

> the distinction between the public and the private is a distinction internal to bourgeois law, and valid in the (subordinate) domains in which bourgeois law exercises its "authority." The domain of the State escapes it because the latter is "above the law": the State, which is the State *of* the ruling class, is neither public nor private; on the contrary, it is the precondition for any distinction between public and private. The same thing can be said from the starting-point of our State Ideological Apparatuses. It is unimportant whether the institutions in which they are realized are "public" or "private."[104]

(Interestingly, Althusser does not indicate here from which of Gramsci's writings these conclusions have been drawn.)

In these two passages, Althusser makes use of Gramsci by ignoring or at least obscuring Gramsci's (admittedly multivalenced) distinction between civil society and the state, securing, for example, such institutions as the church and schools—institutions that, we recall, Gramsci casts as part of *civil* society—for Althusser's Ideological *State* Apparatuses. Althusser thus attempts in these passages to create a homology of sorts between his Ideological State Apparatuses and Gramsci's civil society. Given the ways in which Gramsci's *Prison Notebooks* continually redefine and reimagine the distinction between civil society and the state, it would be imprudent simply to dismiss Althusser's reading as "wrong"—"partial" though such a reading might be.[105] However, in this particular instance, such an interpretation of Gramsci serves chiefly to shore up in Althusser's text the locating of power primarily in the state, and to circumvent attempts to theorize in a more fluid, dynamic, and complicated manner questions of power, resistance, hegemony, and social transformation—the very thing that many theorists argue might be accomplished through a reading of Gramsci. What is muted in Althusser's reading of Gramsci, is, for example, Gramsci's notion of "common sense" and its ability to act as a starting point for social transformation, for, if common sense is, in Althusser's formulation, a product of the Ideological State Apparatuses and an instantiation of state power (as Althusser argues, State power is exercised in the Ideological State Apparatuses),[106] how can it possibly be developed "to construct an intellectual-moral bloc which can make politically possible the intellectual progress of the mass"?[107] Althusser's notion of the relative autonomy of the Ideological State Apparatuses does recognize that "the resistance of the exploited classes is able to find means and occasions to express itself there."[108] But, given Althusser's casting of the state, why should this necessarily be the case? Althusser seems to suggest, quoting the above-cited passage from *A Contribution to the Critique of Political Economy*, that resistance is expressed on the level of ideology simply because Marx said it was so.

More to the point, what is still left unanswered is the very question of *why* Ideological Apparatuses belong to the state rather than civil society (though, admittedly, Althusser would find this question irrelevant, given his subsuming of civil society under the state). The precondition of Althusser's collapsing of the distinction between the public and the private, and the subsequent attributing of the ability to draw "artificially" such a distinction to the state, is an (Althusserian) investiture of the state with the power to draw such distinctions. In other words, Althusser's analysis suggests that because the state is all-powerful, it is responsible for the production of the artificial and "unimportant" distinctions between public and private, civil society and the state, "repressive" and "ideological" apparatuses.

As Robert Paul Resch has recently argued, Althusser's "notes" on the Ideological State Apparatuses lead to the conclusion that "all ideologies, it would seem, are appendages of the state, and the latter assumes an almost monolithic aura of invincibility."[109] Resch's conclusion here gives credence to a refusal to embrace an Althusserian conception of ideology, for such a conception of ideology necessarily locates power primarily in the state, and assumes that political resistance must largely take the form of a struggle against the state. As I have already noted, both Foucault and Wallerstein have argued the limitations of this account of political resistance and struggle.

What is particularly lost in the appropriation of Gramsci's position by Althusser is what Marcia Landy has characterized, in a different context, as Gramsci's account of "civil society as a crucial political element in the war of position and in the forging of hegemony."[110] As Landy has suggested, such an account is crucial to an understanding of, for example, how forms of popular culture might constitute a possible arena of resistance to prevailing structures of domination. For these reasons I will make use, in a subsequent chapter, of Gramsci, while largely steering clear of ideology, at least as Althusser defines it.[111] Before turning to Gramsci and questions of resistance and the political, however, I would like to consider in my next two chapters the possibilities and problematics involved in an "ethical" resistance to what we might term, after Foucault, the forms of power that produce the subject as subjugated.

Chapter 2

Gay Pornography and Nonproductive Expenditure

I

In an essay written in the mid-1930s, the French renegade surrealist author and "pornographer" Georges Bataille divides human consumption into two parts: one part moves toward the conservation and continuation of life and human activity; the second part, "nonproductive expenditure," moves toward loss, waste, and often violent pleasures.[1] Examples of nonproductive expenditure are luxury, mourning, spectacle, the arts, and so-called perverse sexual activity; in all of them, "the accent is placed on a *loss* that must be as great as possible in order for that activity to take on its true meaning."[2]

Because production is the basis of social homogeneity, nonproductive expenditure represents a threat to the continued maintenance of what Bataille terms "homogeneous society"—"productive society, namely, useful society."[3] The homogeneous realm attempts to establish a homogeneity of social relations so that production might be possible. For Bataille, the foundation of social homogeneity is money, "namely, the calculable equivalent of the different products of collective activity. Money serves to measure all work and makes man a function of measurable products. According to the judgment of *homogeneous* society, each man is worth what he produces . . . he is no more than a function, arranged within measurable limits, of collective production."[4] Money thus establishes a homogeneity between various social elements. Wallerstein has offered a related account of this relationship between capitalist (homogeneous) culture and money: "We talk of capitalist social relations as being a 'universal solvent,' working to reduce everything

28

to a homogeneous commodity form denoted by a single measure of money."[5]

Homogeneous society attempts to exclude useless, nonproductive elements from its homogeneous part. In contemporary society, the homogeneous part of society "is made up of those men who own the means of production or the money *destined for their upkeep or purchase.*"[6] According to Bataille, industrial civilization is characterized by a distinction between the producer and the owner of the means of production. Since the owner, in Bataille's terms, "appropriates the products for himself," it is the owner, and not the producer, who founds social homogeneity. Thus, for Bataille, "in the contemporary period, social homogeneity is linked to the bourgeois class by essential ties."[7]

Nonproductive expenditure is characterized not only by its wastefulness but by the high degree of affect it releases. It forms part of what Bataille characterizes as the heterogeneous world, the world of the Other, both sacred and profane. Bataille terms these two types of heterogeneity "imperative" (sacred) and "impure" (profane).[8] Although homogeneous society attempts to exclude both the noble and the filthy, it often necessarily deploys the noble: because "only the rejection of impoverished forms has a constant fundamental value (such that the least recourse to the reserves of energy represented by these forms requires an operation as dangerous as subversion)," homogeneous society uses what Bataille terms "free-floating imperative forces" in order to combat the elements that are most incompatible with it—that is, such "transgressive" cultural forms as nonproductive, "perverse" sexuality.[9]

Bataille argues that although some conservation is necessary in order to assure the continued maintenance of human culture, this conservation ought ultimately to be subordinated to the principles of nonproductive expenditure: "Men assure their own subsistence or avoid suffering, not because these functions themselves lead to a sufficient result, but in order to accede to the insubordinate function of free expenditure."[10] Interestingly, class struggle represents for Bataille "the grandest form of social expenditure."[11]

In his brilliant study of the formation of the modern subject, *Discipline and Punish*, Michel Foucault argues that modern subjects are produced through a number of historically specific practices of subjection and subjugation. Foucault names these practices as disciplines. Foucault defines disciplines generally as "techniques for assuring the ordering of human multiplicities."[12] Historically linked to such institutions as the army, the monastery, and the workshop, and deployed in the modern period through anonymous practices of child rearing, pedagogy, and the physical training of the body, disciplines "made possible the meticulous control of the operations of the body, which assured the constant subjection of its forces and imposed upon them a relation of docility-utility" (137).

One of the most striking characteristics of modern disciplinary practices is their reliance on what Foucault terms an "economic" deployment of power. Not only do disciplines train "docile" bodies to respond "economically," that is, with a minimum expenditure of energy, resulting in a maximum efficiency; additionally, they rely on what Foucault terms processes of normalization, processes that are themselves "economical" in that they teach the body to respond to "internal" forms of coercion. In other words, they need not rely on a wasteful expenditure of external force in order to accomplish their goals, but rather establish the normal as a principle of coercion to which the subject accedes (184). As Foucault argues, "Discipline increases the forces of the body (in economic terms of utility) and diminishes these same forces (in political terms of obedience)" (138). Disciplines thus work to assure the continued "economical" production of a homogeneous social body via the category of the normal.

To return, then, to the discussion with which I began: In their emphasis on an economical deployment of force, as well as the production of subjects who expend "economically," disciplines are thus opposed to Bataille's notion of nonproductive expenditure. They seek to enforce, and are made possible by, a restrained deployment of force as opposed to the antiproductivity of free expenditure. Disciplines thus privilege conservation rather than loss. They attempt to regulate unnecessary and inappropriate displays of affect, and to produce the body as something useful.

In what follows, I would like to argue, theoretically and polemically, for an understanding of both gay sexuality in general and gay pornography in particular as instances of nonproductive expenditure, cultural forms that on a phantasmatic level counter modern disciplinary society's "economical" deployment of the body in the service of subject formation. Such cultural forms attempt to resist specifically those forms of power that produce the (subjugated) subject. I deploy the terms "counter" and "resist" rather than, say, "overcome," in order to emphasize the way these cultural forms do not overthrow disciplinary means of subject production, but rather respond to their force with a counterforce, attempting to reverse the strategic relation of discipline to body. I will thus be suggesting that gay sexuality and pornography are both theoretically "transgressive" in Foucault's use of the term, in the sense of acting as a testing of a limit's density *as well as necessarily a reinscription of that limit*. As Foucault argues, the relation between limit and transgression "takes the form of a spiral which no simple infraction can exhaust."[13] Thus, while gay sexuality and pornography do not simply escape the limit and move beyond the practices of modern disciplinary society to a utopian place free from constraint, they similarly do not *merely* reinscribe the limit and the homogeneous social that the limit seeks to protect and preserve.

I realize that a certain danger exists in attempting to valorize gay sexuality and pornography as nonproductive expenditure. In his analysis of fascism, Bataille's work reminds us that the lines between an "impure" filthy heterogeneity and an "imperative" sacred one are unstable and easily crossed. Bataille's favored example here is the body of Christ, which, in its bloodied and crucified form, represents an impure heterogeneous element that is then mobilized and transformed, via the Resurrection, into an imperative form.[14] The ever-present danger that an "impure" heterogeneity might be "elevated" to an "imperative" form, which might then serve the needs of homogeneous culture, suggests a number of caveats for a cultural criticism claiming to be "transgressive." For example, in the specific setting of the university, postcolonial homogeneous culture seems currently to need "privileged marginals"—privileged members of cultural minorities—whose (disciplinary) role is to contain the threat of a much more radical deployment of difference that might destabilize homogeneous intellectual culture. Such containment works through a process of assimilation in which the privileged marginal operates in a largely specular relationship to the dominant, failing to challenge, for example, the current regime of truth in which knowledge is produced. A "transgressive" critical response to this (academic) privileging of marginalization requires that the "marginalized" critic engage in a scrupulous and protracted deconstruction of his or her privileged positioning, not simply abandoning that positioning, but attempting to deploy it as a kind of counterlogic of the supplement by elaborating and interrogating its contradictory conditions of possibility.[15] For example, those involved in the formation of the "emerging" discipline of gay and lesbian studies would do well to examine the ways in which their own intellectual production might inadvertently collude with the dominant structures of oppression that it is in their interest to oppose, and to attempt to interrupt such collusion. Obviously, in the very writing of this study, I myself must confront such a challenge. Such are the requirements of what I have termed an ethics of marginality.

Placing this proviso alongside the vocabulary provided by Bataille, we might argue that the problem for a "transgressive, ethical" criticism, a "transgressive" criticism on the side of the Other, thus becomes how to make use of Bataille's theme of nonproductive expenditure and impure forms of heterogeneity, given that such a critical valuation always runs the risk of elevating the nonproductive into something useful, that is, always runs the risk of transforming impure forms of heterogeneity into imperative forms in the service of homogeneous culture. How might criticism conserve only what makes a continued expenditure possible?

My very provisional answer to such a dilemma is to suggest that because a valorization of transgression, a valorization of otherness, always runs the risk of making productive the antiproductive, criticism must always search for new forms of resistance, once the old forms have been rendered culturally useful. Criticism must fluctuate according to the cultural moment, strategically critiquing the antiproductive most recently raised to the status of the useful, and valorizing tactically the currently nonproductive. Such a criticism must thus, perhaps paradoxically, resist the continued attempts of liberal culture to bring the Other into the center, and move us instead toward the impossible project of thinking through a radical heterogeneity.[16] For the privileged marginal critic, this means, among other things, attempting to put on the table the problematic of one's having been produced as a subject who both is and is not (marginalized, privileged). Such will be the challenge of the following three chapters of this study.

I turn now to questions of gay sexuality and pornography, arguing against what I read as a recent critical attempt to rehabilitate pornography, to transform the threat of its antiproductivity into something useful. Such a transformation moves to conserve the subjugated modern subject rather than attempt to counter its current (disciplinary) formation. In particular, it bears witness to a desire to conserve the subject's sovereignty by referring to a universal humanity that we are all presumed to share. The attempt to rehabilitate gay pornography to a useful end reminds us that, in this historical moment, pornography is itself an unstable form. Like the body of Christ, like other forms of spectacle, pornography seems to be a heterogeneous form that crosses back and forth between the impure and the imperative. Pornography's status as commodity is obviously significant here, for, while it re-presents the sexual body as nonproductive, it simultaneously "produces" tremendous monetary profits. It circulates in and through various and varying relations of power. These relations, though not existing in total isolation from one another, are not identical. This account of power-in-relation suggests that forms of nonproductive expenditure are clearly commodifiable but are not *merely* commodifiable. The meaning of pornography is neither opposed to, nor exhausted in, its status as commodity. It thus seems ethically appropriate, if not imperative, to counter strategically—and not simply oppose—pornography's impending rehabilitation (which may or may not be related to its increasing commodification).

II

In his essay "Coming to Terms," Richard Dyer argues that pornography "can be the site for 're-educating desire' and in a way that constructs desire in the body, not merely theoretically in relation to, and often against, it."[17] Dyer's essay defends pornography in general, and gay male pornography in particular, on the grounds that "an art rooted in bodily effect can give us a knowledge of the body that other art cannot." This defense privileges gay male pornography as a genre; it does so, however, not for what the pornography currently does, but for what it might do in the future. For although such pornography currently provides a knowledge of the body, "it is mainly bad knowledge, reinforcing the worst aspects of the social construction of masculinity that men learn to experience in our bodies." Dyer is thus both critical and prescriptive, suggesting that gay pornography currently mirrors prevailing cultural understandings of masculine sexuality but need not do so in the future. Dyer's position thus announces itself at the outset as rehabilitative. It seeks to transform what Dyer reads as a "negative" cultural practice into something more culturally (and, Dyer might claim, politically) useful.

Dyer is one of the most influential British film critics of his generation. Up until recently one of only a handful of openly gay scholars in film studies, Dyer's most recent work has concentrated specifically on questions of gay spectatorship and gay film production. Precisely because Dyer's contribution to gay film studies has been particularly noteworthy, I will be critiquing his reading of pornography extensively here, for, as I will be suggesting throughout this chapter, Dyer's work represents one of the most celebrated "liberal" attempts by a gay film critic to deal with questions of cultural marginality and the gay and lesbian subject.

Dyer's desire to rehabilitate pornography comes as no surprise to the reader in light of the way "Coming to Terms" fronts its feminist and "socialist" (Dyer's term) politics. From feminism, Dyer borrows a commitment to overthrowing what he terms "the gender role system" that he sees embodied in contemporary gay pornography. From socialism, he adopts the understanding of all cultural texts as marked by "moments of contradiction" from which change might be effected, so that even an apparently "reactionary" genre such as pornography might be the starting point for cultural transformation (289). (I will have more to say later about both this feminism and this socialism.) Dyer's model for what pornography might do is thus (not coincidentally) the "lesbian" sequence from Chantal Akerman's *je tu il elle*, which, according to Dyer, breaks with the "bad knowledge" offered by gay male pornography while still providing an occasion for a bodily knowledge of the body.[18]

What is this "bad" knowledge that gay male pornography currently affords its spectators? According to Dyer, what characterizes gay male pornography is its narrative drive. All gale male pornography is structured around the desire to have an orgasm, and thus embodies what Dyer terms, after David Bordwell and Kristin Thompson, "a classic goal directed narrative":

> The desire that drives the porn narrative forward is the desire to come, to have an orgasm. And it seems to me that male sexuality, homo or hetero, is socially constructed, at the level of representation anyway, in terms of narrative; that, as it were, male sexuality is itself understood narratively. . . . The goal of the pornographic narrative is coming; in filmic terms, the goal is ejaculation, that is, visible coming. If the goal of the pornographic protagonist (the actor or "character") is to come, the goal of the spectator is to see him come (and, more often than not, to come at the same time as him). (293)

The problem with this goal, the thing that makes it "bad" for (Dyer's) feminist-inflected gay liberation politics, is that it necessarily reinstantiates "the masculine model of gay sexuality, a model that always implies the subordination of women" (294). Dyer does not elaborate on the relation of a "narrative" masculine model of gay sexuality to the subordination of women, apparently considering the relation self-evident. Nevertheless, it seems clear that what Dyer objects to in gay pornography is its driving desire to expend in orgasm, and to expend in a way that seems politically suspect.

One of my most serious reservations concerning Dyer's analysis of pornography is that such an analysis relies on a theory of reading problematized by poststructuralism, a theory that understands reading as a process whereby what is "structured" in the text is transmitted to the reader. Dyer does not hold that there is a single "right" reading for every text. Nor does he treat the text as a completely open field for the play of meaning. Rather, Dyer attempts to account for the multiplicity of readings to which a given text might give rise with reference to the real (historical) circumstances in which that text is produced and read.[19] For Dyer, ideological contradictions in the real produce the text itself as contradictory and thus make possible a variety of readings, "resistant" and otherwise. Unfortunately, because Dyer fails to recognize how the itinerary of the reading he brings to pornography necessarily produces what he is able to read, he is led to offer an extremely monovocal reading of pornography, a reading that cannot adequately acknowledge the heterogeneous weaving of the porno text. In other words, Dyer's model of reading, with its emphasis on the text itself, obscures the readings brought to bear on porno texts as themselves contested spaces of and for the production of cultural explanations. It fails to take up how the production of explanations of texts might itself be, in Dyer's sense of the term, "ideological." It also makes no productive use of the deconstructive tenet that "every interpretation must make systematic omission of incompatible, though no less possible, interpretations."[20] I want now to suggest at some length that such a tacit rejection of deconstruction renders Dyer's project at odds with itself.

It is perhaps a stretch to extrapolate from Derrida's analysis in "Structure, Sign, and Play in the Discourse of the Human Sciences" to Dyer's analysis. Derrida deals with questions raised by Lévi-Strauss's structuralist anthropology, whereas Dyer takes up questions of narrative and genre.[21] However, a kind of structuralism operating in Dyer's text makes such an extrapolation plausible, provided we define structuralism broadly as the attempt to provide an "objective" description of "a unit composed of a few elements that are invariably found in the same relationship within the 'activity' being described."[22] Dyer's contention that all film pornography is structured as a narrative of movement towards orgasm corresponds roughly to the structuralist's attempt "to reconstruct (*reconstituer*) an 'object' in such a way as to manifest thereby the rules of its functioning (the 'functions') of this object."[23]

To place Dyer's analysis alongside Derrida's account of structure, then: Dyer's analysis is totalizing. (Recall that the premise of Dyer's argument is that all filmic pornography is structured as a narrative, and the very same narrative at that.) The analysis is, with apologies for the awkwardness of this term, "pre-poststructuralist," if not exactly structuralist. That is, its account of porno as narratively structured and orgasm-centered conforms to certain aspects of Derrida's account of classical notions of structure. For example, Dyer provides pornography with a narrative structure by assigning it a fixed center: "the goal of the pornographic narrative is coming; in filmic terms, the goal is ejaculation, that is, visible coming."[24] As Derrida argues, such an assignation of a center to a structure serves "not only to orient, balance, and organize the structure"—Derrida's vocabulary reminding us of why arguments like Dyer's are often labeled "formalist"—but also works "to make sure that the organizing principle of the structure would limit what we might call the free play of the structure." According to Derrida, the center qua center "is the point at which the substitution of contents, elements, or terms is no longer possible. At the center, the permutation or the transformation of elements . . . is forbidden."[25] This is precisely the point of Dyer's analysis: regardless of how the individual porno texts may vary, regardless of the multiple interpretations to which the free-play of the porno text might give rise, the orgasmic centeredness of the porno narrative always remains the same. In this sense, Dyer's analysis is pre-poststructuralist, prior to the thinking through of what Derrida terms the structurality of structure.[26]

The problem with Dyer's analysis is not, however, that it is merely what I have called pre-poststructuralist, but that such an attitude renders

Dyer's analysis at cross purposes with itself. Dyer claims that, in the act of analyzing pornography, he is "constantly looking for moments of contradiction, instability and give in our culture, the points at which change can be effected."[27] Yet, by assigning a center to the structure of porn, he is necessarily limiting the free-play of the porno text, its moments of instability. Dyer's analysis thus evokes what Derrida terms "the concept of centered structure," in which, in this particular instance, the individually variant porno texts and the multiple meaning-effects such texts might produce are held in check through recourse to "a freeplay based on a fundamental ground, a freeplay which is constituted upon a fundamental immobility and a reassuring certitude, which is itself beyond the reach of the freeplay." Derrida argues that with this (critical) certitude, "anxiety can be mastered, for anxiety is invariably the result of a certain mode of being implicated in the game, of being caught by the game, of being as it were from the very beginning at stake in the game."[28] Later in this chapter, I will argue that the anxiety that Dyer's analysis attempts to evade is the anxiety provoked by gay pornography's recourse to nonproductive expenditure, and its accompanying critique of the sovereign subject. Dyer's centering of the porno narrative around orgasm—a centering that his analysis paradoxically seeks to undo through the evoking of a utopian, nonorgasmic pornography to come—is a centering of the subject that reassures the certitude of sovereignty by bracketing off the wasteful, nonproductive threat to the disciplined body re-presented by orgasm. Dyer's critical position vis-à-vis pornography is thus conservative, and precisely in the way most liberal positions usually are.

In what follows, I will counter Dyer's reading of pornography with a reading teased out by the implications of his own position in order to open up the possibility of thinking differently about pornography. As I have already suggested, I will thus have recourse to close reading even as I call such close readings into question (for Dyer's analysis is itself dependent on a close reading of pornography). Such a strategy will inform the remainder of this study as well. Beginning wherever I am, as someone trained in the study of English and film at a particular moment in history, in a text where I already believe myself to be,[29] I will be attempting to act as a *bricoleur*, "someone who uses 'the means at hand,' that is, the instruments he finds at his disposition around him, those which are already there, which had not been especially conceived with an eye to the operation for which they are to be used and to which one tries by trial and error to adapt them, not hesitating to change them whenever it appears necessary, or to try several of them at once, even if their form and their origin are heterogeneous—and so forth."[30] This attempt to act as bricoleur will be tempered with the recognition of the limits of such activity. "It is a question of putting expressly and systematically the problem of the status of a discourse which borrows from a heritage the resources necessary for the deconstruction of that heritage it-self."[31] Thus, I will both use the means at hand provided to me by my po-sition as a subject of both modern disciplinary society in general and an aca-demic discipline in particular, as well as attempt to complicate and interrupt such a use.[32]

III

Early in his essay, Dyer defines the "narrative elements" of the porno film as involving some kind of "beginning" where one or more characters "enter" the scene, a "middle" consisting of sexual contact, and an "end" consisting of coming. According to Dyer, even the most "minimal" porno film—an ac-tor masturbating for the camera—contains these narrative elements, and even the ubiquitous porno "loop" popularized by the quarter movie arcade is structured in such a way that, no matter at what point individual viewers "enter" the narrative, they will be "conscious of where the narrative has got to" and will be able to reconstruct the narrative's elements.[33]

Dyer's analysis, however, fails to account for why these three particu-lar elements—entering, masturbating, coming—should constitute the events of the porno narrative, and precisely how the reader determines them. It seems to argue that the "beginnings" and "ends" of a narrative are self-evi-dent, structured into a text, and empirically verifiable. One might compli-cate Dyer's reading, however, with recourse to something as apparently ma-terially obvious as the porno "text itself," deploying a formal analysis like Dyer's to contrary ends. For example, many porno films "begin" in medias res—and Dyer himself acknowledges that they do—with characters already undressed and engaging in sexual activity, so that the beginning of the nar-rative appears arbitrary, constituted by the mechanical act of turning on the camera. Of course, it is possible—perhaps even necessary—for the spectator to construct a plausible "beginning" to this narrative in order to make it intelligible. Such a construction, however, might at least theoretically move in an infinite regress so that no "origin" to the narrative is ever ultimately reached. Dyer's own argument, in its insistence that the spectator who has never seen a particular film before will nonetheless be "conscious of where the narrative has got to" (292), thus paradoxically suggests that a produced reading of the narrative is *not* fundamentally dependent on the materiality of the film itself. This result in turn suggests that narrative itself is a practice of reading, a historically constituted framework of intelligibility, and not merely "structural."

Similarly, few porno narratives end at the moment of orgasm. Some feature the actors kissing and holding one another following ejaculation.

Others may feature them engaging in some other activity together, such as jumping into a swimming pool. In *Hot on His Tail*, the end of one particular sequence—which seems to conclude, contrary to Dyer, with one of the actors engaging in the wasteful and perverse (not to mention acrobatic) act of licking the head of his own penis following ejaculation—is deliberately complicated by what appear to be outtakes of the beginning of the same sequence reedited into the film. A voice-over explains that these shots represent future encounters between the same two partners. To say that this sequence "ends" with orgasm seems to be inaccurate, or at least to overlook a significant aspect of this text that a formal analysis such as Dyer's would presumably take into account. As is the case with beginnings, however, there is no necessary reason for casting the "literal" end of the film as the closure of the narrative. If narratives can begin in medias res, they can also end in some unspecified, perpetually-projected-towards future.

Additionally, Dyer assumes that the goal of the porno narrative—supposedly, orgasm—is also self-evident, structured into the film. One wonders about the source of this conclusion. Unlike many Hollywood films, in which characters' goals are often aurally articulated through such things as dialogue or voice-over narration, the "goal" of coming is seldom spoken by the porno protagonists, and when it is spoken, it is usually announced immediately prior to orgasm, at which point the declaration is somewhat redundant. In fact, the frequently commented-on redundancy of much pornography—in particular, the extreme close-ups, in gay pornography, of oral and anal penetration, and the frequent repetition of identical shots—might be argued to be the result of porn's interest not in ejaculation, but in an almost obsessive desire to document the repetition of the sexual act. This redundancy, combined with the (apparent) hesitancy of the characters to verbalize their (alleged) goal of orgasm, suggests that porn might in fact privilege the deferring, rather than the achievement, of orgasm. Much more common in pornography than verbal articulations of the desire to achieve orgasm are explicit commands such as "Fuck me" and "Suck my dick," commands that also seem to privilege a deferring of orgasm by doubling the image text, slowing down the chain of signification by augmenting and insisting on what is already excessively obvious.

In other words, gay pornography's verbal commands are precisely not on the order of commentary. They do not attempt to fill a lack, revealing and specifying for the very first time what the image has actually signified all along. They are, rather, anti-interpretations, attempts to thwart the lack that makes signification possible. Such a thwarting pursues, in pornography, a strategy of mimicry. Perhaps the redundancy of the porno text, its repetition and deferment of orgasm, is not a desperate attempt to cover over lack under the guise of the sexual. Perhaps, rather, it suggests a mimicry of what is often called the sexual, a mimicry that deconstructs the claims of the sexual to complete the subject in the Other through the act of reproduction. Perhaps such a mimicry opens up, in gay pornography, the fantastic possibility of an endless and nonabating expenditure—deferring as long as possible, but not ultimately rejecting, that small (conservative) productivity represented by nonprocreative ejaculation—by unveiling, rendering obvious, the lack that makes signification possible. Such a deferring mimicry conserves perhaps just enough of the subject to make a continued expenditure possible.

Although the porno text does not seem to articulate the goal of orgasm overtly, it might be argued that such a goal is implanted in the text by the spectator through recourse to something like a transtextual system of conventions. It might be argued that, having seen a number of porno films that "end" in orgasm, the spectator determines that this film will probably end similarly, and thus rightly imputes this goal to the narrative. But this interpretation only emphasizes that narrative is a learned way of reading, and not something "inherent" to the text. In other words, the porn reader constructed in Dyer's analysis must approach the porno text with the assumption that it is moving toward orgasm in order to read it in this way. An event is not in and of itself a goal without recourse to some divine system in which all ends are predestined and predetermined. Dyer's analysis of orgasm as end is in fact made possible by a teleology that posits sexuality as moving toward orgasm—the very position Dyer claims to want to contest in his vision of a new and improved pornography. The "physical evidence" of the porno text, with its multiplicity of possible endings, is in fact much more heterogeneous than Dyer's analysis allows.

Dyer's insistence that the spectator is supposed to come with the actor seems extremely speculative and idiosyncratic, not even based on a reading of any kind of textual "evidence." Moreover, Dyer's narrative analysis fails to mention either that, on many occasions, more than one actor comes (and they rarely do so simultaneously) or that sometimes one of the actors doesn't come at all. Even if we were to adopt Dyer's reading of the porno film narrative as moving towards orgasm, we would at the very least have to speak of multiple desires and goals and "false" closures. This requirement is particularly significant for the representation of anal sex. According to Dyer, "Particularly significant here is the fact that although the pleasure of anal sex (that is, of being anally fucked) is represented, the narrative is never organized around the desire to be fucked, but around the desire to ejaculate (whether or not following on from anal intercourse" (294). This reading unravels in a number of different directions. First, in some sequences in some porno films, men are fucked who do not come. To insist that the narrative is not organized around their desire is to be locked in advance within a specular logic of orgasm that would assume that the partner who ejaculates in these kinds of sequences is the one whose desire is being pursued in the narrative and with whom the spectator is supposed to identify. Again, such a privileging of ejaculation is precisely what Dyer claims to want to contest in his pursuit of a reeducation of male desire through porn. Second, men being fucked often lose their erections in porno films. How is this event to be read? Although Dyer's reading would suggest that these are moments of displeasure, or at least interruptions of much-desired narrative movement, at least some discourse in a gay male community suggests that it may in fact be pleasurable to be fucked without an erection.[34]

What "alternative" does Dyer propose to gay pornography? Recall here his contention that Akerman's film in particular represents a possible foil for this masculinist model of sexuality embodied in gay male pornography. What is the basis for such a claim, and what does this "alternative" pornography look like? According to Dyer, the lesbian sequence at the end of *je tu il elle* "does not have the narrative drive of male porn. It starts in medias res."[35] As I have already argued, and as Dyer's own argument concedes, Akerman's film does not, so far, seem very different from a number of gay male porno films.[36] Dyer goes on to say that "there is no sense [in *je tu il elle*] of a progression to the goal of orgasm."[37] One has to wonder what might "count" here as "evidence" of a progression toward orgasm. Is the assumption that women don't "need" to have an orgasm during sex what allows Dyer to produce this reading of the women making love as *not* moving toward orgasm? Finally, Dyer asserts that there is no

> attempt to find visual or even (as in hetero porn?) aural equivalents for the visible male ejaculation. In particular, there is no sense of genital activity being the last, and getting-down-to-the-real-thing, stage of the experience. It is done in three long takes—no editing cuts across a sexual narrative (as in gay porn . . .); the harsh white lighting and the women's white bodies on crumpled white sheets in a room painted white, contribute to the effect of representing the sexuality as more dissolving and ebbing than a masculine thrusting narrative. (293-94)

I have written elsewhere of the dangers of arguing that female orgasm represents a "problem" for pornography that male orgasm does not. Only from within a certain specular logic can it be assumed that the male orgasm is "essentially" more visible than the female orgasm.[38] As I will suggest at greater length later in this chapter and subsequently, the problem of visibility is a vexing one, for while the production of disciplinary subjects requires ever-increasing forms of surveillance, such surveillance also makes possible a "reverse discourse" whereby subjects might resist disciplinarity.

The analysis of pornography, I will argue shortly, depends on an acknowledgment of this predicament. I would only want to add that the commonplace assumption that hetero porn uses sound to "make visible" the "invisible" female orgasm does not consider the fact that most gay male porno films also feature a great deal of aural "evidence" of pleasure.

What Dyer's formal analysis fails to explore here is the "bodily effect" of the specific cultural imagining of sexuality deployed by *je tu il elle*. Dyer himself defines pornography as *"any* film that has as its aim sexual arousal in the spectator."[39] Dyer's analysis, however, cannot account for how the critic as viewer manages to diagnose whether or not a given film *intends* to arouse. Apparently, this intention is self-evident to the critic. One wonders if Dyer was in fact aroused by Akerman's film. If he was, how does he account for the fact that the majority of other male viewers, according to the implications of Dyer's own argument, are not? (If they were already aroused by the film, desire would be in need of no reeducation—at least not the kind of reeducation that Akerman's film could provide.) If Dyer was not aroused by the film, on what "bodily" basis does he determine that the film should act as a model for gay pornography?[40] More to the point here, Dyer does not explore how a representation of a "dissolving and ebbing" sexuality in a film like *je tu il elle* might come into conflict with pornography's "goal" of arousing the spectator. Implicit in Dyer's analysis is a biologism that assumes both that (at least politically efficacious) female desire *is* aroused by ebbing and flowing, and that male ejaculation does not involve the same.[41]

Dyer tacitly assumes here that the project of "reeducating desire" through pornography must involve teaching (male) spectators to desire differently, in a way that Dyer (among others) would find less politically offensive. How does Dyer want to use porno to reeducate desire? Near the end of his essay, Dyer spells out what he finds most valuable in a particular gay porno film, the final sequence from a film entitled *Wanted*, in which actor Al Parker "licks the semen off [Will] Seagers' penis."[42] Admitting that "some men I know who've seen the film find this final sequence too conventionally romantic (which it is—that's why I like it)," Dyer argues that what he finds most promising in this film is "an explicit and arousing moment of genital sexuality that itself expressed a tender emotional feeling—through its place in the narrative, through the romanticism of the setting, through the delicacy of Parker's performance. If porn taught us *this* more often. . . . " (296; emphasis in original). Apparently, *this* is the familiar humanist model of sexuality as the appropriate consummation of a relationship of romantic love or friendship, a consummation that allows for the expression of feelings of tenderness. According to Dyer, then, what porn apparently ought to teach gay men is how to be more romantic—while still giving good head.

Dyer's conclusion should come as no surprise, considering the antipornography feminists he cites approvingly in his essay, as well as his statement that "I do not feel as out of sympathy with, say, Andrea Dworkin's work as many people, and especially gay men, that I know" (290). At this point in the history of the feminist debates in pornography, it should be unnecessary to state that Dyer's imagining of sexuality in "Coming to Terms" is not the only one espoused by feminism. In fact, a significant body of feminist work would argue that pornography has value for women because it offers them something other than the historically familiar view of feminine sexuality as tender, romantic, "ebbing and flowing."[43] Moreover, Leo Bersani, who does not explicitly define his position as feminist, has argued persuasively that much of the pornography debates articulates a certain cultural revulsion around sexuality, thus demonstrating sexuality's threat to culturally sanctified notions of a self and its boundaries.[44] Thus, what Dyer laments in pornography, a certain refusal of romanticism and tenderness, is exactly what Bersani values.

My point here is not primarily that there is something inherently wrong with the model of sexuality espoused by Dyer (though as I have already suggested, via Bataille, it is a model that I would strategically argue against). Rather, what seems lacking in Dyer's analysis is some kind of interrogation of this model, and the ways in which it necessarily produces Dyer's reading of pornography. Dyer's cultural understanding of sexuality—one clearly not idiosyncratic to Dyer, but also not the only one available—is one of the conditions of possibility for an analysis of desire as in need of reeducation. Yet no real *argument* is forthcoming in Dyer concerning this model of sexuality. The implication is that a (feminist-inflected) politically oppositional theory/practice ought "naturally" to argue for a liberal humanist understanding of both gay male sexuality and pornography as in need of a romantic redemption. Dyer's argument presupposes an apparently self-evident "incorrect" masculine sexuality, which gay pornography currently mirrors, and a corollary "correct" sexuality that porno texts ought to reflect, once desire has been reeducated (though, admittedly, Dyer does seem to suggest that there is a kind of reciprocal reflection between texts and "the real"). One of the results of this stance is that "Coming to Terms" can appeal to a disturbingly familiar understanding of sexuality in order to make its plea for the reeducation of desire, an almost "natural" model that sees an aggressive and destructive masculine sexuality as in need of a feminine (and not necessarily feminist) domestication, and that seeks to rein in the antiproductive possibilities of sexuality. Dyer's analysis seems in fact to be an argument against the impure heterogeneous elements in pornography, for what Dyer seems to object to is pornography's "waste," its emphasis on a nonproductive expenditure not linked to the theme of romantic love.

Many attempts to differentiate between pornography and eroticism draw their distinctions along the lines of the "impure" and the "imperative," with pornography clearly representing the "impure" side of this coupling. For example, Gloria Steinem associates pornography with "force, violence, or symbols of unequal power," while linking eroticism with "a mutual pleasure and touch and warmth, an empathy for each other's bodies and nerve endings, a shared sensuality and a spontaneous sense of two people who are there because they *want* to be."[45] Steinem's analysis privileges sexuality "as a form of expression, a way of communicating," as well as "a way of bonding, of giving and receiving pleasure, bridging differentness, discovering sameness, and communicating emotion."[46] The emphasis here is clearly on the use-value of sexuality, a use-value associated with the potential of the sexual to annihilate difference and provide the imaginary unification of the subject in the Other. This cultural imagining of sexuality as unification has been seriously called into question by a Lacanian-influenced psychoanalytic feminism. As Jacqueline Rose insists:

> Sexuality belongs in this area of instability played out in the register of demand and desire, each sex coming to stand, mythically and exclusively, for that which could satisfy and complete the other. It is when the categories "male" and "female" are seen to represent an absolute and complementary division that they fall prey to a mystification in which the difficulty of sexuality instantly disappears. . . . Lacan therefore argued that psychoanalysis should not try to produce "male" and "female" as complementary entities, sure of each other and of their own identity, but should expose the fantasy on which this notion rests.[47]

Steinem's reading of sexuality—which admittedly predates Rose's formulation by three years—seems to rest on precisely such a fantasy. She contrasts "erotic" representations of mutuality and connection with pornography's "obscene" and "filthy" representations, which always feature scenes of domination.[48]

As the debates in feminism around questions of sexuality suggest, sexuality itself is a highly contested discursive arena, one in which (ethical) struggles over intelligibility occur. It, too, is textual, a heterogeneous weave of competing practices "open" to competing explanations. It is not simply "prior" to representation, pornographic or otherwise, but is "invented" over and over again through the mobilization and remobilization of historically discontinuous discourses producing a multiplicity of subject-effects.

The difficulties of writing about pornography today are enormous. On the one hand, the field is fraught with overzealous valorizations of pornography that, in their desire to argue the benefits of the genre, necessarily reinstantiate a subject who freely "chooses" to watch or participate in the production of porno films. Such valorizations often fail to take into account such things as pornography's status as commodity, its contradictory articulations of gender roles and sexualities, and its privileging of sexuality as a locus of the truth of the individual.[49] They necessarily conserve the figure of the intentional subject, a conservation that a more "transgressive" understanding of pornography might seek to interrupt. On the other hand, many arguments against pornography make sweeping conclusions about pornography's purported violence without specific reference to a single text, treat the genre in such a way as to deny its significant heterogeneity, employ the most mechanistic notions of causality when describing the relationship between pornography and its spectator, and seem uninterested in working to articulate the ideologies around sexuality and theories of power on which they are premised.[50] They, too, often seek to conserve the sovereign subject, in this particular instance, with reference to a subject untouched by the purported evils of power. Such arguments specifically often attempt to call up a mythic eroticism opposed to power. As Judith Butler has argued in response to this position, "If sexuality is culturally constructed within existing power relations, then the postulation of a normative sexuality that is 'before,' 'outside,' or 'beyond' power is a cultural impossibility and a politically impracticable dream, one that postpones the concrete and contemporary task of rethinking subversive possibilities for sexuality and identity within the terms of power itself."[51]

An alternative position to either one of these is the current flurry of "academic" studies of pornography like Dyer's, studies that are admittedly more careful than most "popular" discussions in that they often address some of the problems mentioned above. These studies are often, however, most useful for what they tell us about how individual disciplines construct their objects of study and methods of analysis. Formalist readings of pornography seem to want to instantiate a method of reading pornography that has little in common with its "nonacademic" modes of reception, a "professional" method that must be learned through a kind of codified disciplinary training in film studies. The securing of pornography as a "serious" and useful object of study for the humanities has seemed historically to require this approach. Perhaps responding to forces outside of the university that might challenge the universal humanism on which such things as canon formation depend, the humanities have found, in pornography, one of many means of containing the threat of difference. This is one way to understand the recent flurry of academic studies of pornography.

Given the ways in which Foucault invites us to reimagine power, however, such a containment is always limited, and makes possible new forms of resistance. The "normalization" of academic studies of pornography makes possible certain "aberrant" studies in this same location. Readings of pornography might in fact make a productive use of the hybrid position of (necessarily "fictive") gay intellectuals within the academy. Pornography in particular seems currently to provide a means whereby gay and lesbian subjects can utilize their multiple positionings in order to call into crisis a discipline's production of textual explanations. Specifically, the subject-effect we might loosely and provisionally name "homosexual" has access to a realm of discursive practices that might suggest the absurdity of subjecting porno films to the kinds of extensive formal analyses often popular in academic film circles. Although Dyer's work is formal analysis, "Coming to Terms" also contains an attempt to call into crisis this kind of analysis through, for example, the "commonsense" observation that the modes of reception of gay porn are quite different from those of other kinds of films. In other words, Dyer's (discursive) "experience" of porn calls into crisis his own disciplinary training as a film scholar. For example, as Dyer's own analysis implies, the porno film is often merely a kind of alibi that makes possible the securing of sexual activity. As Dyer himself argues, "Watching porn in gay cinemas usually involves having sex as well—-not just self-masturbation but sexual activity with others."[52] These conditions of reception significantly challenge analyses of pornography that assume that readers make sense of porno films through the reading of such cues as editing, lighting, or mise-en-scène. If anything, the "distracted" television spectator, whose viewing processes are interrupted by such activities as domestic chores, a ringing telephone, and the like, is a much more appropriate model for the porn spectator than the (relatively) "immobilized" film spectator posited by certain incarnations of reception theory.[53] Although the films may increase the arousal level of the men engaging in sex in the video booths, they may also be ignored completely. To subject these kinds of films to a close analysis would seem, in this instance, absurd.[54] The "gay intellectual," who has access (has acceded?) to these two sets of reading practices—"academic" and "experiential"—might thus use his "experiential" knowledge as a lever, enabling an interrogation of the means by which disciplines produce explanations of their objects.

Following Dyer's example, I would like, in what follows, to "use" my having been produced as a "gay" subject to interrupt and complicate the disciplinary production by film studies of explanations of pornography, particularly around questions of visibility and pornography. Specifically: Psychoanalytic film criticism, a highly defined, refined, and contested method of reading films, has appeared to some theorists to be the most appropriate reading framework through which to approach pornography, since both pornography and psychoanalysis take sexuality and gender as their objects of interest, if not study. Yet at least one incarnation of psychoanalytic film criticism has seemed strangely ill equipped to describe the relationship between pornography and the spectator. In particular, psychoanalysis's casting of "the gaze" as sadistic and controlling is, to say the least, inadequate to an understanding of the pornographic spectator.

Much has been made in psychoanalytic film criticism of scopophilia—the sexualizing of the drive to see—and the relationship between scopophilia and sadism. What most psychoanalytic analyses of pornography take for granted is the genre's desire to record visual evidence of bodily pleasure, to see more of such pleasure, and to see it better. This is one way of reading pornography's (supposed) interest in the visual evidence of orgasm represented by the "money shot," in which penetration is interrupted in order to make ejaculation visible.[55]

As I have already suggested, this desire to make of the body a field for visual pleasure must be considered alongside modern disciplinary society's insistence that the subject render itself increasingly visible. Concerning this relationship between disciplinary society and visibility, Foucault writes, "It is the fact of being constantly seen, of being able always to be seen, that maintains the disciplined individual in his subjection."[56] This point will be argued at some length in the next chapter in a discussion of cultural minorities and visibility. As Foucault's reformulation of power reminds us, however, this increasing demand for visibility also necessarily produces resistance. One such resisting counterstrategy might be to make an undisciplined use of the visible body. Pornography must thus be considered alongside both of these factors. It is neither simply a machine in the service of disciplinary society, nor simply an attempt to evade such disciplinarity. Thus the position that "film pornography can be viewed as an important mechanism in the wholesale restructuring of the experience of sexuality into a visual form"[57]—a position often attributed to Foucault—only tells half the story, at least as Foucault would have it.[58]

My own cultural understanding of pornography—an understanding arrived at through watching pornography both by myself and with other men, in situations that might be described as both overtly sexual and not—suggests that pornography is an instantiation not merely of the desire to see visual evidence of bodily pleasure, but of the desire to see in a certain way, from a certain angle, a certain part of the body or activity, depending on the sexual proclivities of the spectator.[59] This proliferation of ways of seeing the sexual body might be understood as both an instantiation of, and attempt to counter, the power of the disciplinary gaze through a multiplication of looks. Such a proliferation opens up the gaze to the threat of a heterogeneity that it perhaps cannot contain.

Specifically: In pursuit of its desire to render the body ever more visible, pornography fragments and magnifies the body, offering it up to an intense and studious gaze. Given the limits of the filmic medium, however, such a gaze is necessarily circumscribed to a limited area of the body. In other words, film cannot simultaneously present part and whole. During a close-up, for example, the fragmentation of the body necessitates that most of the body remain outside the field of vision. This fragmentation, an attempt to view the body more closely, thus necessarily produces a certain resistance to the gaze. In a desperate attempt to capture the body, the pornographic gaze must oscillate uneasily between looking over the whole of the body and examining in detail a variety of isolated parts. This is why the gaze must never come to rest on any particular activity, angle, body, or body fragment for too long. (Note the large number of edits in many porno films.) Otherwise, as I will discuss shortly, the body threatens to evoke a certain resistance to the gaze that renders that gaze "boring." Such an oscillation might in some cumulative sense render the body increasingly visible, but in specific and isolated moments it necessarily thwarts the disciplinary gaze. Filmic pornography, with its introduction of the mobile, temporally continuous gaze, is thus both inferior and superior to, for example, still photography: inferior in that, in its fragmentation of the body, it necessarily thwarts the desire to see, and superior in that, in its fragmentation of the body, it promises an ever-expanding field of visual pleasure. The pleasure of pornography is thus intimately bound up with its unpleasure. It always fails, and yet it always succeeds.

In general terms, the pleasure pornography *as a commodity* strives to offer is the pleasure of seeing in a way that might be most pleasurable to a wide variety of spectators. This wide variety of spectators is necessarily positioned, however, within the competing versions of the gaze unleashed by pornography's "frenzy of the visible."[60] Historical subjects are situated "between," as it were, these heterogeneous versions of the gaze, finding pleasure—and unpleasure—in them. The textual field of the sexual is heterogeneous enough to suggest a number of different historically specific possibilities of visual pleasure. This is one way to make sense of the genre's use of such apparently "unnecessary" devices as editing, lighting, mise-en-scène, costume, and so on, which would seem superfluous to the desire *merely* to render a nonresisting body increasingly visible.[61]

The pornographic gaze's frenzied pursuit of the body is further complicated by pornography's status as commodity. Over, as it were, the competing versions of the gaze operating in pornography—competing versions set into motion by the play of power and resistance—the commodification of pornography attempts to institute a universal, and thus commodifiable, gaze. This commodifying, universalizing gaze must find, in its increasing pursuit of consumers, a method of normalizing, or at least systematizing, the heterogeneity of the pornographic gaze. Such a project is necessarily complicated by the play of power and resistance. This is yet another way of understanding the commonplace that much of pornography is redundant, even boring. The reason much of pornography might seem boring to an individual viewer is that, in a given moment, it is in fact soliciting a particular way of seeing that does not arouse that particular spectator. In other words, the pornographic text, in its desperate pursuit of a variety of competing normalized ways of looking, passes the spectator by, as it were; it fails to solicit the *appropriately* normal gaze for that historical spectator. In order to find pleasure in the porn, the spectator must wait out the film, hoping to find in it the particular image that will be most arousing. The normalized, commodified pornographic gaze seems not so heterogeneous that it will not, eventually, solicit the visual pleasure of the pornographic spectator. Or so is the lure of pornography as a commodity. Pornography as a commodity thus promises what we might term a normalized or contained heterogeneity of gazes.

But the continued unfolding of the image required by the filmic medium seems, as I have already suggested, to be somewhat ill suited to pornography's desire to see in, and catch the spectator up in, particularized (heterogeneous) ways. Anyone who has attempted to "get off" on pornography realizes that it is rare that one can manage to achieve orgasm at the moment of maximum arousal, because, unless one is watching on a video player with an extremely high-resolution pause feature, the image necessarily changes. Even such an attempt to freeze the image necessarily disrupts that pleasurable and unpleasurable oscillation of the gaze that defines most film pornography.[62] Also, many times in the course of the porno film, one is subject to images that are not only not arousing but absolutely distracting. (For example, a sequence in *Best of Surge II* in which three men are having sex is interrupted by a shot of a tire, perhaps in order to reestablish that the men are in a trucking garage, or to suggest a temporal ellipsis; when the camera returns, the three men are in a different sexual position.) Yet the lure that pornography offers the viewer is the possibility of using particular images to achieve the maximum pleasure, and of timing one's orgasm to coincide with the appropriate image.[63]

All of this suggests the inadequacy of naming the relationship between the pornographic spectator and the image as "sadistic" or "controlling." The discursive conditions of reception of pornography "outside" academicist circles suggest a very set different set of conclusions concerning the relationship between porno text and spectator than those suggested by, for example, the Mulvian paradigm of psychoanalytically inflected film theory.[64] If one wanted to make use of a psychoanalysis here, it seems to me that theories of a masochistic spectator might be much more appropriate, since the porno film seems to require its spectator to "submit" to the will of the text.[65] As I suggested above, this is not to argue that there is no relation whatsoever between the historical development of visual pornography as a genre and what Foucault has characterized in *Discipline and Punish* as the tendency of modern disciplinary society to make of the body an object of ever-increasing knowledge and, in particular, to privilege and instantiate a visual knowledge of the body emblematized for Foucault in the architecture of the panopticon. But to move from a recognition of this relationship to a labeling of the relationship of porno spectator to text as "sadistic" is to invoke a model of power that *Discipline and Punish* seeks to interrupt, a model of power that fails to account for the reversibility of relations of power. As I have suggested, Foucault's account of power might insist that pornography must represent not only a historically specific technique for gaining a visible knowledge of the body through an investiture of that body by/with power, *but also* a possible site of resistance to such an investiture. In any case, my point here is that the hybrid positioning of what I have, not unproblematically, named a gay intellectual—a subject-effect produced in two differing, heterogeneous, although not necessarily discrete discursive arenas, one that I might unrigorously label "gay" and the other "intellectual"—this positioning might be used productively to read pornography and, in particular, to interrupt (academic) disciplinary readings of pornography in order to interrogate their assumptions.[66]

In what follows, I will continue to "use" this "hybrid" positioning in order to describe and analyze a number of historico-discursive practices circulating within, among other locations, the urban gay ghetto, pornography being just one of these practices.[67] This positioning will let me articulate both a reading of these practices and a polemic concerning sexuality, a polemic that will significantly differentiate my position both from Dyer's and from those of most antiporn critics. I will, however, be arguing a position that might seem, in at least one sense, analogous to Dyer's. I, too, want to argue here for pornography, as well as other sexual practices associated with the urban gay ghetto, as possible sites for the production of a bodily knowledge of the body. But what I hope this knowledge might make possible is not, as in Dyer's case, a reeducation of desire, but a reimagining of the role of the sexual. Specifically, I will argue for the sexual as a kind of foil for modern practices of disciplinary subject formation, and for gay sexuality in particular as providing the epistemological conditions of possibility of an ethical counterlogic of the supplement, a counterlogic that attempts to resist the forms of power that subjugate. Additionally, I will be suggesting, after Bataille as well as Bersani, that the use-value of the sexual may in fact be its uselessness, its resistance to being dislocated from the antiproductive to the productive, the impure to the imperative.

IV

I want provisionally to argue the following: As a textualized realm, a realm subject to competing cultural explanations, the sexual contains the conditions of possibility for a critique of the sovereign subject. That is, sexuality may be an arena in which it is possible to work towards a bodily knowledge of the critique of the subject, and a countering of its continued disciplinary production. In order to move the sexual toward such an arena, it is necessary to interrupt the familiar humanist model of sexuality as consummation and communion. To return to the vocabulary of the beginning of this chapter: If sexuality is a heterogeneous form that risks being "elevated" from the impure to the imperative, what follows is an attempt to undo the force of that risk.

Earlier, I suggested that Dyer's "liberal" attempt to rehabilitate pornography shares with a feminist-inflected antipornography position a desire to conserve the sovereign subject, a desire emblematized in the move to argue against the wasteful, orgasmic, and violent expenditure that current pornography often privileges. I want to turn now briefly to an example of the gay antipornography position, John Stoltenberg's essay "Gays and the Propornography Movement: Having the Hots for Sex Discrimination." Ostensibly an argument for why it is in the interests of gay men to support the antipornography movement, this essay makes its claims by appealing to a model of sexuality that current pornography does not—according to Dyer—and cannot—according to Stoltenberg—articulate. This is obviously what differentiates Dyer's "liberal" position from Stoltenberg's, for whereas Dyer believes that pornography is capable of redemption and recuperation, Stoltenberg clearly does not.

The problem with gay pornography, according to Stoltenberg, is that it necessarily communicates to its spectators a "sexual disconnecting."[68] The explicit sexual scenes, the frequent close-ups of genitalia, the multiple shifts in camera angles, the "excessive" use of editing, the fragmented bodies—all of these signal to Stoltenberg a sexuality devoid of "communion," "remembering who you're with," "forging a connection," "being there." Instead of offering its spectators images of "a kind of overwhelming blending or a deeply mutual and vigorous erotic melding," an "eroticized empathy," "eroticized equality" (253), and "eroticized justice" (255), pornography sexualizes power disparity and subordination (253). It is this model of eroticism as "alienation" (261) that Stoltenberg explicitly rejects. In other words, pornography details the risk of sexuality as nonproductive expenditure, waste, and loss, all accompanied by violent pleasure. As in the case of Steinem's analysis, Stoltenberg holds out the hope of a conservative eroticism that opposes itself to pornography point by point.

It should be obvious that Stoltenberg embraces a model of sexuality that is fairly familiar, almost "natural"—a model that emphasizes "respect" for the individual rights of both sexual partners, that insists on (an undefined) mutuality during sex, that banishes certain "inappropriate" kinds of sexual fantasies and activities (these apparently include spanking, transvestitism, leather, and perhaps even "ass-fucking," among others),[69] and that seems to comply fairly closely with a Judeo-Christian morality—except of course that the partners involved are queer. Lest the "normality" and "universality" of this model be lost on the reader, Stoltenberg ends his essay with a pathos-wrenching assertion that such a model is so self-evident, so "rational," it ought not to need analysis:

> We are, after all, human. We have feelings. We bleed. We weep. Our hearts need not always have theories in order to have real reasons. We might simply out of our own frail humanity feel grief and pain when another human being is degraded, put down, sexually abused, sexually violated, not cared for. We might simply out of our own experience of what it means to be vilified feel rage against anyone who peddles sexualized hate. We might simply out of a passion for justice—the queerest passion of all—want sex to be about equality instead of hostility. Why indeed should we need an analysis of our political self-interest when it is so obviously in the interest of our own best selves simply to do right by other human beings?[70]

Here we see the familiar (anti-intellectual) attempt to silence theoretical debate through the appeal to an allegedly empirically verifiable and self-evident universally shared humanity. Suspiciously—or perhaps, symptomatically—absent from Stoltenberg's list of bodily fluids are the ones that flow from our genitals.[71] Concerning Stoltenberg's appeal to justice, one hardly needs to be a Foucauldian to ask whose interests justice usually serves. And, regarding the difficulty of recognizing one's own political interests, apparently it is just a matter of sitting down and having a heart-to-heart talk with someone like Stoltenberg, someone in a position to rein in our politically suspect desires through an appeal to our shared humanity.

What we see operating in Stoltenberg's analysis is in fact an attempt to wrestle sexuality in general, and gay sexuality in particular, away from impure forms, to elevate and ennoble it into imperative forms in the service of a homogeneous society and its corollary sovereign subject. The appeal to a "natural" shared humanity in this context is perhaps an attempt to bring gay men into the family of nations, to respond to their cultural othering by appealing to the liberal discourse of inclusion, for the "we" who might inhabit Stoltenberg's rhetoric is apparently not crossed by competing interests and desires, but remains the sovereign yet empathetic human whose "soul" responds with rage at the nonproductive expenditure, the passion for waste, ritualized in pornography.[72] But the rage and passion that Stoltenberg claims pornography unleashes always runs the risk of dis-integrating into an end in itself, rather than being harnessed in the service of "justice," as Stoltenberg desires.[73] The very melodrama of Stoltenberg's appeal inadvertently calls up the threat of nonproductive expenditure that his analysis works to hold in abeyance.

Clearly, there are a number of problems with Stoltenberg's model of sexuality, not the least of which is that it may not sound too terribly sexy to some. But what strikes me as particularly interesting is its linking of self-presence to (a politically correct) eroticism. In Stoltenberg's version of sexuality, the presence of two individuals present to each other as well as to themselves is what makes a "healthy" sexuality possible. The risk of the loss of the self that sexuality might entail, the threat of losing one's self in the constant plugging and unplugging, connecting and disconnecting, the fantasies of incorporation and annihilation, the forgetting of boundaries, the mistaking of one's partner's body for one's own, of forgetting who, where, and with whom you are—all of these are banished from the sexual by Stoltenberg. It is this cultural imagining of sexuality as dis-location or desubjectivization that Stoltenberg (rightly, I think) argues is made available by and through, among other things, pornography.

Throughout what follows, I want to continue to argue for the value of such an imagining of sexuality as nonproductive expenditure. My position is in some ways similar to that of Leo Bersani, who argues, through the mobilization of a psychoanalytic paradigm, that the value of the sexual is its promise of "a breakdown of the human itself in sexual intensities . . . a kind of selfless communication with 'lower' orders of being."[74] According to Bersani, male homosexuality in particular "advertises the risk of the sexual itself as the risk of self-dismissal, of losing sight of the self."[75] In a world in which "the sacrosanct value of selfhood" has been "promoted to the status of an ethical ideal" such that it becomes "a sanction for violence," Bersani argues that sexuality may thus represent "our primary hygienic practice of nonviolence."[76]

The primary difference between my position and Bersani's is that I want to argue for the sexual as differently textualized and more heterogeneous than Bersani's psychoanalytic paradigm allows. I am not interested in arguing that the sexual *does* advertise the value of the loss of an oppressive and oppressing selfhood, but rather that such a reading of the sexual might be made available through historico-discursive struggles. In other words, I am less interested than Bersani in re-presenting psychoanalysis as the science that articulates the truth about sexuality, and more interested in the discursive effects its "truth" might produce.[77] My position is undoubtedly closer to that of Foucault (whom, I would argue, Bersani grossly [under]reads in this context), in particular, the Foucault of the interviews following the first volume of *The History of Sexuality*.[78] That Foucault sees the sexual textually in these interviews, as a site in which struggles over intelligibility must occur, is emblematized elegantly for me in his contention that the problem for so-called gay subjects is not to recognize or discover their "essential" sexuality, but rather to "work" at "becoming" gay.[79]

I turn now to other discursive practices within the gay male ghetto that, like pornography, suggest certain conditions of possibility for a sexuality re-presented as a kind of desubjection and desubjugation, a practice of undermining the sovereignty of the subject and resisting normality. I will use the "abnormal" location of the Other strategically, arguing implicitly for the impossible attempt to glimpse the heterogeneous. I am not arguing that these practices "really" function in this way. Rather, I am interested in thinking through how they might be mobilized in the service of a critique of the sovereign subject in the particular realm of the sexual. (That is, I am making a "theoretical" rather than an "empirical" argument.) I understand that the "choice" of the sexual as a site in which to explore such a critique is highly overdetermined and in need of ideological investigation. But it is, for a number of reasons that I might rapidly and not unproblematically code as "historical," one of the sites in which my own intellectual work has been, and is currently, located.

Throughout what follows, I will be weaving Foucault's texts into my own, taking up some of the themes presented in these highly suggestive and scandalously underread interviews, and building upon them.[80]

In a number of interviews, Foucault notes, through a reading of certain practices within the gay ghetto, the historical potential in gay sexuality to make of the body "a field of production for extraordinarily polymorphous pleasure."[81] This practice, which might be described as a "de-Oedipalizing" of the body—Oedipus understood here as the cultural and historical genital organization of sexuality in the West—proceeds in two directions simultaneously: it seeks to eroticize areas of the body other than the genitals, while attempting to desexualize physical pleasure itself, creating, through the negation of sexual pleasure, new, "monstrously counterfeit" forms of physical pleasure.[82] Foucault reads s/m sex as a particularly privileged network of discourses for the production of what I am calling this de-Oedipalized body.[83]

A number of discursive practices circulating within the gay ghetto might be read as efforts to de-Oedipalize, and thus denormalize, the (fictive) gay body. These discourses appear in a number of different discursive arenas simultaneously—on the bodies of members of the ghetto, in the practices of s/m sex, and in "pornographic" books, photographs, films, and videos. They include, but are not limited to: body shaving, especially the shaving of the testicles; the manipulation of the testicles and/or penis through the use of cock rings and vacuum pumps; anal sex; manipulation of the anus with objects; nipple piercing and clamping; spanking or pummeling certain areas of the body; the manipulation of the skin through the application of hot wax; fist fucking; and water sports.[84] Some of these practices circulate widely; others appear more infrequently. What is especially interesting to note about what we might call, after Foucault, these "technologies of the self,"[85] is the fact that they are done *to* the self, often *by* the self, and are often accomplished through the intervention of devices and machines. In other words, they foreground the production of pleasure as an "unnatural" act and refuse certain humanist understandings of sexual desire and excitation as resulting from "natural" biological urges and drives. Instead, these technologies insist on pleasure as arising from willed manipulations of the body. At a time in history when yet another "scientific" theory is attempting to argue for an understanding of homosexuality as biologically determined—I am referring of course to the "small brain" theory—I am obliged to read these "unnatural" manipulations of the body as attempting to activate an "oppositional" explanation of homosexuality and homosexual activity.

Concerning s/m sex, Foucault is especially interested in reading s/m as a site through which to analyze strategic relations of power. Regarding what s/m may teach us about the relation of pleasure to power, Foucault remarks that what strikes him about s/m is how different it is from social power:

> What characterizes power is the fact that it is a strategic relation that has been stabilized through institutions. So the mobility in power relations is limited, and there are strongholds that are very, very difficult to suppress because they have been institutionalized and are now very pervasive in courts, codes and do on. All that means that the strategic relations of people are made rigid.[86]

In contradistinction to social power, where strategic relations are fixed, s/m represents a strategic relation that is more mobile. "Of course there are roles," Foucault insists, "but everybody knows very well that those roles can be reversed. . . . Or, even when the roles are stabilized, you know very well that it is always a game" (29). Foucault rejects the idea that s/m is a reproduction, inside the erotic relationship, of the structure of power. Instead, he calls it "an acting out of power structures by a strategic game that is able to give sexual pleasure or bodily pleasure" (30). Foucault sees s/m as a process of invention that uses strategic relationships as a source of pleasure. It is "the real creation of new possibilities of pleasure, which people had no idea about previously" (27), a technology of the self applied to the body.

I have a number of conflicting responses to Foucault's reading of s/m.

While I am uncomfortable with his contention that those participating in s/m "know very well" the multiple and conflicting ideologies in which they are positioned, I read this insistence as a kind of strategic impatience before intellectuals who might apply an "armchair" psychoanalysis to s/m, and read it as a "perversion" of the "natural" sexuality someone like Stoltenberg has in mind. I would want perhaps to temper Foucault's assertion with the (Foucauldian) reminder that the "subjugated knowledge" activated in s/m is exactly that—subjugated—and requires intellectual work in order to deploy it in specific local struggles. It is not available to the knower merely by virtue of the fact that he or she, for example, dons leather. Concerning the relationship drawn in many antiporn analyses between s/m fantasies and "real" violence, I am reminded of the commonplaces that there are far more s/m "bottoms" than "tops," and that the "top" often has to be "coerced" into this position. Also pertinent here is the observation that a strict code of rules usually operates in most gay s/m scenes, and a violation of the rules is highly discouraged. The most common of these rules is in fact the respecting of mutually agreed-upon limits.[87] I am concerned that Foucault fails to mention here how strategic relations between men and women are in fact highly stabilized through a number of institutions—much more so, perhaps, than relations between people of the same sex—so that gender differences in "straight" s/m scenes might in fact be quite rigid. But here again, I am reminded of the commonplace that there are far more dominatrixes than dominators, far more female "tops" and male "bottoms" than vice versa (though of course this commonplace must itself be scrutinized). And as far as the question of power goes, I would want to agree with Foucault that if we understand power in its most "microcosmic" form as the ability to act on another, then power is not automatically bad, and s/m doesn't automatically represent an "abuse" of power. Obviously, s/m is not a univocal phenomenon. Rather than traffic in opinions here, I would suggest that, like all texts, s/m needs to be read carefully and closely in specified and particular historical incarnations in order to articulate what readings might be produced of it, the rules of formation from which such readings arise, and the multiple ideologies embedded in those rules.

One of the most interesting characteristics of s/m scenes is in fact their deployment of such nonproductive forms of expenditure as ritual and spectacle. The emphasis on costuming, role playing, and theatricality all attest to the high degree of affect unleashed by s/m. The emphasis on a strict set of rules, as well as Foucault's casting of s/m as a "game," suggests Bataille's contention that what characterizes nonproductive expenditure is its insistence on the possibility of loss. For Bataille, this loss must be as great as possible for the activity to take on its fullest meaning.[88] One way of understanding the historical relationship between gay and lesbian sexuality and s/m is to note their shared status as incidences of nonproductive expenditure, and the shared threat to a normalized subjectivity they re-present.

Foucault characterizes the sexual activities that occur at gay bathhouses as "the affirmation of non-identity." Foucault reads, in the baths, the potential for "de-subjectifying" oneself, for "de-subjugating oneself to a certain point, perhaps not radically, but certainly significantly." At the baths, gay subjects are "reduced" to "nothing else but other bodies with which combinations and creations of pleasure are made possible. You quit being held prisoner by your own face, your own past, your own identity."[89] This affirmation of nonidentity represents for Foucault an opportunity for a kind of pleasure he characterizes as "de-sexualized." He argues, "It's a very important experience, inventing shared pleasures together as one wants. Sometimes the result is a sort of de-sexualization, a kind of deep-sea dive, if you will, so complete that it leaves you with no appetite at all, without any kind of residual desire."[90]

Although I am suspicious of the utopianism of this description of "nonidentity"—a utopianism I read as not unrelated to the kind of utopianism implicit in Bersani's privileging of both "self-debasement"[91] and animality in his account of sexuality as advertising the risk of the loss of the self—this articulation of sexuality seems a significant counter to the one offered by Stoltenberg. And although I would want to note that Foucault's description of the baths is notably different from one provided by Bersani, in which the baths represent "one of the most ruthlessly ranked, hierarchized, and competitive environments imaginable,"[92] my argument here concerns not the "reality" of the baths, but the conditions of possibility they suggest, and the kinds of struggles for which they might provide a site.[93]

The de-Oedipalization of the body, s/m sex, and the sexual practices of the baths are just some of the discourses that meet in photographic and cinematic pornography. As a representation and articulation of these discourses, pornography might be imagined as a site from which to "reeducate" the body in terms not of its use-value but of its potential for expenditure. Articulating highly competing and contradictory representations—for, contrary to Stoltenberg and according to Dyer, the genre is heterogeneous enough to tolerate even images of a "romantic" sexuality—pornography represents one of the most complicated and contested sites from which to read historico-discursive imaginings of the sexual. In fact, I am increasingly led to the position that the debates around pornography are far more interesting than the individual texts analyzed. But, of course, one of the conditions of possibility of this position is my own "hybrid" disciplinary predicament, a predicament that sometimes makes possible the active forgetting of the multiple roles pornography has played in the articulation of my own sexuality and subjectivity.

Chapter 3

"Anthropology—Unending Search for What Is Utterly Precious": Race, Class, and *Tongues Untied*

Ethnology—like any science—comes about within the element of discourse. And it is primarily a European science employing traditional concepts, however much it may struggle against them. Consequently, whether he wants to or not—and this does not depend on a decision on his part—the ethnologist accepts into his discourse the premises of ethnocentrism at the very moment when he is employed in denouncing them.

Jacques Derrida[1]

I

At the 1990 meeting of OUT WRITE, a first-of-its-kind national conference of gay and lesbian writers, the African American poet and essayist Essex Hemphill spoke with several other writers on a plenary panel entitled "AIDS and the Responsibility of the Writer." Hemphill's talk was a draft of his introductory essay to *Brother to Brother*, an anthology of new writings by Black gay men.[2] Although the talk dealt with a number of different concerns, the part of the essay that struck me as most interesting at the time was his discussion of the photographs of the late Robert Mapplethorpe. Mapplethorpe's name came up in a number of different contexts at the conference: Senator Jesse Helms's then-recent assault on his work was considered by many to be the beginning of a full-scale attack on "the lesbian and gay community's freedom of expression."[3] Hemphill in fact was critical of Mapplethorpe, whose work he argued "*artistically* perpetuates racial stereotypes constructed around sexuality" by representing the Black male as little more than "a big, black cock."[4] Hemphill's talk thus sought to situate Mapplethorpe's photographs as another moment in a long history of the white gay community's tendency to treat Black men as "sexual objects."

According to Hemphill, Mapplethorpe's fragmentation of the black male torso, "close-up and close-cropped to elicit desire," was an attempt to reduce the Black man's "identity" to his penis, so that "the minds and experiences of some of his [Mapplethorpe's] black subjects are not as important as close-up shots of their cocks." As Hemphill argued, "Mapplethorpe's eye pays special attention to the penis at the expense of showing us the subject's face, and thus, a whole person." For Hemphill, this refusal "to not look at the black male as a whole being but as selected parts" is a racist practice as old as the slave trade.[5]

During his speech at OUT WRITE—admittedly, only a portion of his speech dealt with the Mapplethorpe photographs—Hemphill began to cry. I remember that these tears elicited at least two different responses from those gathered at the conference. At the time of Hemphill's talk, the audience was largely enthusiastic, vocally encouraging him to continue to speak in the face of his emotion. At some point later in the day, I overheard one attendee say that this moment represented a kind of high point of the conference, a moment in which gay culture was forced to recognize its racist and exclusionary practices, and, hopefully, to begin to develop ways of addressing this past injustice. This attendee praised Hemphill's speech for forcing us to be accountable to gays and lesbians of color. Although I agreed with much of the substance of this person's comments concerning race relations in the gay and lesbian community, I was suspicious of the almost masochistic pleasure released in and through this public declaration of white culpability.

At the time of Hemphill's talk, I also witnessed another response that was, to my knowledge, not discussed at the conference.[6] One person, someone who had refused the elegance of the grand ballroom of the hotel in which we were gathered by bringing his bicycle with him, booed Hemphill's speech and the wave of enthusiasm it provoked. The booing was directed in particular at Hemphill's reading of the Mapplethorpe photographs. It was not loud enough to interrupt the speech, nor even to be heard by Hemphill, but several of us gathered around the man on the bicycle noticed, though no one to my knowledge either encouraged or discouraged his "inappropriate" response.[7]

I have to admit that I admired the bravura of the lone booer. I disagreed with Hemphill's readings of the photographs, and felt that his tears were an attempt to shame the audience into refusing to interrogate the terms of his address. If, as Gayatri Spivak has suggested, we might term the politics of an explanation the means by which it secures its particular mode of being in the world,[8] the politics of Hemphill's reading of Mapplethorpe might be described as the politics of tears, a politics that assures the validity of its produced explanation by appealing to some kind of "authentic," universal, and (thus) uninterrogatable "human" emotion or experience.[9] I agree with Hemphill that, given that both sexuality and race relations act as particularly dense transfer points for relations of power, gay culture often eroticizes racial difference. This eroticization necessarily engages questions of the relation of sexual to social power. I am much less certain, however, that the terms of this eroticization are as monolithic as Hemphill was suggesting, or that any easy analogy can be drawn between the sexual and the social.[10] What struck me most about Hemphill's analysis at the time was its resemblance, almost word for word, to a certain critique of pornography, the critique discussed in the previous chapter. The characterizing of pornography as exhibiting a lack of respect for the "whole" person, an "objectification" of the body, and a "reduction" of the "minds and experiences" of the model to his or her genitals, as well as the positing of a largely untheorized relation between desire, representation, and the political—these are some of the rhetorical strategies deployed in perhaps different but related ways by such foes of pornography as Dworkin, Stoltenberg, and Hemphill.[11] As I have already suggested, this antipornography discourse is itself inflected by a certain model of "appropriate" sexuality, a model that seeks to conserve the sovereign subject by bracketing off the possibility of the sexual as an instance of (in Bataille's terms) nonproductive expenditure.

The connection between Hemphill's discourse and that of the antiporn position was made all the more clear to me recently by Laura Kipnis's "(Male) Desire and (Female) Disgust: Reading *Hustler*." This essay, which provides an excellent summary and analysis of the terms of the antipornography debates, begins with an account of author Robin Morgan's appearance in the antipornography documentary *Not a Love Story*:

> Posed in her large book-lined living room, poet-husband Kenneth Pitchford at her side, she inveighs against a number of sexualities and sexual practices: masturbation—on the grounds that it promotes political quietism—as well as "superficial sex, kinky sex, appurtenances and [sex] toys" for benumbing "normal human sensuality." She then breaks into tears as she describes the experience of living in a society where pornographic media thrives.[12]

Reading this account, I was in fact reminded both of Hemphill's reading of Mapplethorpe and of its accompanying tears. Kipnis goes on to argue that a contemporary feminist disgust with pornography—a disgust she finds evident in the antiporn position—might itself be located historically in terms of class. Arguing from a position informed by Bakhtin and Norbert Elias, Kipnis provocatively suggests that "gestures of disgust are crucial in the production of the bourgeois body, now so rigidly split into higher and lower stratum that tears will become the only publicly permissible display of bodily fluid."[13] The congruence of Hemphill's and Morgan's tears, and the similarity between Hemphill's and, say, Stoltenberg's readings of pornography, suggest the hybrid quality of Hemphill's (discursive) position, a position that exceeds the nominations "Black" and "gay." Reading Kipnis alongside Hemphill, we might note a certain (middle-) class component operating in Hemphill's analysis, a class component left largely unarticulated yet perhaps present nonetheless, carried along inadvertently by the antiporn discourse his analysis of Mapplethorpe employs.

In chapter 2, I attempted to make a limited use of my having been produced as a subject-effect through a number of disciplinary practices—disciplinary in the sense of Foucault's disciplinary society, as well as in the sense of academic disciplines—in order to argue for an understanding of pornography as a discursive practice that might resist the specific technique or form of power that produces the (subjugated) subject. My argument concerning pornography was that, in its "wasteful," noneconomic deployment of the body, it suggests a certain transgression of, and resistance to, the economic practices of modern subject formation. Such transgression and resistance clearly does not undo or overthrow the form of power that subjugates and makes subject to, but rather seeks to enter into a struggle with that power.

I want to reemphasize here that my argument is an attempt to engage with pornography specifically around questions of subjectivity (and not, say, politics or economics). In Foucault's terms, it is an attempt to intervene in a specific struggle—the struggle "against subjection, against forms of subjectivity and submission."[14] Here, I would want to second Foucault's assertion that struggles take a variety of forms that might be productively differentiated from one another. According to Foucault, we may conceive of struggles broadly as occurring against "forms of domination (ethnic, social, and religious)," "forms of exploitation which separate individuals from what they produce," and "the forms of subjection—against the submission of subjectivity."[15] While these forms of struggle might, in particular historical moments, intersect in a variety of ways, they are not simply substitutable for, or equatable with, one another. For example, although struggles "against" subjectivity and struggles against political domination might, in a specified instance, be related, they are not identical. Thus far, my argument throughout this study is largely—although not exclusively—concerned with Foucault's third form of struggle.[16]

One of the problems with the expression "The personal is political" is that in recent discussions of, for example, the relationship between individual acts of transgression and larger political movements, a seamless fit is posited between questions of subjectivity and questions of politics, as if resistance to the forms of subjectivity automatically leads to political resistance. A slogan like "Black Men Loving Black Men Is *the* Revolutionary Act," or the assumption that in engaging in unlawful sexual practices, such as tearoom sex, one is necessarily resisting *political* power, is made possible by this equating of resistance to the forms of subjection with resistance to forms of (political and social) domination. (Some of the conditions of possibility of these two specific examples will be explored at some length in this and subsequent chapters.) In their refusal to think through the move from subjectivity to politics, such formulations risk, among other things, emptying out the collective from the political. In what is sometimes referred to in recent gay and lesbian criticism as a "politics of style," the emphasis is usually placed on style, "politics" in some sense being largely taken for granted—as if an individual stylistic expression of one's cultural marginality were equivalent to political activism or resistance.[17] Such a politics works hand in hand with capitalism's increasing identification and individuation of a specifically gay and lesbian market of consumers, luring queer buyers with the promise that one's "unique" political sympathies might best be expressed through the purchasing of such commodities as rainbow flags, pink triangle pins, and Madonna wannabe junk jewelry.

In these formulations, identity is often the "glue" linking subjectivity and politics: individual subjectivities will be "sutured" into political practices as a result of their identifications. Identity as a critical concept thus seeks to explain how resistance on the level of individual subjectivities might be bound to political struggles. For example, in his recent talk "Migrant Identities: The Arrival of an Enigma," Stuart Hall has argued for an understanding of identity and identification as necessary for the undertaking of certain real political struggles.[18] By identification, according to Hall, subjectivities temporarily locate or suture themselves into specific historical and material practices. Although no identity is ever commensurate with the multiple and fractured experience of the subject, identities are necessary in particular historical moments. They are stories we tell about our origins that make possible certain political practices, stories that must be deconstructed from the inside in order to insist that although such stories are a kind of necessary political settlement through which to construct a cultural politics, they are never wholly adequate to, and always discontinuous with, the subject.

I have several reservations concerning this account of identity. I am uneasy with the description of identification as something the subject wills or enacts. An emphasis on the role of agency in identity formation neglects the complex ways in which subjects can be positioned in identities regardless of their own wishes or desires. For example, someone caught by the police engaging in same-sex sexual activity in a public rest room might be positioned in, say, a news article, as "homosexual," regardless of the individual's insistence that this identity is incommensurate with his experience. This "refusal" to recognize oneself as homosexual is obviously a historical possibility, owing to the continuing presence of a historically prior discourse of same-sex sexual practice, a discourse that did not recognize the distinct "morphology" of the homosexual. As Foucault has argued, "Homosexuality appeared as one of the forms of sexuality when it was transposed from the practice of sodomy onto a kind of interior androgyny, a hermaphrodism of the soul."[19] The discursive remains of this earlier discourse, in which sodomy was "a category of forbidden acts" whose perpetrator was "nothing more than the juridical subject of them," allow for the historical possibility that subjects might be positioned in this early discourse, that is, not "recognize" themselves as homosexual.[20]

An emphasis on identity as produced through the agency of the subject seems unable to take fully into account the material—not to mention the political—effects of identities not willed or chosen. It suggests identity is a kind of "shell" or "role" one might inhabit and discard at will. It also confuses a more properly psychoanalytic definition of identification with a sociological one. "Suture" is, in psychoanalytic terms, an effect of discourse. It is not something that the subject wills or does, but is rather something done to the subject, regardless of his or her conscious intentions. What specifically troubles me here is that in order to use the concept of suture as a way of understanding the operations of the subject within the realm of "conscious" willed political activity, Hall must defer a more persistent critique of the sovereign subject—a critique that I would argue must take place alongside any account of politics.

The attempt to hold a critique of the subject alongside an account of identity politics is always fraught with difficulties. In his *Hart Crane and the Homosexual Text*, for example, Thomas E. Yingling maintains that "gay writers have historically hidden, erased, universalized, or otherwise invalidated not only their homosexual desire but also the shape (or mis-shape) their lives have taken as a result of the social taboo against it."[21] He argues that until quite recently it was impossible for the homosexual to "speak of itself coherently except in a vocabulary of remorse." Here, Yingling takes issue with Foucault, whom he reads as arguing that "it is in the discursive practices of the nineteenth century that the homosexual 'begins to speak on its own behalf.' " For Yingling, the years around World War II seem a "more meaningful date for such watershed events as homosexual self-articulation in its more contemporary (American) sense" than Foucault's date of the nineteenth century (26).

Yingling's disagreement with Foucault relies on a reading of a passage from Foucault's first volume of *The History of Sexuality*. What Yingling and Foucault mean by homosexuality's "speaking on its own behalf," however, are very different things. For Yingling, such speaking means speaking "coherently" through "positive self-representations" (26). Foucault, on the other hand, argues that the creation of the personage of the homosexual in the nineteenth century via discourses of psychiatry and jurisprudence provided one of the conditions of possibility for both "a strong advance of social controls into this area of 'perversity' " and "a 'reverse' discourse" whereby "homosexuality began to speak in its own behalf, to demand that its legitimacy or 'naturality' be acknowledged, often in the same vocabulary, using the same categories by which it was medically disqualified."[22] Foucault says nothing here about speaking "coherently," nor does he equate homosexuality's speaking in its own behalf with Yingling's "positive" (self-validating) "homosexual autobiography."[23] Foucault's observations are drawn from a section of his text that argues against a model of power as purely negative—the very model of power that I would argue provides the conditions of possibility for Yingling's contention that "positive" and "coherent" homosexual "self-articulation" is disallowed until the years following World War II. Foucault's understanding of power would argue that Yingling's "social taboos" do not simply cause gay writers to hide, erase, universalize, or invalidate homosexual desire, but rather provide the very conditions of possibility for the articulation—"self" or otherwise—of that desire. In other words, homosexual desire does not preexist the cultural prohibitions against it but rather is produced concurrently with its prohibition. Foucault's account of the homosexual as subject suggests, in this instance, that the alterity represented by homosexuality is not "outside" of a normal that seeks to repress it, but rather is made possible by the deployment of that normality, set into motion by the play of power and resistance. It is thus impossible to formulate, from within his model of power, the statement that gay writers have historically "hidden" their desire, since any act of hiding is necessarily also an act of revelation. Yingling's concern with "positive" self-representations—absolutely crucial to identity politics in particular—evidences a humanism that requires the positing of a normalized, prescriptive gay desire that would escape the play of power and resistance by overcoming social taboos (in other words, a "healthy" gay desire that might escape the "unhealthy" effects of, for example, repression). This demand for a homosexual subject who speaks positively, coherently, openly, and without remorse is significantly at odds with a Foucauldian understanding of the homosexual subject.

Similarly, Jeffrey Weeks's account of the history of sexuality attempts to deploy a critique of the subject through the critique of sexual essentialism.[24] Weeks's work is perhaps one of the strongest versions of what is called the "social constructionist" position in sociology vis-à-vis sexual identity—a position that, incidentally, is often misattributed to Foucault. Arguing against an essentialist understanding of sexual identity as transhistorical, Weeks insists that sexual identities are the result of particular historical circumstances, with specific identities "emerging" at a given moment in history. Unfortunately, in Weeks's version of social construction theory, what history seems to construct is not a range of subject-effects, but the historically emerging identificatory "choices" available to a humanist subject.

Weeks, like Stuart Hall, argues that identities are "provisional, ever precarious, dependent upon, and constantly challenged by, an unstable relation of unconscious forces, changing social and personal meanings, and historical contingencies" (186). Weeks augments this position by casting identities as involving choice or self-creation, though on grounds "not freely chosen but laid out by history" (209). But, while claiming to understand a homosexual identity as historically contingent, Weeks can simultaneously offer the observation that "many homosexual people have been content to 'pass for straight' throughout the century" (193). It is hard to imagine how one could offer such a formulation without at least acknowledging that because of the continued presence of the discursive remains of an earlier discourse of sexuality, the discursive formation "homosexual people" is itself crossed by competing discourses, so that what looks to Weeks like "passing" may in fact be a lack of fit between subjects positioned as "homosexual" and subjects positioned in the traces of that historically prior discourse of sexuality in which homosexuality was a behavior rather than an identity. In other words, only an "essentially" real homosexual can be said to willfully "pass" for straight. Weeks's account seems to depend on the idea that a homosexual identity "solidifies" at some point in history, that identity becoming not exactly an essentialist category, but perhaps a fixed or stable one—even if for only a specified historical moment. This is presumably one of the conditions that make possible a subject's "choice"—or refusal—of a homosexual identity. Thus, the (historical) *contingency* of identity is precisely what is lost in Weeks's formulation.

Specifically: In Weeks's account, the search for the historical emergence of a gay identity necessarily precludes an examination of identity as discursive production subject to, among other things, "failure." Weeks's focus on the production of "real" gay subjects under the guise of history necessarily assumes that such production is, once it has been initiated, accomplished—again, even if only for a (historical) instance. In other words, history allegedly provides that identity with a kind of stable reality. In Weeks's account, it is thus possible to chart the historical "emergence" of the homosexual subject. The production of such a "historical" (homosexual) subject, however, cannot, by definition, be *discursive*. As Joan W. Scott reminds us, "Subjects are constituted discursively, but there are conflicts among discursive systems, contradictions within any one of them, multiple meanings possible for the concepts they deploy."[25] Such an account of subject constitution reminds us that although subjects will be positioned in and constituted by discourse, such positionings will always necessarily be contingent, provisional, subject to slippage—that is, subject to deconstruction—*regardless of the agency of such subjects*, so that it becomes impossible to speak of something like "the homosexual" except as a determined and vacant place in a discourse, a place that, by definition, cannot be filled once and for all.[26] Weeks's casting of identity not as discursive but as "historical" necessarily ushers in a subject who, while purged of an essentialist sexual identity, is nonetheless sovereign, capable of either *choosing* his or her identity from the supermarket of history or rejecting such an identity—while still, in some sense, *being* homosexual (recall here Weeks's notion of "passing for straight").

In a discussion of recent developments in feminist theory around questions of identity and difference, Christina Crosby notes a similar deployment, often in those very accounts of gender that claim to be "historical," of the figure of the sovereign subject.[27] Crosby's argument is that despite recent efforts by feminist scholars to historicize difference, "women's studies often runs willy-nilly in the circles of historicism" (137). Borrowing a phrase from Althusser, she argues that feminist theory is too often "reduced . . . to a reflection on the presence of real history in all its manifestations." According to Crosby, "The problem is that differences are taken to be self-evident, concrete, *there*, present in history and therefore the proper ground of theory" (134). One of the results of this refusal to interrogate, for example, "how 'differences' is constituted as a concept," is a residual historicism that confuses the specification of identity with its historicization—a historicization that would take as object of inquiry the discursive production of subjects in difference.[28] In my introduction to this book, I argued that Teresa de Lauretis's account of gender, with its emphasis on real (historical) women as agents, deploys a kind of essentialism. Crosby's analysis suggests that what might instead be operating here is a certain historicism. If we understand the (historical) production of woman as historically contingent, we must, for example, acknowledge the possibility that a (non)female "body" might be rendered discursively as female subject in some unforeseen future, if not present, discursive context. Although such a rendering is (historically) unlikely, given the historical entrenchment of the discursive formations of sexuality, gender, and biology, we cannot rule out such a possibility—unless, that is, we are willing to deploy what I called previously a kind of essentialism, an essentialism that depends on the notion that once the historical production of gender has been initiated, it must be "successful," that is, continue to produce "woman" as we know her.[29] Tania Modleski's call to promote the study of the actual female reader depends on such a historicist familiarity with woman. Crosby notes that one of the results of this historicism in feminist theory is an account of the subject in which "the differences which seem to refract and undo a substantive identity actually reflect a multifaceted, modified but all-too-recognizable subject."[30] This, I would argue, is also the case in Weeks's account of the gay subject. Weeks's "historical" understanding of homosexuality as a social construction is in fact dependent on the intentional subject, though perhaps in his more (post)modern, less "coherent," incarnation. In any case, it is perhaps not too spurious to note here recent developments in science that suggest the impossibility of stabilizing—even under the guise of history, and through such categories as "actual women"—the contingent relationship between, for example, female bodies and bodies gendered as female.[31]

Weeks's argument ultimately rests on his contention that (homosexual) identities are political necessities, "necessary in the contemporary world as starting points for a politics around sexuality."[32] For Weeks, "a struggle for identity, a development of sexual communities, and the growth of political movements" are today each necessary to the others: "The sense of community is the guarantor of a stable sense of self; while the new social movements have in an important way become expressions of community strength, emanations of a material social presence" (195). We might ask a number of questions of Weeks's text here. Given his notion of the unconscious, as well as his recognition of the historical contingency of identity, how is it possible for a community to "guarantee" a stable sense of self? Secondly, what is the necessary relationship between sexual communities and political action? How does the material social presence of, say, gay men as consumers translate into politics? More importantly, though, Weeks's analysis begs the question of why, in the contemporary world, we should *need* a politics around sexuality. The argument is in fact circular, suggesting that, because the category of the homosexual exists, we must have a politics around sexuality, and because we have a politics around sexuality, the category of the homosexual must exist. Such an argument assumes a bit too readily the continuing efficacy of identity politics.[33]

In the following sections of this chapter, I would like to continue a discussion of subjectivity, resistance, (identity) politics, and sexuality by offering a reading of *Tongues Untied*, a film by Marlon Riggs that features some of the poetry of Essex Hemphill. This reading will allow me to explore questions of race and class as they might intersect with questions of subjectivity and sexuality, as well as to critique what I am obliged to read as one of the failings of the film: its refusal to interrogate its own discursive conditions of possibility, as well as its politics of explanation—the means by which it as-sures and secures its particular mode of being in the world. Specifically, I will be arguing that although the film attempts to mobilize a kind of "au-thentic" Blackness in order to make its argument that Black men loving Black men is "*the* revolutionary act," the film necessarily employs a hybrid weave of discursive practices, some of which find their conditions of possi-bility in the intellectual history of the white, European West. An exploration of the hybrid and contradictory subject positionings deployed by the film allows me to dis-articulate some of the discontinuous determinants in its production of subject-effects, and to interrogate the limits of its politics of explanation, as well as to de-scribe the possibilities of my own reading. I will thus be attempting here, as I did in the previous chapter, to use the contra-dictions of my own (subjugated) subject position—this time, in order to counter what I read in *Tongues Untied* as a desire to conserve the sovereign subject. My argument will be that such a conservation is made possible by the deployment of the rhetoric of the antipornography movement, a rhetoric that, as I have suggested in my discussion of gay pornography, seeks to "el-evate" the "impure" heterogeneity of the sexual (what I have termed the pornographic) into "imperative" (erotic) forms in the service of a cultural homogeneity.

II

Marlon Riggs's 1989 video *Tongues Untied* has been characterized as a "very personal essay,"[34] a documentary,[35] and an experimental video.[36] Combining the poetry of Riggs, Essex Hemphill, and a number of other Af-rican American gay poets[37] with images shot in a variety of filmic styles, the video draws on an extremely mixed set of filmic, visual, and linguistic dis-cursive practices. A partial genealogy of the discursive practices deployed by the video might include cinema verité, music videos, the African American church, choral speech and singing, slave chants, gospel music, modernist American poetry, overtly "political" rhetoric from both the Black and gay and lesbian civil rights movements, and the disco music of Sylvester.

Although all texts inevitably refer to a wide weave of intertextual sources, much recent work in theories of postcoloniality has focused on the necessarily hybrid quality of diasporic cultural production, which often fea-tures elements culled from both the "native" and colonizing cultures.[38] Much of this theoretical work has privileged both conscious and uncon-scious attempts by diasporic cultures to resist, appropriate, negotiate, and creolize the discursive practices in which they have been violently situated. Less attention has sometimes been paid to some of the ways in which the discursive effects of given practices are beyond the control of any individual cultural producer. In other words, discourses are not simply "available" for a simple appropriation. They carry with them struggles, struggles for power, knowledge, and intelligibility. Their meaning-effects are multivalent, contradictory, and contested. As Derrida has suggested in a slightly different context, the oppositional elements of a system of discourse are necessarily part of that system.[39] Because discursive appropriations "are not elements or atoms and since they are taken from a syntax and a system, every particular borrowing drags along with it the whole" of that system. Thus, in order to understand the struggles embodied in a given text, a careful de-scribing is necessary, an exploration of one's position as a reader vis-à-vis the discursive practices it deploys, and an attempt to understand the conditions of possibility of one's reading, writing, and speaking.

In *Tongues Untied*, one of the consequences of failing to dis-articulate, in one's reading, the hybrid weave of discursive practices deployed by the film might be the erasure of what I would term certain discontinuities of class, race, and imperialism as they might interweave with the necessarily inadequate nominations "Black" and "gay." For example, much of the film seems to employ a set of discursive practices historically familiar to a middle-class audience, Black and non-Black alike. The film tends to privilege the (discursive) "experience" of middle-class Black gay men, and is largely articulated from that position. The film privileges poetry, and in particular, a poetry that seems to owe as much historically to Walt Whitman and William Carlos Williams as to Langston Hughes or Countee Cullen; moreover, the film's more overtly political rhetoric seems culled from organized urban struggles in the gay as well as Black communities, struggles often headed by largely middle-class people. For example, a parody of an ad for a telephone dating line features the following dialogue: "B.G.A.—Black Gay Activist, thirtyish, well read, sensitive, pro feminist, seeks same for envelope licking, flyer distribution, . . . assembly, demonstration companion, dialogical theorizing, good times, and hot safe sex." As the actor speaks into his combined telephone and answering machine, the camera reveals the decor of his apartment, featuring a typewriter, a magazine entitled *A Critique of America*, and two art posters of Black men embracing, posters that appear to be stills from Isaac Julien's film *Looking for Langston*. While locating such a "fantasy" in terms of class might be difficult, the rhetoric employed in the ad, the three-dollar-per-minute phone charges that often accompany the placing of such ads, and the fact that such phone lines are often accessible only to persons with credit cards, suggest a certain class component to this fantasy.

Another moment in the film that suggests a certain middle-class position is arguably one of the central images of the film, a series of documentary style shots of what appears to be a Gay Pride Day march in Manhattan. A group of Black gay men carry a banner that reads "Black Men Loving Black Men Is a Revolutionary Act," apparently echoing the rhetoric of early middle-class American feminism. Furthermore, the men who carry this banner are arguably marked as middle class, their bodies sculpted into the bulging, muscular style so prominent in the gay ghettos of San Francisco and New York. (I will return to a more extended discussion of this image later in this chapter.)

The word *class* is in fact rarely used in the film, one notable exception being a moment in Riggs's poem "Tongues Untied." The six sections of the poem are interspersed throughout the film, usually accompanied by images of Riggs himself reading the poem intercut with other images that illustrate or comment upon the words. *Class* appears in the first section of the poem, which describes the alienation a bright middle-class Black boy feels at a school in Georgia, where he is called "muthafuckin coon" by whites and "Uncle Tom" by Blacks. The boy is hated by other Blacks who assume he is "uppity" because of his class.[40]

Additionally, it might be argued that the discursive style of the film, with its radically hybrid weave of filmic discourses, suggests a middle-class audience, or at least an audience somewhat familiar with experimental or "art" cinema. (Recall here the film still from *Looking for Langston* featured in the phone sex sequence of *Tongues Untied*.) The video uses both black-and-white footage and location and studio shots and has an extremely layered soundtrack featuring a variety of combinations of diagetic and nondiagetic sound. Much of the video consists of close-ups of various actors reading poems, which are then intercut with a wide variety of images. Many of these poems take up the subject of being Black and gay in a hostile culture. This "talking head" style of filmmaking arguably positions the film closer to experimental documentaries than to, say, MTV.

To point out that Riggs's film seems to privilege the (discursive) experience of largely middle-class urban Black gay men and to employ conventions of filmmaking familiar to a middle-class audience is not, in and of itself, a criticism of the video. However, *Tongues Untied* seems insufficiently attentive to the numerous contradictions in which it is necessarily embroiled. It addresses self-representation, a historically familiar problem particularly common to identity politics.[41] *Tongues Untied* attempts to situate itself within a history of marginalized peoples historically denied access to certain powerful and capital-intensive means of self-representation such as film, peoples who have then seized these means in order to counter existing stereotypes. In intervening on the level of filmic representations, such attempts have necessarily to enter into a certain ontology of the visible that assumes that "truth" is a primarily a problem of visibility, and that increased visibility is desirable. (I will have more to say about this shortly.) Many "subaltern" groups have situated their earliest efforts at self-representation in a predominantly realist mode, attempting to displace "stereotypical" representations with more "realistic" ones. Unfortunately, as I have already suggested above, the discursive practices in which marginalized people attempt to achieve self-representation are not "free" of ideology.[42] This is one way of reading Audre Lorde's insistence that "the master's tools will never dismantle the master's house."[43]

In a deconstructionist reading of Lorde's words, the master's tools can never dismantle his house in some "ultimate" sense, but we need not therefore abandon such tools as useless. That "the opposition is part of the system" does not render such opposition completely ineffectual. Rather, it acts as a check on a practice that might fail to remember this. As Derrida argues in the case of ethnography, "The ethnologist accepts into his discourse the premises of ethnocentrism at the very moment when he is employed in denouncing them. This necessity is irreducible; it is not a historical contingency."[44] Derrida responds to this charge, however, with the realization that "if nobody can escape this necessity, and if no one is therefore responsible for giving in to it, however little, this does not mean that all the ways of giving in to it are of an equal pertinence."[45] The suggestion here is that there are ways of using the master's tools, and ways of using the master's tools. In the face of this dilemma, Derrida suggests, using Lévi-Strauss as a model of sorts, that what is required is the conservation of "all these old concepts, while at the same time exposing here and there their limits, treating them as tools which can still be of use. No longer is any truth-value attributed to them; there is a readiness to abandon them if necessary if other instruments should appear more useful. In the meantime, their relative efficacy is exploited, and they are employed to destroy the old machinery to which they belong and of which they themselves are pieces."[46]

Dismantling the master's house with his tools is perhaps, however, a different project from rendering oneself visible to, or vocal before, the dominant culture. Deconstruction instead might complicate the clean line that identity politics often seeks to draw between visibility and invisibility, sound and silence, margin and center. This is perhaps one of the reasons why deconstruction as a theoretical enterprise seems to offer so little promise to a politics rooted in identity. In some sense, then, my theoretical project here—reading *Tongues Untied* "against itself"—is necessarily at odds with its stated political project: rendering Black gay men visible.

One of my fears concerning a project like *Tongues Untied* is that, historically, the desire of marginalized groups to render themselves visible has not necessarily brought with it a particular commitment to economic transformation and broad-based social change. For example, many gay men are willing to march every year in Gay Pride celebrations, but they seem as a whole—and I know this is a generalization—to be less willing to work in broad-based collectives, if the recent fracturing of various chapters of ACT-UP along lines of race, class, and gender is any indication.

Additionally, the desire of cultural minorities to achieve increased visibility *must* be considered alongside modern disciplinary society's demands for a normalization linked to increased forms of surveillance. As Foucault reminds us, the production of modern (subjugated) subjects requires a continued increase in mechanisms of surveillance extended throughout the social body. Unlike premodern forms of power, which were manifested in, and depended on, such spectacular visual displays as public torture, disciplinary power

> is exercised through its invisibility; at the same time it imposes on those whom it subjects a principle of compulsory visibility. In discipline, it is the subjects who have to be seen. Their visibility assures the hold of the power that is exercised over them. It is the fact of being constantly seen, of being able always to be seen, that maintains the disciplined individual in his subjection.[47]

Foucault's description of disciplinary society reminds us that although cultural visibility makes possible the articulation, by minority groups, of a "reverse" discourse in which it might be possible to counter existing cultural representations, such a "reverse" discourse is necessarily implicated in the continued production of modern subjects. It cannot place itself outside of the hold of power, nor can it cleanly separate itself from the continued enforcement of standards of the normal. In other words, it necessarily works to instantiate a normalization of the Other, countering "stereotypes" with "positive" images that strive to interpolate the Other.

In a related vein, Joan Scott has argued that histories that strive to make visible the previously neglected "experience" of the Other necessarily reinstantiate the very epistemological categories it is in their interest to displace.[48] Scott suggests that the project of rendering the lives of once-overlooked historical subjects visible fits conformably within the established protocols of orthodox historiography, which frequently corrects and revises the historical narrative on the strength of "new evidence" (24). According to Scott, the danger of this approach is not only that it reinvigorates the myth of the individual subject as agent, but also that it necessarily leaves behind certain questions, questions about "the constructed nature of experience, about how subjects are constituted as different in the first place, about how one's vision is structured—about language (or discourse) and

71

history"(25). In their eagerness to re-present the formerly undocumented lives of the Other, such histories necessarily abdicate the project of resisting what Scott terms the very "ideological system" that produces the Other as abject in the first place. It would seem that an interrogation of the (discursive) system that represents the categories of race, gender, and sexuality as fixed identities, "its premises about what these categories mean and how they operate, its notions of subjects, origin, and cause," would be of particular pertinence to a film like *Tongues Untied*. In the rush to represent the Other, however, a critical resistance to these categories is necessarily left aside.

Deconstruction as practice of reading makes possible both representation *and* resistance by suggesting that no representation can possibly disentangle itself from the history in which it is located: in this particular case, the history of modern disciplinary practices and their role in ongoing processes of subject formation. What becomes necessary then is not to cease to represent, but to attempt to work through, the historical contradictions in which one is necessarily situated. Throughout this study, I have been referring to this attempt to "work through" as the project of exploring one's own necessarily discontinuous position as subject-effect. The inevitable failure of this attempt (if success is gauged by the overcoming of contradiction) presents a problem primarily for the deliberative consciousness, which imagines for itself some kind of transcendental "wholeness" in which contradiction disappears.

In my reading of *Tongues Untied*, I have been attempting to use my own position as a kind of lever into the film, a lever that opens up the film's contradictions. This seems to be one of the options available to me "between" a pious liberal respect that refuses to speak back to the film or take it seriously, and a critique that merely judges the film according to (allegedly) "disinterested" formalist paradigms. I want to continue in this vein temporarily, deferring until later a necessary exploration of the conditions that have made my position itself possible. Such an exploration will force me necessarily to engage with the thorny question of what it means to be (discursively produced as) "white" and "gay" in relation to this film.

A lack of awareness of the discursive historical contradictions in which it is necessarily situated sometimes positions a film like *Tongues Untied*, for a non-Black audience in particular, as what Spivak has termed a "native informant." The native informant acts as a privileged member of an exotic "Other," carrying news of the colonized to an audience of colonizers eager to partake of foreign fruits. The sometimes "essayistic" structure of certain sections of the film particularly encourages this reading, such as the "essay," complete with subtitles and demonstrations, on the various nuances of SNAP! culture, as well as the section on voguing. A failure to interrogate its own discursive status as native informant necessarily positions the film within a long history of imperialist cultural domination, in which privileged marginals acted as go-betweens for the colonizing culture, rendering up the cultural products of the colonized for the continued delectation of the West. That the film seems unaware of its role in this highly contradictory process is emblematized in the claim made by a voice in the film that declares enthusiastically, "Anthropology—unending search for what is utterly precious." What seems missing in such an enthusiastic claim is some kind of attempt to chart the historical relationship between, say, anthropology and colonialism.

I am not suggesting here that any cultural producer working within the situation of postcoloniality could possibly escape the contradictions necessarily arising from this situation. In fact, I am suggesting the opposite— the situation of postcoloniality *necessarily* renders a video like *Tongues Untied* as a kind of native informant. Following Derrida's suggestion, however, we might explore some of the specific ways in which *Tongues Untied* is required to "give in" to this situation. What thus seems missing in *Tongues Untied*, from the position from which I am obliged to read, is an interrogation of its own conditions of possibility, one of which is, necessarily, the interlocking histories of Western racism and imperialism. The film could not possibly free itself from this history, no more than the recent multicultural movements in canon reformation can possibly divorce themselves from the imperialist practices of rendering up the texts of the world for Western enjoyment and appreciation. This judgment obviously does not mean either that films like *Tongues Untied* have no value, or that canon reform should not occur. Rather, it is to suggest the importance of the attempt to trace out the relation of these textual practices to the history of imperialism, and to elaborate those ways in which such "liberatory" or "affirming" projects may inadvertently and necessarily be at odds with themselves.

Concerning the actual representation of working-class Black gay culture in *Tongues Untied*, the film seems to inform not only to a non-Black audience but to a Black middle-class audience as well. Hemphill's prose piece "Without Comment" listens in on an interchange between two Black gay men on a bus, whose speech patterns (" 'You my bitch!' 'No! uh uh. We are bitches!' 'No! You listen here. *I* ain't wearing lipstick, *you* are! I ain't no bitch! I fucked *you!* You *my* bitch!' ")[49] are markedly different in diction and grammar from the voice that recounts the episode. Working-class drag queens are photographed in slow motion, accompanied by the romantic strains of Billie Holiday and Nina Simone, their movements rendered a tragic and beautiful spectacle. Only one of the poems, Hemphill's "Black Beans," appears to represent working-class Black gay culture, but the diction of the poem, heavy with alliteration, seems at odds with the working-class images—a "meager meal," a "hand-me-down sofa," "chipped water glasses."[50] The self-consciousness concerning class status, and the willingness to treat poverty as if it were inconsequential before love, seem in keeping with a middle-class romanticization of working-class culture, similar to the romanticization operating in the portrayal of the drag queens.

One of the most interesting moments in the film in which questions of class are occluded is the section dealing with vogue dancing. In this section of the film, preceded by the intertitle "Listen," two apparently working-class Black gay men fill the audience in on how voguing started, and of what it consists. This is followed by a demonstration by a number of voguers, including Willi Ninja, whose rise to fame as a kind of voguing star of the fashion world is detailed in Jennie Livingston's *Paris Is Burning*, a film I will discuss at length in the following chapter. In a largely positive review of Livingston's film, Hemphill comments on the attempts by white culture to appropriate Black cultural production, especially

> the recent appropriation of rap by white rapper Vanilla Ice or the
> appropriation of voguing, originally a Black gay dance, by Madonna.
> Vanilla Ice and Madonna ruthlessly continue the tradition of exploiting and
> stealing from Black culture. They are clearly descendants of Elvis Presley
> and other culture vultures that have gone skipping to the bank trading on
> their imitations and appropriations of Black culture for fame and fortune.[51]

Clearly, a Black and gay identity politics is operating in Hemphill's reading of voguing. In Hemphill's analysis, the practice "belongs" to all Black gays, regardless of their class background. Questions of racial and sexual identity seem to override questions of class for both Hemphill and Riggs in the moment of "appropriating" voguing in *Tongues Untied*. Also neglected is an exploration of the relation of New York Puerto Rican culture to this cultural form.

Again, I am not suggesting here that *Tongues Untied* ought not to have represented working-class black gay culture—or, for that matter, that there is some kind of simple "equivalence" between Madonna's and Riggs's "appropriation" of voguing. Rather, I am trying to draw attention to the way terms like "race" and "class" are discontinuous, so that an elaboration of, say, Black gay visibility is necessarily complicated by questions of class. One of the results of this discontinuity might be the overlooking of the specific politics of explanation involved in attempts by, say, middle-class Blacks to render working-class Black life visible. I am thus most interested here in exploring the means by which a video like *Tongues Untied* secures its explanation of Black working-class gay life, and the ways in which, in such a video, interests of race and class might be at odds with one another.

I want now to read another moment in the film around questions of race and class, one that significantly illustrates how calls for an "authentic" Blackness may be entangled with the continued production of both middle-class values and assumptions around sexuality, and modern disciplinary subjects. This moment of the film deals with interracial love and sexuality. It will perhaps be cause for suspicion to some that, as someone (culturally produced as) white, I choose to concentrate on a moment in the film dealing with interracial relationships.[52] I am perhaps susceptible to the charge here that I am complicit with rendering Blackness invisible in my reading of the film by focusing on whiteness, or of misreading the film by failing to take up a proper "sympathetic" position. I can respond to this charge only by stating that although I admire and enjoy a great deal of *Tongues Untied*, its eloquence, its visual style, its spirit, that admiration and enjoyment is necessarily linked to the historical situation in which the film and I meet, which necessarily positions me as anthropologist looking in on a "foreign" culture. One way of resisting that historical positioning is to focus on those places where I "am" (discursively) "in" the text, and attempt to account for how I read myself. I obviously cannot pretend to be a Black gay man, however "sympathetic" or benevolent such a pretending may claim to be. I would also want to remind the reader that racism can appear under benevolent guises as well as hostile ones, and, as a (however resistant) member of the liberal academy, my position as subject in/of that academy is perhaps more susceptible to the former than to the latter.

I will be attempting here to offer what in some ways resembles a "close" analysis of the film, an analysis made possible to some extent by my disciplinary training in film studies. I am aware that other readers may not have read this section of the film in this way, and so want to stress the fact that my discursive positioning as "white" is overlaid with a number of simultaneous discursive positionings, including "male," "gay," "classed," and "intellectual," and, in particular, someone trained in film studies at a specific moment in the discipline's history. I provide these nominations as shorthand to an exploration of the conditions of possibility of my reading here, only some of which I am capable of glimpsing in this historical moment. I am attempting here to make use of these conditions of possibility, deploying the "ruins" of, among other things, my training, in order to enter into a local, specific struggle against the forms of subjection that I would argue the film perhaps unwittingly privileges and supports.[53]

The second section of Riggs's poem "Tongues Untied" tells of a Black adolescent "rescued" from his sense of isolation from both Blacks and whites by a "whiteboy."[54] He then pursues, in the poem's third section, white lovers in the Castro area of San Francisco. Eventually, he leaves behind the Castro and white men, eventually discovering, in the final sections of the poem, the beauty in men of his own race, to which he had previously been "blind" (205).

The last sequence in the first section depicts in words and images a fag bashing and ends with a frozen frame of the victim's outstretched arms. As the soundtrack begins playing Roberta Flack's "The First Time Ever I Saw Your Face," the image dissolves to a small, wallet-sized picture of a white adolescent. The camera slowly zooms in to the photo, and Riggs begins reading, from off screen, his poem. The white boy is dressed in a jacket and tie and looks directly into the camera. The pose and dress of the boy, as well as his out-of-fashion, longish haircut, suggest a school photograph. As Riggs reads the poem, the image dissolves back and forth between Riggs's face, in close-up, reciting the poem, and the photograph, each time repeating the zooming movement in. As Riggs, now on camera, comes to the last line of the poem, "What a curse," in which he expresses his ambivalence at the fact that he was "seduced" "out of his adolescent silence" by a white boy, the music stops for a moment.[55] The image dissolves back to the photograph and zooms out, while the music begins again.

There is an abrupt transition here to the music of Sylvester singing "Do You Wanna Funk with Me?" The image track changes to a series of rapid shots of photographs of the faces and upper torsos of white men. They all look directly into the camera, as did the boy in the school photograph, but these men are clearly porno models. The cutting is punctuated by the disco beat of the music. The camera sometimes zooms into the photographs, just as it did in the preceding section. This movement suggests some kind of parallel between these men and the white boy in the second section of the poem.

The music continues, and the image changes first to a panning left shot of the New York skyline and then to a zoom-in shot of the Castro Street Theater. Another cut reveals two shirtless white men dancing at what appears to be a Gay Pride event. The image then shifts to a series of slow-motion shots apparently taken at the same location where these two men were dancing. The camera explores the bodies of a number of men, many of them shirtless, many dressed in leather harnesses or chaps or both, some of them with their asses exposed. Men, alone and in small groups, are pictured laughing, talking, eating, and cruising. The camera often fragments their bodies, focusing on their muscled torsos, panning and tilting on them. None of the men seems aware of the presence of the camera moving into and around their bodies. While the camera lingers on the muscled back of a man in a harness, Riggs begins reading the third section of the poem, which describes how it was in California that he realized "adolescent dreams" of intimacy with "white boys" (202). Underneath the images, the music fades, and a voice begins to chant, faster and faster, "Let me touch it, let me taste it, let me lick it, let me suck it" as the camera continues to cruise the white bodies, tilting up and down, lingering on a naked chest, an ass in torn jeans, a muscled back.

The chant gives way to a heartbeat, and Riggs's voice, off camera, begins the second stanza of the poem, while the fragmented shots of the white bodies continue. This section of the poem describes the speaker as "immersed in vanilla," refusing the cruising glances of other Black men. The poem then describes how the speaker deliberately avoided acknowledging the lack of "black images" in gay advertising and art, and even in the speaker's "own fantasies." On the image track, a number of shots of a cover of *Blue Boy* magazine's "Pick the Man of the Year" issue. The cover is filled with photos of models, all of them white.

The poem then recounts how the speaker sought not to notice popular images of Blacks. As Riggs begins the line, the image track cuts to a shot of three greeting cards featuring two Aunt Jemima figures and an obese Black woman whose naked ass is exposed. As he continues to read, the video cuts to an obese woman in a polka-dotted bikini with a surf board, and then to another representation of Aunt Jemima. When the line is finished, there is a pause, in which only a heartbeat is heard. There then occur three separate shots of images of Black men, presumably from gay "pornography." The first is a photograph of a naked muscular man shackled around his neck. One white hand reaches into the frame to hold his head down. Another, its wrist wrapped in a leather band, squeezes his left pectoral muscle. Across the top of the photograph appears, in red letters, "Slaves for sale." The second image, a drawing, depicts a naked, muscled white man wearing only black boots, who is whipping a muscular Black man hanging from a tree. The third image is a cartoon of a Black man with exaggerated muscles, penis, and nipples. The camera slowly pans up this figure.

Following this third image, the shot dissolves to a shot of Riggs walking in the Castro. The poem continues, recounting the speaker's growing frustration at his continuing search for his own reflection in the eyes of white men (203). Eventually, the image freezes, and superimposed over it is the face of the adolescent white boy, once again suggesting a parallel between the adolescent love of a white man, and white images of desire. There is then a cross fade to Riggs's face, continuing the poem. Accompanying these images, Riggs's voice describes the speaker's discontent with gay life, insisting that, in the gay ghetto, "I was a nigga, still" (203). The poem concludes with the speaker describing his flight from the Castro.

What troubles me about this section of the film is the way Riggs's camera eroticizes the fragmented bodies of the white men at the Gay Pride gathering, and then attempts to dispel and critique this eroticism by evoking a sense of shame and disgust at the depiction of the Black men and women.[56]

The camera lures the spectator with a series of playful, sexy images of largely white gay men. It peeps in like a voyeur on the decadent, carnivalesque atmosphere of the Gay Pride parade, and then juxtaposes these "documentary" images with the "degrading" images of Black women and men, drawing a kind of equivalence between the two sets of images, and suggesting a causal connection between the licentious behavior of these white men and the representations of Blacks. The suggestion is that while Rome burned, these white men in leather were obviously fiddling. Even the nonsexual friendship of the adolescent white boy of the second section of the poem is implicated here, when his faced is superimposed over Riggs's flight from the Castro.

This reading of the film positions the spectator, who might have found the images of these white men arousing, to be "caught looking," implicating and judging the viewer by suggesting that the same kind of eroticism evoked in the viewing of these white bodies is similarly operating in the admittedly disturbing images of the Black men in particular, all of which seemed culled from the most racist kinds of "pornography" available. And it is undoubtedly no coincidence that the white men's bodies whom the gay spectator is positioned first to admire and then reject in horror are men predominantly dressed in leather.

In this respect, the film's vision seems reminiscent of that of the antipornography feminists, who frequently display the most brutal and violent images as if they were somehow representative of all pornography, and who draw a series of facile equivalences among pornography, s/m sex, and "real," nonconsensual violence.[57] In fact, as has often been noted, most pornography is not of this variety. Additionally, we might wonder at the three representations of Black men from white gay culture that Riggs's camera chooses, two of which draw an equivalence between interracial sex and violence. In what sense, if any, are these "representative" of interracial pornography? Are Black men always eroticized as the "passive" partner, as these images suggest, or doesn't Hemphill's contention that Black men are frequently "reduced" in pornography to "big, black dick" suggest instead that racial inequality is often sexualized in such a way as to gratify white men's desires for, and fantasies of, submission? Only a more careful exploration of the historical representation of interracial eroticism could possibly answer these questions. Unfortunately, the film eschews such an exploration, which would undoubtedly complicate the film's claim to be both "documentary" and "poetry" simultaneously.[58]

I am obviously not denying that racism exists in the white gay community, a racism in which I am obviously discursively implicated, even as I view *Tongues Untied*. But I am interested here in exploring the rhetoric the film deploys to produce its explanation of this cultural phenomenon and, in particular, the ways in which the film depends on evoking in the spectator a sense of shame. My position here requires me to notice the congruence between the disgust *Tongues Untied* expresses for "deviant" sexual behavior, emblematized in the film's rejection of s/m gay white men in particular, and the disgust of the white middle-class antiporn feminists described by Kipnis in her essay on reading *Hustler*. This congruence suggests that, like the white antiporn feminists whose rhetoric they sometimes share, intellectuals like Riggs and Hemphill may in fact be expressing in *Tongues Untied* a (middle-) class-inflected sense of disgust related to sexuality—obviously, not related to all sexuality, but to a particularly culturally problematic kind. It is perhaps thus not a coincidence at all that the rhetoric deployed by Hemphill in his reading of Mapplethorpe should be so similar to that of Dworkin, Stoltenberg, and even Jesse Helms.[59]

As I have suggested in my discussion of gay pornography, this rhetoric represents an attempt to conserve the threat of nonproductive expenditure represented—on a culturally phantasmatic level—by both gay sexuality and gay pornography. In this instance, it seeks to conserve the sovereign subject by reining in the excesses of gay interracial sexuality, as well as the threat of self-annihilation it seductively re-presents, perhaps to both parties. Its emotional appeal relies on a realist ontology of the image that would banish considerations of spectacle and melodrama from a reading of interracial pornography (as well as greeting cards).[60] As I will argue shortly, such rhetoric's demonization of white gay s/m queers allows for them to be constructed as an "Other." This casting of white gay s/m men as "Other" in turn makes it possible for the video to posit and deploy universalist conceptions of a humanity of which these white boys are obviously not a part. Finally, this rhetoric suggests—perhaps rightly—that the antiproductivity of sexuality is antithetical to the goals of identity politics.

To return to the terms laid out by Scott: My argument here is that *Tongues Untied* does not take sufficient pains to interrogate the ways in which its vision of white gay s/m men is necessarily structured in and by a history of the vilification of these same men by straight culture. Its untheorized deployment of experience acts as an alibi for a refusal to examine how the film's vision is necessarily structured by (a certain) homophobia. This deployment of experience necessarily precludes an exploration of how, for example, (gay white) s/m queers are constituted as "different," the grounds on which they are constituted as different, and the film's role in (re)producing them as different. Such an exploration would seem to be in the film's stated political interests, given the fact that Riggs's film often plays for a predominantly heterosexual (and not always queer-friendly) Black audience,[61] as well as the tendency of the religious Right—which presumably finds African American and white queers, dressed in leather or otherwise, equally disgusting—to deploy, in a manner somewhat like that of *Tongues Untied*, titillating and terrifying images of gay (and lesbian) s/m culture.

Near the end of the film, the fragmented, politically incorrect images of the white boys dressed in leather at a Gay Pride parade are replaced with a series of images of Black gay men at a similar parade. These men are photographed chiefly from the sidelines of the parade. The camera does not fragment their bodies nor move among them to tilt and pan; but sticks largely to the familiar *plan americain* shot, photographing them from the knees up. There is an emphasis in the scene on community, as opposed to the more disorganized wanderings of the white men depicted earlier at that other Pride parade. Instead of moving around among themselves, talking, laughing, and admiring each other's bodies, these men chant political slogans, sing, and carry banners, one of which, as I've stated above, reads, "Black Men Loving Black Men Is a Revolutionary Act." Riggs's film in fact ends with this statement. It appears in intertitles, one word at a time, at the film's conclusion, except that "a" has been amended to "the," the "the" underlined for emphasis.[62] The slogan is then punctuated by a cartoon of a Black man snapping. Here, the threat of sumptuous expenditure represented by gay sexuality and demonstrations of gay pride has been relegated to the more productive end of organized and orderly demonstration.[63]

How are we to account for the deployment in *Tongues Untied* of this middle-class-inflected sense of disgust around questions of interracial sexuality, as well as the film's overall failure to address sufficiently questions of what I have been referring to as the discontinuities of race and class? In pursuit of such a question, I will have to shift my argument slightly here from questions of subjectivity to questions of forms of domination. One possible explanation is provided by Immanuel Wallerstein in his account of historical capitalism's pairing of racism and universalism. According to Wallerstein, racism has assisted historical capitalism by socializing groups "into their own role in the economy":[64]

Racism was the mode by which various segments of the work-force within the same economic structure were constrained to relate to each other. Racism was the ideological justification for the hierarchization of the work-force and its highly unequal distributions of reward. What we mean by racism is that set of ideological statements combined with that set of continuing practices which have had the consequence of maintaining a high correlation of ethnicity and work-force allocation over time. The ideological statements have been in the form of allegations that genetic and/or long-lasting "cultural" traits of various groups are the major cause of differential allocation to positions in the economic structures.[65]

Wallerstein's analysis of racism suggests that in a film like *Tongues Untied* race and class ought to work in tandem with one another. Because racism as an ideology works, among other things, to socialize people into their "proper" (inferior) position within the work force, race correlates on some level with class. Wallerstein's analysis thus seems unable to account for the recent "upward mobility" of some contemporary African Americans, a class mobility that *Tongues Untied* celebrates. Throughout this chapter, I have been attempting to use my own position as reading subject—a position I have sought at some lengths to disclose—to suggest not that such a celebration should necessarily be abandoned but that its conditions of possibility must be elaborated and explored. Wallerstein's suggestion of the correlation between race and class seems initially unable to account precisely for the noncongruence, in *Tongues Untied*, of interests of race and class.

Wallerstein's analysis also reminds us, however, that racism has often functioned in tandem with the apparently contradicting ideology of universalism. Universalism is the belief that "there exist meaningful general statements about the world—the physical world, the social world—that are universally and permanently true, and that the object of science is the search for these general statements in a form that eliminates all so-called subjective, that is, all historically-constrained, elements from its formulation."[66] According to Wallerstein, universalism serves the needs of capitalism by assisting in the commodification of everything. In a world economy built on the endless accumulation of capital, the freer the flow of goods, capital, and labor power in a world market, the greater, presumably, the degree of commodification.[67] Universalism assists the flow, making possible the continued expansion of the capitalist world market all over the globe through what has been called variously "Westernization," "modernization," or, more critically, cultural imperialism.

Universalism is the ideology whereby indigenous cultural practices and beliefs in the periphery have been discredited and devalued by those who wielded economic and political power in the capitalist world system. In the name of supposedly universal truths shored up by such ideological creations as scientific progress and the brotherhood of man, universalism invited its recipients to reject their own indigenous culture as prescientific, mystical, or primitive. According to Wallerstein, the ideology of universalism served the needs of accumulators of capital in at least two specific ways. On the one hand, it socialized workers into their proper roles and functions in the processes of production by teaching them the requisite cultural norms, as well as eradicating competing cultural norms.[68] Concurrently, it allowed for the formation of Westernized "elites"—privileged marginals—who, it was presumed, would be separated from the masses of workers, and so less likely to revolt. Through the ideology of universalism, the Other is thus not posited in this particular instance in a relationship of absolute alterity to the homogeneous, but rather is deployed in a way that is useful for capitalist concerns. To place Wallerstein's analysis alongside Bataille's, we might suggest that racism-universalism makes a limited use of the heterogeneity represented by the Other by placing the Other both "inside" and "outside" homogeneous culture simultaneously.

What I have been referring to variously throughout this chapter as the figure of the privileged marginal or native informant is thus made possible by the extension of universalist premises to *token* members of a cultural minority. Such an extension works, as Wallerstein suggests, through a process of meritocracy that denies the structural inequalities underlying the system. Meritocracy serves to shore up the ideology that success is a matter of individual will and determination, pointing to the privileged marginal or native informant and insisting, for example, "If Oprah did it, anyone can." Thus, according to Wallerstein, the particular combination of racism-universalism has in fact best served the needs, historically, of accumulators of capital.[69] As I have suggested throughout this chapter, the mode of address of a film like *Tongues Untied* is often, but not exclusively, that of the native informant. (In other words, I do not mean to suggest here that *resistance* to racism-universalism is not also present in the video.)

Returning briefly to Foucault, we might argue that in the period of historical capitalism characterized by colonialist expansion, racism-universalism as an ideology works in tandem with the forms of subjection (as well as the other forms of power), normalizing, through modern practices of subject formation such as education, "token" individuals in such a way as to make possible a continued flow of goods, capital, and labor power. This is not to suggest that in the period of historical capitalism Foucault's three forms of power—(colonialist) domination, (economic) exploitation, and (disciplinary) subjection—are identical to one another, but, rather, that such different techniques of power might be mobilized in the service of one another. In the period of historical capitalism, the ideology of racism-universalism might thus represent a strategy whereby these three forms of power might be wedded into a (more or less) "coherent" project, the project of securing the periphery for a continued capitalist expansion (the "more or less" reminding us that, wherever there is power, there is also necessarily resistance). Employing a Gramscian vocabulary alongside Foucault here, we might suggest that hegemony works in this historical instance to mask the relationships between domination, exploitation, and subjection, substituting "consent" for "force" by wooing the privileged marginal into assenting to the forms of power that subjugate and subject. The brutalities of domination and exploitation thus find an alibi in the ideology of universalism, that "gift of the powerful to the weak"[70] wrapped ("economically," as Foucault reminds us) in the promise of a "universal" (Western) subjectivity.

The reliance in *Tongues Untied* on universalist precepts is most apparent in those sections of the film just discussed, sections that deploy what I have been referring to schematically as a middle-class feminist position against pornography. As I have already suggested, in *Tongues Untied*, the "bestiality" of white men in leather is deployed to shore up the "humanity" of the Black "victim" of both pornography and interracial sex. Such a position necessitates that these white men, as well as, by implication, all those who continue to find pleasure in pornography, be vilified as nonhuman, or at least inhumane. As I suggested in the previous chapter, in his critique of pornography, John Stoltenberg makes explicit the connection between universalist precepts and the antiporn position. (Recall Stoltenberg's insistence that "we are, after all, human. . . . We might simply out of our own frail humanity feel grief and pain when another human being is degraded, put down, sexually abused, sexually violated, not cared for.")[71] Apparently, in Stoltenberg's account, those who are interested in exploring the value of pornography are clearly lacking in humanity. The similarity between Stoltenberg's rhetoric and that deployed by *Tongues Untied* is thus no mere coincidence. Both Stoltenberg's and Riggs's projects necessarily work to secure the Other for a contained use by the normal, relying on universalist precepts that attempt to guarantee a certain (admittedly limited) subjectivity to the figure of the Other. In other words, both projects seek, through universalist precepts, to make the Other over in the image of a (universalist) human subject. Unfortunately, such a rhetorical strategy depends on the positing of certain "Others" as less human, more other, than others. In both Stoltenberg's and Riggs's accounts, that "Other of the Other" is the white peruser of pornography (who is also, by implication, a practitioner of s/m sex). In the situation of colonialism, that "other" Other is the (undisciplined) mass of workers presided over by cadres of colonial elites.

In the conclusion to an essay on racism, sexism, and universalism, Wallerstein provocatively suggests that what is currently required of theoretical work is a discussion of "whether and how we shall invent new systems that will utilize neither the ideology of universalism nor the ideology of racism-sexism."[72] Wallerstein's analysis suggests some of the limits of the continued attempt, by a "liberal" feminism, gay and lesbian studies, and Black studies, among others, to utilize the discourse of universalism to remake the Other in the image of the same. It suggests the need to be vigilant in our attempts to interrogate the ways in which such disciplines might inadvertently collude with the securing of the Other as a (limited) place of normality, and invites us to resist the attempts by liberalism to bring the Other into the fold of the normal, the universal, the homogeneous.

Wallerstein's analysis of the particular historical convergence of universalism-racism in the period of historical capitalism implies that we might also productively interrogate the particular historical combination of what we might term universalism-homophobia. Such a combination allows for the continued cultural production of a sexual Other over and against which "universal" man might be constructed, while at the same time allowing for an increasing commodification of gay middle-class culture. In other words, universalism-homophobia manages to cast gays and lesbians (at least partially and provisionally) outside the realm of the human, while simultaneously keeping them inside the circuits of consumption. Through a process of meritocracy, certain gay and lesbian persons are granted a (limited) subjectivity, a subjectivity that allows them to be produced as, among other things, consumers. This granting of a subjectivity necessarily depends, however, on the figure of the undisciplined gay and lesbian body, who continues to act as a foil for a normal that can make sense only in terms of what it is not. Wallerstein's analysis suggests that gays and lesbians in positions of privilege in particular must attempt to resist and transgress, on the level of subjectivity, the increasing normalization of the gay subject. The goal is not to produce the gay body as a universal, normalized (capitalist) subject, but attempt to use the "contaminated" position of the gay subject to thwart disciplinary society and the congruent attempts by accumulators of capital to secure other forms of domination and exploitation.

III

Considering Hemphill's contention that Mapplethorpe's photographs reduce the Black man to the image of a big, black dick, emphasizing a fragment of his body at the expense of his personhood, it is perhaps surprising that Hemphill's poetry in fact contains numerous references to dicks—presumably black ones, and some of them big. In addition to the section from "Heavy Breathing" already cited, several other poems display the penis prominently. "The Tomb of Sorrow" describes a figure beneath a moonlit tree clothed in military fatigues, with a "dick" of proud length; the penis is characterized as a "warrior," and it nods "knowingly" to the narrator.[73] The figure's face (and thus, according to Hemphill's own logic, personhood) is never described.[74] Another poem, "American Wedding," describes a symbolic wedding in which a ring is placed on a cock.[75] Concerning the fragmentation of the body and its "objectification," one poem in the collection, "Le Salon," describes a sexual encounter at an adult movie arcade in which the speaker describes his sexual partner as "another mouth";[76] another, "Object Lessons," I read as celebrating the speaker's willingness to fetishize his own body as an object of pleasure.[77] Such images seem surprisingly out of character for Hemphill, given his critique of Mapplethorpe.

It could be argued that I have read these images of penises "empirically," and outside of the context of the poems in which they originally appeared. The same might be argued of Hemphill's reading of Mapplethorpe, which deliberately brackets a consideration of the photos of Black men in relation to the remainder of Mapplethorpe's oeuvre, or even the particular exhibits or books in which these photos appeared. Significantly, the ambivalence on which a poem like Hemphill's "The Tomb of Sorrow" depends, in which the lover is portrayed as simultaneously monstrous and alluring, is unfortunately absent from Hemphill's reading of Mapplethorpe's photographs.

Clearly, I draw attention to these images from Hemphill's poems not to implicate Hemphill in the very fragmenting of the "whole" person of which he accuses Mapplethorpe, but rather to draw attention to the ways in which both *Tongues Untied* and Hemphill's reading of Mapplethorpe seem driven by a realist ontology of the photographic image. Behind Hemphill's call for a representation of the "whole" person, one hears the discursive traces of both the very familiar Western desire for mimesis, as well as American ego psychology's emphasis on a subject not split, but unified. One wonders if Hemphill might bring the same reading paradigm he brings to Mapplethorpe to his own poetry. I suspect a poet would not demand that a poem convey an image of a "whole" person, whatever that might entail. The continued reliance by identity politics on "positive," "realistic" representations to counter stereotypes necessitates a certain faith in the ability of photographic images to "capture" faithfully the oppressed, in their many states of "being."[78]

My reading here also draws attention, however, to the ways in which Hemphill's poetry—perhaps "against" his best intentions—also necessarily resists the attempt to make of the Black body a proper, disciplined subject. Hemphill's attempt to render that body visible necessarily brings with it the fragmentation, "objectification," and dispersal of the body that his reading of Mapplethorpe seeks to contain. These poems thus contain the conditions of possibility not only for an inscription of the Black body as subject but for a resistance to that normalization, a resistance that I have associated here and in the preceding chapter with pornography. (And surely it is significant that for some readers Hemphill's poems will not seem very different from either pornography or Mapplethorpe's images.) In other words, my reading of these poems reminds us again that the project of rendering Black bodies visible—a project in which both Hemphill's poetry and *Tongues Untied* partake—necessarily produces possibilities for resistance and transgression. These texts thus do not merely render these bodies useful for a contained capitalist consumption. They also necessarily participate in the continued attempt to maintain such bodies in their "useless," nonproductive, transgressive state.

In an essay in *Ceremonies*, "Miss Emily's Grandson Won't Hush His Mouth," Hemphill describes some of the criticism he received for speaking out against Mapplethorpe's photographs:

> Maybe grandmother knew that the editor of a Black literary journal based in the United States would call me and tell me that I should stop making public criticisms about the work of Robert Mapplethorpe regarding images of Black males. Even though the editor said that he agreed with my point of view, he didn't feel that the climate was appropriate for my statements and warned that Senator Jesse Helms and company would use my commentary to continue attacking the NEA.[79]

The editor in question then warned Hemphill that, because his journal was funded in part by the NEA, he might not be able to print Hemphill's work in future issues. In the tradition of an identity politics wedded to American ego psychology, Hemphill attributes this editor's statements to his status as "a cowardly, closeted faggot," the implication being that his individual "internalized homophobia" produced his comments. What this interchange unfortunately obscures is the ways in which Hemphill's and Helms's readings of Mapplethorpe might inadvertently share a similar politics of explanation, in that they rely on a similar rhetorical strategy—that of the antiporn movement—in order to secure their authority. It is one of the unfortunate ironies of history that a similar rhetoric will eventually be deployed by Helms against *Tongues Untied* when the question of the public funding of PBS comes before the U.S. Senate.

Throughout the writing of this chapter, I have had to struggle with the question of the politics of my produced explanation of *Tongues Untied*. I have had to face not only the question of what makes it possible for me to read this video in this way, but why I might strategically "choose" to do so, in as much as I am capable of understanding such a choice. Part of my willingness to engage with the film results from my insistence that Hemphill, Riggs, and I share a certain status as privileged marginals. Riggs was trained at Harvard and Berkeley. Hemphill's work has appeared beside my own in John Preston's anthology *Hometowns: Gay Men Write about Where They Belong*. We share a certain position, although, given the discontinuities of race, class, and sexual orientation, we obviously share that position unevenly. I have attempted here to critique the film not for its reliance on "indigenous" or "native" discourses, but rather for its apparently unacknowledged debt to Eurocentric discursive practices such as anthropology, as well as its implication in ongoing processes of subject formation. This critique is rooted in an ethical commitment to making as legible as possible the means by which I have produced my explanation of this text, given both my status as someone working within the liberal academy who is attempting to understand and make some tentative use of both its limits and possibilities, as well as my own ongoing production as a subject who both is and is not marginalized.

A continued commitment to the poststructuralist critique of the intentional subject requires an insistence that I cannot know or manipulate adequately the multiple and conflicting interests that move through me as I produce this explanation of the video. To claim even this final gesture as necessarily inadequate is perhaps our current disciplinary predicament.

Chapter 4

"I Just Wanna Be a Rich Somebody":
Experience, Common Sense, and
Paris Is Burning

I

At a recent committee meeting in my department, the chair of the committee, a professor in a field other than my own, and one whom I had not yet met, began with the familiar gesture of suggesting that we introduce ourselves to him. For years, I have been uncomfortable with such gestures. In addition to the fact that they seem painfully artificial, they necessarily force me to confront my shyness, a shyness that I have struggled for some time to overcome, and that today still reveals itself in such awkward social situations—this despite several years of acting training deliberately designed to overcome such feelings. I also must admit that I was a bit nervous when I arrived for the meeting; it concerned the job search on which I was about to embark. As I went on to introduce myself, my voice, not uncharacteristically, cracked, so that my name was apparently unclear to the chair, for, following my introduction, he repeated what he thought to be my first name, "Jan."

Now I know full well that this name is one of a handful—Pat, Kim, Leslie, Terry, for example—that might be shared equally by both men and women. But one of the reasons I have always been uncomfortable meeting people for the first time is that from as early as I can remember up until I was seventeen or so, I was often mistaken for female. Though this happened in a variety of different situations, one of the most painfully embarrassing and shameful instances of this occurred in high school my freshman year, when, on the first day of band practice, the band director responded to one of my questions with, "Yes, ma'am."

I could never understand how people managed to make this mistake. I didn't see myself as particularly effeminate, although I was shorter and of a slighter build than most other boys my age. And I did everything I could to mark myself as male so that this fateful error might not occur. I tried, unsuccessfully, to lower the pitch of my voice. (These attempts resulted in a case of chronic vocal strain that led people to ask me if I was suffering from a cold, or if I always spoke that way.) I refused to shave the soft coating of brown hair covering my upper lip. I tried to leave the first few buttons of my shirt undone, so that it would seem obvious that I was breastless. (Only my self-consciousness about my slight build kept me from going completely shirtless in many situations.) But these techniques only seemed to work sporadically, and couldn't actually guarantee that someone wouldn't make this terrible and humiliating error.

At thirty-three, it has obviously been many years since anything of this kind has happened to me. I suppose I just grew out of whatever it was that had led people to mistake me for female. And at nineteen, just to ensure that I would no longer have to deal with such worries, I grew a beard and mustache, some version of which I wore sporadically throughout my twenties. But just before the departmental meeting in which I was mistaken for "Jan," I had, for the first time in seven years or so, shaved my mustache. In that moment of being called by a name other than my own, a name that could or could not have referred to someone female, years of self-doubt, humiliation, and embarrassment flowed back to me—so much so that it was difficult for me to concentrate on the remainder of the meeting until the chair excused himself, and I could be absolutely certain that there wasn't anyone left in the room who might be unsure of my gender. Of course, I reassure myself that it is highly unlikely that this man could have mistaken someone my age, with my thinning hair, my razor stubble, and my recently gym-tailored swimmer's build for a woman. But a small enough doubt remains to act as a reminder of how absolutely terrifying and shameful it is in this culture to be a man mistaken for a woman.

As might be expected, given my approving citation of Joan Scott's work in the previous chapter, I am extremely wary of the recent tendency in gay and lesbian studies to deploy largely untheorized notions of autobiography and experience. I am particularly suspicious of the eagerness with which the liberal academy has lent its benevolent ear to our stories as of late. Replacing the psychiatrist's couch with, for example, the podium at an academic conference or the pages of a dissertation seems to leave too much the same.[1] I am less certain than some of my colleagues that the casting of ourselves as an object of knowledge for the disciplines of English or film studies is necessarily a gain, political or otherwise. The rapidity with which "queerness" in particular has become grist for the academic mill—evidenced, for example, in the current plethora of "queer" panels and papers at the recent annual meetings of both the Modern Language Association and the Society for Cinema Studies—should at the very least invite us to examine the facility with which the academy manages to interpolate allegedly oppositional cultural practices.[2] In the wake of the work of such theorists as Foucault and Derrida, it is difficult to cling to the idealist precept that knowledge (in this particular instance, knowledge of the Other) is simply made available by the academy for an unproblematic and disinterested use, benevolent or otherwise, even under the guise of the "appreciation" of difference. Add to this questions of the relationship between the humanities and broader political and economic concerns, and it becomes increasingly impossible to maintain a happy outlook concerning the liberal academy's continued pursuit of knowledge of the Other.[3]

Additionally, in the current historical moment, practitioners of gay and lesbian studies seems particularly vulnerable to being seduced by the academic star system. The relative newness of the discipline, combined with the liberal academy's desperate attempts to contain the threat of difference by creating and celebrating privileged marginals, has allowed a handful of highly visible scholars in the field to claim their place in the academic pantheon. Unfortunately, as might be expected, the logic of scarcity still prevails, suggesting that the discipline will tolerate only a certain small number of scholars in the field. Although most universities claim, falsely or otherwise, to have nothing like the financial resources necessary to begin programs in gay and lesbian studies in these times of programmatic cutbacks, there are already rumors of an impending turf war between various factions in the emerging discipline. Autobiographical narratives in particular unfortunately make possible, given both this current state of academic affairs as well as U.S. culture's fantasies concerning the lures and powers of the individual personality, a kind of fetishization of the gay and lesbian academic body.[4] They might unwittingly contribute to the continued production of gay and lesbian subjects as marginalized by privileging the personal experiences of only a handful of the chosen few. As Spivak might have it, this placing of token gay and lesbian subjects within the academic star system necessarily obscures the shifting differences and distinctions between representation as proxy and representation as portrait, the gay academic representing, in both his corporeal body and the body of his work, an image that is perhaps unwittingly but necessarily also a politically and economically interested proxy.[5] Gay academic stars perhaps too readily stand in for the interests of an often unspecified otherness (or, rather, an otherness specified exclusively by sexual orientation), an otherness that, if more carefully plotted, would necessarily be crossed by competing interests of class, gender, and race, to name only the most obvious. The token presence of highly visible gay and lesbian scholars might obscure the question of in whose political interests they speak when they claim to be speaking as gay and lesbian.[6]

Thirdly, for reasons outlined in the preceding chapter, I am uncomfortable with the continued reliance by identity politics on a strategy of visibility, a strategy that sometimes privileges experiential, testimonial accounts of oppression over intellectual interrogations of positioning, and that seems particularly susceptible to being embraced by the most recent wave of anti-intellectual, antitheoretical academicians. The continued holding of the body of "experience" over the head of "theory," as if experience were some kind of self-evident answer to the difficult questions posed by poststructuralism, particularly around questions of identity, agency, and the political, is a strategy shared (although shared unevenly) by certain academic critics on the Left as well as the Right. I would only want to add here that such testimonial accounts necessarily rely for their political force on an unproblematized conflation of the two senses of *representation*, a conflation of which Spivak reminds us to be wary. The testimonial necessarily stands in for an experience of oppression "larger" than the individual, the native informant acting as the vocal and visible representative of the (largely silent, largely invisible) collective. The testimonial is thus an individual and privileged representation of experience (portrait) that works to represent (by proxy) the political interests of the group to which the informant claims to belong. This seems a fairly apt description of, say, a work like Riggs's *Tongues Untied*. Although it is impossible to separate cleanly and finally these two senses of *representation*, it is perhaps possible to be (scrupulously) ethically attuned to the problematics engaged in the act of representing.[7] As I have suggested in previous chapters, perhaps only a continuously unfolding deconstruction of one's privileged position as native informant might complicate and undercut the claims of one's own experiential account of oppression (representation as portrait) to represent adequately (as proxy) the interests of the Other.

Yet, given the current political and intellectual climate, it seems impossible merely to reject narratives of experience outright, as much as we might be tempted to do so. Many marginalized groups outside of the academy continue to rely on experience to counter and resist the dearth of "negative" representations that greet them in their everyday lives. As much as we need to continue to problematize the relation of image making to the political, given the difficulty of forging a collective politics, narratives of experience—even if that "experience" is understood, as in the case of identity, to be both discursively and textually produced—might make possible some kind of collective struggle. If intellectuals working within the academy want their discourse to be understood and made useful and available—as problematic as these terms might be—in the service of struggles for social justice, it is imperative that poststructuralist thinkers find some way to speak of, through, and to the discourse of experience, given the fact that (political) subjects continue to invest so heavily in the category.[8] The discourse of experience might thus provide a bridge between the academy and other places where struggles for social change occur, a common discursive ground.[9]

A sustained discussion of the category of experience might engage productively with questions of representation in the two senses of that word, questions that obviously can't be willed away by refusing to treat experiential narratives as anything other than "false consciousness" or something of the like. One cannot simply choose not to represent, to avoid and escape the perils of the shifting distinctions between the two senses of the term. This is not to suggest that silence and invisibility might not be appropriate responses in specific and local situations. I would suggest polemically that the specific political effects of the rage to represent (and self-represent) need to be thought through a little more carefully by culturally marginalized peoples. We need not automatically assume that, for example, increased representation is equivalent to better and more effective representation. It is not too outlandish to suggest that perhaps the cultural practices and productions of the marginalized should not be made available for the delectation of the mainstream, that, for example, certain literatures and films should not be served up to students, even under the guise of a benevolent and appreciative multiculturalism.[10] As I have argued in previous chapters, however, power engenders its own specific forms of resistance. Sometimes the master's tools are the most efficacious ones at hand. In a culture that so heavily invests in the myth of experience, perhaps there are ways, perilous though they might be, to make use of the category of experience and the narratives to which it sometimes gives rise.

I want now to recast the problem of experience through a number of thinkers, and to examine how this recasting of experience might inflect a discussion of some of the relationships between gender, sexuality, subjectivity, and what we might broadly designate as the political. I take the risk, then, despite my hesitations, of beginning with what remains for me an embarrassingly personal anecdote, in order to set the stage for a meditation on questions of experience, subjectivity, agency, politics, and gay men and the feminine.

As I have already implied in my discussion of the attempts by marginalized peoples to combat "negative" mainstream representations, one of the most obvious things at stake in a discussion of experience is the status of what has been variously termed the lived, the actual, or the (however inadequately empirically verifiable) real (although these terms are obviously not interchangeable). The past twenty years of debates in criticism affiliated with the culturally marginalized are fraught with discussions of the real, discussions that often pit what for the sake of polemic we might term a humanist identity politics against a more deconstructive or Foucauldian-inflected position. Judith Butler has recently offered this excellent intervention into the debate as it has inflected feminism:

> A contemporary feminist interrogation of representation is inevitably caught up in a set of persistently ambivalent ontological claims. Recent feminist criticisms of poststructuralism and poststructuralist feminism take issue with what appears to be a refusal to grant a pre-given, pre-linguistic or self-identical status to the real. The so-called deconstruction of the real, however, is not a simple negation or thorough dismissal of any ontological claim, but constitutes an interrogation of the construction and circulation of what counts as an ontological claim. The critical point is to examine the exclusionary means by which the circumscription of the real is effected. And in a sense, this particular move to problematize the real has been part of feminist practice prior to there being any question of its status as a poststructuralist intrusion.[11]

Butler's text reminds us that the struggle of marginalized groups to gain access to the means of self-representation is necessarily implicated in the (so-called) deconstruction of the real, for, by insisting that their reality has historically been blocked or thwarted by the existing structures of power, such groups necessarily contest "the exclusionary means by which the circumscription of the real is effected." The difference between, say, a more rigorously poststructuralist deconstruction of the real and one still wedded to identity politics is perhaps that the position aligned with identity politics sometimes imagines that there is some place beyond exclusion, some place where, if everyone were given "equal" access to the tools of self-representation, representation might accurately reflect the reality of lived experience in all its "diversity." This is in fact one of the reigning definitions of the term "multiculturalism." The assumption here is that the removal of the constraints currently operating in the production of cultural self-representations will make it possible for minority communities to use the category of experience to displace the current, exclusionary "reality" with a more varied, "authentic" multiplicity of realities.

But poststructuralist thinkers such as Foucault have drawn attention to some of the limits of this utopian imagining of a field of unconstrained (discursive) representation. In "The Discourse on Language," Foucault suggests that "in every society the production of discourse is at once controlled, selected, organised and redistributed according to a certain number of procedures, whose role is to avert its powers and dangers, to cope with chance events, to evade its ponderous, awesome materiality."[12] According to Foucault, a number of rules necessarily operate in the production of discourse: rules of prohibition, which dictate when, where, how, and by whom something can be spoken; rules of division, which oppose reasonable discourse to folly; and rules that separate true discourse from false.[13] For Foucault, there is no place "beyond" these rules where discourse might be "freely" entered.[14] This suggests that even discourse about the self, the kind of discourse associated with what we term "personal experience," is itself necessarily constrained by a number of historically specific procedures.[15]

In a slightly different but related vein, Foucault's work in *The Archaeology of Knowledge* suggests that a number of historically specific discursive preconditions must exist even if one is to make a statement about one's self in which that self functions as the subject of that statement—in other words, the kind of statement we often associate with what we term "personal experience."[16] For Foucault, the subject of the statement refers not to its "cause, origin, or starting point," but to the place from which the statement is uttered, a place that, Foucault argues, is necessarily *assigned* by the statement. In this passage, Foucault is concerned with "what position can and must be occupied by any individual if he is to be the subject" of a statement. This again suggests that the production of even those statements we might term "personal experience" is subject to a number of constraints. "Personal experience" thus does not simply emerge from the desire to tell the truth about one's self (nor can the "truth" of the statement be separated out from the history of truth in which such a statement is situated). Rather, the "truth" of the self can be produced only through a historically specific set of discursive constraints.[17] One of the problems with the genre of the testimonial is that it often willfully forgets that the discourse of the native informant is itself subject to a multiplicity of discursive constraints. The myth that the native informant can somehow manage to transcend the particular and historic conditions of possibility of his or her own discourse, revealing, in his or her personal testimony, a "truth" that manages to escape the constraints typically operating in the production of truth, represents one of the most familiar and pernicious castings of the (limited) subjectivity of the Other. Such a casting calls forth the Other as that noble savage whose connection to nature (often figured as prior to the perils of signification) renders him or her more "authentic" than his or her benevolent and appreciative (mainstream) listeners, in greater proximity to a prelapsarian (unconstrained) truth. It is perhaps not too crude to suggest a genealogical link between today's privileged native informant and yesterday's noble savage (or at least to suggest that the two figures often signify similarly in the contemporary multiculturalism debates).

Foucault's later work takes up the problem of truth at some length, but here the analysis has shifted from an exploration of the statement to what Foucault terms the "regime of truth":

> Truth is a thing of this world: it is produced only by virtue of multiple forms of constraint. And it induces regular effects of power. Each society has its regime of truth, its "general politics" of truth: that is, the types of discourse which it accepts and makes function as true; the mechanisms and instances which enable one to distinguish true and false statements, the means by which each is sanctioned; the techniques and procedures accorded value in the acquisition of truth; the status of those who are charged with saying what counts as true.[18]

As I have argued in my first chapter, the intellectual *must* challenge the rules operating in the regime of truth so that the conditions of possibility of a new politics of truth might emerge. In the context of this discussion, this requirement means, among other things, complicating the easily assumed authenticity of the native informant's discourse. Foucault imagines the intellectual saying, "I would like to produce some effects of truth which might be used for a possible battle, to be waged by those who wish to wage it, in forms yet to be found and in organizations yet to be defined."[19] This image suggests again that "true" statements about the self—and it is difficult to posit the category of experience except in relation to the question of the "truth" of the self—need themselves to be disengaged from the current regime of truth, if they are to bring about change. Such a disengagement is particularly crucial in light of Foucault's insistence that the subject is historically produced through processes of subjection and subjugation. If one is to effect some kind of change in the production of subject-effects, one of the crucial historical questions to pose must be "How does it happen that the human subject makes himself into an object of possible knowledge, through which forms of rationality, through which historical necessities, and at what price?" (245). Given the concerns of this present study, it might be particularly fruitful to explore the ways in which "emergent" subjects such as native informants make themselves into objects of knowledge for, among other things, the liberal academy (and, as Foucault suggests, through which historical necessities, and at what price).

Finally, as I have argued throughout this study, Foucault's reformulation of power suggests that margin and center are unthinkable except in relation to one another. To extrapolate this condition to the question of experience and the real: Foucault's argument suggests that what we call the real is itself possible only as a result of what Butler terms "the exclusionary means by which the circumscription of the real is effected." The concept of the real would fail to make sense were it not posited in relation to something which it is not. As Butler suggests, "We can understand the 'real' as a variable construction which is always and only determined in relation to its constitutive outside: fantasy, the unthinkable, the unreal."[20] As I suggested through my reading of *Tongues Untied*, one of the problems with the category of experience is that it necessarily relies on an often untheorized deployment of the real. Experience is hauled into court in the service of one reality in order to discredit a competing one.[21] In the case of the struggle for marginalized groups to achieve the means of self-representation, one version of reality—the "negative," "stereotypical" portrayal of a marginalized group—is replaced with a "positive," "realistic," and self-constructed image. But one of the limits of such an approach is, as Butler has suggested, that "to prove that events are real, one must already have a notion of the real within which one operates, a set of exclusionary and constitutive principles that confer on a given indication the force of an ontological designator; and if it is that very notion of the real that one wants, for political reasons, to contest, then the simple act of pointing will not suffice to delimit the force of the indexical."[22] Thus, simply substituting one version of reality for another is not sufficient to challenge the grounds, or, in Foucault's terminology, the regime of truth, on which the initial, competing reality is posited. As Butler argues, "To change the real, that is, to change what qualifies as the real, would be to contest the syntax within which pointing occurs and on which it tacitly relies" (107). As I have suggested at various moments throughout this study, one of the perils of a criticism affiliated with the culturally marginalized is that it too often seeks, with recourse to, for example, identity politics, to re-create the marginalized in a specular image to the dominant, as if, say, substituting gay bodies for straight ones, and giving such bodies "equal" re-presentation, would significantly and decisively alter the current regime of truth. Such a move circumvents the possibility of a more radical epistemological rupture impossibly suggested by the place of the Other.

Gramsci's theme of "common sense" adds to poststructuralism a slightly different way of rewriting the discourse of personal experience. Common sense, we recall, finds at least one of its conditions of possibility in the problematic of the relationship between intellectual work and social change. According to Gramsci, philosophical activity is not merely "the 'individual' elaboration of systematically coherent concepts," but rather involves "a cultural battle to transform the popular 'mentality.' "[23] Intellectual work thus has an active role to play in the transformation of culture. The role of the intellectual is to provide for his or her social group a sense of homogeneity as well as "an awareness of its own function not only in economic but also in the social and political fields."[24] To do so requires that intellectuals maintain contact with, as Gramsci puts it (in quotation marks), the "simple," so that a social bloc might be formed "which can make politically possible the intellectual progress of the mass and not only of small intellectual groups."[25]

One of the ways through which such intellectual work might be accomplished is the path of "common sense," the existing, "indigenous" form of philosophical activity. Common sense is a kind of reservoir of historically discontinuous and disjointed ideas. Gramsci refers to this reservoir as "the most widespread conception of life and of man" (326n). Gramsci stresses that there is not a single common sense (325). As the "folklore" of philosophy, common sense necessarily takes a variety of forms, its most fundamental characteristic being its "fragmentary, incoherent and inconsequential" character, which is "in conformity with the social and cultural position of the masses whose philosophy it is."[26] According to Gramsci, every philosophical movement of any historical effectivity leaves behind "a sedimentation of 'common sense.' "[27] Common sense thus might be characterized as the "philosophy of non-philosophers."[28]

Gramsci suggests that the role of the intellectual is to make of this non-philosophical philosophy a "unitary and coherent" intellectual activity, so that it might help to advance social change.[29] As Gramsci argues,

> A philosophy of praxis cannot but present itself at the outset in a polemical and critical guise, as superseding the existing mode of thinking and existing concrete thought (the existing cultural world). First of all, therefore, it must be a criticism of "common sense," basing itself initially, however, on common sense in order to demonstrate that "everyone" is a philosopher and that it is not a question of introducing from scratch a scientific form of thought into everyone's individual life, but of renovating and making "critical" an already existing activity."[30]

A critique of common sense that nonetheless recognizes the philosophical activity involved in such thinking acts as the starting point of critical intervention. Gramsci also argues that this interrogation of "common sense" must then itself be followed by an autocritique of the history of philosophy, an autocritique that recognizes the historical limits of philosophy as well as determining how it may be activated in the analysis of contemporary problems.

I am extremely suspicious of a number of recent attempts to rewrite Gramsci through poststructuralism in such a way as to erase the problematic of class from his work by transforming "social bloc" into something like a "coalition" made up of various "identities" such as women, gays and lesbians, people of color, and so forth. A poststructuralist acknowledgment that one is positioned within a multiplicity of discursivities that we might inadequately name as class, race, gender, and sexuality—to name only the most obvious—does not require that one pose an isomorphic analogy between these competing discourses, nor that one "choose," in the last instance, one of these competing discourses as "true" or fundamental. While we might at strategic points choose to argue polemically for the primacy of one of these discourses over the other, such a choice is necessarily crossed by competing interests that we can never adequately know and manipulate.

I am also not arguing here for some kind of ahistorical fetishization of Gramsci's project that would wrestle Gramsci's writings out of their historical context and treat Gramsci as a prophetic figure, a poststructuralist *avant la lettre*, whose writings provide, for example, an adequate political program for the present. My method of attempting to circumvent this kind of ahistorical fetishization has been, perhaps paradoxically, to attempt to make a productively presentist use of Gramsci, a use that requires that I read Gramsci perhaps idiosyncratically, or at least selectively, largely leaving behind such questions as what is the real in Gramsci, and how is it different from that of other Marxists, as well as a more extended examination of the differing defining conditions of both Gramsci's context and our present one. What I am most interested in retaining from Gramsci in this instance is the attempt to think through a relationship between the intellectual work he characterizes as common sense, and the ways in which such intellectual work might be activated in the service of present collective struggles, struggles that pursue as their end a society in which relations of power are more fluid, more easily reversible, and in which relations of production are made more egalitarian as a result of this fluidity. My use of Gramsci here might thus be characterized as an instance of an admittedly tentative, strategic, and provisional attempt to bring together what I would call considerations of both the ethical and the ideological as they intersect with questions of cultural marginality.

Perhaps, then, given the necessity here of addressing questions of difference in addition to class, it is permissible to speak of the "common sense" of women, of people of color, or of gays and lesbians, if we acknowledge that such common sense is extremely heterogeneous (as Gramsci himself suggests), crossed by competing interests, all of which carry traces of other "philosophical" currents, and which are subject to highly contested historical interpretation. Such a formulation of common sense might allow the poststructuralist critique of experience to reformulate experience as a kind of common sense, finding in the discourse of experience the traces of an intellectual activity that might form the basis of social change. An elaboration of this experience might then provide the conditions of possibility for a consideration of common sense as a form of cultural explanation, a form of cultural explanation that must be subject both to ethical elaboration and ideological critique.

This recasting of experience as common sense allows us to retain the (so-called) poststructuralist deconstruction of the real in such a way as to insist that all ontological claims are themselves made possible through existing discursive structures. Experience would thus be cast not as some kind of immediate and unproblematized encounter with an empirical reality that is knowable (even partially or provisionally), but as a discursive mapping, a structure of interpretation that necessarily renders that which we designate as the real as intelligible. Experience thus makes possible, among other things, not a greater access to an existing (if misrepresented) reality, but a critical interrogation of the regime of truth that makes possible concepts such as reality and experience.

Secondly, experience reformulated as common sense might take into account Foucault's critique of the historical role of the intellectual without necessitating the positing of a unified and fully intentional subaltern consciousness. The intellectual's role vis-à-vis common sense is not to discredit such thinking as false consciousness, but to suggest ways in which it might be made more systematic and less impressionistic so that it might be made more politically useful, that is, assist collective struggles against various forms of power. The intellectual uses his or her historic positioning to tease out some of the implications of common sense. As Gramsci insists, such a teasing out requires that the intellectual maintain contact with the discursive milieu in which common sense is produced. Ideally, this contact would necessitate the continued production of what Gramsci terms organic intellectuals. Although, as I suggested earlier, given the very different historical situations in which Foucault and Gramsci are writing, it would be unwise to propose an exact analogy between Gramsci's "organic" and Foucault's "specific" intellectuals, both theorists are concerned here with how intellectual activity might be marshaled in the service of struggles. Both theorists also recognize the historical limits of the role of the intellectual. Common sense might provide a means for reinvigorating the role of the intellectual while acknowledging the problematic of what Deleuze has termed the indignity of speaking for others.[31]

This suggests the third, and perhaps most urgent, reason for recasting experience as common sense. In the previous chapter, I noted that there has been a tendency in certain incarnations of cultural criticism to equate the struggle against the forms of power that produce the subject with political struggle. This equation often forges the link between subjectivity and politics with recourse to the concept of identity. Experience plays a particularly vital role in this argument. Specifically, the link between subjectivity and politics is produced with recourse to experience wedded to identity. In other words, individual subjects (allegedly) "suture themselves" into political practices through a shared identity shored up by a common experience. This is in fact one of the founding fictions of identity politics: that a shared identity rooted in a shared experience (often cast as the experience of community) will produce a shared political commitment. In the case of a minority politics, experience and identity mutually reinforce one another. A shared experience of cultural domination (and subcultural affirmation) produces a shared identity; a shared identity in turn makes possible a shared body of experience, which acts as the basis for political dissent (as well as subcultural celebration). Thus, if identity provides the "glue" that links subjectivity to politics, experience might be said, in discussions of identity politics that privilege experience, to provide the glue that links individual subjectivities to identity.

For example, in the context of *Tongues Untied*, the statement "Black Men Loving Black Men Is *the* Revolutionary Act" depends for its rhetorical force on a resistance to the lures of interracial s/m sex and the threat to subjectivity such sex re-presents. This resistance is shored up with recourse to a homogeneous identity—gay Black man—wedded to a common (communal) experience—the experience of first giving in to, and then rejecting as inappropriate, one's desire for white gay men.[32] As I have suggested in my reading of the video, crucial to the forging of this homogeneous Black identity is the erasure of questions of class.[33] At the conclusion of *Tongues Untied*, the casting of loving Black men as *the* "revolutionary" act completes the chain linking subjectivity to politics through identity and experience, equating the resistant sexual subject with the resistant (revolutionary) political subject.

This equating of subjectivity and politics is unfortunately a familiar gesture in (middle-class) gay activist rhetoric (and, as I suggest in my reading of *Tongues Untied*, one can't help noting here the presence in the video of certain discursive traces of this rhetoric). As Leo Bersani notes, "There has been a lot of confusion about the real or potential political implications of homosexuality. . . . Thanks to a system of gliding emphases, gay activist rhetoric has even managed at times to suggest that a lust for other men's bodies is a by-product or a decision consequent upon political radicalism rather than a given point of departure for a whole range of political sympathies."[34] According to Bersani, such rhetoric forgets that "many gay men could, in the late '60s and early '70's [sic], begin to feel comfortable about having 'unusual' or radical ideas about what's OK in sex without modifying one bit their proud middle-class consciousness or even their racism."[35]

This conflation of (resistant) subjectivity and politics in gay activist rhetoric has been particularly prevalent in discussions of resistance to gender norms. Bersani rightly critiques the efforts of Jeffrey Weeks and Richard Dyer to read the hypermacho style of urban gay (largely white) ghetto culture as politically oppositional. Specifically, Bersani takes issue with Dyer's contention that "by taking the signs of masculinity and eroticizing them in a blatantly homosexual context, much mischief is done to the security with which 'men' are defined in society, and by which their power is secured."[36] Bersani rightly wonders how much mischief can be accomplished through the deployment of a style of dress that is often largely limited to Saturday nights in the ghetto, and that many straight people perhaps read as a poor imitation of the real (masculine) thing. To add my own anecdotal evidence of this equating, in certain sectors of the gay community, of gender experimentation with political intervention: At the 1991 meeting of the Gay, Lesbian, and Bisexual Caucus of the Society for Cinema Studies, an enthusiastic young scholar suggested that a proper "political" intervention at the next year's annual meeting of the society might consist of having all members dress in drag for the presentation of their papers. Such a suggestion fails to consider, for example, how the liberal academy might actually privilege and even valorize such easily containable isolated gestures of token opposition, for such gestures do not seem to challenge, in any substantial way, for example, the way the academy is invested in relations of power that pursue goals other than the production of the gendered subject.

Interestingly, this "system of gliding emphasis" that Bersani notes in the rhetoric equating homosexuality with radical politics also occurs in recent discussion of the relationship between reading and politics, in which the resistant (or nonresistant) reader of a text is conflated with the resistant (or nonresistant) political subject. Consider, for example, Cornel West's recent contention that the major shortcoming of Derridean deconstruction is that the works of Derrida and his followers "too often become rather monotonous, Johnny-one-note rhetorical readings that disassemble texts with little attention to the effects and consequences these dismantlings have in relation to the operations of military, economic, and social powers."[37] Only through a massive sleight of hand can one move from a discussion of literary criticism to a discussion of military, economic, and social power without arguing what the causal links might be between these realms. Although Foucault has often been accused of theorizing power as a totalizing force from which nothing can escape, he is at least careful to distinguish different forms of power. The conception of power in West's account of Derridean criticism suggests that there is virtually no difference between the power of the literary critic and the power of, for example, the military dictator, except perhaps in terms of the (undefined) quantity of power that they both wield.

My argument here is clearly not that resistance is not operating in such practices as, say, "perverse" sexual activity, Black men loving Black men, drag, or even a certain reading strategy. Rather, I want to insist that not all resistance is resistance to the same thing. Foucault's account of power obliges us to think of power not as a monolith, always and everywhere the same, but as a series of forces that pursue different strategies, that invest different (social, political, and human) bodies, and that necessarily bring with them different forms of resistance. What is lost when resistance on the level of subjectivity is equated with political resistance is, for example, a notion of collective political struggle that might resist forms of power *other* than those linked to the production of the subject. The equating of the form of power that subjects and subjugates the subject with all other forms of power perhaps inadvertently makes possible the deployment of a liberal individualism that privileges individual acts of transgression and resistance as "political." Such (allegedly politically) resistant subjects are (perhaps literally) not in a position to thwart, for example, what Foucault has termed "forms of exploitation which separate individuals from what they produce,"[38] for they are not resisting in the realm where such relations of power are most concentrated.

All of this suggests, among other things, the need to engage with forms of struggle that move beyond (but do not abandon) the production of the subject. In other words, my assumption here is that in its privileging not only of experience but also of an equating of the resistant disciplinary subject with the resistant political subject, identity politics has often assumed erroneously that struggles against power are always and everywhere the same. Thus has arisen, perhaps, a situation in which struggles against the forms of subjection have taken the place of, or been substituted for, other kinds of struggle, struggles I will schematically characterize as political: struggles against what Foucault has termed the other forms of power, that is, forms of ethnic, religious, and social domination, and forms that alienate the subject from his or her labor. Though it is perhaps premature to cast struggles against all other forms of power as political to the exclusion of struggles against the forms of power that subjugate, I tentatively do so because this present study is so heavily indebted to the forms of struggle against subjectivity. In order to differentiate my position from one that would equate all struggles over power with politics, I want to define the political strategically as the collective struggle against forms of power other than those disciplinary practices that subject and subjugate. Or perhaps I would reserve the term for those struggles that, in addition to engaging the form of power that subjects, also engage with other forms of power. Perhaps, then, we ought to rewrite the slogan "The Personal Is Political" as "The Personal Is Politicized." Such a rewriting may circumvent the attempt to equate all resistance with political resistance, at the same time insisting, among other things, that struggles against the forms of power that subject might usefully be connected up with other kinds of struggle.

A turn to a Gramscian account of common sense, then, might allow us to wrestle the category of experience away from identity politics, and find a way to deploy it in struggles against forms of power in addition to those associated with the production of the subject. However, once the category of identity has been put under erasure (and not simply erased or banished), some other critical concept might be deployed to fill the gap between subjectivity and politics. A name might be given to the means whereby the personal might be strategically politicized, whereby resistance on the level of subjectivity might become attached to other forms of resistance. Throughout this study, I have been tentatively proposing the category of ethics as the means whereby subjectivities might be compelled to engage in collective political practice. I say "might be compelled to engage" rather than "sutured" in order to emphasize ethics as that which names one's political affiliations and commitments. My hesitancy to deploy the term *suture* alerts us to the fact that, for example, the resistant sexual subject must work at becoming a resistant political subject, that such resistance is not automatic, but willed. A commitment to the critique of the intentional subject that insists that political intervention, though necessarily taking place on the level of willed activity, cannot sufficiently control the effects and ends of that activity, suggests both the possibilities and limits of the ethical. Ideology critique must thus interrupt the ethical, attempting to provide a glimpse of the competing economic interests that move through the production of any ethics. Thus there must be two different kinds of critique, ethical and ideological. One concerns itself primarily with the forging of shared concerns, stated goals, expressed sympathies, and articulated strategies for the achievement of a more "free," more egalitarian social arrangement in which relations of power might be made more easily reversible. The other attempts to call into crisis those concerns, goals, sympathies, and strategies, by struggling to know the competing (economic) forces and interests that inadvertently move through, disrupt, way-lay, and de-rail even the most purportedly radical and just solutions to the problems of inequity, domination, and alienation. Because of what we might schematically refer to as history, that numerous, impossible to disentangle, and always inadequately named weave of causal forces, I have been produced as a certain kind of reader of texts in a specific location. This position has afforded me the opportunity to focus throughout this study primarily on the ethical, while still marking a place for another kind of analysis, an analysis that points toward considerations of the ideological.

The forging of a shared ethics on which a politics might be based will require the opening up of cultural spaces in and beyond the academy in which experience might be considered as common sense, and in which common sense might be elaborated as a basis for continuing political intervention. In a decidedly anti-intellectual, anticollective culture, this is a difficult task. In the following section of this essay, I would like to discuss how an inflection of the discourse of experience through the problematic of common sense might make possible a reading of a text of popular culture, Jennie Livingston's film *Paris Is Burning*; I also wish to respond to some of the criticism of the film. Marcia Landy has recently argued for the necessity and appropriateness of using a Gramscian understanding of common sense to analyze texts of mass culture.[39] I hope the following analysis is an effort in this direction.

The mass reception of a text of popular culture such as a film suggests that it might form one of the beginning points for an elaboration of ethics. In the *Prison Notebooks*, Gramsci suggests that "culture, at its various levels, unifies in a series of strata, to the extent that they come into contact with each other, a greater or lesser number of individuals who understand each other's mode of expression in differing degrees, etc."[40] The forging of a shared cultural "climate" is thus vital to the bringing about of collective activity in the service of social change. As Gramsci argues,

> An historical act can only be performed by "collective man," and this presupposes the attainment of a "cultural-social" unity through which a multiplicity of dispersed wills, with heterogeneous aims, are welded together with a single aim, on the basis of an equal and common conception of the world, both general and particular, operating in transitory bursts (in emotional ways) or permanently (where the intellectual base is so well rooted, assimilated and experienced that it becomes passion). (349)

My assumption here is that, as a mass-distributed cultural artifact that records and deploys the widely disseminated mode of expression termed by Gramsci as "common sense," *Paris Is Burning* might be mobilized in the formation of a collective "ethico-political" will.[41] Sue Golding has recently argued for the central importance of Gramsci's notion of the will.[42] According to Golding, the will for Gramsci "was precisely the *creative component* of practical/political activity. But, at the same time, the will marked the terrain or boundary of that practical/political activity, a terrain made coherent or unified precisely through political struggle" (73; emphasis in original). In Golding's reading, the will for Gramsci is neither psychological nor metaphysical, but political in the strongest sense of the word. It is a conceptual category that denotes the combined ability to grasp the historical present and to begin to work toward the possible. Neither pregiven nor continuous, but rather immanent, it must become directed or focused in the service of change. In a passage entitled " 'Creative' Philosophy," Gramsci defines the will "in the last analysis" as practical or political activity based on historical necessity.[43] This will must be diffused as a form of "good sense," "in such a way as to convert itself into an active norm of conduct" (346). In reading *Paris Is Burning*, I am attempting to suggest how the film and the narratives of experience it deploys might be put to use in such a way as to enable the forging of an ethico-political will, a will that might animate a collective struggle against the forms of power that subject, exploit, and dominate.

II

"I remember my dad would say, you have three strikes against you in this world. Every Black man has two. That you're Black and you're male. But you're Black and you're male and you're gay. You're gonna have a hard fuckin' time. And he said, if you're gonna do this, you're gonna have to be stronger than you ever imagined."

Paris Is Burning

Paris Is Burning focuses on the lives of a number of poor Black and Puerto Rican gay men living in New York City in the late 1980s. The film documents "the ball circuit," a series of competitions held in ballrooms and Elks lodges, in which gay men of color costume themselves according to certain preordained categories such as "High Fashion Winter Sportswear," "Going to School," "Executive Realness," and "Butch Queen First Time in Drag at a Ball." Because many of the competitors are "performing" in drag, such categories provide them with, among other things, a means of resisting, at least in the moments of the ball, a normalized, gendered subjectivity. This resistance apparently extends for many participants "outside" the world of the competition, where many of the competitors live either in various degrees of drag, or as women.[44]

Dressed according to their chosen categories, the competitors walk the floor in the manner of runway models, performing for the assembled crowd. The walkers are awarded scores by a panel of judges who hold up numerical values from one to ten in a kind of parody of the Olympic games. The highest scorers are then awarded trophies for their efforts.

The balls have given rise to a number of "houses" named after ball walkers who have won a significant number of trophies. A house is described variously in the film as a family for a lot of children who don't have families, and as a "gay street gang." Dorian Corey, one of the older members of the ball circuit, explains "A gay house street-fights at a ball . . . by walking in the categories." The leaders of the houses are described as "mothers," irrespective of either their biological or their "adopted" gender.

(For example, the "feminine" Pepper LaBeija and the mustached Willi Ninja both describe themselves as "mothers.") One of the members of one house in fact compares his ill treatment by his real mother with his treatment by his house mother, who always remembers his birthday. The film suggests that many of these men, rejected by their biological families because of their sexuality, have found a surrogate family in their house. The members of the various houses take the name of the house as their last name, and appear either to retain their given first name or to choose one more to their liking.

The film is divided into two sections. The first is a long segment beginning with an intertitle "New York 1987" and closing with a long fade to black. The second, brief section, "New York 1989," follows up on the lives of three of the men detailed in the first section. The intertitles that divide the first section either introduce by name one of the men being interviewed, or list an aspect of ball-culture vocabulary. For example, the intertitle "BALL" appears, followed by a voice-over, "This movie is about the ball circuit and the gay people that's involved in it."

The film is organized largely by these intertitles and by the actual words of the men interviewed in the film. No single omniscient voice-over unites the documentary. Three or four times during the film, a woman's voice, presumably that of the director, asks a question, or, in one instance, responds from off screen to a question asked by one of the men during his interview. The voice is usually clearly audible, but significantly softer than the voice of the person being interviewed. (In other words, the effect of this offscreen voice is not that of the "voice of God" often deployed in documentaries: its deployment seems somewhat random and inadequately marked in volume level.) Most of the film consists of four types of interviews: "talking head" type interviews with subjects who look either directly into the camera or slightly off to one side of the frame; subjects interviewed in their bedrooms or presumably homes, sometimes reclining, sometimes performing activities related to the balls, such as sewing costumes or applying makeup; group interviews conducted in a cinema-verité on-location style; and interviews that act as voice-overs over shots of the balls or other images.

The film's heavy reliance on the filmed testimony of the men involved in the ball circuit, who appear at times to be recounting and "performing" their lives before the camera, leaves the film open to the charge by bell hooks that "it is easy for viewers to imagine that they are watching an ethnographic film documenting the life of black gay 'natives' and not recognize that they are watching a work shaped and formed."[45] I will return to hooks's critique at some length in the third section of this chapter, but here I want to echo her concern that the film does not seem to interrogate sufficiently its "benevolent" attempt to carry news of subaltern Black gay culture to a largely privileged audience, and seems to position the viewer un-problematically as investigating subject without sufficiently paying attention to the ways the film's "vision" of Black life—even as that vision is articulated on some level by "authentic" subalterns—is necessarily "shaped and formed" by a number of discursive constraints. But this difficulty in itself does not seem sufficient reason to discount the film's discursive power to intervene in discussions of oppression, economic inequity, and social justice.[46]

I turn now to several aspects of this film in order to consider its experiential accounts provided by its subjects as "common sense," in Gramsci's use of the term. I will be arguing that there is a "core" of "good sense" in the accounts presented by these men, a core that might act as the basis of a more developed critique of the place of poor, Black gay men in contemporary consumer culture. My assumption throughout will be that this critique might serve to compel in some readers an ethical commitment to reversing the strategic relations of power that make possible, among other things, the continued poverty of these men. I will also be arguing that at several significant points *Paris Is Burning* does not merely record this common sense as is, but seeks to transform it, by both elaborating upon it and critiquing it through its juxtaposition with the image track. Because I will be concentrating here on the relationship between experience and common sense, I will be focusing largely on the words of the men in the film, their produced accounts of their lives. But the film itself might similarly be treated as a kind of common sense, in light of Gramsci's insistence that the philosophy that opposes itself to common sense must itself be subject to autocritique if such a philosophy is to play an active role in the transformation of thought.[47]

At several points in *Paris Is Burning*, the men in the film speak of the relationship between poverty and the balls, suggesting that walking in a ball is a specific response to conditions of economic exploitation. Pepper LaBeija explains that the balls represent the walkers' fantasies of being a superstar or runway model. As she/he insists, "A lot of those kids in the balls don't have two of nothing. Some of them don't even eat. They come to balls starving. . . . They don't have a home to go to. But they'll make, they'll go out and they'll steal something and get dressed up and come to a ball for that one night and live the fantasy." When the question is raised as to how ball participants support themselves financially, Venus Xtravaganza, a petite blonde preop transsexual, states, "Ninety percent of drag queens are hustlers." Another subject, one of the apparently few "natal" female interviewees, describes their profession as "showgirls." Similarly, another voice, presumably that of the young Octavia, another preop transsexual, explains

I'd always see the way rich people live, and I'd feel it more, you know, it would slap me in the face, I'd say, "I have to have that," because I never felt comfortable being poor, I just don't, or even middle class doesn't suit me. Seeing the riches, seeing the way people on *Dynasty* lived, these huge houses and I would think, these people have forty-two rooms in their house, oh my God, what kind of house is that, and we've got three. So why is it that they can have that and I didn't? I always felt cheated. I always felt cheated out of things like that.

Over this voice, the image track features a number of images of white high fashion. First comes a series of images from magazines: a white European model on the cover of *Dépeche Mode*; a white couple embracing, the woman draped in fur. Various shots of haute-couture boutiques are then followed by a shot of a white woman receiving a makeover at a cosmetics counter, an ad for an expensive home, a magazine story on *Dynasty*, and a photo of a white man and woman in English riding gear. The film suggests that these images are what "inspire" the walkers to compete in the balls and to aspire to the status of models.

The film's relationship to this common-sense desire for wealth and fame is necessarily ambiguous and complicated. Although the interviewed subjects often speak of their desires for wealth and glamour, the film portrays, in what in this context seems a highly critical light, white consumer culture, its distance from their "real" lives, and the lures that it continues both to hold out and to deny to them. Although none of those interviewed critiques the balls for their (supposed) capitulation to the ideals of white conspicuous consumption (I will complicate this reading of the balls later in this chapter), the juxtaposition of the men's expressed desires with the realities of their economic interest suggests a critique of the ideology in which the balls are necessarily positioned. The balls' necessarily contradictory relationship to wealth is highlighted when one voice explains,

This is white America. Any other nationality that is not of the white sect knows this and accepts this till the day they die. That is everybody's dream and ambition as a minority, to live and look as well as a white person is pictured as being in America. Every media you have from TV to magazines to movies to films, I mean, the biggest thing that minorities watch is, what, *Dynasty* and the Colbys."

Over this voice are a number of images of Black men competing in what appears to be the "Town and Country" category at a ball, men dressed in English riding suits. These images then cut to images of "real" white opulence in the streets of New York, followed by the cover of *Forbes* magazine proclaiming "What I Learned in the 1980s," surely a reference to the 1980s as the "me" generation. The voice continues, describing the opulence of TV ads and noticing the absence of images of blacks. The image shifts to a tall Black man in a military coat and hat walking the floor at a ball. He is draped in an American flag. The voice continues:

> We as a people for the past four hundred years is the greatest example of behavior modification in the history of civilization. We have had everything taken away from us, and yet we have all learned how to survive. That is why in the ball room circuit it is so obvious that if you have captured the great white way of living, of looking, or dressing, or speaking, you is a marvel.

Eventually, the man walking the floor drops the flag from around his shoulders, and stands on top of it. In these sequences, the film augments its discussion of subjectivity and economic exploitation with an account of ethnic domination/racism. The film suggests here, as does Wallenstein, that racism is a form of economic exploitation.

That the balls are an attempt to unravel the logic cleanly dividing representation from "reality" surfaces most powerfully in the film's discussion of "realness." Many of the categories in which these men compete at the balls—"Schoolboy/Schoolgirl Realness," "Executive Realness," "Town and Country," the various categories of military dress—suggest a critique of white consumerist culture that seeks to reverse and displace the binaries "essence/appearance" and undermine the logic that equates the visible with the true. This deconstruction of the real occurs not only at the level of gender, but along a number of different registers as well. As Dorian Corey, dressed here as a woman, explains in an interview:

> In real life, you can't get a job as an executive unless you have the educational background and the opportunity. Now the fact that you are not an executive is merely because of the social standing of life. . . . Black people have a hard time getting anywhere. And those that do are usually straight.

The image track cuts here to shots of two Black men competing in an "Executive Realness" competition. They are both dressed in conservative business suits and carry briefcases. There is little in their appearance to suggest that they are "dressing up" or performing. Only the circumstances of the ball, and the panel of judges rating their realness, suggests that they are not actually businessmen. Corey's voice continues, "In a ball room, you can be anything you want. You're not really an executive, but you're looking like an executive." The image cuts back to his face and continues to alternate between shots of his face and the competition, as he suggests, "And therefore you're showing the straight world that I can be an executive. If I had the opportunity, I could be one. Because I can look like one. And that is a fulfillment. Your peers, your friends are telling you, 'Ooh, you'd make a wonderful executive.' "

Another voice explains, over a series of images of a man dressed in a yellow coat stamped with the words "Merrill Lynch World Financial Center Project," "It's not a takeoff or a satire. No, it's actually being able to be this."[48] Realness represents a kind of postmodern parody, what Fredric Jameson has termed "pastiche," a form of parody that does not produce laughter.[49] The balls thus refuse a parody that might suggest that there is some "real" place beyond representation where the ontological persuasiveness of the real cannot be destabilized through laughter.

Realness is also linked by the ball participants to a strategy of survival. It is described as a way for gay men to go back into the closet, to hide those signifiers of gayness that might cause one both physical and mental anguish. As one man states, "When you're a man and a woman you can almost have sex in the streets. . . . But when you're gay, you monitor everything you do. You monitor how you look, how you dress, how you talk, how you act, did they see me, what do they think of me." By capturing a masculine realness, one manages to avoid the shame and violence that sometimes greet gay men perceived as effeminate. And, as Corey explains, those "Femme Realness" queens—those who dress at the balls, and perhaps in their "real" lives, as women—are those who are able to emerge from a ball and into the subway and arrive home without being bloodied in the process.

The film's "common sense" critique of consumer culture also deploys considerable irony, an irony sometimes produced by combining the expressed common sense of one of the men being interviewed with a series of images. For example, one of the film's subjects, the thin and beautiful Octavia, goes to some lengths to describe her desire to be some day in the same photo spread as her idol, supermodel Paulina. Pointing to the various photos of the model she has attached to her bedroom wall, she exclaims, "I just wanna be a rich somebody." Such a desire reads as perhaps ridiculous, given the realities of the modeling industry, despite Octavia's beauty, as well as her insistence that "This is not a game for me or fun. This is something I want to live." Later, the film recounts an actual search held by Eileen Ford of the Ford modeling agency for the "supermodel of the year." The search, held in New York's Bloomingdale's, invited young women to meet Ford and a number of her models in order to discuss the prospects of a future modeling career. *Paris Is Burning* records not only the model search but the media hype surrounding the search, highlighting, among other things, an interview with

Eileen Ford in which she counsels would-be models never to tell the truth when someone asks how they are feeling that day, as well as a reporter who continually asks, and is never answered, "How does all this square with women's lib?" Most interesting are the shots of Octavia, who has managed to "pass" as a "real" would-be model. We notice Octavia's face in the near background as a camera crew reports on the event, and see her meet with one of the Ford models to discuss her possible career. She leaves Bloomingdale's completely undetected by either Ford or her models. Here, the film critiques the modeling profession by insisting on the inabilities of the various players to manipulate sufficiently the lines between "fiction" and "reality." Ironically, Octavia "passes" those who one would expect would have the keenest eye for "real" "beauty"—Ford, her models, and the media assembled for the event.

Some might argue that the film's critique of white consumerist culture is insufficiently elaborated, in that it relies too heavily on the "common sense" accounts of the ball participants, and does not "speak" (literally) a critique of their aspirations for wealth and fame. But this seems ultimately to be a poor reading of the film: it does not take into account the necessarily hybrid quality of common sense, its combining of both "progressive" and "reactionary" elements. Paris Is Burning elaborates the core of good sense in common sense but also suggests some of its limits. Without positing a savvy subaltern consciousness that could effortlessly "tell it like it is" to a white audience, the film suggests that certain members of the ball circuit are positioned in what we might term, after Foucault, a subjugated knowledge of their circumstances, a knowledge that might become activated in historical struggles against economic and racial oppression. But the film also contrasts the knowledge of the older figures such as LaBeija and Corey, who speak the most articulately about the disparity between the material poverty of this segment of Black gay life and the ball circuit, with the fantasies of the younger figures of Octavia and Venus, who detail their plans and dreams for a life of stardom. The first section of the film concludes with alternating shots of Octavia and Venus, each posed in their respective bedrooms. Venus explains, "I want a car. I want to be with the man I love. I want a nice home away from New York. . . . I want my sex change." The image then cuts to Octavia, who describes her aspirations for "a normal happy life," whether that consists of marrying and adopting children or of becoming famous and rich. The image track continues to cut back and forth between the two as they describe their desires to be famous models, with Venus concluding that she wants to be married in church, dressed in white.

This sequence brings to the foreground a critique of drag-ball culture and suggests some of the limitations of that culture's deployment of common sense. Octavia and Venus both appear to believe that their resisting of gender norms will bring them economic advantages. Like many of the participants in the drag balls, they respond to the (relative) nonreversibility of the power relations that operate on them in the arena of the economic with a resistance directed against the forms of power that subjugate. In other words, racism / economic exploitation is countered, in ball culture, with drag. The conclusion of the film will highlight the limits of such a strategy of resistance.

The final section of the film, following the long blackout and beginning with the "New York 1989" intertitle, contrasts these dreams with Willi Ninja's description of his rise to fame as a voguer. (As Ninja explains, voguing is a form of competitive dance that developed in the ball circuit.) Unlike either Octavia or Venus, Ninja does not desire a sex change, nor does he ever appear in the film dressed as a woman. Yet he has managed to find a certain fame as a dancer, choreographer, and runway model. As proof of his success, he gestures towards a large Gaultier earring dangling from his ear, exclaiming that he bought it himself. This image of Ninja as a privileged marginal—gendered, not coincidentally, as masculine—who has managed to find success contrasts with the film's account of Venus, who we learn from Angie, the mother of the House of Xtravaganza, has died. As the film cuts back and forth between shots of Angie and shots of Venus talking with friends on a pier of the Hudson River, Angie details how Venus was found dead under a bed, strangled. Angie's voice over the footage of Venus stops long enough for us to hear Venus exclaim, "I'm hungry." The film then cuts back to Angie, who tells us that the death of Venus is "part of life as far as being a transsexual in New York City and surviving." This sequence is a haunting reminder of the limits of a resistance directed primarily toward the forms of power that subject and subjugate. The film concludes by returning us to the familiar shot of Dorian Corey at the makeup table, talking about his/her life, and exclaiming, "If you shoot a arrow and it goes real high, hooray for you."

In its depiction of drag-ball culture, *Paris Is Burning* is thus concerned with a variety of forms of power, including the forms of power that produce a normalized gendered subjectivity, the forms of power that exploit, and the forms of power that dominate. It reads ball culture as a "common sense" response to these forms of power, while also suggesting the hazards and limitations of such a response. In particular, its account of the death of Venus draws attention to the near-impossibility of countering economic exploitation and ethnic domination with a resistance on the level of subjectivity.

In the previous chapter, I suggested that the ideology of universalism provided a means, in the historical moment of colonialism, of linking up a number of forms of power so that they might be mobilized in the service of one another. Such an ideology deploys a "universal" subjectivity in the service of domination and exploitation. Here, I would suggest that the ideology of the balls—an ideology linked to the ideology of consumer capitalism— also provides a means for linking a variety of forms of power so that their interrelations are obscured. In the case of the balls, the ideology that one can "dress for success" displaces a resistance to the forms of power that dominate and exploit with a resistance at the level of subjectivity, the ball participants believing that, for example, their appearance might transform them into "a rich somebody." Arguing from these two examples, we might propose that *ideology*, provisionally, should name here the means by which the relations between a variety of forms of power are obscured. Ideology critique would thus be the attempt to disentangle and make legible these relations. Such an account of ideology does not require that we revert to a notion of ideology as "false consciousness." In fact, the ball participants are in some sense correct: in certain instances, one's appearance can translate into economic advantage. What the ideology of the balls can't explain, for example, is how relations of power work to afford such an advantage for some and not for others, and how the processes of meritocracy and tokenization act as an alibi for the continuing nonreversibility of relations of exploitation and domination.

In this limited sense, then, I would name my project throughout this study as, among other things, a kind of ideology critique, for I have sought throughout to use my position strategically in order to differentiate and discuss a variety of powers and some of the resistances to which they give rise. I have sought concurrently neither to privilege the economic as the final instance nor to ignore its role in the functioning of power. (Recall here Foucault's insistence that power cannot be made sense of outside of economic processes and the relations of production.)[50] I realize that, in offering yet another name for this project I am perhaps pushing the concept-metaphor of catachresis to its limit, and risking incoherence. My hope is that such a frequent (re)naming signals to the reader the difficulty of this project, a difficulty that arises from the attempt to bring together a more Foucauldian analysis with a (however nascent) materialist critique. *Paris Is Burning*, with its emphasis on subjectivity, economic exploitation, and ethnic domination, seems a particularly appropriate site from which to stage such an attempt.

III

In her essay "Is Paris Burning?" bell hooks critiques *Paris Is Burning* on the grounds that its maker, Jennie Livingston, a white lesbian, has not paid sufficient attention to "either the political and aesthetic implications of her choice as a white woman focusing on an aspect of black life and culture or the way racism might shape and inform how she would interpret black experience on the screen."[51] Because hooks's charge seems to resemble my critique of Marlon Riggs's film in the previous chapter, in that we are both faulting a film for failing to interrogate sufficiently some of its enabling conditions of possibility, I would like to spend some time exploring the differences in our two methods of producing explanations.

One of the major differences between hooks's analysis and mine is that we are operating with what are perhaps opposing understandings of textual production and reception. Rather than interrogating the film's refusal to consider the hazards of its project by analyzing specific moments in the film, hooks concentrates much of her attention on the filmmaker herself, particularly on Livingston's expressed understanding of her project as evidenced in a number of interviews. The result may be in conflict with hooks's stated project of exploring the film's racism and classism. By focusing on the "strengths" and "weaknesses" of the filmmaker, hooks's analysis perhaps inadvertently suggests that racism is not systematic but a problem of the individual that might be overcome, or at least thwarted, by sufficient reflection. That is, hooks performs a particular version of ideology critique here, in which the knowing critic manages to diagnose and correct the "false consciousness" that produced the film. This kind of ideology critique manages to inaugurate the return of the sovereign subject in the figures of both the critic who knows, and the filmmaker who ought to have known better. Wanting to hold Livingston personally responsible and accountable (hooks's terms) for the film's shortcomings, hooks suggests that with "progressive critical reflection" (63), Livingston might have made "a progressive vision of 'blackness' from the standpoint of 'whiteness'" (61). The implication here is that a more critically informed filmmaker might have managed to escape the difficulties of the film's project.[52]

The first chapter of this study highlights some of the shortcomings of this version of ideology critique. What is significant for my purposes here is that such a deployment of ideology critique also depends on a kind of untheorized faith in experience and its abilities to represent, unproblematically, the real. That is, hooks's analysis is unable to respond to the objections raised earlier in this chapter to an untheorized deployment of both the category of experience in general and the genre of the testimonial in particular. I would like now to turn to hooks's reading of the film in some detail in order to contest some of the guiding assumptions of her critique.

For hooks, what is missing from Livingston, at least the Livingston represented in various interviews and reviews of the film, is a kind of declaration of her "interest and fascination with black gay sub-culture."[53] The assumption here is that such a declaration would have produced an adequate response to the difficulties involved in making a film such as *Paris Is*

Burning.[54] hooks similarly suggests that Livingston ought to have been asked by her reviewers "to speak about what knowledge, information, or lived understanding of black culture and history she possessed that provided a background for her work or to explain what vision of black life she hoped to convey and to whom." While such a questioning would undoubtedly have provided important material for critical elaboration, and helped to make possible some kind of analysis of Livingston's (commonsense) "experience" making the film, I am less certain than hooks that such information would necessarily have accomplished that for which hooks had hoped—an interrogation of the filmmaker's positioning as a white woman filmmaker documenting the lives of Black gay men. Additionally, the suggestion that Livingston *could* have provided satisfactory answers to such questions blunts the force of hooks's critique by implying that the problems the film confronts are idiosyncratic to Livingston's experience, and that the "false consciousness" that Livingston's responses manifest could be corrected through a declaration of interest. This privileging of the filmmaker's testimonial also suggests that the hazards of the shifting distinctions between the two forms of representation necessarily involved in the making of this film might be sufficiently thwarted with recourse to the category of experience. In hooks's analysis, the problem for both the critic and the filmmaker seems not to be to draw attention to the ways in which the film is both necessarily, though not unproblematically, a portrait of, and proxy for, its subjects. Rather, hooks's desire that Livingston state her interest in making such a film as *Paris Is Burning* evidences a faith that such testimonial might have adequately transformed the film into a representation not distorted or perverted by racism.[55]

When recounting how the film text might have engaged more fully with the problematic of presenting a representation of Black culture to a largely white audience, hooks suggests that Livingston's physical presence in the film might have allowed viewers to "recognize that they are watching a work shaped and formed from a perspective and standpoint specific to Livingston" (62). hooks suggests that because we hear Livingston ask questions of her subjects but never see her, the film "assumes an imperial overseeing position that is in no way progressive or counterhegemonic." The implication here is that the bodily presence of Livingston in the film would have disrupted its colonizing impulses, as if the problems of representation of the Other could be overcome with recourse to a spectatorial "experience" of Livingston the historical person. A certain faith in the visible is operating here, a realist ontology of the photographic image that is at odds with hooks's own stated intellectual project, which is the attempt to call into crisis the "truth" of Livingston's documentary representation. Although hooks's analysis wants to marshal here the suggestion from a feminist- and

Brechtian-inflected film theory that the "passive," voyeuristic pleasure of the spectator must be disrupted if theoretical reflection is to occur, the analysis concurrently relies on a faith in the ontological power of the image, a faith interrupted by this same film theory. Here we see another instance of the limits of what I have discussed earlier as an identity-politics-inflected deconstruction of the real.

My critique of hooks's project should not obscure her important insistence that Livingston's project is necessarily implicated in the project of imperialism, nor her contention that the "current trend in producing colorful ethnicity for the white consumer appetite . . . makes it possible for blackness to be commodified in unprecedented ways, and for whites to appropriate black culture without interrogating whiteness or showing concern for the displeasure of blacks" (63). One of the major differences between hooks's perspective and my own is that although she faults Livingston for approaching her subject matter "as an outsider looking in" (62), I would insist that no other vantage point is available to her from which to view drag-ball culture. hooks's faith in the category of originating experience makes possible the suggestion that Livingston could somehow have gotten sufficiently "inside" the world of the drag balls to overcome certain problems of racism and classism. I would instead critique the film by proposing that its highly complicated discursive circumstances perhaps require a greater attentiveness to the (discursive) constraints operating in the genre of the testimonial than the film seems willing to allow. Nonetheless, hooks's queries regarding questions of the location of the filmmaker, as well as the film's intended audience, remain.

Additionally, I would suggest that hooks's failure to sufficiently theorize her own "common sense" experience of watching the film severely limits the explanatory power of her posited explanation. hooks's refusal to theorize her own positioning as a reader in relation to *Paris Is Burning* necessitates that she deny the force of Livingston's film by ignoring the possibilities it contains for a reading that might highlight the very political situation she had hoped it would have explored. Yet her explanation of the film perhaps inadvertently suggests, in certain instances, another reading. For example, hooks describes the film as "a graphic documentary portrait of the way in which colonized black people (in this case black gay brothers, some of whom were drag queens) worship at the throne of whiteness, even when such worship demands that we live in perpetual self-hate, steal, lie, go hungry, and even die in its pursuit" (61-62). Yet, simultaneously, she insists that "the film in no way interrogates 'whiteness' " (61). hooks's reading seems not to be able to mean what it says, for it is difficult to understand how a film could both fail to interrogate whiteness and simultaneously be a graphic documentary that implicates whiteness in the continued oppression of blacks.

There are other instances in hooks's text where her analysis seems, in spite of itself, to be arguing the "progressive" politics of Livingston's film.[56] hooks notes two competing narratives in the film, one focusing on the spectacle of the drag balls, the other reflecting on the lives of the participants (64). According to hooks,

> This second narrative was literally hard to hear because the laughter [of audience members] often drowned it out, just as the sustained focus on elaborate displays at balls diffused the power of the more serious critical narrative. Any audience hoping to be entertained would not be as interested in the true life stories and testimonies narrated. (64)

It could be argued here that part of the intellectual work of viewing this film is the struggle to read its counternarrative. Such a struggle would in a sense place the spectator in a position analogous to that of the ball participants, whose poverty is covered over by the spectacle of the balls, as well as allegorize for the spectator the labor of reading both "reality" and the core of good sense operating in common sense. Although such a reading would posit the film as perhaps complicitous in this attempt to erase the signs of material poverty from these men's lives, to do so does not, in itself, foreclose the possibility of reading the signs of such complicity. hooks's awareness of these competing narratives, and the difficulty of hearing the narrative of oppression, might in fact be precisely what the film necessarily solicits. To argue that the oppression of the men depicted in the film should (or could) be clearly visible is perhaps to reinforce a simple understanding of the real that the film seems anxious to complicate, and to fail to consider the limits of a politics of visibility. Such an argument once again reinscribes the category of experience (the experience of the men expressing the conditions of their lives, as well as the experience of the audience "accurately" reading such conditions) as something that might manage to escape the constraints operating in the production of discourse.

hooks seems particularly disturbed by the pleasure produced in watching the film. She describes in some detail her experience of viewing the film, particularly her discomfort with the assembled audience's laughter, which led her to ask aloud in the dark "What is so funny about this scene? Why are you laughing [sic]" (63). A failure to elaborate this experience theoretically leads in hooks's essay to what I read as its most serious and consequential abandonment of a theory of the production of cultural explanations.

hooks appears here to assume that laughter automatically means derision. Additionally, she negates the power of spectacle to invigorate "progressive" political change, once more calling up a realist ontology of the image—for hooks, spectacle equals a depoliticized "illusion" opposed to "reality" (64)—by casting it in opposition to ritual: "Ritual is that ceremonial act that carries with it meaning and significance beyond what appears, while spectacle functions primarily as entertaining dramatic display" (62). The assumption here is that meaning and significance are diametrically opposed to entertainment and display.

Yet hooks's analysis undoes these binaries in her discussion of the death of the character of Venus, for hooks faults the film for withholding scenes in the wake of Venus's death:

> There is no mourning for him/her in the film, no intense focus on the sadness of this murder. Having served the purpose of "spectacle" the film abandons him/her. The audience does not see Venus after the murder. There no scenes of grief. [*sic*] To put it crassly, her dying is upstaged by spectacle. Death is not entertaining. (64)

The implication here is that the film ought to have represented such scenes. But here, again, the analysis seems not to be able to mean what it says, for to solicit such scenes from the film is to risk "spectacularizing" them in hooks's sense of the word, to risk turning them into material for "entertaining, dramatic display." *Paris Is Burning* is, after all, a movie. Whatever "meaning and significance" it may embody necessarily engages questions of spectacle, and death is in fact extremely entertaining, at least as a cinematic representation. hooks's analysis suggests that her desire to see beyond the death of Venus may itself be in conflict with her insistence that the film not "exploit" its subject matter in this way. The melodrama that hooks's analysis solicits in the moments following Venus's death may be in this moment precisely what the film wants to thwart, particularly given its interest in excess and spectacle throughout the rest of the film, and its refusal to make a spectacle of the mourning of Venus.

I want to argue polemically here that hooks's refusal to interrogate her experience of watching this film inadvertently positions her analysis to invigorate the heterosexism and oppression of gay men that her analysis and, according to my reading, Livingston's film seek to interrupt. This placement is particularly evident in hooks's reading of drag, which I will consider shortly, but is similarly operating in her reading of the film's audience. hooks's account of her experience of watching the film names the audience as "yuppy looking, straight acting, pushy, predominantly white folks" who gush approval over a film that hooks feels should not have produced pleasure in its spectator (61). There is little or no consideration of how subjects produced in excess of heterosexuality might have read and responded to *Paris Is Burning*, the pleasure they might have felt, and the source of such pleasure.[57]

I am particularly interested in hooks's contention that "*any* audience hoping to be entertained would not be as interested in the true life stories and testimonies"[58] recounted in the film as they might be in the spectacle of the drag balls. hooks can assume an opposition between these two aspects of the film because she also assumes an antithesis between laughter and seriousness. The analysis is incapable of theorizing something like camp or melodrama, in which in fact these apparently conflicting affective responses might be deployed concurrently, and to what some have argued are politically "progressive" ends. Much work has in fact been done to suggest that representational strategies employing a heavy dose of affect, such as masquerade, parody, and creolization, are means whereby colonized and oppressed peoples negotiate and resist, on the level of subjectivity, structures of oppression. hooks's reading seems to ignore some of the multivalences of a hybrid cultural practice like drag. In what follows, I will be arguing another reading of drag that might complicate hooks's inability to read spectacle as "progressive."

hooks reads drag in *Paris Is Burning* as something retrograde, an indication of the false consciousness of its practitioners that betrays their lack of self-love (64). According to hooks, drag is acceptable as long as it recognizes the limitations of fantasy, but it unfortunately holds out to its practitioners the politically unhealthy lure of abandoning or betraying their true selves.[59] The status of drag itself, however, is not sufficiently theorized in hooks's essay. Near the end of the essay, hooks mobilizes readings of drag in order to call for a "politically correct" deployment of drag, one that encourages gender bending while managing to hold in abeyance the guilty pleasure of identifying with "negative," "oppressive" images of women. Opposed to this deployment is the kind of drag represented in *Paris Is Burning*, in which, according to hooks, the subversive power of drag "is radically altered when informed by a racialized fictional construction of the 'feminine' that suddenly makes the representation of whiteness as crucial to the experience of female impersonation as gender, that is to say when the idealized notion of the female/feminine is really a sexist idealization of white womanhood" (61). According to hooks, within the world of the black drag-ball culture depicted in Livingston's film, "the idea of womanness and femininity is totally personified by whiteness. What viewers witness is not black men longing to impersonate or even to become like 'real' black women but their obsession with an idealized fetishized vision of femininity that is white" (61).

This discussion evidences a significantly unelaborated understanding of drag in general and gay drag in particular (and, like certain incarnations of gay activist rhetoric alluded to above, it draws a facile equation between resistance to gender norms and political resistance). While straight transvestites might be content to dress as, say, working women or housewives, their goal being to "pass" as "average" women, gay drag privileges not only femininity, but femininity as spectacle. It emphasizes excess and artifice, deploying the cultural trappings of femininity in order to put into play an abundance of affect. This is one of the reasons why drag is often tied to questions of star impersonation. No gay drag queen in her right mind would dress as a "typical" woman, Black or white, at least as that typicality is defined by many media representations. For gay drag is as much about glamour and spectacle as it is about gender.

That drag's representation of femininity is often racist is obvious. But I would locate one of the sources of this racism in the media's historical refusal to glamorize images of Black women. In other words, gay drag may mirror the racism of a Eurocentric culture, but its deployment of white idealizations of beauty is inexorably tied to a racist history of what constitutes the glamorous. As that history shifts, and the media represent increasingly a glamorous image of Black women, gay drag will perhaps continue to reflect an idealized, fetishized vision of femininity, but one that is no longer exclusively white. *Paris Is Burning* in fact features, in its credit sequence, a drag performance of a man dressed as Patti LaBelle singing her remake of Judy Garland's "Over the Rainbow." Other "typical" Black celebrities emulated by drag queens today include Diana Ross, Donna Summer, Whitney Houston, Dionne Warwick, and Eartha Kitt.[60] Diana Ross is pictured on Octavia's wall in *Paris Is Burning*; while Pepper LaBeija refers to the desire of young drag queens to emulate the Black model Iman.[61]

Symptomatic of hooks's refusal to theorize drag as a cultural practice is her reliance in her essay on a long quotation from Marilyn Frye's essay "Lesbian Feminism and Gay Rights." Considering the amount of work that has been done recently on questions of drag and gender fluidity,[62] it is curious that hooks would cite Frye's essay and its singularly wrongheaded reading of drag. hooks quotes Frye, in part:

> As I read it, gay men's effeminacy and donning of feminine apparel displays no love of or identification with women or the womanly. For the most part, this femininity is affected and is characterized by theatrical exaggeration. It is a casual and cynical mockery of women, for whom femininity is a trapping of oppression, but it is also a kind of play, a toying with that which is taboo. . . . What gay male affectation of femininity seems to be is a serious sport in which men may exercise their power and

control over the feminine, much as in other sports. . . . But the mastery of the feminine is not feminine. It is masculine.[63]

Frye's analysis has several flaws. In its conflation of effeminacy and drag, it assumes that gay men willfully assume the feminine; it ignores the way gay men often find themselves positioned within the feminine against their will and even in spite of their own expressed wishes, and it can't account for the feelings of shame I described at the beginning of this chapter that occur when one is, against all acts of agency, still mistaken for, or positioned as, feminine. For many gay men, being called effeminate is a drag, and effeminacy is not something one might court comfortably. Thus there is great emphasis in *Paris Is Burning* on "realness," and such "masculine" categories as the schoolboy, the military man, the executive, and the street gang member.[64] Additionally, Frye's analysis cannot distinguish different contexts in which drag might occur, or show how such contexts might shift the risks and pleasures arising from drag. Frye's reading is typical of a certain kind of popular gay liberationist discourse in that it can account for gendered behavior through only two rubrics: choice, as in Frye's analysis; or that often-cited flip side of choice, biology.[65]

Frye's analysis, easily equating affectation with contempt, also cannot explain why drag queens would emulate women they admire. I am not suggesting that a certain kind of misogyny does not often surface during drag shows. But this misogyny is complicated by questions of ambivalence, as well as a historical theatrical tradition of the burlesquing of the body.[66] Drag appears not so much to mock the feminine as to express an ambivalence toward it, an ambivalence we might expect, given the contradictory ways in which gay men are positioned vis-à-vis the feminine. If gay men merely adopted drag in order to mock the feminine, it is difficult to see why they would go to such great lengths to imitate the stars they adore, rather than the "average" women whom hooks would have them emulate.

Frye's analysis also shows the limits of her 1970s feminism, which can imagine femininity only as oppression. For at least the past twenty years, lesbian feminists in particular have attempted to interrupt theoretical positions like Frye's, positions that have attacked the style of butch/fem lesbians as politically incorrect, and isolated them from the lesbian community.[67] Given the continuing importance of these debates, it is vexing that hooks would choose to cite such a monolithic understanding of femininity and feminine drag as Frye's.

Following her approving quotation of Frye, hooks claims that this reading of drag "remains one of the most useful critical debunkings" of the "myth" that queens are both antiphallocentric and antipatriarchal (though hooks provides no exploration of what this might mean). She adds that *no* viewer of Livingston's film can deny either the film's treatment of the drag ball as a competitive sports event, or the way in which "the male 'gaze' in the audience [of the drag balls? of the film?] is directed at participants in a manner akin to the objectifying phallic stare straight men direct at 'feminine' women daily in public spaces."[68] hooks here ignores the implications of her own analysis, which suggests, interestingly, that straight men might direct their "objectifying, phallic" gaze at a sports event in the same way as they might stare at a woman. Additionally, her deployment of the metaphor of the male gaze ignores those members of the audience who might identify with, rather than "objectify," the depicted drag queens. In other words, again, a heterosexist presumption allows hooks to ignore—as if all men "looked" the same—those audience members who might want to be, rather than possess, the depicted drag queens.

hooks's reading of drag in *Paris Is Burning* fails to recognize how this very idealized, fetishized, sexist version of femininity is what Livingston's film both celebrates *and* critiques, insisting on the pleasures it provides, while also implicating it in such things as the death of Venus near the conclusion of the film. It fails to recognize that in its deployment of "experiential" commonsense renderings of drag articulated by members of the ball culture, the film must necessarily court both "progressive" and "reactionary" ideologies. In order to theorize specifically how drag as spectacle might combine a variety of affective responses, including pleasure and critique, and how the pleasure of viewing *Paris Is Burning*'s spectacular deployment of drag might be intimately linked to its transgressive, if not oppositional, status, *as well as to those elements hooks would characterize as "reactionary,"* we might turn once again to the writings of Georges Bataille. This admittedly brief theorization of drag I will propose via Bataille will insist on understanding drag as a practice of resistance to forms of subjectivity, and not as something that resists the forms of power in their several incarnations. Following my polemical insistence that all struggles against subjectivity not automatically be named as political, I would suggest here that drag is not a politically oppositional practice, but one that might be mobilized in the service of, and connected up to, struggles both politically oppositional and reactionary.

Recall, from my discussion of pornography, the following: In his essay "The Notion of Expenditure," Bataille argues that what links such apparently disparate cultural practices as (so-called) perverse sexual activity and spectacle is their status as "nonproductive expenditure."[69] Placing Bataille's notion of nonproductive expenditure alongside Foucault's account of modern subject formation as necessarily involving an "economical" deployment of forces in the service of a "docile body," we might once again theorize, as in my discussion of pornography, nonproductive expenditure as a counter to

122

modern subject formation, this time, in the guise of drag. In its excessive deployment of both costuming and affect, drag displaces the disciplined, re-strained, and efficient body of the modern gendered subject with an image of the body as melodrama. The modestly gendered body of the disciplinary subject is countered by one ostentatiously dressed and excessively sexual-ized, a body whose gestures are both extravagantly stylized and wastefully deployed. As an instance of nonproductive expenditure, drag is necessarily characterized by the fact that "the accent is placed on a loss that must be as great as possible in order for that activity to take on its true meaning" (118). We might be reminded here of Corey's insistence, in *Paris Is Burning*, that the stakes involved in losing a drag-ball competition are quite high, so high that competitors will go to great lengths to attempt to secure the disqualifi-cation of the competition. Additionally, as an instance of nonproductive ex-penditure, drag features the discharge of "affective reactions of varying intensity" that are themselves highly unstable and subject to transforma-tion.[70] This is one explanation of how *Paris Is Burning* might unleash in its spectators the contrary emotions of joy and sadness, and might provoke a critical response of both valorization and critique.

But recall that the danger represented by (heterogeneous) nonproduc-tive expenditure, a danger implied in hooks's critique of the film, is that it might move in two directions at once, toward the "elevated" and the pro-fane, what Bataille terms the "imperative" and "impure." As Bataille ar-gues, homogeneous society must be constantly protected from the unruly elements—the poor, for example—who do not benefit from production, or those cultural others who "cannot tolerate the checks that homogeneity im-poses on unrest" (139). Homogeneity, however, does not banish the hetero-geneous, but deploys imperative elements of heterogeneity in the service of "obliterating the various unruly forces or bringing them under the control of order" (139). Bataille's analysis thus warns of the problematic relation-ship between impure and imperative forms of heterogeneity, between, say, drag as spectacle and the spectacle of fascism.[71] Although *Paris Is Burning* struggles to maintain the impure heterogeneity of its spectacle, overwhelm-ing the spectator with an "excess" of pleasurable affect released by the wan-ton expenditure and glamour of the drag balls, and representing a number of (subaltern) "unruly elements"—drag queens of color, transsexuals, and thieves, all of whom smile into the camera—the film also necessarily, and simultaneously, runs the risk of valorizing the media's "exalted" and "noble" images of conspicuous consumption, images often mirrored in drag. Both the balls themselves and *Paris Is Burning* as an instance of the film medium, necessarily court this danger. Placing my analysis of the film alongside hooks's, we might notice that although the two readings of the film argue their positions from opposite views, both attempt on some level to maintain the Other in its "improper," impure heterogeneity. What troubles me about hooks's analysis is what I read as its efforts to render the film "useful" for a homogeneous society that needs exalted forms of heterogeneity such as the figure of the noble, sovereign subaltern (as well as the privileged marginal critic) in order to bring under control the unruly forces of the Other. What might trouble hooks about my analysis is its refusal to address sufficiently how my valorization of the film's "filthy" status might overlook the ways in which even "filth" (here, in the form of unruly drag queens) might be rendered useful—commodifiable—for (homogeneous) conspicuous capitalist consumption.[72]

I argue that the complicated discursive web in which *Paris Is Burning* is necessarily situated requires it, as both an instance and a representation of nonproductive expenditure, to court a transgression of cultural norms around gender, sexuality, and glamour (an "impure" heterogeneity), *as well as* a continued privileging of useful capitalist consumption (an "imperative" heterogeneity). This double heterogeneity is perhaps best emblematized in the title of the film. Near the beginning of her essay on *Paris Is Burning*, hooks states, "When I first heard that there was this new documentary film about black gay men, drag queens, and drag balls, I was fascinated by the title. It evoked images of the real Paris on fire, of the death and destruction of a dominating white western civilization and culture, an end to oppressive Eurocentrism and white supremacy."[73] hooks admits that this fantasy "gave me a sustained sense of pleasure." Here, recalling the rhetoric of "Burn, baby, burn," hooks allows herself to indulge in a fantasy of nonproductive expenditure of which Bataille himself might be proud.

Yet, in the film, when Willi Ninja describes his desire to make Paris burn through his work as a vogue dancer, he is referring not to a literal destruction, but to the bringing of a certain (contained) excitement to the Paris fashion world, and to the gaining of a certain "burning" notoriety and fame (not to mention capital) as a result of his work. Ninja's use of the term "burning" might thus be described as the exalted complement of hooks's, "burning" here embodying the dual nature of heterogeneity—burning as (in the case of hooks's analysis) destruction, and burning as (in the case of Ninja's use of the term) elevation.

Ironically, although the conclusion of the film does in fact detail Ninja's rise to fame, it is perhaps a modest fame, much more modest than the one he had initially dreamed. For although voguing has reached an international audience, it is not via the name of Ninja, but via that perhaps "imperative" form of cultural heterogeneity, the figure of Madonna.[74] This state of affairs reminds us again of the dual nature of heterogeneity (emblematized in the very name "Madonna"), the instability of that easily crossed line between the impure and the imperative, and, thus, the perils of valorizing forms of nonproductive expenditure as "transgressive." It also suggests the continued necessity of interrogating gay men's differing relationships to consumer culture, and white gay men's status as middle-class consumers—a status that is perhaps best emblematized in their continuing love/hate relationship with the Material Girl.[75]

Coda

It was only after completing an initial draft of this study in its entirety that I read Butler's *Gender Trouble*, a text that can provide us with a slightly different account of the troublesome laughter often unleashed by drag performance. Butler's study is a critique of identity politics, and is particularly concerned to disrupt the idea that a stable identity must be in place prior to political action. (I associate this position in the previous chapter with the work of Jeffrey Weeks, among others.) According to Butler, identity politics assumes a bit too readily that political agency can follow only from a preconstituted identity. As Butler has it, "My argument is that there need not be a 'doer behind the deed,' but that the 'doer' is variably constructed in and through the deed."[76] Butler argues against the positions that "(a) agency can only be established through recourse to a prediscursive 'I,' " and "(b) that to be *constituted* by discourse is to be *determined* by discourse, where determination forecloses the possibility of agency" (143; emphasis in original).

Butler's argument is that identities in general, and gender identities in particular, are constituted discursively and are thus necessarily contingent. According to Butler, disciplinary society, in its production of the normalized subject, attempts to effect

a false stabilization of gender in the interests of the heterosexual construction and regulation of sexuality within the reproductive domain. The construction of coherence conceals the gender discontinuities that run rampant within heterosexual, bisexual, and gay and lesbian contexts in which gender does not necessarily follow from sex, and desire, or sexuality generally, does not seem to follow from gender. (135)

Butler argues that gender is not "essential" but rather performative in that the essence or identity it purports to express is what she terms a "fabrication" (136). That is, gender as performance is not the true expression of some interiorized prediscursive femininity or masculinity, but is rather the continual resignification of an identification for which no original exists—an imitation without an origin, a simulacrum. According to Butler, certain cultural practices, such as drag, foreground gender as performance, implicitly revealing "the imitative structure of gender itself—as well as its contingency" (137). The laughter in response to *Paris Is Burning* that bell hooks finds so troubling arises, in Butler's account of drag, from "the recognition of a radical contingency in the relation between sex and gender in the face of cultural configurations of causal unities that are regularly assumed to be natural and necessary. In the place of the law of heterosexual coherence, we see sex and gender denaturalized by means of a performance which avows their distinctness and dramatizes the cultural mechanism of their fabricated unity" (137-38). According to Butler, drag's attack on the normal, as well as its accompanying recognition that the normal is itself a fabrication, can itself be an occasion for laughter. What hooks reads as "reactionary" Butler might thus read as "subversive." Butler is careful, however, to argue that not all drag is subversive; she insists that only a careful interrogation of the context and reception of a parodic display of gender can help us to understand which acts of performance are "effectively disruptive, truly troubling," and which "become domesticated and recirculated as instruments of cultural hegemony" (139).

I find Butler's critique of identity politics careful and convincing and her account of identities in discourse congruent to mine, but I am suspicious of the move in her text "from parody to politics"—the title of her last, and perhaps too brief, chapter. One of my hesitations concerning Butler's account of gender as performance is that it seems unwilling to differentiate between "willed" and "accidental" acts of gender subversion. I understand this hesitancy, given her study's refusal to discuss agency with reference to a preconstituted subject. In fact, one of the strengths of Butler's account of gender as performance is that it does not throw us back on a notion of the intentional subject, the gendered subject as deliberate performer. As Butler is careful to suggest, one can "signify" gender in a number of ways, many of which might escape or exceed one's intentions and desires. Recall here the "fabricated" autobiographical account of gender with which this chapter began. Regardless of how "subversive" my youthful signification of gender might have been, it certainly was not intentional—at least not on a conscious level. I am thus left wondering, however, how these kinds of significations can produce a politics. Butler's account of gender subversion here is a bit reminiscent of the one implied by Kaja Silverman in the concluding chapter of her *Male Subjectivity at the Margins*, in which "some" gay men's "unconscious" identifications with the feminine are strangely valorized as "political."[77]

Given my argument in the third chapter of this study, I think the reader will not be surprised to learn that I am less certain than Butler that, as a result of a parodic staging of the "failure" of gender through practices such as drag, "a new configuration of politics" will "surely emerge from the ruins of the old."[78] Even if we grant, rightly, I think, Butler's contention that political interests are elaborated not by a prior identity, but in the performative signification of identity, it is still difficult to follow how the performance of *gender* as pastiche will particularly establish as *political* "the very terms through which identity is articulated" (148). The subject is, after all, produced along a variety of different registers. There is no guarantee that mischief in the register of gender will necessarily alter the production of, for example, the classed subject. I am not maintaining that class or the economic is the sole or determining element of politics. But I mistrust the historical tendency in gay and lesbian studies to make class disappear from discussions of the political. Even if, as Butler suggests, we rewrite the definition of politics from "a set of practices derived from the alleged interests that belong to a set of ready-made subjects" to one that acknowledges subjects as always (already) in production, the vexing category of interest still remains, its role largely unelaborated by Butler. Perhaps the problem is that we have no clear sense from Butler of what she means by politics. In any case, this seems at least to be one of the lessons of *Paris Is Burning*: It is difficult to understand theoretically how the production of gender as fabrication, for example, will subvert the production of the subject along lines *in addition* to those of gender. My fear is that the new configuration of politics that might emerge from the subversively gendered subject would leave too much the same.

I am also uncomfortable with Butler's insistence that such a practice as the gay appropriation of the feminine "works to multiply possible sites of application of the term, to reveal the arbitrary relation between the signifier and signified, and to destabilize and mobilize the sign" (122). The obvious question here is, for whom, and where? Who are the "we" who recognize drag as the subversion of gender norms, and insist that the "real" is itself an imitation? Butler seems to have conflated here what I might call a theoretical argument with an "empirical" one. In fairness to Butler, we ought to recall her insistence that such questions can be answered only in specific contexts and circumstances. But if this is the case, why does Butler attempt to theorize the political in the context of a study such as *Gender Trouble?* What would a political intervention look like that was not tied to a specific time, place, and location? As careful and valuable as Butler's project is, I fear that it (perhaps necessarily) reflects the increasing tendency by academics to claim too readily a certain political status for their own sites of theoretical inquiry.

The euphoria with which queer academics have embraced Butler's work suggests to me that we ought to recall Bersani's warning that gay activist rhetoric has historically been marked by a certain will to believe in the subversive powers of style. Butler's conclusions are, after all, not very dramatic. They arise from a careful rereading of a number of psychoanalytic, poststructuralist, and feminist texts. They offer up certain conclusions that (again, as Bersani reminds us) gay and lesbian theory has been positing for some time. Queer academics, feeling politically disenfranchised, have apparently seized on Butler's account, with its legitimating recourse to a sometimes unnecessarily tortuous philosophical language, as evidence that a politics of style does in fact translate into some kind of "subversion" "beyond" the subjective. Throughout this study, I have been (strategically) opposing this argument, not to suggest that subjectivity has nothing whatsoever to do with politics, but to defer, and to suggest some of the current limitations of, a quick slide from discussions of one to discussions of the other. In the following and final chapter, I add a discussion of history to this deferral.

Chapter 5

Conclusion: On the Uses and Disadvantages of a History of the Other—An Untimely Meditation

If you are to venture to interpret the past you can do so only out of the fullest exertion of the vigour of the present.

Friedrich Nietzsche[1]

In the second of his "untimely meditations," Friedrich Nietzsche attempts to read the value of both the historical and the unhistorical for his time. According to Nietzsche, culture needs both historical and unhistorical elements if it is to survive, for, although history provides to every person and nation, "in accordance with its goals, energies and needs, a certain kind of knowledge of the past" (77), the unhistorical makes possible an act of forgetting that allows the present to rid itself of "a huge quantity of indigestible stones of knowledge" (78), "stones" that inhibit cultural development by fetishizing the past. The problem for the historian thus becomes the determination of "the boundary at which the past has to be forgotten if it is not to become the gravedigger of the present" (62). Nietzsche thus invites his reader to meditate on the proposition that "the unhistorical and the historical are necessary in equal measure for the health of an individual, of a people and of a culture" (63). In accordance with the vocabulary of Bataille, we might cast the problem as the necessity of determining how small a conservation of the historical is necessary if we are to lavish in the sumptuous expenditure represented by what Nietzsche so recklessly terms "life."

Nietzsche calls his meditation "untimely" because it argues primarily for the value of the unhistorical at a time when the historical sense is being employed by "toothless and tasteless greybeards" against the vitality and exuberance of youth:

We know, indeed, what history can do when it gains a certain ascendancy, we know it only too well: it can cut off the strongest instincts of youth, its fire, defiance, unselfishness and love, at the roots, damp down the heat of its sense of justice, suppress or regress its desire to mature slowly with the counter-desire to be ready, useful, fruitful as quickly as possible, cast morbid doubt on its honesty and boldness of feeling; indeed, it can even deprive youth of its fairest privilege, of its power to implant in itself the belief in a great idea and then let it grow to an even greater one. (115)

Nietzsche contrasts the figure of this instinctive, immoderate, coarse and vital youth, a youth racked by an "intense feeling of life" (121), with the "greybeard," the scholar, the man of science, "and indeed the most speedily employable man of science, who stands aside from life so as to know it unobstructedly . . . the precocious and up-to-the-minute babbler about state, church and art, the man who appreciates everything, the insatiable stomach which nonetheless does not know what honest hunger and thirst are" (117). Counterposing the wild expenditure of youth with the pedantic conservation of the greybeard, Nietzsche highlights the necessity of interrogating particular deployments of the historical sense for their differential values for use in the present.

"I have striven to depict a feeling by which I am constantly tormented; I revenge myself upon it by handing it over to the public" (59). So Nietzsche confesses at the outset of his untimely meditation, and so must I likewise confess that this present meditation originates in a kindred sentiment, a certain reckless and impatient intolerance concerning the question of the uses of history in our own time. For although we in English and film studies are boldly called upon to "Always historicize!" it seems that what this might involve is still often left largely unexplored. Specifically, although we are acquainted with a variety of powerful critiques of traditional historiography, we often, under the pressure to appear historical in the eyes of our disciplines, bracket such critiques in our daily critical and pedagogical practice. To offer a preliminary anecdote, one that admittedly I will perhaps grant too much authority in order to continue my ruminations: Twice this past year, during the course of job interviews, I asked candidates how they responded in their undergraduate teaching to the critique of historiography. This was not intended as a hostile question (though of course we in the humanities have come recently to linger, and linger at some length, on the banks of that gulf that often opens up between our best intentions and their perilous effects). It was certainly not a question to which I myself had an easy answer. I assumed that my colleagues shared with me a certain vexing conundrum: How do we in English, who have not been trained as historians, manage to do justice in our work to the tremendous problematization of historiography accomplished by our colleagues in, for example, the discipline of history?[2]

Unfortunately, both times, my question was answered with what my admittedly prejudiced ears were obliged to hear as "The critique of historiography has not influenced the teaching of undergraduates in the least." Perhaps the question was too broad in scope (one might have rightfully asked, "Of what particular critique of historiography do you speak?"); perhaps the candidates, hearing a certain eager anticipation in my voice, mistook what was intended as a generous question for the kind that often surfaces during these admittedly nerve-racking proceedings, the kind of question that is meant to force the candidate to show publicly his or her tattered underwear, as it were. In any case, the effect of these two instances was to heighten my growing sense of discomfort concerning the role of the historical sense in both English and film studies.

Perhaps my perspective is too local. Perhaps my contention that there has recently occurred a return to a simpleminded historicism is the result of, say, my too avid perusal of those film history survey textbooks written for undergraduates that have recently crossed my desk. If this should be the case, I am eager to be corrected. And it may partly exonerate me if I give an assurance that the tormented feelings that lead me to put forth the ideas here are mostly my own, and that I have drawn on the experiences of others only for the purposes of comparison. But until such time as I am publicly instructed and put right about the character of our own time, I will continue in this vein, attempting to commit to print a number of rumors concerning the uses and disadvantages of our current historical sense.[3]

Today, we might recognize Nietzsche's "greybeard" in, among others, the figure of the humanist archivist, who seeks to establish a linear causal connection between the past and the present by endlessly poring over historical documents ranging from the "elevated" to the mundane, from canonical works of art to last week's *TV Guide*, from nineteenth-century composition textbooks to *The Young and the Hung*, and who, invigorated by the recent fashion for microcosmic histories that acknowledge the necessity of detailing ad nauseam a multiplicity of historical determinants, constructs a totalizing narrative of, say, French film of the 1930s, or 1950s muscle-culture magazines, a narrative that encompasses questions of politics, economics, ideology, race, class, gender, sexuality. Such activities make possible a situation in which what began as a critique of the limits of causal thinking becomes transmogrified into the most self-assured, pedantic, and ironclad causality.[4] I would venture that this situation has given rise in our time to a rampant historicism that has little to do with history as a force intervening in the life of the present, but instead resuscitates history as a series of dry and deadly facts designed to ossify knowledge, and to further the production of modern disciplinary subjects by creating a coterie of disciplinary authorities whose role is to enact a pedagogy of examination. Such a pedagogy quizzes students on the minutiae of yesterday's news, and implants in them a sense of shame at their inability and reluctance to memorize and know the details of a dusty past, while at the same time failing to offer them a means to deploy a knowledge of the past in present struggles. The current undergraduate education in history leaves the status of the event largely unchallenged, and continues as if no one had ever questioned the instability of the cultural opposition between fact and fiction, or the necessary presence of the tropological in historical narratives, or the limits of a " 'documentary' or 'objectivist' model of knowledge that is typically blind to its own rhetoric."[5] Some brief attention might be paid to the names of Foucault, Benjamin, and even Hayden White, but when push comes to shove, undergraduate education still casts history as a series of "what happeneds" and "whens." "Genealogy" loses its Nietzschean sense and comes to stand in for any history of the everyday. When historiography "discovers" subaltern subjects, they are made to fit neatly within the established protocols of the discipline.[6] The humanist ideology that insists that unless we know the past we will be condemned to repeat it, has been parodied to the point where it suggests that cultural change for the better requires both a pedant's knowledge of that past and an "adequate" understanding of causality. Such a mechanistic understanding of change forgets the commonsense wisdom that suggests that you don't need to know why the horse kicked you to know to stay out of its way.

But there is perhaps equally in our time a certain dangerous and haphazard refusal to think historically. Hourly television news renders the immediate past ever more obsolete, erasing historical memory with a flood of new information, an ecstasy of communication. Current struggles are displaced to a distant past (emblematized in the familiar claim made by our students that feminism was a problem for the 1950s), while the specificities of present conflicts are elided. Saddam Hussein is compared to Adolf Hitler, Kuwait to Vietnam, and Bill Clinton to Jimmy Carter. Here again, the ideology of history repeating itself operates, acting as an alibi for all sorts of mischief, and making possible a kind of talismanic thinking that assumes that a superficial resemblance to things past will magically bring about a recurrence of the same, as if "the Pythagoreans were right in believing that when the constellation of the heavenly bodies is repeated the same things, down to the smallest event, must also be repeated on earth."[7] Televised docudramas deploy the recognition that what we call history is always also narrative, not by interrupting the ease with which the culturally sanctioned lines dividing the fictive and the factual are drawn, but rather by treating the historical as fiction dressed up in the most lurid and sensational of outfits.

The ideology of the visible remains firmly entrenched; the historical real is that which is seen, if not for the first time, at least in simulation. When asked to think through the limits of their historical positionings, students exclaim assuredly that anyone on the face of the earth can be made to understand the phrase "I ate a hamburger yesterday." When asked to think through the limits of such historical categories in film history as German expressionism and the French New Wave, they express their dismay at having to write critical essays rather than answer a simple exam consisting of names and dates, and complain that three whole class periods have been devoted to a discussion of Weimar cinema.[8]

Throughout this study, I have attempted to elaborate how an ethical commitment to what I have been terming at times an impure heterogeneity might inflect a study of subaltern textual production and reception. I have remained resolutely presentist, focusing on questions of how my own critical intervention as a reader might bring to the fore some of the limits of what I read as "liberal" responses to the culturally marginalized. In other words, I have focused on the value of the unhistorical in order to suggest some of the ways in which it might interrupt and complicate recent theorizations of cultural difference, as well as attempts by the academy to "manage" such differences.

I want now to turn to questions of history and the Other, using Nietzsche's three modes of history described early in his essay on the uses and disadvantages of history for life. Nietzsche characterizes these modes as the monumental, the antiquarian, and the critical. Each of them suggests a different conceptualization of the relationship between history and human life: the monumental understands the living human being as "a being who acts and strives"; the antiquarian as "a being who preserves and reveres"; and the critical as "a being who suffers and seeks deliverance."[9] These modes are not mutually exclusive; elements of all three might be found in any single history. The danger of the modes, the disadvantages they might represent for a history that privileges use for life, occurs when one of them dominates the other two (just as when the historical sense overtakes and disarms the unhistorical).

After a brief exploration of each of these modes of historical thinking, I will suggest how they might produce a variety of histories of the Other. Specifically, I will theorize monumental, antiquarian, and critical histories of homosexuality. This is not to suggest a homogeneity between all forms of cultural otherness. As I have suggested throughout this study, the discontinuous discursivities we designate as race, class, gender, and sexuality do not cast their subjects identically. Or, to state this another way, cultural othering works along a variety of axes. Nonetheless, this condition should not obscure the ways in which cultural homogeneity depends upon the production of the normal, which itself can only occur in tandem with the production of an Other. As I have argued throughout this study, the "margin" and "center" are necessarily codependent upon one another. This relation suggests that, if the normal is consolidated and made homogeneous through an encounter with the Other, this encounter might make possible a variety of resistances or reverse discourses, all of which share *a certain* relation to the normal. That certain shared relation to problems of history is what I want to begin to explore here.

The question I will thus ask is, What use is history, given my emphasis throughout this study on questions of nonproductive expenditure, modern subject formation, resistance, and the Other? What small use ought to be reserved for history so that it might allow for a future of sumptuous expenditure argued from the place of the Other? Or, to put the question in Nietzsche's terms, how might we hold together the use of the historical and the unhistorical? How might the risk of "free" expenditure threatened by youth hold in abeyance the overly conservative impulses of the greybeards?

I

I have no wish to conceal from myself that, in the immoderation of its criticism, in the immaturity of its humanity, in its frequent transitions from irony to cynicism, from pride to scepticism, the present treatise itself reveals its modern character, a character marked by weakness of personality.[10]

Nietzsche

According to Nietzsche, monumental history supplies a lethargic or uninspired present with material for reanimation by arguing that "the greatness that once existed was in any event once *possible* and may thus be possible again." The monumental thus understands history as a series of great events presided over by a noble hero: man. It relies on a universal humanism that argues that "the great moments in the struggle of the human individual constitute a chain, that this chain unites mankind across the millennia like a range of human mountain peaks, that the summit of such a long-ago moment shall be for me still living, bright and great" (68).

Nietzsche suggests a number of hazards confronting this monumental history. The monumental runs the risk of falsifying the past by concentrating on only its most noble aspects. Because it hopes to lead the present into glory, it has no use for the errors, mishaps, and blunders of the past. Monumental history thus always runs the risk of beautifying the past, of rendering the past into an object for aesthetic contemplation, and of transforming historiography into "free poetic invention" (70). Such an aestheticization of the past forgets, among other things, that there is no record of civilization that is not also a record of barbarism.[11]

Additionally, monumental history struggles to cover over the fissure dividing the past and the present, relying on a perhaps too facile comparison between the two, and forcing simplistic analogies. It abandons causal thinking, substituting for a careful exploration of historical causality a privileging of "effects in themselves" plucked from history and held up as worthy of imitation in the present.[12] For Nietzsche, a more careful exploration of the "historical *connexus* of cause and effect" would reveal the limits of monumental history, for such an elevation of effects ignores the fact that "the dice-game of chance and the future could never again produce anything exactly similar to what it produced in the past" (70).

Finally, the monumental risks stifling the creativity, ingenuity, and hazard of the present by holding up the past as a kind of corrective. For "the impotent and indolent" (71) in particular, the monumental past is conservative, acting to hold in check the excesses of present expenditure. For these tired greybeards, monumental history is "the masquerade costume in which their hatred of the great and powerful of their own age is disguised as satiated admiration for the great and powerful of past ages." Nietzsche ascribes to such greybeards the motto "let the dead bury the living" (72).

A monumental history of homosexuality might seek to establish a link between great homosexuals of the past and present fags and dykes, animating the poverty of present buggery with inspiring examples from days gone by. It might conduct a tireless search through the archives for "positive" role models, role models whose lives would be celebrated in books, plays, and films, and whose photographs would be displayed proudly in parades and festivals. This pantheon of positive role models would counter the popular associations of homosexuality with deviance by doubly canonizing those already noteworthy contributors to culture who were also homosexual. Popular wisdom would be shocked to learn from the monumental historian of homosexuality that one of the great romantic composers who left a brilliant symphony unfinished was also queer, or that a famous king of England was executed for his love of another man, or that one of the most important American poets of the nineteenth century *wanted* to have sex with another woman, even if she never managed to leave her room long enough to do so. You may already love your little Marcel, the monumental historian of homosexuality might say, but wouldn't it surprise you to learn that he was gay? And think of how the greatness of Gertrude is inseparable from her love for Alice. How can you celebrate such monumental works as the "1812 Overture," *The Waves*, the *Phaedrus*, or *October*, without acknowledging our contribution to human culture?

135

This monumental celebration of the gay spirit would in turn produce an exhaustive historical search for all those great men and women whose homosexuality has not yet been uncovered. A series of exhaustive debates animated by a perpetual search through the archives would pose that vital question: Was s/he or wasn't s/he? The search for such evidence could occupy a lifetime of archival research, interviews, and renewed close readings. Of course, this quest for present role models from the past would necessitate the positing of some kind of "essential" transhistorical queerness that makes possible the establishing of a link between such heroes and heroines as, say, Alexander the Great and Keith Meinhold, between Sappho and k. d. lang, between Aristotle and Allan Bloom, so that the great moments in the struggle of the gay, lesbian, and bisexual human individual might constitute a series of individual flames that unite gay, lesbian, and bisexual humankind in a blaze of glory across the millennia.

But what of the ordinary folk who "just happened to be gay"—a phrase that would never be allowed to be invoked in relation to any of the "great" homosexuals or lesbians of the past (or present, for that matter)? What is the monumental to do with them? The recent demand that homosexuality be acknowledged as the most "elemental" aspect of one's personality[13] would encourage monumental historians to argue for some kind of intrinsic greatness—an aestheticized nobility—to all expressions of gaiety. Such an argument would require a massive prettification of queer sexuality, in which, for example, idyllic scenes of lesbians frolicking in Sapphic splendor would replace all historical knowledge of butch dykes who pierce their clits and wield dildos, in which the shabby life of an Italian hustler-painter would be recreated in Cinemascope for the delectation of the art house audience, and in which gay men who liked to get fucked might be championed for their libidinal, political (!), unconscious identification with "lack."

This is the greatest danger represented by a monumental history of homosexuality: that it necessarily strives to make imperative the impure heterogeneity of homosexuality's nonproductive expenditure through an aestheticization and heroicization of queerness. The monumental historical approach runs the risk of rendering the lives of historical gay and lesbian subjects useful for homogeneous culture, turning a knowledge of their transgressive sexual practices into material for coffee-table books and music videos, rewriting gay and lesbian subjects in an image palatable for middle-class consumption by focusing on their "artistic" production or heroic actions at the expense of an insistence on their wasteful carnality. Such an aestheticization of gay and lesbian sexuality blunts whatever transgressive threat such sexual practices and institutions might represent to the historically familiar by situating these within a noble, elevated, and conservative past.

Perhaps it is possible to imagine a monumental history of homosexuality that attempted to wrestle from the past not a number of noble homosexuals, but a multiplicity of ignoble (homo)sexual acts. It would undoubtedly be a perilous adventure, this attempt to animate the poverty of contemporary sexual practices with an exploration of the sexual excesses of the past, given the dangers of the monumental approach. Such a history would need to be ever vigilant, ennobling and conserving just so much of a wanton past to make possible in the present a continued expenditure.

II

He or she who looks to the past with love and loyalty, preserving and revering all that once was for the benefit of those who are yet to come, is the man or woman dedicated to an antiquarian history. Nietzsche's antiquarian historian serves life by "tending with care that which has existed from of old" and preserving for those who come after him those same abiding conditions under which he himself came into existence. Content with his homeland and customs, he abhors the "restless, cosmopolitan hunting after new and ever newer things." Instead, this historian feels as comfortable in her past as the tree in its roots. "The happiness of knowing that one is not wholly accidental and arbitrary but grown out of a past as its heir, flower and fruit, and that one's existence is thus excused and, indeed, justified"—these are the felicitous conditions that make possible an antiquarian history.[14] In our present conditions, in which such phenomena as the hourly news update threaten to obliterate any knowledge of the workings of the past in the present, the antiquarian might serve to keep alive the very possibility of memory and history.

But as is the case with the monumental, the antiquarian historical sense faces a number of dangers. Seeking to judge the value of the present with reference to the past, the antiquarian historian must overlook those unpleasant aspects of history that might counter his happy vision.[15] This desire to embrace the past so warmly and generously sometimes leads to a situation in which everything in the past is treated with equal importance, whereas all that is new is suspect. The greybeards, walled up in their precious archives, manipulate the historical sense so that it no longer serves life, but mummifies it, substituting "an insatiable thirst for novelty" for a true concern with history as a force that might enrich an understanding of the present. As soon as antiquarian history loses its contact with the present and life, it degenerates into the most pedantic and self-indulgent forms of navel gazing.[16] This antiquarian sense fears the arrogance of a youth impatient with the past. Like the monumental, it, too, is conservative, protecting the sanctity of history from a youth who, filled with fire and defiance, might recklessly squander its riches.

An antiquarian history of homosexuality might preserve from the past *all* extant accounts of same-sex interaction, carnal or otherwise, elevated or profane. Unlike the monumental, the antiquarian would not discriminate between "great" and "mundane" gays. Recognizing that the "sexual" is a fairly recent historical phenomenon, it would pore over the totality of the archive, searching the past not only for divinations of that ancient embryonic figure who will one felicitous day in the nineteenth century emerge, as if from a millennial sleep, from the psychoanalyst's couch as the modern homosexual, but also for evidence of any ancient homoerotics that might have anticipated our present happy condition. The ancient precursor to such contemporary figures as the drag queen, the butch dyke, the sweater boy, and the lipstick lesbian would be located in such unlikely places as Renaissance England and the pre-Columbian Americas, among the sadhu of India and the Oriental mystics.

This celebration of antiquarian homosexualities might inspire a rage to collect and preserve the artifacts of our ancient heritage. Contemporary gay men and lesbians might furnish their homes with carvings from primitive cultures, outfitting their coffee tables and bookshelves with giant phalluses and voluptuous breasts, and covering their walls with erotic images from Greek vases and Chinese paintings. And if authentic examples of such exotic goods are exorbitantly costly, no one will turn his nose up in disgust at the tiny plaster reproduction of Michelangelo's *David* adorning his host's bathroom shelf, or begrudge her neighbor her miniature of an Aegean kitchen goddess. Such examples of queer household pride will announce to all visitors one's veneration of, and reverence for, that glorious gay past.

This rage to collect might concurrently inspire a wave of pilgrimages to our ancestral homes. Gay- and lesbian-owned travel agencies might inaugurate a series of gay-only tours to such places as Morocco, Lesbos, Mykonos, Pompeii, San Francisco, Amsterdam, and Northampton, Massachusetts. Invigorated by the sense of queer history saturating such locales, the gay sojourner would find in such lands an antiquarian history of himself. Returning from the diaspora to the city of his true queer origins, "he reads its walls, its towered gate, its rules and regulations, its holidays, like an illuminated diary of his youth and in all this he finds again himself, his force, his industry, his joy, his judgment, his folly and vices" (73). As Paul Monette exclaims in his memoir, *Borrowed Time*, "The moment we set foot in Greece I was home free. Impossible to measure the symbolic weight of the place for a gay man. . . . When I ran in the grassy stadium high on the mountain where the Pythian Games were held, their heroes sung by Pindar, I knew

I was poised at the exact center of my life. I belonged at last to a brother-hood whose body and spirit were one."[17]

For those who might reject such bourgeois and dilettantish displays of queer pride, other means might allow them to capture that antiquarian sense of gay history. The search for the primitive roots of one's sexuality might lead to an exploration of cultures skilled in the ancient arts of tattoo-ing and body piercing. Travelers to a gay metropolis might find, on their way to a chic cafe, a gilded parlor where modern heirs to a primitive queer-ness adorn their ears, noses, nipples, and genitalia with a variety of loops and studs, and decorate their bodies with a panoply of colorful representa-tions. Only a few brief moments of pain separate the modern queer from the primitive lurking within. Such a sacrifice to one's ancestral gods might evince that veneration for the past that characterizes the antiquarian sense of history.

As was the case with the monumental, the antiquarian risks conserv-ing and revering a past that might obstruct the continued expenditure of the present. Although an antiquarian history of the homosexual Other makes possible a sense of pride that might engender and animate present struggles, creating out of the accidents of history an imaginary collectivity, it also nec-essarily relies on an essentializing and normalization of the gay subject. It dangerously courts a proximity to certain disciplinary institutions and prac-tices, the past providing a normalizing model for present queer conduct, as well as assisting in the forging of a place from which gay subjects might oc-cupy the subject of the statement "We Are the World." Queer U.S. culture's multiple relationships to the project of imperialism must continue to be elaborated and explored. The failure to interrogate the contradictions in-volved in the forging of a transnational "Queer Nation" might have serious consequences for a gay and lesbian politics that seeks something other than a simple "liberation" of gay sexuality, reduced to a freedom from govern-mental interference in (allegedly) private sexual conduct. Recent disputes and complaints concerning the (supposedly) overly inclusive agenda of the 1993 Gay, Lesbian, and Bisexual March on Washington suggest how the continued deployment of an antiquarian queer history might not be in the best interest of queers crossed by the competing agendas of race, class, gen-der, and nationality, to name only the most obvious.

III

Alongside the monumental and antiquarian modes of historical sense, Nietzsche posits the necessity of a third, which he characterizes as the criti-cal. Unlike both the monumental and the antiquarian, critical history is not conservative. It neither offers up to the present a noble past as a model of right conduct, nor preserves and reveres a past that provides the present with a sense of its felicity. Rather, critical history requires that the historian "break up and dissolve" a part of the past. The critical historian makes use of the past for life by "bringing it before the tribunal, scrupulously examining it and finally condemning it." Such a destruction of the past is ruled over not by any sense of justice, but by "life alone, that dark, driving power that insatiably thirsts for itself."[18] Of the three modes of history offered by Nietzsche, the critical thus represents the closest approximation to Bataille's theme of nonproductive expenditure. It lays waste the past so that the present might be free of its burdens. Although it works in tandem with the unhistorical sense, privileging the necessity of forgetting for life, it "suspends" such forgetting long enough to contemplate how greatly a certain aspect of the past deserves to perish (76). Critical history is thus an attempt to free oneself from the burden of the past by subjecting it to a lingering and perhaps protracted destruction. To return to the vocabulary supplied by Bataille: The critical historical sense perhaps argues for that small conservation of history required by life so that it might ultimately continue to expend, forget, and waste. Critical history provides the fuel whereby the past might continue to burn away. Into the time of now, it blasts out of the continuum of history a memory flashing up in a moment of danger, a memory that might bring about in the present a real state of emergency.[19]

The "dangerous and endangered men and generations"[20] who wield this critical history must, as in the case of both the monumental and antiquarian, be wary of a certain hazard. This hazard is the folly of attempting to free oneself too easily and completely from history. As Nietzsche warns,

> Since we are the outcome of earlier generations, we are also the outcome of their aberrations, passions and errors, and indeed of their crimes; it is not possible wholly to free oneself from this chain. If we condemn these aberrations and regard ourselves as free of them, this does not alter the fact that we originate in them. The best we can do is to confront our inherited and hereditary nature with our knowledge of it, and through a new, stern discipline combat our inborn heritage and implant in ourselves a new habit, a new instinct, a second nature, so that our first nature withers away. It is an attempt to give oneself, as it were a posteriori, a past which one would like to originate in opposition to that in which one did originate: always a dangerous attempt because it is hard to know the limit to denial of the past. (76)

In drawing attention to one of the hazards of the critical historical sense, Nietzsche refuses the move to situate the subject outside of the constraints of historical causality, a move that would suggest that one could free oneself wholly from the weave of historical forces in which one is necessarily positioned. Yet, at the same time, Nietzsche does not abandon the possibility of a subject who acts. Faced with this awareness of the difficulty of freeing ourselves from the past, Nietzsche argues that "the best we can do" is both to confront our knowledge with the possibility of its nonknowledge, its inability to transcend the chain of historical aberrations, passions, errors, and crimes of and by which it is constituted, and to confront also the difficulty of determining how much of the past must be forgotten for life. This declaration suggests that although the subject is "chained" within an imperfectly known causal nexus that he cannot sufficiently manipulate, the subject is not merely chained, but might deploy knowledge in order to maneuver to some degree within such a nexus. Nietzsche thus provides here a critique of the subject that does not foreclose the possibility of agency.[21] As I have argued similarly in the case of Foucault's critique of the subject, this Nietzschean critique obviously does not paralyze. Rather, it suggests some of the limits of the subject's (in this case, historical) knowledge, and the perils of ignoring such limits. Spivak might characterize this move to confront historical knowledge with an awareness of its limits in the knowing subject as an effort "to question the authority of the investigating subject without paralyzing him, persistently transforming conditions of impossibility into possibility."[22]

In the work after *Discipline and Punish* in particular, Foucault will take up the Nietzschean suggestion that through the elaboration of "a new, stern discipline," a discipline that I would argue Foucault terms "ethics," subjects might resist the disciplinary practices of modern subject formation. As I have already suggested in an earlier chapter, this resistance occurs through what Foucault terms practices of the self, practices that seek to "implant" in the subject what Nietzsche calls "a new habit, a new instinct, a second nature," a "fictive past in which one would like to originate." Ethics thus designates a resistant disciplining of the self by the self made possible by the practices of subjection and subjugation, a disciplining that resists discipline by countering these practices. Foucault's work in the second and third volumes of *The History of Sexuality* is crucial here.[23] Those critics who claim that Foucault "is wrong" about the Romans and Greeks seriously misread his intellectual project. Foucault is not an antiquarian historian in these texts. He is rather a critical historian forging a historical fiction that might produce a number of effects of truth in the present.[24] It might be argued that in his "historical" studies of sexuality, Foucault is perhaps even interested in a critical destroying of the historical past through a deliberate (mis)reading of the Greeks and Romans that attempts to substitute a "fictive" history for the "true" one of the monumental and antiquarian historiographers. Following Nietzsche, Foucault wants to make use of the material of the past to suggest a new instinct and a second nature, one that might be given to oneself through practices of the self.

This theme arises a number of times in Foucault's discussions of homosexuality, in which he suggests that the historical legacy of the discourse of homosexuality contains the possibilities for the formation and transformation of a self. As Foucault argues, "To be 'gay' I think, is not to identify with the psychological traits and the visible masks of the homosexual, but to try to define and develop a way of life."[25] Foucault thus recognizes the discourse of homosexuality as providing the preconditions for the development of a new sexual instinct and nature that does not ask "Who am I?" and "What do I secretly desire?" but rather attempts "to use sexuality henceforth to arrive at a multiplicity of relationships."[26] Such an attempt is imperative, given the way disciplinary society and its institutions have attempted to shrink the possibilities of "a rich relational world."[27]

A critical history of homosexuality might hold up historical models of gay sexuality and subjectivity only to destroy them. It suggests that rather than adopting current historical models of right homosexual conduct, we must "work" at becoming gay,[28] forging a new, as yet unanticipated, way of life. Such a history would thus reject the efforts of both the monumental and antiquarian to posit some kind of transhistorical gay sensibility. While it might turn to the past for inspiration, it insists on that past as a fiction. It shows no reverence for such a past, but seeks to employ it, strategically. It might deploy the errors and blunders of the past as well as its more "noble" elements. It seeks not to situate gay and lesbian subjects within a chain of humanity united across the millennia, but might strive instead to interrupt that chain by suggesting the discontinuities of what is called the human, and, in the name of an impossible freedom, contesting the ways in which that thing called the human has been produced historically through the subjugation and subjection of Others who are not. It might counter the overly conservative elements in both the monumental and antiquarian by insisting on the poverty of all previous models of gay subjectivity, promising a future of sumptuous expenditure that pays as little regard as possible to the historical. The irony deployed in my earlier descriptions of the possibilities of a monumental and antiquarian history of homosexuality was an effort to employ such a critical historical sense against these two perhaps dangerously conservative modes of analysis. Perhaps, in our own time, the monumental and antiquarian approaches threaten to overtake our sense of the historical, so that we forget the necessity of both the critical and the unhistorical for life.

Following Nietzsche, I would want to repeat the caution that our time might need all three of these modes of historical inquiry, but that all three pose certain dangers to the unhistorical, which similarly remains necessary for life. The three modes thus must not dominate either one another, or the unhistorical. The specific question animating the following section thus becomes, in light of the rest of this study, How might all three forms of history serve the Bataillian theme of nonproductive expenditure as it might be mobilized as a counter to the economic practices of modern subject formation, especially given the fact that the monumental and antiquarian move toward conservation rather than loss and waste? What is that small amount of history we must preserve in our present moment, if we are to continue to consume and resist?

I now discuss a film that combines, in varying degrees, Nietzsche's three modes of historical analysis. I will be reading this film in the service of a polemic concerning the current value of nonproductive expenditure. *Urinal* employs the three models of the historical sense in order to argue, on a variety of levels, for the value of the filthy for history in general, and, in particular, for a useful history of the Other.

IV

An intertitle announces a date, June 28, 1937. A group of artists has met under mysterious circumstances in the garden of an abandoned church shared by two Canadian sculptors, Florence Wyle and Frances Loring. The guests have all received forged letters of invitation to a phony conference of some sort, all signed with the names of the two sculptors. The guests include the Mexican painter Frida Kahlo, the African American poet Langston Hughes, the Japanese novelist Yukio Mishima, and Dorian Gray. The assembled artists wonder aloud who has summoned them here and for what purposes. Kahlo is just finishing a portrait of Gray when the next guest, the Soviet filmmaker Sergei Eisenstein, arrives. As Kahlo completes the painting of the nude Gray, an earthquake occurs, followed by a knock on the door. Eisenstein wonders who the next guest could be. Thomas Mann? Kahlo hopes it is Gertrude Stein. One of their hostesses reappears with a tape recorder that has been left at the door. After announcing the date as June 28, 1987, a voice on the tape recorder exclaims "Happy Lesbian and Gay Pride Day, everyone." Apologizing for gathering everyone together under false pretenses, the voice explains the true purpose of this meeting: "We have chosen you as outstanding lesbian and gay artists to help us resolve a crisis, a crisis between the police and the gay community. In the province of Ontario, hundreds of men are arrested each year for having sex in public washrooms. Your mission, if you should choose to accept it, is to research this problem through the next seven days and propose solutions." The voice then warns, in proper *Mission Impossible* fashion, "This message will self-destruct in ten seconds." The naked Gray now places a police cap on his head. Resembling one of the stars of a porno film (perhaps *Young Cadets* or *Young Guns*), he smiles into the camera. (This same image accompanies the film's opening credit.) A blackout follows, followed in turn by another intertitle, giving the date, June 28, 1987.

Beginning their assigned quest, the guests divide up the topic of tearoom sex between the seven of them. Six will present their research in a series of reports to the others; Gray will infiltrate the (contemporary) police, who have already been warned by the locals of the "half a dozen hippies" assembled in the abandoned church where (the now dead) Loring and Wyle live. Each of the ensuing seven days is announced by an intertitle, as are the titles of the reports presented by the various artists. The film is organized largely through these reports, which range in topic from "historical" matters to present-day discussions. The reports include Loring's "Selective Social History of the Public Washroom," which explores the history of waste disposal, cleansing strategies, and the sex-segregated washroom; Mishima's "Dramatic Reading of Toilet Texts," which features a section of a novel, a sociological study, a police report, and a porno story, all of which discuss washroom sex; Eisenstein's "Guided Tour of Toronto's Hottest Tearooms," in which the filmmaker explains in detail how to pick men up in a public washroom; Hughes's "Survey of Small Town Washroom Busts in Ontario," which recounts police surveillance of public men's rooms in seven small towns, the arrests that accompanied such surveillance, and the consequences of such arrests, which, in at least one instance, included the suicide of the accused; Wyle's "Policing of Washroom Sex in Toronto," in which local gay activists discuss Canadian laws relating to (so-called) public indecency; and Kahlo's "Policing of Sexuality in Society"—arguably the denouement of the film—which I will discuss at some length shortly. The reports feature a voice-over of their "author" accompanied by a variety of images, though the reports are sometimes interrupted by documentary footage in which the "characters" of the artists do not appear. For example, Eisenstein's description of how to pick up men in a rest room is accompanied by still images of the filmmaker demonstrating the intricacies of his newly discovered technique; the image and voice-over are themselves accompanied by the synthesized strains of "The Internationale." This report is intercut with "straight" documentary footage of men recounting their experiences of tearoom sex, one of whom was arrested by police in a bust that featured video surveillance.

The reports are interspersed with brief scenes of how the guests spend their leisure time in the church. Such time is usually spent debating "contemporary" topics such as the Spanish Civil War, and attempting to seduce one another. Much of the group's socializing takes place in the downstairs washroom, where Kahlo's portrait of Gray is first hung. In a parody of Wilde's novel, the actors admire the portrait; Eisenstein suggests, "Wouldn't it be wonderful if he was always like this, but the picture withered?" Later, as he zips up in front of the urinal, Hughes exclaims of the portrait, "It's almost like he's watching us." "Isn't he?" Eisenstein responds.

In parallel to the artists' search, the film details the activities of the police, who have kept the artists under surveillance. Tracking Wyle, in pursuit of her research, to the library, the police discover that she has conducted a subject search under the heading "urinal." The police conclude that this is an anagram for "Uranian Resistance Initiative of the Nonpartisan Action League." (These two policemen are continually satirized in the film. They are portrayed by what appear to be deliberately "bad" actors, and are shot in an extremely unflattering, flat video. Not uncoincidentally, I would suggest, this footage resembles cheap gay pornography.)[29] As the narrative progresses, the police increase their efforts, forcing Gray into cooperating with them in the continued surveillance of the artists, which eventually includes the installation of a camera in the upstairs washroom. The activities of these "fictive" police are thus paralleled in the reports by both Hughes and Wyle in particular of "real" police activities. The film culminates in the revelation that Gray has been working for the police. Without completely giving away the end of the film, I will only indicate that it once again parallels Wilde's novel in that the portrait has changed, is first covered and then removed by Gray, and is eventually destroyed by him.

John Greyson's *Urinal* attempts to make a critical use of a history of the Other for life—specifically, by using the material of a history of (homo)-sexuality in the service of a contemporary polemic concerning surveillance, sexuality, and resistance. This polemic is largely detailed in the reports presented by the artists. I will take up this polemic at some length momentarily, but I want to begin my discussion of the film by highlighting some of the ways in which it suggests that the material of history might be made suitable for use in the service of life.

Greyson's film attempts, in a number of ways, to make a critical use of the past in the present. *Urinal* is burdened with a history that has often imagined the media as capable of recording with some accuracy a present reality, a reality that will one day become the historical past. A realist ontology of the image, naive or otherwise, has made possible the continued understanding of film as both art and science, "fiction" and "fact," invention and trace.[30] Although the history of film theory is marked by attempts to complicate a simplistic understanding of film as recorder of the real—attempts that range from Arnheim's insistence that the filmic image is significantly different from perceptual reality, to Bazin's account of the phenomenological density of deep space / deep focus photography, to Baudry's analysis of the "ideological effects" of the apparatus[31]—there has nonetheless existed a tendency to treat film as some kind of mechanical reproducer of some version of the real. With "historical" films, whether they be understood as fictive or documentary, such a tendency has often privileged what might be characterized as the monumental and antiquarian tendencies of the media, the abilities of film to preserve and conserve both the noble and everyday of the past. The biopic and the documentary recounting the life of the great historical figure represent instances of the former; the historical melodrama and preserved home movie, the latter.[32] *Urinal*'s hybrid generic status—part fiction film, part biopic, part documentary, part melodrama, part avant-garde art film, partly a remake of a filmic adaptation of Oscar Wilde's *Picture of Dorian Gray*, partly an essay on the ins and outs of anonymous tearoom sex—highlights the ways in which the film must necessarily be implicated in this history. This status suggests some of the historical difficulties of employing the medium of film toward a critical historical end.

Urinal attempts, however, to interrupt this historical imagining of the media as a recorder of a monumental or antiquarian history by complicating its own ontological status as film. Its mixed-media narrative is presented in a combination of moving and still images shot in film and video. These images are culled from a variety of sources. Some are staged. Others are shot with a hand-held camera in a live, on location, cinema-verité style. Some feature human beings, whether those human beings be actors, unwitting passersby, or willing documentary subjects, some of whom are heavily disguised by false wigs, glasses, and noses.[33] Others deploy such inanimate objects as dolls, a Scrabble board, and food. Drawings, photographs, and a variety of written texts—newspaper headlines, biographies punched up on a computer screen, fictive memoirs, an essay report—also appear in the film. Some of the images are obviously archival, such as photographs of the "real" historical artists, and drawings culled from the history of plumbing. Some are contemporary. But on top of and across these images, *Urinal* also deploys computerized video imaging techniques that alter the image, changing either sections of the image or the whole frame, freezing, moving, multiplying, decorating, and coloring over it. At times, it is as if the spectator were watching a *bricoleur* at work, constructing, rearranging, altering, and defacing the images gathered from both the waste dump of history and yesterday's garbage pail. This continual manipulation of the image interrupts the traditional vocabulary of film analysis, creating effects for which there is no handy vocabulary.[34] In an attempt to counter the historical tendency of the media to stabilize, conserve, and ossify both the past and the present as future past, there is, in *Urinal*, a constant refusal to leave the image alone, a perpetual construction and destruction of the visual field that highlights the immediacy of the image, its potential for deployment in the present. The surface of *Urinal* might thus be described not as a window into a preexisting world, nor even a canvas on which the past has been recorded, but perhaps as a kind of flatbed on which has been assembled a collection of artifacts that, though necessarily linked to the aberrations of the past, might be deployed to implant the "new instinct" required by Nietzsche's critical historical sense.[35]

Urinal's hybrid visual style, its collage aesthetic, its narrative deployment of "fictive" and historical figures, as well as its very title—surely a reference to that infamous readymade of Marcel Duchamp's—suggest the necessity of considering the film's formal qualities in relation to questions of modernity, history, politics, and aesthetics. Such a consideration will require a brief historical detour through the writings of Walter Benjamin. Benjamin's "The Work of Art in the Age of Mechanical Reproduction" remains one of the most fruitful and compelling attempts to describe a relationship between art and politics.[36] In this essay, Benjamin charts some of the ways in which, in the period of modernity, technology has altered both art and perception.

Benjamin's argument begins with the assumption that the organization of human sense perception is determined by both natural and historical circumstances. According to Benjamin, art (dialectically) reflects and organizes historical changes in human modes of perception, changes that themselves occur in dialectical tension with social changes. Benjamin's essay argues that the conditions of mechanical reproducibility attack the authenticity of the art object, rendering that object capable of being more easily detached from its originating circumstances, and complicating the distinction between "original" and "copy." Benjamin defines the authenticity of the object as "the essence of all that is transmissible from its beginning, ranging from its substantive duration to its testimony to the history which it has experienced" (678). The spatiotemporal mobility of the mechanically reproduced art object serves to detach the artwork from the domain of tradition, and allows it to "meet the beholder or listener in his own particular situation." The conditions of mechanical reproduction concurrently substitute a plurality of copies for the unique art object, complicating the question of authenticity even further. Benjamin subsumes under the term "aura" that which "withers" as a result of this attack on the authenticity of the artwork inaugurated by the conditions of mechanical reproduction.

This withering of the aura of the artwork occurs in tandem with a historical shift in perception. The "contemplative" spectator of the unique art object is replaced by the "distracted" spectator of modernity. These two factors change the function of art. "For the first time in world history," writes Benjamin, "mechanical reproduction emancipates the work of art from its parasitical dependence on ritual" (681). For Benjamin, this emancipation introduces politics as the basis of art.

In Benjamin's formulation, the historical sense in the period of modernity is also necessarily structured by the shift in perception that accompanies the withering of the artwork's aura. This shift inaugurates "a tremendous shattering of tradition which is the obverse of the contemporary crisis and renewal of mankind" (678-79). Benjamin views this shattering of tradition and its accompanying crisis dialectically, that is, in terms that cannot be assigned a clearly "negative" or "positive" value: the shift in perception inaugurated by modernity and its accompanying technological developments requires a shift in the historical sense, a movement necessarily implicated in both the rise of fascism and historical materialist responses to that rise.

A similar vocabulary of rupture thus structures Benjamin's "Theses on the Philosophy of History," differentiating what Benjamin terms a historicism that might be enlisted in the service of fascism from a resistant historical materialist practice of historiography. In the "Theses," Benjamin describes how the materialist historian must "seize hold of a memory as it flashes up at a moment of danger. Historical materialism wishes to retain that image of the past which unexpectedly appears to man singled out by history at a moment of danger."[37] While historicism calls up an eternal image of the past, a historical materialist practice works "to blast open the continuum of history" (262). (This trope of "blasting" is in fact repeated several times in the "Theses.") Historical materialism "cuts through" (255) a historicism content to establish a causal connection between various moments in history (263). It attempts "to wrest tradition away from a conformism that is about to overpower it" (255), and to use the past critically in the service of present struggles. (Recall here Nietzsche's similar use of tropes of rupture in his account of how the critical historian must from time to time "employ the strength to break up and dissolve a part of the past" and "take the knife to its roots.")[38]

In his historical circumstances, Benjamin argued that the critical historical sense of the historical materialist must be deployed against the rise of fascism; "it is our task to bring about a real state of emergency," he insists. "One reason why Fascism has a chance is that in the name of progress its opponents treat it as a historical norm."[39] According to Benjamin, fascism specifically introduces the aesthetic into political life by organizing the newly created proletarian masses—masses whose creation has been made possible by, among other things, the new modes of perception structured by new technologies of mechanical reproduction—*without* affecting any change in property relations. Fascism "expects war to supply the artistic gratification of a sense perception that has been changed by technology." In the period of modernity, the self-alienation of humankind is such that "it can experience its own destruction as an aesthetic pleasure of the first order."[40]

But Benjamin the dialectician does not propose that historical materialism respond to the threat of fascism by attempting to recuperate the lost aura of the artwork. The implication of Benjamin's argument is not that the transformation of sense perception by technology is simply historically reversible.[41] Rather, Benjamin proposes that historical materialism—here named as "communism"—respond to fascist aestheticization of politics with a politicization of aesthetics. As one of the recent art forms produced by technologies of mechanical reproduction, film in particular has a vital role to play in the politicization of art, one necessarily (dialectically) made possible by the destruction of the aura of the artwork—although (or because) the withering of aura has required the severing of the artwork from the domain of tradition. About film, Benjamin thus insists, "Its social significance, particularly in its most positive form, is inconceivable without its destructive, cathartic aspect, that is, the liquidation of the traditional value of the cultural heritage."[42]

Benjamin is sensitive to the facility with which culture might transform a politicization of aesthetics into an aestheticization of politics. (Recall here also the "proximity" of Bataille's two forms of heterogeneity, the ease with which the "impure" might be elevated to the "imperative," as well as his insistence that fascist culture makes use of imperative forms like an aestheticized politics.) In "The Author as Producer," Benjamin contrasts "the revolutionary strength" of a politicized art movement such as dadaism, which used techniques of assemblage and bricolage to challenge the autonomy of the work of art, with then-contemporary efforts in photography.[43] Such efforts render photography "ever more *nuancée*, ever more modern," resulting in an aestheticization of, for example, poverty. The ease with which photography "has succeeded in transforming even abject poverty, by recording it in a fashionably perfected manner, into an object of enjoyment" (230), alerts Benjamin to the necessity of examining what he might term the politics of form, for, as Benjamin asserts, "the bourgeois apparatus of production and publication can assimilate astonishing quantities of revolutionary themes, indeed, can propagate them without calling its own existence, and the existence of the class that owns it, seriously into question" (229). Form for Benjamin, however, is not limited to what we often think of as the formal qualities of an artwork, its aesthetic properties, its method of addressing the spectator, its status as a realist or antirealist text, and so on (though, as Benjamin's valorization of Brecht's epic theater in this same essay reminds us, such considerations are always also involved in a discussion of form). Benjamin's argument also concerns itself with the position of the artwork in the relations of production of its time. The politicization of aesthetics thus involves a consideration of the artwork in relation to existing *forms of production* (a phrase that includes the formal qualities of the artwork).[44] In other words, Benjamin insists that there is a necessary relationship between the formal qualities of the work of art and the forms of production in which it originates and is positioned.

This long digression has introduced some of what might be at stake in any attempt to read *Urinal*'s politics of explanation, the means—"formal" and otherwise—by which it assures and secures its particular mode of being in the world. The film's overt references to techniques of assemblage and its self-reflexive foregrounding of its own status as mechanical reproduction, as well as its attempts to take up, on the level of content, questions of politics, police, and resistance, suggest that it might be fruitful to explore whether *Urinal* might ultimately suggest either a politicization of aesthetics or an aestheticization of politics—although such an either/or formulation is unsatisfactory, particularly in light of Benjamin's emphasis in "The Work of Art in the Age of Mechanical Reproduction" on dialectical analysis. The fact that the film courts both of these possibilities simultaneously is perhaps emblematized in its combining in a single film of, for example, the politically committed Sergei Eisenstein and the eternally aesthetic Dorian Gray. I will, however, leave a more extended exploration of the politics of the form of *Urinal* for later in this chapter.

In its attempt to suggest a critical usefulness of history for life, *Urinal* sometimes collapses and confuses historical temporality. The film's narrative seems to move from 1937 to 1987 and back again, at least according to its intertitles. This movement is not narratively motivated, even on a fantastic level. In other words, there is no "event" that "logically" causes this movement, such as the placement of the characters in some kind of time-travel device, or the intervention of a supernatural being who acts in a particular moment to transport the artists into the present (though it might be inferred that Dorian Gray, as a "fictive" character, is capable of moving the scene to 1987, since the narrative ultimately reveals that he has in fact gathered the artists together; and there is also the unexplained earthquake). Nor is there even a formal device such as a dissolve or some other special manipulation of the image to suggest that the movement in time occurs. Instead, the movement of past to present to past again occurs simply through the insertion of intertitles. The first claims it is 1937. This image is eventually followed by the voice on the tape recorder announcing that it is "in fact" 1987. The film does not attempt to resolve the contradiction between the intertitle and the voice on the tape recorder until the end of the sequence, when a new intertitle stating the date as 28 June 1987 appears. Similarly, the movement at the end of the film "back" to 1937 is apparently motivated only by the passage of the seven days promised by the voice on the tape recorder. Again, there are no formal devices to suggest how this movement back in time occurred; only the presence of an intertitle reestablishes the year as 1937. There is apparently no concern here for an antiquarian sense of the historical past that might dictate that proper historical chronology be defined and maintained.

Throughout most of the film, it appears to be 1987. As I will discuss shortly, the guests interact with the world of 1987, even going so far as to read and criticize a number of their own biographies and to rent a video of a Hollywood movie of Mishima's life, which leads Frances Loring to scold him for what will be his life's outcome—a failing attempt to lead a right-wing coup, followed by ritual suicide. Yet, at times, it appears to be 1937 and 1987 simultaneously. At one point in the film, Mishima reads from his novel *Forbidden Colours*, which he explains he has not yet written. (*Forbidden Colours* was written in 1951-53.) Similarly, the assembled guests discuss not only their current research but such "contemporary" events as the Spanish Civil War and relations between Mexico and the Soviet Union. This refusal to grant a simple autonomy to either past or present suggests, in *Urinal*, the possibility that the past might be deployed in the present towards a critical rather than conservative end.

Another way in which *Urinal* pursues its suggestion that the historical might be useful for contemporary life occurs in the film's frequent staging of a confrontation between the two realms through the figures of the seven resurrected artists. (For the sake of discussion here, I will treat Dorian Gray, as the film does, as a historical personage.) This confrontation occurs hand in hand with the film's continued attempt to unravel the "common sense" opposition between (historical) fact and (contemporary) fiction. As I have suggested above, the film does not simply collapse the past into the present, nor project the present back into the past—in other words, it does not simply reverse the binaries—but continually seeks to undo the opposition between the two. For example, when the actors playing the six "historical" artists are first introduced, that introduction is interrupted by the insertion of a still photograph apparently shot in video of the "real" Mishima, Hughes, Kahlo, and so on, into the film. (At several points, *Urinal* features what appears to be video footage reshot on film.) Similarly, a number of the artists' reports combine "real" historical persons or places with the "fictionalized" artists. Eisenstein's report, which presents in images and describes in words a number of "real" popular Toronto tearooms, also includes actual accounts of men who have engaged in tearoom sex. We learn from Wyle that the research for her report led her to attempt to interview the actual attorney general of Ontario and the police chief of Toronto, both of whom refused (presumably) to appear in *Urinal* when they learned of the film's topic; instead, "real" gay activists appear to discuss the legal ramifications of tearoom sex.

In addition to these more serious encounters with reality, the film details how Hughes takes a trip one afternoon with Loring and Wyle to the Art Gallery of Ontario, which is featuring a retrospective of their sculpture. We see the three "artists" wander through the exhibit, admiring the women's work. But the film does not simply supplant contemporary "fiction" with historical "reality." Following the screening of the Hollywood biopic on Mishima's life, when Loring scolds the present Mishima for being a fascist in the future, Mishima insists, "But Hollywood doesn't know anything about postwar politics, about Japan, about the samurai tradition. Clearly, neither do you Americans." Such a remark draws attention not only to the limits of historical fiction but also to the ways in which historical accounts of Asia produced by the West are necessarily shaped by Western belief systems. When Loring replies that she is now a Canadian, Mishima retorts, "You all look the same to me," parodying the historical tendency of the West to treat the "Oriental" Other as an undifferentiated mass.

Perhaps the most interesting and terrifying confrontation between the past and the present occurs in Hughes's report. Hughes's exploration of small-town washroom busts in Ontario leads him to St. Catharines, a town where a police video surveillance team arrested thirty-two men for engaging in tearoom sex. According to the film, local newspapers were flooded with letters in support of the police efforts, until one of the accused, a married man with children, killed himself by dousing his body with gasoline and lighting himself on fire. Hughes explains that when he tried to visit this infamous tearoom, which was attached to a restaurant, he was stopped by the restaurant's owner, who called him a "queer-lover," took down his license plate number, and called the police. On the image track, we see a "real" person, presumably the restaurant owner, heading toward the camera and mouthing angry epithets. Hughes's report concludes with a written text that informs us that a 1988 Ontario court of appeals case "upheld the constitutionality of most washroom arrests and police video surveillance." In Hughes's report, the past confronts the present critically, holding up an image not of a past worthy of noble or antiquarian conservation, but a past that, after having been scrupulously examined and condemned, must be annihilated in the service of life.

Although *Urinal* sometimes employs both the monumental and antiquarian historical sense, it does so toward parodic and critical ends. For example, although the film calls up from the past a number of "monumental" (supposedly) gay and lesbian artists, it simultaneously attempts to undercut the nobility of these characters, as well as any simple attempt to assign them a stable sexuality or sexual identity. The characters are often depicted bickering with one another over politics and sexuality. They are reluctant heroes and heroines at best, not eager to embrace either the tenets of modern gay liberation or a contemporary gay "sensibility" or "identity." Early in the film, Kahlo chides Hughes, who is moping because someone has let his "secret" (homo)sexuality out of the bag. Hughes in turn reminds her of her husband and male (as well as female) lovers, insisting, "You hardly seem to qualify as a card-carrying lesbian." Similarly, when Mishima flirts initially with Eisenstein, the filmmaker insists that "my private life is exactly that—private." He seems uncomfortable with Mishima's desire to discuss sex under socialism. Later in the film, when a "reformed" Eisenstein confesses to Hughes his desire to make gay-themed films, Hughes responds that gay art seems "superficial." "You can't compare Jim Crow with cock sucking," he insists. When the police, who not coincidentally control the flow of biographical information on the artists, consult their computers for information, calling up encyclopedialike entries (though these are themselves somewhat ironic, defining, for example, Loring as "Lesbian. Bohemian. Conversationalist," and detailing Mishima's fascination with blood, sex, and suicide), most of the artists are listed by their apparent biographers as "suspected" homosexuals and lesbians. These biographers tell us that Eisenstein, Mishima, and Kahlo were in fact married to people of the opposite sex. No easily identifiable sexual "essence" unites these characters. Loring and Wyle, cuddling in bed one morning, emphasize this fact by referring to their guests as a "crazy bunch of people just to throw together." In the manner of Eisensteinian montage, the image then cuts to a salad being tossed, emphasizing the haphazardness of this collection. The film also foregrounds the characters' different political persuasions—Hughes's communist sympathies, Mishima's extreme right-wing tendencies, Kahlo's support of Trotsky, Eisenstein's relation to Stalin—suggesting that no single political sensibility links these characters named as gay and lesbian.

The characters in fact seem at times to have to be seduced by one another into their (homo)sexuality, a sexuality that grows more seductive as they investigate their assigned topic. Early in the film, Mishima dresses as Saint Sebastian to seduce a somewhat reluctant Hughes, who eventually submits. Later, he joins a cautious Eisenstein in the shower, claiming the political necessity of conserving water, and offering to scrub his back. Eisenstein, carried away by his recent research into the pleasures of tearoom safe sex, will later use his own political rhetoric on Hughes. "It is our last opportunity to experience what they call . . . the new sexual ethics that have resulted from the AIDS crisis," he insists to a sleepy Hughes on the evening of the sixth day. Brandishing condoms and lubricant, he cries, "It is your duty to participate." While Hughes calls this "the worst come-on line I've ever heard," he nonetheless registers no protest when Eisenstein disappears headfirst beneath the covers to place a condom on him. Kahlo first tries to seduce both Loring and Wyle by coyly flopping into their bed one morning under the guise of being consumed with their "fucking mission." Though her advances are rejected, she will have better luck later in the film, when, overcome with curiosity concerning the joys of tearoom sex, she approaches Wyle in the upstairs washroom.

The film similarly employs a parodic sense of the antiquarian. This is especially true in the case of Loring's report, "A Selective Social History of the Public Washroom," which goes to hyperbolic lengths to recount such things as the many names for the toilet, various approaches to elimination, historical methods of cleansing (including such things as corn cobs, the neck of a swan, and the pages of the Sears catalog), taboos associated with waste, modern art and elimination, gender and elimination, and the design of public facilities. Yet, as in the case of the monumental, this antiquarian sense is employed by *Urinal* toward a critical end. Loring's history focuses on how it was initially historically "necessary" to convince and coerce people, who much preferred to eliminate at will wherever possible, to use toilets. The report also mentions the culture of shame, disgust, and fetishization that such coercion has produced in the twentieth century. Loring follows with a discussion of the development in the nineteenth century of communal public facilities for elimination, and an account of how the intervention of state power made possible, in the washrooms, what we might term, after Foucault, a "reverse" discourse. According to Loring's report, the state blamed the supposed immorality of women factory workers for the growing sexualization of the space of the washroom, rather than addressing the economic, social, and sexual abuse of women at the hands of their male employers and colleagues in the workplace. This growing "threat" of sexual play and titillation in communal washrooms led the state to intervene, legislating sex-segregated facilities. But this extension of state power made possible at least two forms of what the film defines as resistance. For women, the state's move entailed the creation of the washroom as a space of isolation from men, a refuge and a social space that was perhaps subversive, in that women were relatively free within its confines from patriarchal surveillance. For men, sex-segregated washrooms created the conditions for (homo)sexual tearoom activities.[45]

At a number of different points, *Urinal* explores, in a variety of different ways and along a variety of different registers, this theme of a counterdiscourse made possible by an extension of power. Though Foucault is never named in the film, it is perhaps inevitable, given the way the themes of power, surveillance, and resistance haunt *Discipline and Punish*, that the film's polemic might be considered alongside Foucault. I will conclude this chapter with such a consideration, but I want briefly here to examine some of the additional ways in which *Urinal* calls up this theme of a counterdiscourse. As I have already suggested, in its perhaps deliberate portrayal of the police through the conventions of cheaply made gay video pornography, a pornography that often features a variety of men in uniform, *Urinal* suggests that the police's eroticization of the gaze—a gaze that in the circumstances of tearoom surveillance is directed, interestingly, toward *male* bodies—makes possible a contrary (homo)eroticization of the figure of the police.[46] Crucial here is the opening credit of the film, in which Gray is pictured naked save for a police hat. The long history of the eroticization of the figure of the police, not only through gay pornography but through the work of Jean Genet and Kenneth Anger, attest to the enormous cultural currency that this figure commands within the (so-called) gay community. By calling this eroticization of the police a counterdiscourse that nonetheless necessarily takes part in that which it opposes, I am once again attempting to remind the reader of the proximity of transgression to its limit, as well as to hold in abeyance the (simplistic) reading of gay male culture's fetishization of the police as "simply" oppressive. In other words, I am insisting on an avoidance of the twin traps of labeling this eroticization either "progressive" or "reactionary," but wish instead to consider it as necessarily multivalent, given the way this study understands questions of power, subject formation, and resistance.[47]

A counterdiscourse to the extension of power is posed again during Eisenstein's exhaustive account of tearoom sex, in which both Eisenstein and an unidentified disguised man describe in detail how to go about picking up a sexual partner in a washroom. (Eisenstein provides step-by-step instructions in the form of an outline, while the man describes and pantomimes his technique for the camera.)[48] This creates a circumstance in which a disabling condition—the situation of the continued policing of tearooms, and the reliance of the police on ever-improving methods of surveillance—makes possible an enabling condition, in which knowledge of transgressive tearoom practices is conveyed to a larger audience. The film in fact suggests, both "didactically," in Kahlo's final report, and, narratively, in the characters' ever-growing enthusiasm for their mission, the necessity of preserving tearoom sex culture and practices. The film thus attempts to counter one of its own conditions of possibility—the extension of the power of the police to gaze on and prosecute male (homo)sexual bodies—with a powerful response that attempts to proliferate such transgressive and outlawed (homo)-sexual behaviors. *Urinal* is necessarily woven into a wildly contradictory set of circumstances. Its conditions of possibility are exactly those that it seeks on some level to resist. Obviously, a film like *Urinal* could not have been made without the continued policing of tearooms. Given these circumstances, the film attempts to use this opportunity to convey to its audience a means of resistance to such policing. The film defines that resistance at least in part as a transgressive knowledge of how to pick up men for sex in a rest room.

But the film's desire to transmit knowledge of "deviant" tearoom practices cannot simply be embraced and hailed as "oppositional," for such a knowledge in turn creates a new counterknowledge that might ultimately serve the police better in their attempts to control and prosecute such practices. This is the risk the Other courts in pursuing cultural visibility, a risk explored earlier in my discussion of *Tongues Untied*. The struggle for the visibility of the Other always risks appropriation and containment, but it is a counterstrategy made possible—perhaps necessitated—by the continued encroachment of power.

One other related example from the film will illustrate the complexities of this attempt to forge and describe critically a counterdiscourse from within the historically specific circumstances of continued police surveillance of tearoom sexual activity. One of the men in Eisenstein's report, a man busted for engaging in washroom sex, describes how, in the course of appealing his conviction, he came to see the police videotape of his sexual activity. Appearing as "himself" in the film, not dressed in any disguise, this man describes how glad he felt, given the circumstances, as he watched himself on camera. "I was delighted by how human and how physical and how sexual and how beautiful I was, and I was surprised." We might read these words in at least two ways. On the one hand, we might read them as an attempt by the subject to forge a counterdiscourse, a counterdiscourse of affirmation, from a set of circumstances in which the subject's body has been subjected to one of the most raw and brutal forms of police surveillance. On the other hand, the subject's affirmation necessitates a certain capitulation to the logic of visibility. Such an affirmation requires that the subject, on some level, be positioned in a network of power relations that he cannot adequately know or control, a network that has implanted in him a desire for visibility. How is the critic to decide between these two readings of the situation, since *both* are *required* by the formulation of power and resistance that I have been invoking throughout this study (in other words, given the fact that these are not two different readings at all, but rather two different faces of the same situation)? Or, to put this another way, which aspect of this reading should the critic emphasize and explore, given the necessity of resisting the ongoing practices of modern disciplinary subject formation, as well as the recent history of criticism, which unfortunately continues to cast the critic in the role of "arbiter" of resistance? (Again, I am referring here to the tendency of critics to name texts as "either" "progressive" or "reactionary," a tendency I noted in passing in my discussion of bell hooks's reading of *Paris Is Burning*.)

My suggestion is that, although *ideology* might be a kind of shorthand for those material, textual forces that the critic cannot adequately know—or, in Nietzsche's vocabulary, the chain of historical aberrations, passions, and errors in which the critic as subject is necessarily positioned—*ethics* names the process whereby the critic determines strategically and contingently, in the act of reading, where the emphasis might be placed: on the ways in which a text such as *Urinal* necessarily reinscribes the sovereign subject and the modern disciplinary forms of subject production, or on the ways in which it necessarily resists the sovereign subject and modern disciplinary forms of subject production. *Ethics* thus names the grounds of choice that can be known. An ethical commitment to an impossible freedom requires that, as a critic, I attempt to specify both faces of this dilemma: the power that extends, and the resistance that such an extension engenders; the limit, and the transgression that explores that limit's density. Thus arises the necessity of developing a critical (and strategic) ethics of marginality, an ethics ever scrupulous in its attempts to seek out new forms of resistance and abandon outmoded ones. Nietzsche's model of critical history—a model that I have argued shapes *Urinal*—might help us to define, in these most untimely of circumstances, how history might serve such an ethical project, and what small amount of history we might need to conserve in order to serve life.[49]

In privileging tearoom sex here as a "wasteful" and "nonproductive" form of resistance to the "economic" practices of modern subject formation, and in mobilizing a reading of *Urinal* that argues a similar stance, I am responding ethically (and strategically) to "liberal" forces within the gay community that see tearoom sex as an aberrant and disgusting form of behavior, which must be negated and purged from the scene of contemporary (homo)sexuality. This liberal argument marshals a discourse of rights to suggest that such "public" displays of expenditure as tearoom sex infringe on the rights of others, gay and straight alike, and it often insists that if gay men can't manage to restrict their sexuality to a single partner, they ought at least to keep their promiscuity quiet, hidden from the public eye.[50] There is significant disagreement among politically active, self-identified, and vocal gays concerning the status of washroom sex. As a gay activist in *Urinal* argues, the gay community has not embraced this sexual practice as part of gay liberation. He suggests that it still represents one of the "taboo areas we have never really come out of the closet on," and argues that there is "still a great deal of self-oppression in this area." Discussing this film with a very close friend, I was amazed to hear him ridicule not only the film's apparently "positive" stance towards tearoom sex, but in particular, the man who described the act of watching himself on video having tearoom sex as a "self-affirming experience." My friend was extremely angered by this man's "irresponsible" position, and found it completely untenable.

That tearoom sex is to this day regarded by some of the most "radical" members of the gay community as an aberration is evidenced in an issue of *The Advocate* from 1992, in which the AIDS activist, playwright, and novelist Larry Kramer is interviewed. Kramer complains of a recent benefit he attended for New York's Gay Men's Health Crisis, where he claims to have seen "4,000 or 5,000 gorgeous young kids on the beach who were drugged out of their minds at high noon, rushing in and out of the Portosans to fuck."[51] Arguing that such behavior would never occur at an event sponsored by a straight organization, Kramer insists, "I think that what has destroyed us has been our determination to celebrate our promiscuity. And I will never change the way I feel about that, I am sorry. It's childish. It has turned out to be unhealthy, and I think that we are capable of much, much more."

What I find most interesting about Kramer's rhetoric here is in fact its polemic against "childish" nonproductive expenditure, emblematized significantly in his moralizing rejection of both drug use and "promiscuous" youthful tearoom sex. Kramer recognizes that fucking in portable toilets may be counterproductive to the incarnation of gay politics that wants gay and lesbian people to behave "appropriately"—like (Kramer's version of) straight people. Symptomatically, Kramer forgets here that sexual practices involving the exchange of certain bodily fluids, and not "promiscuity" per se—whatever that might be—are what have turned out to be unhealthy. Ironically, Kramer appears on the cover of *The Advocate* sporting an elegantly trimmed grey beard.

Also extremely telling in light of my present concern with history is Kramer's reading of a number of largely unnamed gay and lesbian historians:

> When I see the return of essays—the likes of which people like Marty
> Duberman now write—extolling the virtues of gay promiscuity . . . I get
> worried. . . . Second-rate academics affiliated with third-rate educational
> institutions [are] studying our history, telling me that there was no such
> thing as homosexuality before 1890. Fuck them! This is one of the most
> destructive, damaging things—that our own historians refuse to
> acknowledge that homosexuality has existed since the beginning of time.
> . . . You can't tell me that dicks weren't being sucked by male mouths since
> shortly after the Garden of Eden. (47)

Kramer's harangue—which can be described only as a willful misreading of recent histories of sexuality—expresses a longing for an antiquarian gay history that would connect up the gay present to a mythic (post-) Edenic homosexual past. It also rightly recognizes that a more critical historical approach might destroy some of the founding fictions of a gay identity politics. Considering the parodic employment in *Urinal* of the antiquarian historical sense, as well as its polemic in favor of tearoom sex, it is not difficult to guess how a gay political activist like Kramer might respond to the film.

But what of the critical ethics involved in reading the formal aspects of the film? How are we to understand what I have termed, after Spivak, *Urinal*'s (formal) politics of explanation? Earlier in this chapter, I proposed that Benjamin's analysis of the relationship between aesthetics and politics in modernity might provide an important reference point for a discussion of *Urinal*. The film's "blasting" of its cast of characters out of the continuum of history (recall the earthquake with which the film begins); its mobilization of the material of the past in the service of a contemporary struggle; its privileging of mechanical techniques of interruption, appropriation, and assemblage, techniques that might, in terms supplied by Benjamin's reading of Brecht, "alienate" the public "in an enduring manner, through thinking, from the conditions in which it lives";[52] its hybrid combination of genres; its use of an "alienating" humor (as Benjamin suggests, "there is no better start for thinking than laughter"[236])—all of these suggest that *Urinal* pursues Benjamin's goal of politicizing aesthetics with recourse to the processes of mechanical reproduction. Also to be considered is that the film was not produced and distributed through the usual commercial routes. Produced via a more artisanal mode of production than big-budget commercial films, *Urinal* is distributed through smaller "alternative" media exhibitors, such as Frameline. It has played primarily in a handful of gay and lesbian film festivals in the United States and Canada, and is available for video rental only at "alternative" video stores (in other words, such large corporate chains as Blockbuster Video do not carry *Urinal*).

One of the problems with this reading of the film is of course that Benjamin's analysis was written in 1935. In the spirit of Benjamin, it would be "undialectical" to fetishize his account of art in the age of mechanical reproducibility as if it could be applied unproblematically to a contemporary film such as *Urinal*. Additionally, some readers would find Benjamin's account of art in modernity to be an inappropriate analysis of our postmodern condition. (As Andreas Huyssen reminds us, however, for some readers of Benjamin this problem has been alleviated by claiming Benjamin as postmodern *avant la lettre*, an increasingly expanding category that interestingly includes, in Jameson's deployment of it, Marcel Duchamp himself.)[53] Any discussion of the politics of *Urinal* must thus at least provisionally confront questions of the postmodern aesthetic.

But the term *postmodernism* is fraught with difficulties: even those who use it concede that there is, necessarily, a variety of postmodernisms.

For example, Hal Foster writes, in 1983, of two different ones, a postmodernism of "resistance" that "seeks to deconstruct modernism and resist the status quo," and a postmodernism of "reaction" that "repudiates the former to celebrate the latter."[54] Even these two definitions, however, seem too simplistic. How, for example, are we to read a practice like neo-expressionism, which neither resists modernism nor repudiates it but rather attempts, through nostalgia, to recuperate a certain strain of modernist painting and its accompanying values—the originality of the avant-garde, the aura of the work of art, and the cult of the artistic personality, for example.[55] Huyssen problematizes the term *postmodern* by noting the different uses of *modernity* by French and German scholars, the French referring primarily to an aesthetic modernism, the Germans (at least in the guise of Habermas) to theories of the Enlightenment.[56] The implication is that these different understandings must produce different conceptions of the postmodern. Finally, Jameson suggests that if postmodernism is a reaction against modernism, "there will be as many different forms of postmodernism as there were high modernisms in place, since the former are at least initially specific and local reactions *against* these models."[57] Besides these qualified uses of *postmodernism*, consider those who see it as a continuation of the modern and refuse the optimism of such terms as "late capitalism," and it becomes increasingly vexing to attempt to use the term without a more extended consideration of its problems than I am willing to take up here.

Rather than attempt to place *Urinal* in terms of the modern-versus-postmodern debates, I would instead express these cautions concerning the effort to read the film as a politicization of aesthetics. Marcel Duchamp wrote in 1962 of then contemporary art:

> This Neo-Dada, which they call New Realism, Pop Art, Assemblage, etc., is an easy way out, and lives on what Dada did. When I discovered ready-mades I thought to discourage aesthetics. In Neo-Dada they have taken my ready-mades and found aesthetic beauty in them. I threw the bottle-rack and the urinal into their faces as a challenge and now they admire them for their aesthetic beauty.[58]

Duchamp's words remind us that even "politicized" attempts to resist the aesthetic are subject to forces beyond the intention of the individual artist, forces that in this context we might catachretically name "history." In Duchamp's formulation, the bottle rack and the urinal represent "impure" forms of heterogeneity transformed historically into "imperative" ones in the service of, among other things, the increasing market value of, and demand for, what were once received as scandalous aberrations and only later

have become works of art (though Duchamp's narrative, with its valorization of the oppositional gesture of the individual artist, cautions us to interrogate such things as the production of scandal in the age of mechanically
reproduced art, and the relation of the market to the concept of the avant-
garde). Duchamp's complaint suggests, after Benjamin, that the effectivity of
the form of the work of art can be discussed only in relation to its *current*
place in the processes of production. In other words, the political effects of
the film have to be examined in concrete and locally specified situations,
and can't be deduced from a reading of the (phantom) text itself. Such an
examination would in turn require an attempt to totalize relations of production, even at a kind of "microcosmic" level. Because I have concentrated
my efforts here largely on questions of subjectivity and not economics or
politics, I have strategically left behind such a totalization, which requires a
more developed theory of ideology. I have tried here to begin to elaborate
some of what might be at stake in such an examination of the place of *Urinal* in the processes of production.

To this admittedly circumscribed project, I would only want to add the
following: To aestheticize politics would presumably mean, in this instance,
to deploy history monumentally and as an antiquarian, in such a way as to
activate the past for a "conservative" rather than "critical" use in the
present. My reading of the film has tended to privilege its critical tendencies
as overriding its monumental and antiquarian concerns. My position is not
one of relativism, if relativism means the critic is free to decide, for example,
whether the film politicizes aesthetics, aestheticizes politics, or enacts some
combination of the two (dialectically or otherwise). I am rather pointing
here to the limits of intelligibility, the difficulty of charting something like
the place of an artwork in its relations of production, given what Spivak
terms the heterogeneity and systematicity of the economic text, as well as
my own concerns, from Foucault, that even ideology critique is necessarily
structured by the constraints of the *dispositif*.[59]

If, at any point in this study, my position has seemed to be one of relativism, this appearance is perhaps a result of the model of power with which
I have been attempting to work. According to Funk & Wagnalls, one of the
meanings of *relative* is "intelligible only in relationship."[60] My argument
throughout has been that power, as the name given to a series of strategic
relations characterized by their reversibility, cannot be theorized universally,
acontextually, or ahistorically. Its lines of force are intelligible only in a specific posited relationship. The resistances to which it gives rise are produced
relative to power, and not "outside" of it. The difficulty of this theory of
power is its insistence that we think of power relations not as fixed but as
mobile and, as a result, as capable of a strategic reversibility that is not easy
to chart. Such an imagining of power is particularly at odds with a theory of

history that cannot take into account the way the spatiotemporal fluidity of power relations might be at odds with a historicism's attempt to represent such relations as fixed. Benjamin's analysis in "The Work of Art in the Age of Mechanical Reproduction" remains particularly compelling precisely because the essay attempts, in a specified historical moment, to chart the play of power and resistance (and I trust that some readers will have noted, in my account of Benjamin's essay, the traces of an almost Foucauldian discourse).[61]

V

Urinal climaxes with Frida Kahlo's report, which attempts to consider at some length the overall project of the film, at least as this project is reflected in the various artists' reports. Kahlo presents her report in Spanish. An English translation appears along the right side of the frame. Because this report is crucial to an understanding of the film, I quote it here in total:

So. . . . we've put our many differences aside and embraced these reforms, striking a balance between the rights of the individual and the rights of society. We pat ourselves on the back, the "gay" community says "well done" and we go back to 1937, smug as anything, right? I'm not sure. Our research commenced with the toilet, proceeded to the straight and gay men involved, and concluded with the police. But did this progression go far enough? Surely this is the right framework, our gaze coming to rest on the cops. But aren't the police and the courts simply part of a larger state apparatus, which since the 19th century and particularly since the war, is increasingly involved in the regulation of privacy, encroaching on more and more private space through myriad social agencies? Isn't it true that the state has accelerated its project of categorizing, organizing, and defining the realms of the public and private? Indeed, while advanced capitalism seems to encourage a "wealth" of individual responses to social organization, through consumerism, leisure activities, and the dissolution of the nuclear family unit, it is simultaneously in the best interests of the state to reorganize and buttress this plurality of responses, including sexual expression, into a semblance of "order." Thus, "private" life becomes increasingly the object of sophisticated surveillance systems through the state's social agencies, its census taking, its taxation procedures, its insurance programs. Isn't it true that washroom sex poses a greater threat precisely because it is a "public" anonymous activity, where only the crudest and most repressive means of surveillance can be utilized? The subtler means of state regulation no longer work—the heavy hand of law enforcement must be recruited to repair the social fabric. . . . Perhaps, my friends, we have failed, because though the solutions to the problem are important, they are only the first step in challenging the states [*sic*] regulation of our social and sexual realities. Washroom sex becomes not a metaphor, but a concrete example of the battle that lies before us: the battle to emancipate us all as sexual subjects. . . .

I agree with Kahlo's report on a number of points. I find compelling its description of the interplay of power and resistance, which suggests that although what it characterizes as advanced capitalism makes possible resistances to power in the form of "consumerism, leisure activities, and the dissolution of the nuclear family unit"—all of which might be linked historically to tearoom sexual activity—such resistances necessarily create counterresponses that attempt to reorganize and manage them. I would also agree with Kahlo that the solutions proposed by gay activists in *Urinal* to the problem of washroom sex—solutions, detailed in Wyle's report, such as posting signs forbidding loitering in rest rooms, locking rest rooms, using uniformed security guards to patrol problem sites, and issuing trespass notices to offending loiterers—seem ultimately to be reformist, and not to address the more compelling issues involved in the regulation of sexuality by the state. Finally, as I have argued throughout this study, I would want to second an understanding of wanton practices of sexual expenditure such as tearoom sex not as "metaphors" but as strategies of resistance to power, strategies that I want this study, perhaps like *Urinal*, to valorize.

But the difference between Kahlo's position and my own in this study is perhaps one of emphasis. Whereas Kahlo's report emphasizes the role of the state in subjection and subjugation, I have emphasized, after Foucault, the role of disciplines. Foucault clearly does not deny the force of state power. Rather, he takes issue with the attempt to cast all power relations as necessarily instituted by, and emanating from, the state, in a kind of top-down fashion. Foucault's position is that such a formulation fails to take into account power's productivity, its economy of force relations, and the ease with which it invests the subject. Foucault is interested in answering the question of why people appear to say yes to power, to say it willingly, and to say it often. According to Foucault, an account of power as merely repressive cannot answer this question without recourse to a theory of ideology as "false consciousness" that argues that subjects are duped into saying yes to power when it is in their best interests to say no. As I have already argued, Foucault explicitly rejects this conception of ideology, specifically as it animates an account of the relationship between intellectual production and subalternity. According to Foucault, such an account of ideology requires the intellectual or critic of ideology to act as a kind of soothsayer, revealing to "the masses" what their own limited intellectual production cannot. As Foucault suggests, it has been historically advantageous to intellectuals—in their best interests—to act in such a role, and to assist the state in a continued disqualification of "other" forms of knowledge. I have already suggested, through a reading of Spivak, some of the dangers of countering this historical role of the intellectual with the figure of a knowing, self-identical subaltern, but I have nonetheless retained from Foucault an insistence that a model of ideology as false consciousness dangerously reinscribes the sovereignty of the figure of the intellectual.

To return specifically to the questions of state power and *Urinal*, Foucault's position concerning state power is the reverse of what is commonly argued: rather than understanding state power as the source and model of all power relations, Foucault argues that state power must necessarily rely on the "economic" deployment of power made possible by the disciplines. It is, in fact, to the state's advantage to curb the wasteful expenditure required by brutal displays of power enacted in such practices as public execution, practices that always also run the risk of unleashing an unmanageable, perhaps "revolutionary," display and expenditure in return. Disciplines thus invest the subject with power in advance, as it were, of the state (though of course this temporal vocabulary is inadequate, since disciplines and the state work simultaneously on the subject). They do the work of state power economically, freeing up the state so that it does not have to resort to such costly, debilitating, and difficult-to-manage expenditures of power as public execution, mass arrests, the curbing of speech, and the restriction of movement through the imposition of curfews. In surveillance, disciplines move toward an increasingly economical deployment of force, securing the subject's cooperation largely through processes of normalization and the continued threat of exposure. As Foucault reminds us, the penultimately economical surveillance device does not even require any human expenditure, for the panopticon might operate effectively even without the actual physical presence of anyone occupying its center. The threat of detection alone is enough to maintain the subject in his or her subjection.

Urinal, however, attempts to explain why state power, in the form of police surveillance, has in fact increased. It begins from the premise that "state intervention is alive and well and on the rise," as Wyle's report puts it. *Urinal* thus locates its analysis not at the level of the disciplines but at the level of the state, and suggests that when, for reasons left largely unexplored by the film, the state perceives that former means of social regulation are no longer effective, it might have to rely on cruder and more repressive displays of power. According to *Urinal*, the state steps in with "the heavy hand of law enforcement" when "the subtler means of state regulation no longer work."

Is this the case? Have the forces of what *Urinal* calls advanced capitalism destabilized relations of power so that the state's subtler means no longer work? Unfortunately, such a question is not seriously taken up by the film. *Urinal* significantly lacks a theory of the advanced capitalism that it explicitly evokes. Kahlo's report in fact argues from assertion. It relies on the specter of the state as Big Brother, positing an accelerating historicist teleology linking nineteenth-century police practices to contemporary state regulation. It fails to take up at any length the multiple relation among disciplines, surveillance, and the state. It assumes perhaps too readily the model of power that Foucault's account of disciplinary society interrupts, and it abandons an exploration of subjectivity under the banner of the political. Finally, it fails to take into account the implications of its own analysis, which suggests that if one's gaze is to come to rest on the cops, one cannot concurrently insist that the power of surveillance belongs exclusively to the state.

One of the consequences of *Urinal*'s emphasis on state rather than disciplinary power necessitates that the film imagine tearoom sex not as a counterresponse to power, a response that resists modern practices of disciplinary subject formation, but as a practice that might "free" us *as* sexual subjects. The limits of the sexual, sexual liberation, and even subjectivity itself, limits detailed by Foucault in the first volume of *The History of Sexuality*, go largely unheeded. The conclusion of Kahlo's report begins to sound suspiciously like a liberationist discourse, promising that individual acts of resistance in the register of the sexual will somehow battle the state's increasing surveillance activities. But by focusing power largely in the state, the film thus undercuts the very possibility of the resistance that it calls forth, for it is difficult to imagine how "singular" acts "outside" of power such as those occurring in public washrooms (this is the film's formulation of the problem) will adequately redress the state's increasing deployment of surveillance tactics. How can one engage in a battle when one has no power? Such an account obviously fails to consider how the realm of the sexual is itself not "outside" of power, but, as Foucault argues, appears "as an especially dense transfer point for relations of power."[62] Finally, the casting of tearoom sex as a battleground for the emancipation of sexual subjects also displaces the Foucauldian theme of transgression in favor of the theme of revolution.

My reluctance to address questions of politics here makes it difficult to take up the problematic of revolution. However, I would want to insist—again, strategically—that we maintain some kind of distinction between revolutionary and sexual acts. In other words, from my current disciplinary vantage point, I want to argue against statements that fucking someone is a revolutionary act. My current positioning as a scholar working within the fields of English and film studies makes it difficult for me to chart the relation between individual acts—academic or sexual—and what we might broadly designate as the political. This suggestion is not a denial of a relationship between, say, ideology and intellectual or sexual production. It is rather an insistence that such a relationship exists, although an exploration of the relationship is not within the purview of this kind of study. It is also a tactical assertion that the forms of power that subjugate and subject should not be equated with all other forms of power, and that such an equating is perhaps politically disabling.

Perhaps the reason the end of *Urinal* seems so disappointing is that the film undercuts, at the level of subjectivity, the possibility of the very resistance it seems to demand. Near the end of the film, the artists, minus Gray, are once again gathered in the garden of Wyle and Loring's home. Their "mission" is complete, but they are having some difficulty understanding why they have been called here. Wyle expresses her wish that she had never allowed Gray into their home. Dorian's disembodied voice interrupts the sculptor's lamentations: "But you mustn't be so depressed. You haven't failed. Perhaps you were expecting the sort of success that appears in newspaper headlines: Parliament Repeals Antigay Laws, Sweeping Police Reforms Instituted, Discrimination against Homosexuals Is Outlawed. That's not what this is about." Yet Kahlo's report, with its emphasis on power as primarily repressive and the state as Big Brother, and its call to engage in a battle with the state to emancipate ourselves as sexual subjects, suggests in fact that this *is* what the film is about. No wonder the artists are depressed.

Despite its invocation of a model of power that limits the possibilities of resistance, *Urinal* does suggest how the theme of nonproductive expenditure might be deployed towards critical historical ends. Much of the film seems to celebrate the pleasures of wanton expenditure, not only on the level of its polemic in favor of tearoom sex, but through its heavy deployment of spectacle, excess, and even pornography, as well as its calling forth of a variety of affective responses in the spectator. The ridiculously disguised tearoom queens; the continued and playful manipulation of the image; the campy use of G.I.-Joe-type dolls to illustrate tearoom sex activities; the exhaustive history of waste disposal and wiping; the "pornographic" image of a man fellating a crucifix; Yukio Mishima, clothed in a loincloth, pulling himself down on top of a half-clothed Langston Hughes; Frida Kahlo putting the make on Florence Wyle in the upstairs washroom—these tropes and figures seem to demand a myriad of responses, including laughter, disgust, arousal, pleasure, and fear, as well as intellectual contemplation. The choice of these artists for this "mission" seems especially significant. Mishima's fantasies of the torture of Saint Sebastian and his interests in imperial Japan, the samurai tradition, and ritual suicide; "Sir Gay" Eisenstein, the alleged pornographer who supposedly parodied and sexualized the crucifixion in a cartoon; Frida Kahlo, with her "promiscuous" bisexuality—all of these figures seem appropriate poster children for the crusade to encourage nonproductive expenditure. The film perhaps contrasts these figures with Langston Hughes, Florence Wyle, and Frances Loring, who, while chiefly pursuing what might be described as "vanilla" sex during their lifetime, discover, in the course of their mission, an opportunity for new and formerly unanticipated forms of pleasure. Perhaps the next time these artists gather, they will be joined by the likes of Genet, James Baldwin, Kenneth Anger, Audre Lorde, Bataille himself, Divine, Mink Stole, and even the timid Virginia Woolf. In its wanton and "irresponsible" deployment of the refuse of the past, *Urinal* suggests how history might provide the material for a critical resistance to subject formation, suggesting a number of counterstrategies that might greet and respond to disciplinary power. Breaking up and dissolving the past in its willed refusal to treat either the artists it represents, or even its own materiality, as noble, stable, or worthy of preservation in some pristine state, this critical history of the Other demands that history make itself useful for life.

Notes

Foreword

1. For representative accounts of Foucault's "cryptonormativism," see Peter Dews, *Logics of Disintegration: Post-Structuralist Thought and the Claims of Critical Theory* (London: Verso, 1987); Jürgen Habermas, *The Philosophical Discourse of Modernity: Twelve Lectures*, trans. Frederick Lawrence (Oxford: Polity Press, 1987); Nancy Fraser, "Foucault in Modern Power: Empirical Insights and Normative Confusions," *Praxis International* 1 (1981): 272-87. The term performative contradiction refers to Foucault's tacit dependence on such Enlightenment ideals as liberty and social justice in order to reject these same ideals as cognate with disciplinary normalization.

2. Michel Foucault, "Theatricum Philosophicum," in *Language, Counter-Memory, Practice: Selected Essays and Interviews*, ed. Donald F. Bouchard (Ithaca, N.Y.: Cornell University Press, 1977), 168.

3. For a compelling analysis of these statements insofar as they inform Foucault's genealogy of ethics, see Gayatri Chakrovorty Spivak's "More on Power/Knowledge," in *Rethinking Power*, ed. Thomas E. Wartenberg (Albany: State University of New York Press, 1992), 149-73.

4. Jonathan Dollimore, *Sexual Dissidence: Augustine to Wilde, Freud to Foucault* (Oxford: Clarendon Press, 1991), 225.

5. Ibid., *Sexual Dissidence*, 86.

6. Ideology thus becomes the second term ("antiproductive expenditure" was the first) supplementing the ethics of marginality. "Ideology," Champagne explains, "thus interrupts the ethical, flagging the ways in which the economic text might complicate our understanding of ethics in ways we cannot adequately know, given our placement in this text, as well as the limits of that textual mapping we name the economic. In other words, in pointing toward the economic, I am not reverting to a mechanistic account of causality that understands the material as the base that produces all superstructural phenomena, but am instead using the term *ideology* to hold the place specifically of the effects of the economic, with the understanding that even such a limited account of causality must insist on the economic itself as a mapping, an attempt to name inadequately a series of forces that, given the limits of knowledge, can never be adequately named or known."

7. Paul A. Bové, *Intellectuals in Power: A Genealogy of Critical Humanism* (New York: Columbia University Press, 1986), 306.

8. In *The Infinite Conversation* Maurice Blanchot provides a usefully succinct account of a notion of transgression compatible with Foucault's: "Transgression is not an act of which the force and the mastery of certain men, under certain conditions, would still be capable. Transgression designates what is radically out of reach: assailment of the inaccessible, a surpassing of what cannot be surpassed. It opens to man when power ceases to be man's ultimate dimension." Translated by Susan Hanson (Minneapolis: University of Minnesota Press, 1993), 453 n. 3.

Introduction

1. Michel Foucault, "The End of the Monarchy of Sex," in *Foucault Live*, ed. Sylvère Lotringer (New York: Semiotext[e], 1989), 153.

2. James P. Pinkerton, "Gays on the Right: Proposing a Marriage between Unlikely Allies," *Pittsburgh Post Gazette*, 14 June 1993.

3. Interestingly, in light of my discussion that follows, Pinkerton places gays and lesbians not "outside" the legal system, but in a "fugitive" position inside. The Other is thus not posited in a place of absolute alterity, but is rather contained *within* the dominant.

4. Barry Goldwater, *Pittsburgh Post Gazette*, 15 June 1993.

5. For an extended discussion of poststructuralism and the Other, see Robert Young, *White Mythologies* (London: Routledge, 1990).

6. See Gayatri Spivak, "Unmaking and Making in *To the Lighthouse*," in *In Other Worlds* (New York: Routledge, 1988), p. 40. See also Jacques Derrida, "The Supplement of the Copula," trans. James Creech and Josue Harari, *Georgia Review* 30 (Fall 1976): 527-64.

7. We might contrast here Bataille's vocabulary with the one offered by Pinkerton et al., which stresses (re)productivity, conservation, prudence, and use.

8. The outcome of such resistance is often, however, different from what one imagines it will be; thus there is need for a practice of a tactical and strategic criticism that works also to disclose the limits of transgression.

9. For a discussion of ethics and leftist cultural studies, see Jennifer Daryl Slack and Laurie Anne Whitt, "Ethics and Cultural Studies," in *Cultural Studies*, ed. Lawrence Grossberg, Cary Nelson, and Paula A. Treichler (New York: Routledge, 1992), 571-92.

10. E. D. Hirsch, "Three Dimensions of Hermeneutics," in *The Aims of Interpretation* (Chicago: University of Chicago Press, 1976), 90-91 (emphasis in original); cited in Barbara Herrnstein Smith, *On the Margins of Discourse* (Chicago: University of Chicago Press, 1978), 133-34.

11. Such a naming is necessarily inadequate because it (impossibly) suggests the possibilities of a non-figurative use of language. For an introduction to this use of the term rhetoric, see Paul de Man, "Semiology and Rhetoric," in *Textual Strategies*, ed. Josue V. Harari (Ithaca, N.Y.: Cornell University Press, 1984), 121-40.

12. My argument here obliquely indicates some of Foucault's hesitations concerning Lacanian theory. Foucault's analytics of power proposed in the first volume of *The History of Sexuality* specifically works to free itself from a "juridico-discursive" model that in psychoanalytic discourse "governs both the thematics of repression and the theory of the law as constitutive of desire" (Foucault, *The History of Sexuality*, vol. 1, *An Introduction*, trans. Robert Hurley [New York: Vintage Books, 1990], 82). According to Foucault, such an account of power must seriously question the assertions from psychoanalysis that "the law is what constitutes both desire and the lack on which it is predicated" and that "where there is desire, the power relation is already present" (81). Perhaps it is not too farfetched to extrapolate that Foucault's ana-

lytics of power necessarily refuses the psychoanalytic positing of the subject as "lack" in relation to language.

13. Clearly, I am not proposing here that "using" a text and "using" a person involve the same sorts of ethical questions. I am, rather, attempting to respond to Hirsch's use of the term *ethics*, which suggests the analogy between using a person and using a text.

14. Raziel Abelson, "Ethics, History of," in *The Encyclopedia of Philosophy*, ed. Paul Edwards (New York: The Macmillan Company and the Free Press, 1967), 3:81-82.

15. For a discussion of this use of the term *ethics*, see Foucault, "The Ethic of Care for the Self as a Practice of Freedom," in *The Final Foucault*, ed. James Bernauer and David Rasmussen (Cambridge: MIT Press, 1988), 1-20. See also Thomas R. Flynn, "Truth and Subjectivation in the Later Foucault," *Journal of Philosophy* 82 (October 1985): 531-40; Barry Smart, "On the Subjects of Sexuality, Ethics, and Politics in the Work of Foucault," *boundary 2* 18, no. 1 (Spring 1991): 201-25; and Paul Veyne, "The Final Foucault and His Ethics," trans. Catherine Porter and Arnold I. Davidson, *Critical Inquiry* 20 (Autumn 1993): 1-9.

16. Foucault, "The Ethic of Care for the Self," 11.

17. Ibid., 6.

18. Michel Foucault, *The History of Sexuality*, vol. 2, *The Use of Pleasure*, trans. Robert Hurley (New York: Pantheon Books, 1985), 251.

19. In calling this method "deconstructive," I am deploying the term in perhaps a somewhat unorthodox way, borrowing from Gayatri Spivak's reading of Derrida. Spivak suggests that "the greatest gift of deconstruction" is "to question the authority of the investigating subject without paralyzing him, persistently transforming conditions of impossibility into possibility" (Spivak, "Subaltern Studies: Deconstructing Historiography," in *In Other Worlds* [New York: Routledge, 1988], 201). This reading of deconstruction is preceded in Spivak's text by a citation of Derrida from *Of Grammatology*: "Operating necessarily from the inside, borrowing all the strategic and economic resources of subversion from the old structure, borrowing them structurally, that is to say without being able to isolate their elements and atoms, the enterprise of deconstruction always in a certain way falls prey to its own work" (*Of Grammatology*, trans. Gayatri Spivak [Baltimore: The Johns Hopkins University Press, 1976], 24). I find a number of things appealing in these definitions of deconstruction that lead me to attach this label to my own critical practice here. First, they respond to the persistent question of what makes the close readings I will undertake in this study *that* different from the ones I critique with the admittedly impatient reply that they cannot possibly *be that* different. What that (small) difference might be is perhaps for my reader to determine. I use the term *deconstruction* here to indicate a practice of close reading that works to disclose some of the limits of close reading. Such a strategy of reading seeks to respond to what I find to be the increasingly annoying tendency in textual studies to produce close readings as if no argument concerning their viability had ever been produced. I am thus not calling here for an end to close readings. Rather, I am attempting to forge a critical practice that offers up a different kind of close reading. Although I am increasingly disturbed by the demands for theoretical purity that require that I go to such lengths to justify my deployment of a single word—I have considered at some length simply deleting the word *deconstruction* from this text in its entirety so that I would not have to construct such a tortuous footnote—I realize that the protocols of academic writing require that I provide some kind of preliminary definition of this term. It is one of the ironies of the present situation that I have to go to such great lengths to define a practice that the pages of *PMLA* have recently proclaimed is dead. Another irony is, of course, the necessity of attempting to fix the meaning of a term that has historically been used precisely to draw attention to the hazards of such a fixing.

20. Michel Foucault, "The Discourse on Language," in *The Archaeology of Knowledge and the Discourse on Language*, trans. A. M. Sheridan Smith (New York: Pantheon Books, 1982), 215-37.

21. I should probably note at the outset of this study that I will not be using the term *discourse* in the exact sense described by Foucault. For example, I have no particular use for the distinction between the discursive and the nondiscursive, nor would I want to differentiate between what Dreyfus and Rabinow call "serious" and "everyday" speech acts (Hubert L. Dreyfus and Paul Rabinow, *Michel Foucault: Beyond Structuralism and Hermeneutics* [Chicago: University of Chicago Press, 1983], 44-52). My assumption is that, for example, rules for the formation of true and false statements operate everywhere, and, additionally, that discourse is woven through "the world" in such a way as to make the concept of the nondiscursive untenable. The allegedly nondiscursive—institutions, for example—also produce subject positions that must be filled, and from which certain kinds of statements can be uttered as intelligible. I use *discourse* rather than *language* to designate the broader but still specified contexts in which any given statement—"linguistic" or otherwise—*can* make sense, can be rendered as intelligible. My assumption is there can be no intelligible place "outside" of these contexts. *Textuality*—a term I will define in a bit of detail in the next chapter—describes perhaps the more general conditions in and through which discourse circulates. Perhaps of significance here is my lack of particular interest in this study in considering at any length an "earlier" Foucault—the "author" of those texts written before *Discipline and Punish* in particular.

22. Pertinent here is Foucault's characterization of his own penchant to "break loose" (*se déprendre*) from himself as "the ethic of the intellectual. " See Foucault's interview with François Ewald, "Le souci de la vérité," *Magazine Littéraire* 207 (May 1984): 22. Cited in Flynn, "Truth and Subjectivation," 532.

23. Foucault, "The Ethic of Care for the Self," 6.

24. Both Foucault and Spivak offer examples of how critics might strategically intervene in this facile tendency to equate intellectual work and politics. In an interview entitled "The Question of Power," Foucault questions the naming of something one does in one's head in an office as political. He argues that "political action belongs to a category of participation completely different from those written or bookish acts of participation. It is a problem of groups, of personal and physical commitment" ("The Question of Power" [191] and "What Calls for Punishment" [282], both in *Foucault Live*, ed. Lotringer). Similarly, Spivak argues that literary criticism is a relatively trivial discipline when compared to questions of global politics. As she insists, "To think that [literary criticism] is an allegory of any kind of direct political action, I think it's the way most people who are in trivial positions like to imagine that they're in control" ("The New Historicism," in *The Post-Colonial Critic*, ed. Sarah Harasym [New York: Routledge, 1990], 162-63).

25. As Marx and Engels have argued, "*The occupation assumes an independent existence owing to division of labour.* Everyone believes his craft to be the true one. Illusions regarding the connection between craft and reality are the more likely to be cherished by them because of the very nature of the craft" (Karl Marx and Friedrich Engels, *Collected Works* [New York: International Publishers, 1976], 5:92; cited in Spivak, "Explanation and Culture: Marginalia," in *In Other Worlds*, 285 n. 20; emphasis in original).

26. bell hooks, "Marginality as Site of Resistance," in *Out There: Marginalization and Contemporary Cultures*, ed. Russell Ferguson, Martha Gever, Trinh T. Minh-ha, and Cornel West (New York: The New Museum of Contemporary Art, and Cambridge: MIT Press, 1990), 342. In this same essay, hooks quotes a passage from an earlier work in which she emphasizes the need of culturally marginalized people to strengthen "their sense of self" (see 341 in particular).

27. *The Oxford Dictionary of English Etymology* reminds us that *vigilant* comes from the Latin *vigilare* ("to keep awake or alert") and is related to *vigere* (to be vigorous or lively). *Scrupulous*, on the other hand, comes from the Latin *scrupus* (rough or sharp stone). These two words, with their emphasis, in the first instance, on the necessity of inhabiting and working within disciplinary structures of visibility, and, in the second, on the need to be attentive to that small, nagging, and painful reminder of the limits and perils of visibility, describe a tactical critical practice that works to disclose the limits of the critic as knowing subject without disavowing his or her agency (*The Oxford Dictionary of English Etymology*, ed. C. T. Onions [New York: Oxford University Press, 1966], 980, 802).

28. Paul Bové, *In the Wake of Theory* (Hanover, N.H.: University Press of New England, 1992), 78.

29. Melvin Dresher, *Games of Strategy* (Englewood Cliffs, N.J.: Prentice-Hall, Inc., 1961), 1.

30. Edward N. Luttwak, "The Impact of Vietnam on Strategic Thinking in the United States," in *Vietnam: Four American Perspectives*, ed. Patrick J. Hearden (West Lafayette, Ind.: Purdue University Press, 1990), 67.

31. Young, *White Mythologies*, 2.

32. These all-too-familiar attacks on poststructuralism range from the increasingly strident diatribes "against theory" published in books and academic journals to the frequent negative references made to poststructuralism and deconstruction—usually defined in the most superficial of terms—in the pages of the book review section of the *New York Times*.

33. Bové, *In the Wake of Theory*, 49.

34. Ibid., 66.

35. Teresa de Lauretis, "The Technology of Gender," *Technologies of Gender* (Bloomington: Indiana University Press, 1987), 3.

36. I am thus, for example, taking issue throughout this study with R. Radhakrishnan's contention that Foucault's refusal to posit a resistance "outside" the dominant is a "shortcoming" or "blindspot" (Radhakrishnan's words) in Foucault's work. In arguing his position, Radhakrishnan writes, "Contemporary theorists of subjugated subject positions . . . have contested the necessity to conceive of their positions as 'lacks' or 'absences' within the dominant structure. Why not 'think' these spaces as separate and disjunctive from the official body and therefore capable of engendering their own theories? The choice to locate these insurrectionary spaces within the hegemonic totality forecloses possibilities of 'separatist' and 'alternative' historiographies that may have nothing to do with the lacks and insufficiencies of the hegemonic model. Besides, this way of looking at these events exclusively as 'insurrections' foists on them an eternally 'transgressive' and 'reactive' identity that is forced to feed parasitically on what it should effectively forget and 'prehistoricize' " (R. Radhakrishnan, "Toward an Effective Intellectual: Foucault or Gramsci?" in *Intellectuals: Aesthetics, Politics, Academics*, ed. Bruce Robbins [Minneapolis: University of Minnesota Press, 1990], 64). De Lauretis's work is an instance of the kind of theorization of "subjugated subject positions" described by Radhakrishnan here, and is presumably a project he would laud. I would agree with Radhakrishnan that Foucault's project does not allow such wishful thinking. I, however, see this as one of the strengths of his position. It would take me too far afield of my subject to argue in detail why Foucault specifically rejects these possibilities described by Radhakrishnan, but I would remind the reader that Foucault's account of power and resistance specifically prohibits the positing of a resistance "separate and disjuncted" from power. I will have more to say about this in subsequent chapters, and will specifically take up briefly Foucault's account of "transgression." Finally, I would also note that Spivak has taught us to be suspicious of anything that claims to have "nothing to do" with what it opposes. (Reading Radhakrishnan here, one can't help recalling the commonplace charge made by its earliest critics that deconstructive criticism is "merely parasitical," nor Derrida's warning, already cited above, that deconstruction always

necessarily falls prey to its own work.) Perhaps, then, it is a certain "deconstructive" Foucault that Radhakrishnan opposes here, the Foucault "after" *Madness and Civilization* in particular. It is perhaps ironic that later in his essay Radhakrishnan critiques Foucault for positing a "subjugated knowledge" that claims to be "separate and disjuncted from the official body." Specifically, in critiquing Foucault's account of subaltern insurrection in the interchange with Deleuze published in English as "Intellectuals and Power," Radhakrishnan argues that Foucault romanticizes the position of the subaltern. As Radhakrishnan suggests, in this interchange, "the masses have been reified as a pure form of alterity" (73). Radhakrishnan appears to be suggesting here, as I will suggest in the next chapter, that in this interchange with Deleuze, Foucault is perhaps not being Foucauldian enough.

37. De Lauretis argues that gender is part of ideology: as ideology constitutes concrete individuals as subjects, gender constitutes concrete individuals as men and women.

38. De Lauretis, "The Technology of Gender," 26.

39. Tania Modleski, "Feminism and the Power of Interpretation: Some Critical Readings," in *Feminist Studies / Critical Studies*, ed. Teresa de Lauretis (Bloomington: Indiana University Press, 1986), 132; emphasis in original; cited in de Lauretis, "The Technology of Gender," 23.

40. De Lauretis, "The Technology of Gender," 9.

41. I will have more to say about this kind of "historicization" in chapter 3.

42. De Lauretis, "The Technology of Gender," 21. Of course, we might wonder what precisely constitutes the feminist project "per se."

43. I characterize Spivak in this way in order to emphasize her unwillingness to inhabit comfortably a recognizable position as a critic, emblematized in her casting herself as a Marxist-feminist-deconstructionist, as well as her insistence that she is a Europeanist by training and not a "third world" scholar. I have to admit, however, that I was surprised by a number of initial readings of this project that took it to task for its apparent lack of careful critical interest in feminism—as if Spivak's work could not be considered "feminist" except when it explicitly invoked the subject of gender.

44. Tony Bennett, *Outside Literature* (London: Routledge, 1990). I thank Matthew Tinkcom for bringing these ideas of Bennett's to my attention.

1. The Subject and/in Ideology

1. Benedict de Spinoza, *The Ethics* (New York: Hafner, 1966), 133.

2. That woman was largely absent from this narrative is shown by the emergence of at least two feminist projects out of this history: one, a perhaps "phallic" feminism characterized by its desire to extend to woman the sovereignty previously granted only to men; the other, a feminism that would seek to undermine the sovereignty of the male subject. For the sake of polemic, one might characterize, say, such diverse figures as bell hooks, Sandra Gilbert, and Susan Griffin as engaging in the former, and Jane Gallop, Gayatri Spivak, and Luce Irigaray as working towards the latter, though such a polemic necessarily obscures the significant differences between these various theoretical projects. See, for example, bell hooks, *Feminist Theory from Margin to Center* (Boston: South End Press, 1984); Sandra Gilbert, *No Man's Land: The Place of the Woman Writer in the Twentieth Century* (New Haven: Yale University Press, 1988); Susan Griffin, *Woman and Nature: The Roaring inside Her* (New York: Harper and Row, 1978); Jane Gallop, *Reading Lacan* (Ithaca, N.Y.: Cornell University Press, 1985); Gayatri Spivak, *In Other Worlds: Essays in Cultural Politics* (New York: Routledge, 1988); and Luce Irigaray, *This Sex Which Is Not One* (Ithaca, N.Y.: Cornell University Press, 1985).

3. This account of the psychoanalytic critique of the subject is drawn from a number of sources, including Jacqueline Rose's *Sexuality in the Field of Vision* (London: Verso, 1986).

4. Unfortunately, it is often treated by its practitioners, at least in the disciplines of English and film studies, as a kind of master discourse capable of reading and accounting adequately

for all other texts of culture. One of the problematic consequences of such a deployment of psychoanalysis is that it necessarily positions the psychoanalytic critic as the (sovereign) analyst diagnosing the ills of the patient text or its author. Theorists such as Jane Gallop have argued that an attentiveness to the psychoanalytic critique of the subject requires that the psychoanalytic critics' presumptions to knowledge be undone through what Gallop characterizes as "an analysis of the effects of transference in reading," accomplished through a certain critical willingness to inhabit the role of "patient" in relation to the text as analyst (Gallop, *Reading Lacan*, 29–30). Other psychoanalytic critics, however, persist in their belief that psychoanalysis "is the site of a 'knowledge of meaning' " (ibid., 29), granting to both psychoanalysis and their own critical practice a kind of supraphallic mastery that denies the effects of the massive transference onto psychoanalysis that psychoanalytic criticism requires of the psychoanalytic critic. Such a denial threatens to shore up the illusory power of the critic to know, so that the psychoanalytic critique of the subject seems to apply to everyone but the critic as analyst. Symptomatic of this tendency is Kaja Silverman's recent *Male Subjectivity at the Margins* (New York: Routledge, 1992), which attempts to psychoanalyze a number of works of film and literature, as well as their authors. For example, here is Silverman's analysis of T. E. Lawrence, accomplished through a reading of his autobiography: "Lawrence's sexuality—or, to be more precise, his homosexuality—is enormously complex. Blocked at the site of the genitals, it finds expression primarily through the narrowing down of narcissistic object-choice to erotically resonant identification, and through a masochism which is initially 'reflexive,' and later 'feminine.' For most of *Seven Pillars* . . . Lawrence's masochistic homosexuality assumes forms which are surprisingly compatible with the delusions of leadership, and which underwrite rather than challenge his virility. The flagellation and implicit homosexual rape recounted in Chapter 80 of that text, however, effects the radical desublimation of Lawrence's homosexuality, and reconfigures his masochism, thereby calling into radical question his ambition to lead" (Silverman, *Male Subjectivity at the Margins*, 300). Such a psychoanalysis of Lawrence (one for which the "patient" need not be present) seems to replicate the very kind of application of psychoanalysis to literature against which Gallop warns, one in which the critic escapes what Gallop characterizes as the "terror" of nonmastery represented by the position of patient in relation to the text under consideration by "importing psychoanalytic 'wisdom' into the reading dialectic so as to protect herself from what psychoanalysis is really about, the unconscious, as well as from what literature is really about, the letter" (Gallop, *Reading Lacan*, 30). Given the recent (and not so recent) interventions of such figures as Gallop, Luce Irigaray, and Hélène Cixous, it is difficult to sustain the kind of spectacular faith in the psychoanalytic enterprise required of its readers by Silverman's text. See Gallop, *Reading Lacan*, 29–30; Silverman, *Male Subjectivity at the Margins*, 300; Irigaray, *This Sex Which Is Not One*; and Hélène Cixous, "The Laugh of the Medusa," in *Critical Theory since 1965*, ed. Hazard Adams and Leroy Searle (Tallahassee: University Presses of Florida, 1986), 309–20. In critiquing Silverman's position here, I realize that I am treating Lawrence's autobiography as literature, and Silverman's analysis as literary criticism. In so doing, I am following the example of Silverman herself, who reads, for example, the metaphors at work in Lawrence's text (see, for example, Silverman, *Male Subjectivity at the Margins*, 315).

5. Karl Marx, preface to *A Contribution to the Critique of Political Economy*, excerpted in Karl Marx and Friedrich Engels, *Basic Writings on Politics and Philosophy*, ed. Lewis S. Feuer (New York: Anchor Books, 1959), 44.

6. Louis Althusser, "Ideology and Ideological State Apparatuses (Notes towards an Investigation)," in *Lenin and Philosophy*, trans. Ben Brewster (New York: Monthly Review Press, 1971), 154.

7. Ibid., 148. Although Althusser goes to some lengths to differentiate these two apparatuses, the former encompassing such organizations as the military and the judicial system, the

latter including, for example, the press and schools, what is important for my purposes here is the recognition that both Repressive and Ideological State Apparatuses function through the exercise of state power. I will take this fact up at some length later in this chapter.

8. Ibid., 164-65.

9. Gayatri Spivak has offered this warning in a slightly different vocabulary: "the desire to explain might be a symptom of the desire to have a self that can control knowledge and a world that can be known"; thus, "to give oneself the right to a correct self-analysis and thus to avoid all thought of symptomaticity" Spivak characterizes as "foolish" (Gayatri Spivak, "Explanation and Culture: Marginalia," in *In Other Worlds: Essays in Cultural Politics* [New York: Routledge, 1988], 104).

10. See, for example, Spivak, "Reading the World: Literary Studies in the 1980s," in *Writing and Reading Differently*, ed. Douglas Atkins and Michael L. Johnson (Lawrence: University Press of Kansas, 1985), 33.

11. Although Foucault is not named explicitly in Jonathan Dollimore's *Sexual Dissidence*, he is surely implicated in Dollimore's casting of the current intellectual climate as one "in which, more generally, the basis of agency and praxis have been so effectively dismantled; in which desire itself has been powerfully 'rewritten' as the effect of domination rather than a source of resistance to it" (Dollimore, *Sexual Dissidence* [Oxford: Clarendon Press, 1991], 44).

12. Foucault, "The Archaeology of Knowledge," in *Foucault Live*, ed. Sylvère Lotringer (New York: Semiotext[e], 1989), 48. For Foucault, this subject acts as "origin and foundation of Knowledge (*savoir*), of Liberty, of Language and History" (Foucault, "The Birth of the World," in *Foucault Live*, ed. Lotringer, 61). According to Foucault, "This equation of subject-consciousness at the transcendental level is a characteristic of Western philosophy from Descartes to our own time" (Foucault, "An Historian of Culture," in *Foucault Live*, ed. Lotringer, 78; see also "The Ethic of Care for the Self as a Practice of Freedom," in *The Final Foucault*, ed. James Bernauer and David Rasmussen [Cambridge: MIT Press, 1988], 10).

13. Foucault, "The Birth of the World," 61. See also Foucault, "An Aesthetics of Existence," in *Foucault Live*, ed. Lotringer, 313. As Philip Turetzky argues, "For Foucault, the subject is no longer the being which constitutes the lifeworld, but rather is itself constituted and produced in the reciprocal relations of knowledge and power. The subject is an historical formation constituted by specific technologies of power" (Turetzky, "Immanent Critique," *Philosophy Today* 33 [Summer 1989]: 146).

14. For an extensive analysis of these processes, see Foucault, *Discipline and Punish*, trans. Alan Sheridan (New York: Vintage, 1979).

15. Michel Foucault, "The Subject and Power," in Hubert Dreyfus and Paul Rabinow, *Michel Foucault: Beyond Structuralism and Hermeneutics* (Chicago: University of Chicago Press, 1983), 212. As I will argue in a subsequent chapter, Foucault does not equate this form of power with either all power or power in general; rather, he differentiates between three forms of power, forms he associates with subjection, domination, and exploitation. See Dreyfus and Rabinow, *Michel Foucault*, 212-13.

16. Foucault, "Lecture Two," in *Power/Knowledge: Selected Interviews and Other Writings* (New York: Pantheon Books, 1980), 97.

17. Jeffrey Weeks, *Sex, Politics, and Society* (London: Longman, 1981), 8.

18. Foucault, "The Ethic of Care for the Self," 13.

19. Foucault, *The History of Sexuality*, vol. 1, *An Introduction*, trans. Robert Hurley (New York: Vintage Books, 1990), 101.

20. Those who accuse Foucault of political quietism include Edward Said, Marshall Berman, Peter Dews, Jürgen Habermas, and Nancy Fraser. Those who counter such a critique include Ed Cohen, Barry Smart, Robert Young, and Philip Turetzky. For a partial list of sources, see Said, *The World, the Text, the Critic* (Cambridge: Harvard University Press, 1983); Ber-

man, *All That Is Solid Melts into Air: The Experience of Modernity* (London: Verso, 1983); Dews, *Logics of Disintegration: Post-Structuralist Thought and the Claims of Critical Theory* (London: Verso, 1987); Habermas, *The Philosophical Discourse of Modernity: Twelve Lectures*, trans. Frederick Lawrence (Oxford: Polity Press, 1987); Fraser, "Foucault on Modern Power: Empirical Insights and Normative Confusions," *Praxis International* 1 (1981): 283; Cohen, "Foucauldian Necrologies: 'Gay' 'Politics'? Politically Gay," *Textual Practices* 2, no. 1 (Spring 1988): 87-101; Smart, "On the Subjects of Sexuality, Ethics, and Politics in the Work of Foucault," *boundary 2* 18, no. 1 (Spring 1991): 201-25; Young, *White Mythologies* (London: Routledge, 1990); and Turetzky, "Immanent Critique." I find Young's analysis particularly compelling. According to Young, Foucault is interested in "the tactical use of historical knowledge in contemporary political situations. . . . Such politics stress the local or the specific without assuming that they constitute the starting point for a global hegemony into which they will be subsumed. Foucault does not aim to produce 'a' politics any more than 'a' history. It is this factor which, perhaps above all, has enabled the critical use of Foucault's analyses of power in demarcated areas of analysis" (Young, *White Mythologies*, 87).

21. Foucault, "Truth and Power," in *Power/Knowledge*, 126.

22. Foucault, "The Concern for Truth," in *Foucault Live*, 305-6.

23. Foucault, "Truth and Power," 133.

24. Foucault, "The Ethic of Care for the Self," 10.

25. Ibid., 11.

26. Foucault, "An Aesthetics of Existence," in *Foucault Live*, 313.

27. Specifically, those feminisms that have sought to unsettle ahistorical and acultural notions of gender difference by insisting on the production of the female subject as a historically specific phenomenon. See, for example, Judith Butler, *Gender Trouble* (New York: Routledge, 1990); Judith Butler and Joan W. Scott, eds., *Feminists Theorize the Political* (New York: Routledge, 1992); and Teresa de Lauretis, *Technologies of Gender* (Bloomington: Indiana University Press, 1987).

28. David Greenberg, *The Construction of Homosexuality* (Chicago: University of Chicago Press, 1988), 489.

29. Edward Said, *The World, the Text, the Critic* (Cambridge: Harvard University Press, 1983), 243. Foucault's project is frequently read in this kind of "all or nothing" manner, as arguing for either an unconstrained subjectivity, or a subjectivity trapped in a totalizing power. These "all or nothing" readings are perhaps most symptomatic of the current intellectual climate, in which there is a renewed interest in some kind of "pure," totalizing theory that might account for everything. In his essay "On the Subjects of Sexuality, Ethics, and Politics in the Work of Foucault," Barry Smart presents an excellent summary of, and rejoinder to, a number of Foucault's critics. He is especially careful to argue against those who would read Foucault's account of power and the subject as rendering resistance impossible.

30. Gayatri Spivak, "Can the Subaltern Speak?" in *Marxism and the Interpretation of Culture*, ed. Cary Nelson and Lawrence Grossberg (Urbana: University of Illinois Press, 1988), 271-313.

31. Michel Foucault, "Intellectuals and Power," in *Language, Counter-Memory, Practice: Selected Interviews*, trans. Donald F. Bouchard and Sherry Simon (Ithaca, N.Y.: Cornell University Press, 1977), 207; emphasis in original.

32. Michel Foucault, "Lecture One," in *Power/Knowledge*, 82.

33. Foucault, "Truth and Power," 133.

34. Cornel West, "The New Cultural Politics of Difference," in *Out There: Marginalization and Contemporary Cultures*, ed. Russell Ferguson, Martha Gever, Trinh T. Minh-ha, and Cornel West (New York: The New Museum of Contemporary Art, and Cambridge, Mass.: MIT Press, 1990), 19-36.

35. Irigaray, *This Sex Which Is Not One*, 78.

36. For a discussion of organic intellectuals, see Gramsci, "The Intellectuals," in *Selections from the Prison Notebooks*, ed. Quintin Hoare and Geoffrey Nowell Smith (New York: International Publishers, 1971), 5-23. For a discussion of "common" sense, see, in the same volume, "The Study of Philosophy," 321-77.

37. This theme will be taken up at some length in chapter 3.

38. Foucault, "What Calls for Punishment?" in *Foucault Live*, ed. Lotringer, 282.

39. Gramsci, "The Intellectuals," 9.

40. Gramsci, "The Study of Philosophy," 334.

41. For a more extended attempt to bring together Foucault and Gramsci, see R. Radhakrishnan's "Toward an Effective Intellectual: Foucault or Gramsci?" in *Intellectuals: Aesthetics, Politics, Academics*, ed. Bruce Robbins (Minneapolis: University of Minnesota Press, 1990), 57-99. Radhakrishnan's project is siginificantly different from my own, as he explicitly attempts in this essay to theorize politics in a poststructuralist context (57). I would argue that Radhakrishnan significantly underreads Foucault, specifically around the question of power. The "or" in the title of his essay seems particularly telling, for, at least twice in his argument, Radhakrishnan associates positions exclusively with Gramsci that I would argue are in fact shared by the "late" Foucault in particular. Specifically, in opposing Gramsci's and Foucault's projects, Radhakrishnan argues that "the 'constituted' nature of 'man as node' does not preempt the possibility of man functioning as an agent in relatively and historically constituted freedom" (84). My assumption throughout this study is that Foucault's account of power and the subject leads to this very conclusion, a conclusion Radhakrishnan attributes to Gramsci alone. Similarly, Radhakrishnan's contention that "to be located within a relationship does not mean the same thing as being condemned to that complex of relationships in a spirit of passive acceptance" (85) is one shared by, and not opposed to, Foucault's account of the subject, power, and resistance. All of this said, there is nonetheless much that is compelling in Radhakrishnan's analysis of Gramsci, specifically around questions of class and the historical bloc (see especially 93-97).

42. Gramsci, "The Intellectuals," 12. Gramsci is actually writing here of "hegemony" rather than ideology, for reasons I will touch on later in this essay.

43. Unlike Donald Morton and Mas'ud Zavarzadeh, I do not reject the value of interventions by intellectuals in "local" struggles around such issues as child care or equal pay for equal work. Although such an intervention obviously cannot take the place of global struggles, I am suspicious of the (gendered) disciplinary privilege that allows male intellectuals to discredit "local" struggles for social justice while assuming that their own disciplinary sites of intervention must be the most efficacious ones from within which to conduct an interrogation of global politics. See Morton and Zavarzadeh, *Theory, (Post)Modernity, Opposition* (Washington, D.C.: Maisonneuve Press, 1991).

44. Foucault is quoted in Spivak, "Can the Subaltern Speak," 280.

45. Ibid.

46. Foucault, "Intellectuals and Power," 215. These are in fact the words of Deleuze.

47. This is an admittedly elliptical way of indicating the necessity of examining in particular the anti-intellectualism currently flourishing among certain "subaltern" groups, both on the edges of, and within, the academy. See, for example, Wayne Dynes, *Encyclopedia of Homosexuality* (New York: Garland, 1990); Camille Paglia, *Sexual Personae* (New Haven: Yale University Press, 1990); and Allan Bloom, *The Closing of the American Mind* (New York: Simon and Schuster, 1987).

48. See, for example, Foucault, "Friendship as a Way of Life," in *Foucault Live*, ed. Lotringer, 203-4. In an interview recorded on 10 July 1978 and published in the French magazine *Mec*, Foucault argues "against" desire. "I prefer 'pleasure' in order to avoid the medical and

'natural' connotations associated with 'desire.' 'Desire' has been and can get used strategically as a tool, a sign which is easily intelligible, a standard of 'normalcy' " (Jean Le Bitoux, "Michel Foucault, Le gai savoir," *Mec* 5 (June 1988): 32-36). I am greatly indebted to Gerard Koskovich for providing me with a copy of this interview and to Michael West for providing a translation.

49. Foucault, "How Much Does it Cost?" in *Foucault Live*, ed. Lotringer, 248.

50. Foucault, "Intellectuals and Power," 216.

51. For a more extensive discussion of this point, see my "Seven Speculations on Queers and Class," *The Journal of Homosexuality* 26, no. 1 (1993): 159-74.

52. Cindy Patton, "The AIDS Service Industry," in *Inventing AIDS* (New York: Routledge, 1990), p. 13.

53. Foucault, "Intellectuals and Power," 216.

54. Ibid. I realize that I run the risk of dehistoricizing Foucault here, who is obviously speaking from his historical context in general, and the events following the political uprisings of May 1968 in particular. But my goal here is neither to recover nor to dispute Foucault's theoretical project, but to use it—as problematic as this term might be—to think through the problem of the subject today.

55. Foucault, "The History of Sexuality," in *Power/Knowledge*, 188.

56. Foucault, "Truth and Power," 118.

57. See, for example, the Althusser of *For Marx*, trans. Ben Brewster (London: Allen Lane, The Penguin Press, 1969). Spivak has attributed the position that "a scientific politico-economic and socio-cultural explanation can be produced through a rigorous ideological critique" to Althusser (*In Other Worlds*, 111 and 284-85 n. 17). However, she also argues that Althusser "tinkers with the name of science itself, re-constellates it" in such a way as to refigure, over and over again, the opposition between ideology and science (ibid., 293-94 n. 5). Such a reading, however, does not deny that Althusser distinguishes between, or even opposes, the two terms.

58. V. N. Volosinov, for example, specifically invokes scientific knowledge as an object of a Marxist theory of ideologies, comparing it to literature, religion, and ethics. According to Volosinov, all ideological phenomena possess semiotic value (*Marxism and the Philosophy of Language*, trans. Ladislav Matejka and I. R. Titunik [Cambridge: Harvard University Press, 1986], 10-11). All semiotic material is necessarily ideological. Since what we call science is itself composed of semiotic material—in particular, language, "the ideological phenomenon par excellence" (13)—there can be no placing of science "outside" of ideology. As Volosinov argues, a word "can carry out ideological functions of any kind—scientific, aesthetic, ethical, religious" (14; see also 19).

59. Foucault, "Truth and Power," 118.

60. Althusser, "Ideology and Ideological State Apparatuses," 170. Ideology here seems to require a subject capable of articulating the whys and wherefores of his/her behavior. It thus seems to come close to replicating a notion of ideology as "false" consciousness, an "inaccurate" version of the real. Althusser's insistence on ideology as representing "the imaginary relationship of individuals to their real conditions of existence" (162) is perhaps significant here in that it suggests that a "scientific," nonideological discourse might be able to represent the real adequately. As I have suggested above, Foucault explicitly rejects the possibility of such a "scientific" discourse.

61. "What troubles me with these analyses which prioritise ideology is that there is always presupposed a human subject on the lines of the model provided by classical philosophy, endowed with a consciousness which power is then thought to seize on" (Foucault, "Body/Power," in *Power/Knowledge*, 58).

62. Foucault, "Truth and Power," 133. In another account of ideology, Althusser explicitly rejects referring the problem of ideology to consciousness, instead casting it as a problem of the

unconscious. My assumption here is that Foucault would find this equally problematic. An ahistorical notion of the unconscious does not necessarily contradict an understanding of the subject as transcendental. See Althusser, "Marxism and Humanism," in *For Marx*, 231-33.

63. Althusser, "Ideology and Ideological State Apparatuses," 171.

64. Volosinov, *Marxism and the Philosophy of Language*, 11.

65. Foucault, "Truth and Power," 118.

66. Volosinov, *Marxism and the Philosophy of Language*, 17. As Volosinov argues, "No cognitive value whatever adheres to the establishment of a connection between the basis and some isolated fact torn from the unity and integrity of its ideological context" (17-18).

67. Perhaps the reason is that, as he notes, "the name ideology is given both to the necessary superstructure of a particular structure and to the arbitrary elucubrations of particular individuals" (Gramsci, "The Study of Philosophy," 376).

68. Gramsci, "The Intellectuals," 12.

69. I realize that there is a complex relationship in Gramsci among civil society, the state, and hegemony. For a careful account of this relationship, as well as of the varying ways Gramsci uses the term *state*, see Anne Showstack Sassoon, *Gramsci's Politics* (New York: St. Martin's Press, 1980).

70. See Gramsci, "The Modern Prince," in *Selections from the Prison Notebooks*, ed. Hoare and Nowell Smith, 181-82, in which it is suggested that the hegemony of one social group over another is created when "previously germinated ideologies become 'party', come into confrontation and conflict, until only one of them, or at least a single combination of them, tends to prevail, to gain the upper hand, to propagate itself throughout society."

71. Gramsci, "The Study of Philosophy," 377.

72. Gramsci, "The Modern Prince," 161.

73. Gramsci, "Problems of Marxism," in *Selections from the Prison Notebooks*, ed. Hoare and Nowell Smith, 407.

74. The section of Gramsci's essay in which these words appear is in fact entitled "Economy and Ideology."

75. Robert Young, *White Mythologies* (London: Routledge, 1990), 57.

76. Althusser, *For Marx*, 113. Cited in Young, *White Mythologies*, 58.

77. Young, *White Mythologies*, 58.

78. Young is writing here of Althusser's interest in "the possibility of history as a 'process without a subject,' a history characterized by radical breaks and discontinuities, distinct from each other and not totalizing" (53).

79. Spivak, "The Post-modern Condition," in *The Post-Colonial Critic*, ed. Sarah Harasym (New York: Routledge, 1990), 23.

80. Spivak, "Criticism, Feminism, and the Institution," in *The Post-Colonial Critic*, ed. Harasym, 1.

81. Spivak, "The Post-Modern Condition," 25.

82. Said, *The World, the Text, the Critic*, 3.

83. Spivak, "Subaltern Studies: Deconstructing Historiography," in *In Other Worlds*, 204.

84. I am referring here to the curious passages in which Foucault suggests that institutions are nondiscursive (see, for example, "The Confession of the Flesh," in *Power/Knowledge*, 197-98). When his interviewers call into question this seemingly non-Foucauldian distinction between the discursive and the nondiscursive, Foucault uncharacteristically equates discursivity with language: "my problem isn't a linguistic one" (198). See also, in this context, "The Birth of the World," in *Foucault Live*, ed. Lotringer, 59, in which the nondiscursive is described as "political, social or economic practices."

85. In a subsequent chapter, I will have more to say about "knottings" vis-à-vis the problem of identity.

86. Althusser, "Ideology and Ideological State Apparatuses," 150.

87. Young similarly suggests that Foucault rejects Althusser's theory of ideology not simply because it employs a science / not science distinction, but also because "it produces the notion of ideology as a secondary mediation (Althusser's interpellation) in an inside/outside structure between the determinants of power and the individual subject"—as if the processes of interpellation describe the means whereby power seizes upon a subject "outside" its initial purview (Young, *White Mythologies*, 80). For Foucault, there is no subject prior to or outside of power.

88. Foucault, "Questions on Geography," in *Power/Knowledge*, 72.

89. Foucault, "Truth and Power," 122.

90. Immanuel Wallerstein, *Historical Capitalism* (London: Verso, 1983), 8.

91. Ibid., 48.

92. Ibid., 58; emphasis in original.

93. Wallerstein defines labor-socialist movements as those that focused on the conflicts between the wage worker and the owners of the economic structures in which they worked, and nationalist movements as those that focused on the conflicts between numerous "oppressed" peoples and the dominant peoples of a given political jurisdiction (*Historical Capitalism*, 67-68).

94. Ibid., 69.

95. Foucault, "Truth and Power," 122.

96. For an interesting account of Foucault's relationship to Marxism, see James A. Winders, "Foucault and Marx: A Critical Articulation of Two Theoretical Traditions," *New Orleans Review* 11 (Fall 1984): 134-48.

97. Compare, for example, Wallerstein's assertions that "truth as a cultural ideal has functioned as an opiate, perhaps the only serious opiate of the modern world" (*Historical Capitalism*, 81) and that "our collective education has taught us that the search for truth is a disinterested virtue when in fact it is a self-interested rationalization" (ibid., 82) with Foucault's insistence that "the history of the West cannot be disassociated from the way in which 'truth' is produced and inscribes its effects" and that "we live in a society which is marching to a great extent 'towards truth'—I mean a society which produces and circulates discourse which has truth as its function, passing itself off as such and thus obtaining specific powers. The establishment of 'true' discourses (which however are incessantly changing) is one of the fundamental problems of the West" (Foucault, "The End of the Monarchy of Sex," in *Foucault Live*, ed. Lotringer, 139).

98. Foucault, "The History of Sexuality," in *Power/Knowledge*, 193.

99. Wallerstein, *Historical Capitalism*, 84.

100. Ibid., 83.

101. I would immediately want to differentiate my use of *ideology* here from two other recent deployments of the term in texts that take up questions of (homo)sexuality, subjectivity, and resistance. In his essay "Homographesis," Lee Edelman calls for a critical practice that strives "to place the study of rhetoric and tropology at the center of a lesbian and gay criticism." Edelman identifies this "homographesis" as a "rhetorical analysis of the figurations of homosexual legibility" ("Homographesis," *The Yale Journal of Criticism* 3, no. 1 [1989]: 202). Edelman anticipates and counters the argument that such a placement "risks the charge of seeming to advocate or condone an apolitical formalism." Here, he attempts to deconstruct the binary "rhetorical/political": "It is, however, precisely the inescapable politics of any formalism, the insistence of ideology in any and every graphesis of gay sexuality, that the study of homographesis takes as its point of departure. To do otherwise, to remain enchanted by the phantom of a political engagement outside and above an engagement with issues of *rhetoric*, is to ignore the historical conceptualization of homosexuality in a distinctive relation to lan-

guage" (202; my emphasis). Edelman's restaging of this deconstruction of "the rhetorical" and "the political," however, obfuscates that *rhetoric* is what "homographesis" privileges. In other words, Edelman's analysis fails to consider some of the political effects of constructing the rhetorical *as* political. In deploying the false binary rhetorical/political, even to deconstruct it, Edelman seems to be equating what I have been calling textuality with rhetoric. The difference is that the term *rhetoric* tends to conflate textuality with the linguistic text, and thus makes possible the simpleminded accusation that deconstruction "reduces" everything to language. What is perhaps most significantly lost in this equation is, in this instance, the role of the economic in the political. Edelman's easy equating of textuality with rhetoric allows for a slippage whereby ideology—the term is deployed but never defined in Edelman's text—becomes a problem not of class inequity or conflict but of rhetoric. The "absent cause" of ideology appears to be some kind of apolitical, free-floating rhetoric—apolitical in that there is no material relationship between its production and the production of social labor. In the slippage from the textual to the rhetorical, what is lost is the economic text as a determinant. The advantage of a theory of textuality over Edelman's privileging of rhetoric is that such a theory allows for a place to be held for the economic while simultaneously complicating a mechanistic understanding of the causal relationship between economic base and ideological superstructure. A second example: In *Sexual Dissidence*, Jonathan Dollimore argues for an understanding of ideology as that which "fixes meaning, naturalizing or eternalizing its prevailing forms by putting them beyond question, and thereby also effacing the contradictions and conflicts of the social domain" (*Sexual Dissidence* [Oxford: Clarendon Press, 1991], 86). Dollimore rationalizes this admittedly "specific and limited" understanding of ideology, which figures ideology primarily as a problem of "false consciousness," with a footnote explaining that he deploys this understanding of ideology "in order to indicate that a materialist criticism is always finally *also* an ethical perspective" (emphasis in original). Thus, in Dollimore's formulation, an ethical commitment to a proposition magically renders that proposition nonideological. As Dollimore himself argues: "Thus the view that homosexuals are naturally inferior to heterosexuals is (in my sense) ideological; the view that homosexuals are equal with heterosexuals, and deserving of equal rights in law is not, resting rather on an openly admitted ethical commitment to equality (from which the practice of a materialist/political criticism arises)" (86). Leaving aside an interrogation of the limits of a liberal humanist discourse of rights, we would still find in Dollimore a move exactly opposite to the one I suggest throughout this study. For "ethics" in Dollimore can be understood as naming the realm in which, through the overcoming of "ideology" in the limited sense in which Dollimore defines it, "desire" and "interest" coincide: the subject outside of ideology "recognizes" that it is in his or her best interest to desire equality for all. In other words, Dollimore's text argues that "false consciousness" might be overcome in the "transgressive" subject so that his or her desire and interest will not be in conflict. This formulation requires the return of an undivided subject capable of knowing his interest adequately and of aligning his desires with that interest. This position, as Spivak insists, is opposite to what is argued in Marx, who resists the return of the undivided subject through an instance on interest as that which can never be adequately known. I would suggest, contrary to Dollimore, that ethics does not overcome ideology but rather that ideology names a way of mapping the economic that might interrupt the ethical's claims to be impartial, unbiased, and disinterested. In other words, I have wanted to retain the concept of ideology precisely because it might provide a way of thinking through the limits of an ethical criticism.

102. Althusser, "Ideology and Ideological State Apparatuses," 142-43.

103. Ibid., 144; emphasis in original.

104. Ibid., 144; emphasis in original.

105. For a brief gloss on some of the different ways in which Gramsci understands this distinction between civil society and the state, see the introduction, written by Hoare and No-

well Smith, to his notes collected under the title "State and Civil Society" in the *Selections from the Prison Notebooks*, 206-9. Though cautioning that Gramsci's account of civil society "is open to reformist interpretations, involving an under-estimate of the problem of the State in revolutionary strategy," Hoare and Nowell Smith concede that "Gramsci did not succeed in finding a single, wholly satisfactory conception of 'civil society' or the State" (207). Perhaps, following Spivak's lead in her attempt to rescue Althusser from readings that would ignore the way he continually refigures the opposition between ideology and science, we should say that Gramsci continually "reconstellates" his distinction between civil society and the state.

106. Althusser, "Ideology and Ideological State Apparatuses," 148.

107. Gramsci, "The Study of Philosophy," 333.

108. Althusser, "Ideology and Ideological State Apparatuses," 147.

109. Robert Paul Resch, *Althusser and the Renewal of Marxist Social Theory* (Berkeley and Los Angeles: University of California Press, 1992), 215.

110. Marcia Landy, "Cultural Politics and Common Sense," *Critical Studies* 3, no. 1 (1991): 110.

111. I will, however, approvingly cite Wallerstein's use of the term. What I value in Wallerstein's analysis is its insistence on the relationship between the economic and the ideological, its refusal to cast the state as the provenance of all power, and its hesitancy regarding claims of scientificity.

2. Gay Pornography and Nonproductive Expenditure

1. Georges Bataille, "The Notion of Expenditure," in *Visions of Excess: Selected Writings, 1927-1939*, ed. and trans. Alan Stoekl (Minneapolis: University of Minnesota Press, 1985), 116-29.

2. Ibid., 118; emphasis in original.

3. Bataille, "The Psychological Structure of Fascism," in *Visions of Excess*, 138.

4. Ibid.; emphasis in original.

5. Immanuel Wallerstein, "The Ideological Tensions of Capitalism: Universalism versus Racism and Sexism," in Etienne Balibar and Immanuel Wallerstein, *Race, Nation, Class: Ambiguous Identities* (London: Verso, 1991), 31.

6. Bataille, "The Psychological Structure of Fascism," 138; emphasis in original.

7. Ibid., 139.

8. According to Bataille, "Compared to everyday life, *heterogeneous* existence can be represented as something *other*, as *incommensurate*, by charging these words with the *positive* value they have in *affective* experience" ("The Psychological Structure of Fascism," 143; emphasis in original).

9. Ibid., 146.

10. Bataille, "The Notion of Expenditure," 129.

11. Ibid., 126.

12. Michel Foucault, *Discipline and Punish*, trans. Alan Sheridan (New York: Vintage Books, 1979), 218.

13. Foucault, "Preface to Transgression," in *Language, Counter-Memory, Practice*, ed. Donald F. Bouchard (Ithaca, N.Y.: Cornell University Press, 1977), 35.

14. According to Bataille, whereas "the theme of the Son of God's ignominious crucifixion . . . carries human dread to a representation of loss and limitless degradation" ("The Notion of Expenditure," 119), the sovereignty of the resurrected Christ "represents the most profound introjection of the structure characteristic of homogeneity into heterogeneous existence" ("The Psychological Structure of Fascism," 153).

15. See, in this regard, the work of Gayatri Spivak, such as *The Post-Colonial Critic*, ed. Sarah Harasym (New York: Routledge, 1990).

16. As Spivak has argued, "On the general level, the possibility of explanation carries the presupposition of an explainable (even if not fully) universe and an explaining (even if imperfectly) subject. These presuppositions assure our being. Explaining, we exclude the possibility of the *radically* heterogeneous" ("Explanation and Culture: Marginalia," in *In Other Worlds* [New York: Routledge, 1988], 105; emphasis in original). Thus, thinking through the radically heterogeneous is impossible. As I will be suggesting throughout this study, "impossible" is not equivalent to "not worthy of pursuing." It is rather a reminder of the limits of our own presumptions to know, an attempt to acknowledge the critique of the subject without abandoning critical agency.

17. Richard Dyer, "Coming to Terms," in *Out There: Marginalization and Contemporary Cultures*, ed. Russell Ferguson, Martha Gever, Trinh T. Minh-ha, and Cornel West (New York: New Museum of Contemporary Art, and Cambridge: MIT Press, 1990), 291.

18. Dyer goes to some length in this essay to differentiate an "intellectual" knowledge of the body from an "experiential" one. Although these binaries are obviously open to deconstruction, Dyer's aim here is to counter what he sees as the cultural delegitimation of an experiential knowledge of bodily sensation.

19. For a brief introduction to Dyer's understanding of such things as "resistance" and reading, see, in addition to "Coming to Terms," his "Resistance through Charisma: Rita Hayworth and Gilda," in *Women in Film Noir*, ed. E. Ann Kaplan (London: BFI Publishing, 1980), 91-99. See in particular page 93, on which Dyer argues that a film such as *Gilda* makes possible a number of mutually contradictory readings because it is situated within a "terrain of ideological struggle."

20. David Kaufer and Gary Waller, "To Write Is to Read Is to Write, Right?" in *Writing and Reading Differently*, ed. G. Douglas Atkins and Michael L. Johnson (Lawrence: University Press of Kansas, 1985), 69.

21. Jacques Derrida, "Structure, Sign, and Play in the Discourse of the Human Sciences," in *The Structuralist Controversy*, ed. Richard Macksey and Eugenio Donato (Baltimore: The Johns Hopkins University Press, 1972), 247-72.

22. Gayatri Spivak, translator's preface to Derrida's *Of Grammatology* (Baltimore: The Johns Hopkins University Press, 1976), lv.

23. Roland Barthes, *Critical Essays*, trans. Richard Howard (Evanston, Ill.: Northwestern University Press, 1972), 214-15; cited in Spivak, translator's preface to Derrida's *Of Grammatology*, lvii.

24. Dyer, "Coming to Terms," 293.

25. Derrida, "Structure, Sign, and Play," 247-48.

26. Ibid., 249.

27. Dyer, "Coming to Terms," 289.

28. Derrida, "Structure, Sign, and Play," 248.

29. I am paraphrasing and making use of Derrida here (see *Of Grammatology*, 162).

30. Derrida, "Structure, Sign, and Play," 255.

31. Ibid., 252.

32. Spivak describes this deconstructive practice of drawing attention to the limits of one's critical practice as, among other things, an attempt to "take into account the lack of sovereignty of the critic himself" (translator's preface to Derrida's *Of Grammatology*, lxxiv). "Perhaps this 'will to ignorance,' " she continues, "is simply a matter of attitude, a realization that one's choice of 'evidence' is provisional, a self-distrust, a distrust of one's own power. . . . Even so, it is an important enough lesson for the critic, that self-proclaimed custodian of the public 'meaning' of literature" (lxxiv-lxxv). This study must of course largely substitute "film" for literature. Spivak adds, however, that "in the long run the critic cannot himself present his own

vulnerability" (lxxv). It will thus be up to my readers to draw my attention to those places in this text where I have necessarily fallen for the lure of my own critical discourse.

33. Dyer, "Coming to Terms," 292.

34. "The sensation of being fucked may be so intense that, while you enjoy it, you'll lose your erection" (Jack Hart, *Gay Sex: A Manual for Men Who Love Men* [Boston: Alyson, 1991], 18).

35. Dyer, "Coming to Terms," 293.

36. Many porn production companies currently turn out compilation reels that allow them to recycle footage from a number of different films. Often organized around particular sexual acts, these cheaply produced films string sequences together with little attempt to "situate" the actors narratively within the sequences, or to draw any connection between the various sequences. See, for example, such films as *The Best of Surge, The Best of Surge II, Daddies, Hot Bottoms,* and *Lovers Coming Home.*

37. Dyer, "Coming to Terms," 293.

38. See my "Interrupted Pleasure: A Foucauldian Reading of Hard Core, A *Hard Core* (Mis) Reading of Foucault," *boundary 2* 18, no. 2 (Summer 1991): 181-206, especially 201.

39. Dyer, "Coming to Terms," 289.

40. Dyer's analysis begins with a call for a pornography that would provide a bodily knowledge of desire (see especially "Coming to Terms," 290).

41. We might note in the context of this discussion that such a reading of male sexuality attempts to circumvent a reading of male ejaculation as nonproductive expenditure.

42. Dyer, "Coming to Terms," 296.

43. For an introduction to the feminist debates in pornography, see Ann Snitow, Christine Stansell, and Sharon Thomas, eds., *Powers of Desire: The Politics of Sexuality* (New York: Monthly Review Press, 1983), and Carole S. Vance, ed., *Pleasure and Danger: Exploring Female Sexuality* (Boston: Routledge, 1984).

44. Leo Bersani, "Is the Rectum a Grave?" in *AIDS: Cultural Analysis, Cultural Activism* (Cambridge, Mass.: MIT Press, 1988), 197-222.

45. Gloria Steinem, "Erotica vs. Pornography," in *Outrageous Acts and Everyday Rebellions* (New York: Signet Books, 1983), 247; emphasis in original.

46. Ibid., 243.

47. Jacqueline Rose, "Feminine Sexuality—Jacques Lacan and the école freudienne," in *Sexuality in the Field of Vision* (London: Verso, 1986), 56.

48. As in most antipornography discussions, Steinem doesn't take the trouble to define what might constitute scenes of domination and unequal power. There is at least something perhaps rigorous in Dworkin's well-known contention that intercourse itself constitutes domination. At least she is willing to define her critical terms.

49. For a discussion of this privileging, see Michel Foucault, *The History of Sexuality*, vol. 1, *An Introduction*, trans. Robert Hurley (New York: Vintage Books, 1990).

50. Steinem, for example, makes the rather amazing claim that "There is hardly a newsstand without women's bodies in chains and bondage, in full labial display for the conquering male viewer, bruised or on our knees, screaming in real or pretended pain, pretending to enjoy what we don't enjoy" ("Erotica vs. Pornography," 251).

51. Judith Butler, *Gender Trouble* (New York: Routledge, 1990), 30.

52. Dyer, "Coming to Terms," 292.

53. For a discussion of this "immobilized" spectator, see Jean-Louis Baudry, "Ideological Effects of the Basic Cinematographic Apparatus," in *Narrative, Apparatus, Ideology*, ed. Phillip Rosen (New York: Columbia University Press, 1986), 287-98.

54. One obvious theoretical foil for such close readings would be the vocabulary of transtextuality offered by Gérard Genette in *Palimpsestes*, which suggests that the "beginnings"

and "ends" of any text are radically "open" to interpretation. In particular, Genette's conception of paratextuality, which describes the "embeddedness" of a text in a series of other textual "fragments"—from (in the case of a film) the opening and closing credits to the specific material circumstances of reception—calls attention to the difficulty of separating a text from the multiple and multiplying encrustations in which that text meets the spectator (*Palimpsestes: La littérature au second degré* [Paris: Editions du Seuil, 1982], especially 9-10).

55. See in this context Dyer's contention, cited above, that the goal of the pornographic narrative is to see the actor come, as well as Linda Williams's account of the "money shot" in *Hard Core: Power, Pleasure, and the "Frenzy of the Visible"* (Berkeley and Los Angeles: University of California Press, 1989), 93-119. As might be expected, neither of these analyses considers the money shot as a trope of nonproductive expenditure, a kind of visible insistence on sexuality as loss and waste. This reading suggests that the money shot represents not a complete capitulation to disciplinary society's demands for increased surveillance, but a visible use of the visible to counter the usefulness of reproductive sexuality.

56. Foucault, *Discipline and Punish*, trans. Alan Sheridan (New York: Vintage Books, 1979), 187.

57. Williams, *Hard Core*, 48. Williams here is arguing a position influenced by Gertrude Koch. See Koch, "The Body's Shadow Realm," *Jump Cut*, no. 35 (April 1990): 17-29.

58. I realize that, in the following discussion, I am perhaps responding to a Lacanian-inflected argument concerning the gaze with a more properly Foucauldian one. As Joan Copjec has noted, however, the casting of the gaze as "sadistic" in feminist film theory is itself made possible by a reading of Lacan through Foucault. In other words, the psychoanalytic commonplace with which I want to take issue here depends on a conflation of Lacanian and Foucauldian conceptions of the gaze. See Joan Copjec, response to the question of the female spectator, *Camera Obscura* 20/21 (May-September 1989): 122-23.

59. The reading of pornography I offer here obviously requires a different set of conditions of reception from the ones described above in the quarter movie arcade, and perhaps more closely resembles the conditions of home video viewing. I would also draw attention to the multiple positionings from which I read, two of which I have named, in a kind of shorthand, "gay" and "intellectual." This "intellectual" positioning in relation to film was formed at least in part through a schooling in film studies. I thus would not claim that this reading is necessarily that of any fictive "average" spectator.

60. I borrow this term from Linda Williams, who in turn borrowed it from Jean-Louis Comolli. See Williams, *Hard Core*, 30 and 285 n. 2, and Comolli, "Machines of the Visible," in *The Cinematic Apparatus*, ed. Teresa de Lauretis and Stephen Heath (New York: St. Martin's Press, 1980), 121-42.

61. I also wonder if there isn't what might provisionally be termed a heterosexism in the continued theoretical insistence that pornography strives for *visual evidence* of bodily pleasure in general, and female pleasure in particular. One wonders for whom precisely the (visual) *evidence* of pleasure is necessarily a problem. Such a reading of pornography mistakenly assumes that the body's resistance to the disciplinary gaze is bound to questions of gender. Specifically, a biologism is marshaled in order to argue that the female body is somehow more resistant to the gaze. As Linda Williams argues, "The disciplinary practices Foucault describes so well have operated more powerfully on the bodies of women than on those of men" (*Hard Core*, 4). Such a position deploys Foucault to reinscribe a pre-Foucauldian understanding of power that would assert that a quantifiable amount of power is "held" by one group (men) over another (women). While Foucault might argue that strategic relations between men and women are fixed in such a way as to be difficult to reverse, this is a very different argument from one that suggests that men have more power than women. I would then want to amend Williams's po-

sition by suggesting that Foucault allows us to imagine how disciplinary practices might operate *differently* on female bodies.

62. I realize that some filmic pornography today uses a stationary camera and does not feature much editing. I would speculate here that the body's resistance to the gaze has produced a situation historically in which such pornography is rendered increasingly "boring." Williams's historical study of pornography suggests that even "primitive" stag films featured some editing.

63. Here, I am obviously taking issue with Dyer's contention that one is to come "with" the characters. I have no idea how Dyer produced this reading, considering his own admission that viewers in theaters or video booths often "enter" the porno narrative at varying points in the film, and might not have either the time or inclination to wait for the actors to come.

64. Laura Mulvey, "Visual Pleasure and Narrative Cinema," in *Movies and Methods II*, ed. Bill Nichols (Berkeley and Los Angeles: University of California Press, 1985), 303-15. Although Mulvey does not consider pornography here, the "normalization" of her essay within the field of feminist film scholarship has led scholars to assume that the porno gaze is "sadistic." Williams herself describes how she had (wrongly) anticipated such a conclusion prior to undertaking her study of pornography (*Hard Core*, x).

65. For an example of a masochistic theory of the spectator, see Gaylyn Studlar, "Masochism and the Perverse Pleasure of the Cinema," in *Movies and Methods II*, ed. Nichols, 602-21.

66. Interestingly, Bataille's work suggests another way of understanding questions of pornography, sadism, and masochism. In his essay on fascism, he writes, "In individual psychology, it is rare for the sadistic tendency not to be associated with a more or less manifest masochistic tendency. But as each tendency is normally represented in society by a distinct agency, the sadistic attitude can be manifested by an imperative person to the exclusion of any corresponding masochistic attitudes. In this case, the exclusion of the filthy forms that serve as the object of the cruel act is not accompanied by the positioning of these forms as a value and, consequently, no erotic activity can be associated with the cruelty. The erotic elements themselves are rejected at the same time as every filthy object and, as in a great number of religious attitudes, sadism attains a brilliant purity" ("The Psychological Structure of Fascism," 146).

67. "Urban gay ghetto" is obviously a catachresis and should be understood as what Spivak might characterize as a "discontinuous determinant." In other words, the term inadequately names, in this case, a fictive location produced by a weave of forces that might themselves be inadequately named by economics, sexuality, and ethnicity, to name only the most obvious.

68. John Stoltenberg, "Gays and the Propornography Movement: Having the Hots for Sex Discrimination," in *Men Confront Pornography*, ed. Michael S. Kimmel (New York: Crown, 1990), 249.

69. See page 254 of Stoltenberg's essay in particular, in which he recounts a number of personal ads.

70. Stoltenberg, "Gays and the Propornography Movement," 261-62.

71. And, as I will suggest in a subsequent chapter, the presence of tears in particular here is itself worth noting.

72. Foucault in fact suggests, in *Discipline and Punish*, that the "soul" itself is produced through the disciplinary training of the body.

73. According to Bataille, nonproductive expenditures are characterized, at least in primitive circumstances, by having no ends beyond themselves ("The Notion of Expenditure," 118).

74. Bersani, "Is the Rectum a Grave," 221.

75. Ibid., 222.

76. I am uncomfortable with my use of the term *world* in this particular paraphrase, but, as I will argue shortly, Bersani's argument at this point in the essay loses any cultural and historical specificity.

77. Bersani's analysis seems to depend on a faith in the capabilities of psychoanalysis to read the actual correctly. It is thus difficult at times to know whether his argument is an ahistorical and acultural one concerning "human beings" and their relation to sexuality, or whether it is an attempt to explore a more "local" set of relations and practices.

78. See, in particular, Gilles Barbadette, "The Social Triumph of the Sexual Will: A Conversation with Michel Foucault," trans. Brendan Lemon, *Christopher Street* 64 (May 1982): 36-41; Bob Gallagher and Alexander Wilson, "Michel Foucault, An Interview: Sex, Power and the Politics of Identity," *The Advocate* 400 (7 August 1984): 26-30, 58; Michel Foucault, "Friendship as a Way of Life," in *Foucault Live*, ed. Lotringer, 203-9; Jean Le Bitoux, "Michel Foucault, Le gai savoir," *Mec* 5 (June 1988): 32-36, trans. Michael West; James O'Higgins, "Sexual Choice, Sexual Act," in *Foucault Live*, ed. Lotringer, 211-31.

79. Foucault, "Sex, Power, and the Politics of Identity," 27.

80. To give one example of this underreading, Judith Butler mistakenly asserts that Foucault gave a single interview on homosexuality (*Gender Trouble*, 102). Sections of the following discussion appear in a slightly different form in my "Interrupted Pleasure," cited above.

81. Le Bitoux, "Michel Foucault, Le gai savoir," 33.

82. Ibid., 32-35.

83. Ibid., 34; Foucault, "Sex, Power, and the Politics of Identity," 27-28.

84. Although I am speaking primarily of practices associated with gay males, certain similar discursive practices circulate among some lesbians. See, for example, Susie Bright, *Susie Sexpert's Lesbian Sex World* (Pittsburgh: Cleis Press, 1990). This text also (favorably) discusses lesbian s/m and pornography.

85. See Michel Foucault, "Technologies of the Self," in *Technologies of the Self*, ed. Luther H. Martin, Huck Gutman, and Patrick H. Hutton (Amherst: University of Massachusetts Press, 1988), 16-49.

86. Foucault, "Sex, Power, and the Politics of Identity," 29.

87. Limits are established in an s/m scene through the determination of a mutually agreed-upon particular word, which is a signal the partners use when they wish not to go beyond a certain point. This word is not usually "stop," as part of the s/m fantasy may involve the invocation of "theatrical" pleas for release. Often the word may be one or the other of the partner's names, which interestingly suggests, in light of my argument here, the necessity of sometimes reestablishing the "boundaries" of the self through the invocation of the proper name. This information on s/m comes from private conversations with several practitioners.

88. Bataille, "The Notion of Expenditure," 118.

89. Le Bitoux, "Michel Foucault, Le gai savoir," 36.

90. Ibid.

91. Bersani, "Is the Rectum a Grave?" 217.

92. Ibid., 206.

93. Additionally, we might respond to Bersani's reading of the baths with the suggestion from Bataille that, were the baths not an arena in which the threat of "losing" was so great, they would cease to function as an incident of nonproductive expenditure, acting instead as the kind of "community" or "brotherhood" as which other gay theorists cast them, and which Bersani explicitly rejects.

3. "Anthropology—Unending Search for What Is Utterly Precious"

Unfortunately, filmmaker Marlon Riggs, whose work is discussed in this chapter, has recently died of HIV disease.

1. Jacques Derrida, "Structure, Sign and Play," 252.

2. Essex Hemphill, introduction to *Brother to Brother: New Writings by Black Gay Men*, ed. Essex Hemphill (Boston: Alyson Publications, 1991), xv-xxxi. A section of this essay also appears as "Does Your Mama Know about Me?" in Essex Hemphill, *Ceremonies: Prose and Poetry* (New York: Plume, 1992), 37-42. This talk was later adapted for publication in a journal (Essex Hemphill, "The Imperfect Moment," *High Performance* 13, no. 50 [Summer 1990]: 18-19).

3. Address from the Planning Committee, Program Booklet, OUT WRITE '90, 1. Although Mapplethorpe is not named in this introduction to the conference, the senator from North Carolina is.

4. Hemphill, "The Imperfect Moment," 18; emphasis in original.

5. It would take me far afield from my topic here—which will be an examination of the rhetoric in which Hemphill presents his critique of Mapplethorpe's photos—to counter Hemphill's reading. For "alternative" readings of these photographs see Kobema Mercer, "Skin Head Sex Thing: Racial Difference and the Homoerotic Imaginary," in *How Do I Look?*, ed. Bad Object-Choices (Seattle: Bay Press, 1991), 169-210; and Judith Butler, "The Force of Fantasy: Feminism, Mapplethorpe, and Discursive Excess," *Difference* 2, no. 2 (1990), 105-25. Although I disagree with Hemphill's reading, which seems far too monolithic, and which assumes a bit too facilely that "artistically" produced images circulate and are read in the same way as so-called pornographic images (emblematized in Hemphill's unelaborated assertion that Mapplethorpe's photographs were "conscious" attempts to elicit [what Hemphill terms] racist sexual fantasies), Hemphill is responding, in *High Performance* in particular, to Edmund White's equally facile "formalist" reading of the photographs in his introduction to Mapplethorpe's *Black Males* catalogue, a reading that refuses to elaborate any relationship whatsoever among "aesthetic" pleasures, eroticism, and racism.

6. There was in fact no time for discussion following the plenary, and I have to admit that I found the conference itself to be largely not a place in which ideas could be publicly elaborated, contested, and argued. The one notable exception was an excellent panel, "Revis(ion)ing Race," in which a panel of Black and Latino writers were actually willing to publicly disagree with one another concerning the "proper" response of gays and lesbians of color to the continued exclusion of their work from "mainstream" gay journals like *Christopher Street*.

7. A friend of mine recently suggested to me that there was a kind of similarity in the order of these two responses—tears and booing—in that both kept the terms of the discussion in close congruence to the body. Considering the photographs under discussion, perhaps both of these responses are somehow "appropriate."

8. See Spivak, "Explanation and Culture: Marginalia," in *In Other Worlds: Essays in Cultural Politics* (New York: Routledge, 1988), 105-6.

9. I do not share with Hemphill the belief in a deliberative consciousness guiding discursive production, and so am not suggesting here that his talk and its accompanying tears were consciously calculated to produce this result.

10. I would instead second Foucault's observation that, unlike social power, the strategic relations operating in the sexual are relatively fluid, and more capable of reversal.

11. For one feminist response to the argument that pornography "objectifies" the body, see Muriel Dimien's "Politically Correct? Politically Incorrect?" in *Pleasure and Danger: Exploring Female Sexuality*, ed. Carole S. Vance (Boston: Routledge, 1984), 138-48.

12. Laura Kipnis, "(Male) Desire and (Female) Disgust: Reading *Hustler*," in *Cultural Studies*, 373. I thank Paul Smith for bringing this essay to my attention.

13. Ibid., 377.

14. Michel Foucault, "The Subject and Power," in Hubert L. Dreyfus and Paul Rabinow, *Michel Foucault: Beyond Structuralism and Hermeneutics*, 2nd ed. (Chicago: University of Chicago Press, 1983), 212.

15. Ibid., 212-13.

16. Interestingly, Gramsci, like Foucault, also sought to distinguish between varying forms of struggle. Like Foucault, he complicated theories of struggle that emphasized the seizure of state power to the exclusion of all other strategies. Most familiar in this context is Gramsci's distinction between state and civil society—a distinction that, it must be noted, is, as Spivak might say, productively reconstellated throughout the *Prison Notebooks*. (Compare, for example, Gramsci's counterposition, in "The Intellectuals," of civil society and the state as "two major superstructural levels" [Antonio Gramsci, "The Intellectuals," in *Selections from the Prison Notebooks*, ed. Quintin Hoare and Geoffrey Nowell Smith (New York: International Publishers, 1971), 12] with his suggestion, in "State and Civil Society," that the term "State" should include "not only the apparatus of government, but also the 'private' apparatus of 'hegemony' or civil society" [Gramsci, "State and Civil Society," in *Selections from the Prison Notebooks*, ed. Hoare and Nowell Smith, 257-64]). Additionally, Gramsci argued the need to define and develop what he termed "the 'dual perspective' in political action" (Gramsci, "The Modern Prince," in *Selections from the Prison Notebooks*, ed. Hoare and Nowell Smith, 169). This dual perspective recognizes that struggles occur on different levels, levels Gramsci differentiates as "force and consent, authority and hegemony, violence and civilisation . . . of agitation and of propaganda, of tactics and of strategy, etc." (170). It is perhaps not impertinent to hear, in certain passages in Foucault, an echo of Gramsci's words. Foucault's genealogies, defined as "the union of erudite knowledge and local memories which allows us to establish a historical knowledge of struggles and to make use of this knowledge tactically today" (Michel Foucault, "Two Lectures," in *Power/Knowledge: Selected Interviews and Other Writings* [New York: Pantheon Books, 1980], 83) seem not unrelated to Gramsci's proposed analyses of relations of force, in that both argue for forms of knowledge that might be employed tactically in specific struggles. It is also perhaps not too facile to suggest a relationship between Foucault's genealogical union of "erudite knowledge and local memories" and Gramsci's "philosophy of praxis," which attempts to bring "common sense" into dialogue with "a higher conception of life" (Gramsci, "The Study of Philosophy," in *Selections from the Prison Notebooks*, ed. Hoare and Nowell Smith, 332). We might also hear Gramsci's call for concrete analyses of relations of force as a precursor to Foucault's insistence that power be analyzed at its specific points of application. (See, for example, Foucault, "Two Lectures," 97.) Additionally, Foucault's insistence that power produces a multiplicity of resistances resonates with Gramsci's suggestion, in a passage in "State and Civil Society," that political struggle often engages a number of forms of resistance that he allegorizes as war of movement, war of position, and underground warfare (Gramsci, "State and Civil Society," 229-30). Gramsci is here comparing political struggle (which he insists is "enormously more complex" than military war) with colonial wars such as the one India engaged in with the British. According to Gramsci, "Gandhi's passive resistance is a war of position, which at certain moments becomes a war of movement, and at others underground warfare. Boycotts are a form of war of position, strikes of war of movement, the secret preparation of weapons and combat troops belongs to underground warfare" (229-30). Finally, we might note in both theorists a certain polemical rejection of allegedly "disinterested" intellectual practice, and a concurrent demand that intellectual work be deployed strategically and for immediate ends in struggles against forms of power. It would not be wise to make too much of these similarities without a more extensive analysis of, say, the relationship of base to superstructure in Gramsci, and how such an analysis might square with Foucault's insistence that "the State is superstructural in relation to a whole series of power networks that invest the body, sexuality, the family, kinship, knowledge, technology, and so forth" (Foucault,

"Truth and Power," in *Power/Knowledge*, 122). This kind of discussion is clearly beyond the scope of this study, necessitating as it would an extended discussion of, for example, Gramsci's continued efforts to theorize the state in relation to such philosophers as Hegel, Marx, and Croce—a project Foucault explicitly rejects. I cite Gramsci here tactically, primarily to justify a particular strategic activity—the differentiating of forms of power and struggle.

17. I borrow this phrase "politics of style" from a lively discussion that occurred at the 1993 meeting of the Marxist Literary Group at Carnegie Mellon University.

18. Stuart Hall, "Migrant Identities: The Arrival of an Enigma," talk given for the Program in Cultural Studies, University of Pittsburgh, October 1991.

19. Michel Foucault, *The History of Sexuality*, vol. 1, *An Introduction*, trans. Robert Hurley (New York: Vintage Books, 1990), 43.

20. Eve Kosofsky Sedgwick makes a similar argument in axiom 5 of her *Epistemology of the Closet* (Berkeley and Los Angeles: University of California Press, 1990; 44-48). This lack of recognition is obviously not a problem of "false consciousness" on the part of the individual subject. In other words, I am obviously not arguing that the subject who does not "recognize" himself as homosexual in this particular instance is the victim of his own internalized homophobia, or unwilling to acknowledge consciously who he really is, or is somehow unable to bring to consciousness the truth of his being. For that which constitutes consciousness itself is circumscribed by a historically specific range of discourses in which the subject is produced as an effect of those very discourses. Thus it is possible that a subject engaging in homosexual acts might be produced "consciously"—in the discursive space of his own thoughts—as *not* a homosexual, because of, among other things, the historical remnants of this prior discourse, while in the same historical moment the same subject might be positioned in another discursive network—in this example, a news article—*as* a homosexual.

21. Thomas E. Yingling, *Hart Crane and the Homosexual Text* (Chicago: University of Chicago Press, 1990), 26.

22. Foucault, *The History of Sexuality*, vol. 1, *An Introduction*, 101.

23. Yingling, *Hart Crane and the Homosexual Text*, 26.

24. Jeffrey Weeks, *Sexuality and its Discontents* (London: Routledge & Kegan Paul, 1985).

25. Joan W. Scott, " 'Experience,' " in *Feminists Theorize the Political*, ed. Judith Butler and Joan W. Scott (New York: Routledge, 1992), 34.

26. As Judith Butler argues, "Identity is not signified at a given point in time after which it is simply there as an inert piece of entitative language" (*Gender Trouble* [New York: Routledge, 1990], 144).

27. Christina Crosby, "Dealing with Differences," in *Feminists Theorize the Political*, ed. Judith Butler and Joan W. Scott, 130-43.

28. Although I agree with Crosby's contention that to specify is not to historicize, I'm not exactly sure what a historicization of the discursive production of difference might look like. The term *genealogy* is often invoked to counter a historicism that would, in Crosby's terms, specify rather than historicize. It becomes increasingly difficult, however, to recognize a referent for this term. In *Gender Trouble*, Butler, for example, considers her project a genealogy of gender—if I am reading her correctly when she defines genealogy in her preface, after Foucault, as a critique that "investigates the political stakes in designating as an origin and cause those identity categories that are in fact the effects of institutions, practices, discourses with multiple and diffuse points of origin" (x-xi). My sense of genealogy, however—even as it is defined here by Butler—suggests that such a critical practice requires one to trace, in this particular context, throughout the totality of the archive, the discursive "effects" of gender. Butler's project clearly does not set itself this task. It is perhaps a partial genealogy of feminist discourse about gender. In any case, I hope it is clear that, in attempting to specify my positioning as a reader in this

study, I am not claiming to historicize (genealogize?) such a position. At the very least, such a project would require a genealogy of the homosexual subject.

29. In *Gender Trouble*, Butler suggests, through a reading of Simone de Beauvoir, a number of similar conclusions (see 112 in particular). Of especial consequence here is her proposal that gender "ought not to be conceived as a noun or a substantial thing or a static cultural marker, but rather as an incessant and repeated action of some sort."

30. Crosby, "Dealing with Differences," 137.

31. See, for example, Dennis D. Kelly, "Sexual Differentiation of the Nervous System," in *Principles of Neural Science*, ed. Eric Candel and J. Schwartz (New York: Elsevier/North-Holland, 1981), 533-46, as well as Butler, *Gender Trouble*, 106-10, both of which discuss the increasing inability of science to determine once and for all who is "actually" male or female.

32. Weeks, *Sexuality and Its Discontents*, 209.

33. Judith Butler goes to some lengths to problematize the notion that identity must precede political agency (see especially *Gender Trouble*, 142-45). I am tempted to leave behind completely a discussion of identity, given its problematic recurring presence in discussions of cultural marginality in particular. The question "Who am I?" is perhaps itself part of the problem. Constraints of time and space prevent me from engaging adequately with the wealth of literature around this topic; see, for example, Diana J. Fuss, *Essentially Speaking* (New York: Routledge, 1989).

Butler's book also contains a critique of identity with which I largely sympathize. A strategic focus in this study on the critique of the subject also necessitates that I forgo a discussion of the problem of self-identification. I would, however, propose the following provisional understanding of identities: Identities are positionings within specified (discontinuous) discursive networks, provisional and recurring attempts to stabilize (unsuccessfully) the historical contingencies of subject positionings. They signify, in the moments of their articulation, their "truth" or "falsehood," determined not in some ontological realm, but according to the rules of the particular discursive network in which they are activated. (Butler offers a similar statement of this problem: "If the inner truth of gender is a fabrication and if a true gender is a fantasy instituted and inscribed on the surface of bodies, then it seems that genders can be neither true nor false, but are only produced as the truth effects of a discourse of primary and stable identity" [*Gender Trouble*, 136].) Identities are provisional "knottings" in historically contingent weavings of discourse, knottings activated in the service of a subject-effect, knottings that are, by definition, necessarily undone. Drawing on language from Deleuze and Guattari, we might call an identity a "chance" assemblage or arrangement that puts into tentative connection certain multiplicities drawn from a variety of discursive orders (see Gilles Deleuze and Félix Guattari, *A Thousand Plateaus*, trans. Brian Massumi [Minneapolis: University of Minnesota Press, 1987], 23; see also Spivak's translation of this same passage in *In Other Worlds*, 293 n. 6). Such a definition is admittedly undeveloped, but it perhaps captures some of the provisionality and discontinuity of identity. It also blocks the attempt to cast identity as something that is inhabited via the agency of the subject, and refuses to posit an identity's "cause," even under the guise of "history."

Regardless, then, of whether or not the subject locates himself or herself in a particular discursive network, he or she may be located—or, for that matter, may not be. In other words, the will of the subject vis-à-vis these identities is perhaps negligible, since the agency of any individual subject to alter the rules operating in a discursive network is highly constrained. To return to the example of the news story: We might imagine a newspaper as a discursive network woven of a number of highly historically discontinuous discourses that establish a body of rules for the formation of statements—though if we were to read these discourses deconstructively, their edges would show, so that the tightness of the weave might begin to give way, and might begin to suggest ways in which the rules might be altered. The subject positioned in a news story is thus not simply free to alter the rules of that particular discursive network. At the very least, such an alteration is extremely difficult. Thus, the individual subject refusing himself as gay will have great difficulty altering the rules of formation of statements in a news story so as to render his positioning in this discursive network as gay *unintelligible*. (It is obviously not enough that he render this positioning as "false," since, in this particular discursive network, "false" can mean only heterosexual. To attempt to position oneself as heterosexual in a news story is clearly not the same as resisting the rules of formation of that discursive network.) It is thus possible for a subject to enact a deconstructive reading, within a newspaper, of the rules of formation that produce the binaries heterosexual/homosexual as intelligible. But the likelihood that such a deconstruction will be allowed is negligible, considering the historical forces that police the boundaries of what might and might not be articulated in this particular discursive network (forces that of course mobilize the ideology of the popular press to disallow certain discourses as too difficult, too intellectual, too opposed to the common sense of the populace, a common sense that is reluctant to call into crisis the binaries on which sexuality currently depends).

34. The video was called this in the voice-over introduction to its television broadcast over the Public Broadcasting Service.

35. Hemphill, introduction to *Brother to Brother*, xxv.

36. Ron Simmons, "Tongues Untied: An Interview with Marlon Riggs," in Hemphill, *Brother to Brother*, 189-99.

37. These poets include Reginald Jackson, Craig Harris, Steve Langley, Alan Miller, Donald Woods, and Joseph Beam.

38. See, in this context, Kobena Mercer, "Black Hair/Style Politics," in *Out There: Marginalization and Contemporary Cultures*, ed. Russell Ferguson, Martha Gever, Trinh T. Minh-ha, and Cornel West (New York: The New Museum of Contemporary Art, and Cambridge: MIT Press, 1990), 247-64; Mary Louise Pratt, "Arts of the Contact Zone," in *Ways of Reading*, ed. David Bartholomae and Anthony Petrosky (Boston: Bedford Books, 1993), 442-56; and Bill Ashcroft, Gareth Griffiths, and Helen Tiffin, *The Empire Writes Back* (London: Routledge, 1989).

39. Jacques Derrida, "Structure, Sign, and Play in the Discourse of the Human Sciences," in *The Structuralist Controversy*, ed. Richard Macksey and Eugenio Donato (Baltimore: The Johns Hopkins University Press, 1972), 251.

40. A version of this poem appears as "Tongues Untied" in Hemphill, *Brother to Brother*, 200-205.

41. As Riggs suggests, "*Tongues Untied* is a documentary in that it tries to undo the legacy of silence about black gay life. It affirms who we are, what our existence is in all of its diversities, and that we are of great value to our community and ourselves" (Simmons, "Tongues Untied: An Interview with Marlon Riggs," 193). Similarly, Hemphill described the film as "an historic work that captures black gay men in many states of 'being' " (introduction to *Brother to Brother*, xxvi).

42. For an introduction to some of the problems realism has presented to feminist film production, see Christine Gledhill, "Recent Developments in Feminist Criticism," *Film Theory and Criticism*, ed. Gerald Mast and Marshall Cohen (New York: Oxford University Press, 1985), 817-45. See also Butler, "The Force of Fantasy." Concerning realism and representations of gay men, see my "The Celluloid Contradiction: An Other Look at *Parting Glances*," *CineAction!* no. 19/20 (Winter/Spring 1990): 43-51.

43. Audre Lorde, "The Master's Tools Will Never Dismantle the Master's House," in *Sister Outsider: Essays and Speeches* (Trumansburg, N.Y.: Crossing Press, 1984), 110-13.

44. Derrida, "Structure, Sign, and Play," 252.

45. Ibid.

46. Ibid., 254. Although there are significant differences between the theoretical projects of Derrida and Foucault, here is a place where the two critics suggest remarkably similar positions. Compare, for example, Derrida's words here with Foucault's interest in fashioning fictions that might produce specific effects of truth. Andrew Parker notes some of the significant differences between the projects of Derrida and Foucault, pointing in particular to their well-publicized exchange around Foucault's work on madness. In *White Mythologies*, Robert Young offers an interesting reading of this debate, suggesting that Derrida's critique of *Madness and Civilization* allowed Foucault to substitute "the idea of an otherness at work within reason for that of a repressed alterity existing outside or beyond it" (*White Mythologies* [London: Routledge, 1990], 72). It is in fact this Foucault that I invoke in this study (see Andrew Parker, " 'Taking Sides' (On History): Derrida Re-Marx," *Diacritics* 11, no. 4 [Fall 1981]: 57-93). For a passage from Foucault that seems deconstructive, if not Derridean, in its account of rationality's "indispensability" as well as its "intrinsic dangers," see Foucault, "Space, Knowledge and Power," *Skyline*, March 1982, 19 (cited in Barry Smart, "On the Subjects of Sexuality, Ethics, and Politics in the Work of Foucault," *boundary 2* 18, no. 1 (Spring 1991): 220.

47. Michel Foucault, *Discipline and Punish*, trans. Alan Sheridan (New York: Vintage Books, 1979), 187.

48. Scott, "Experience," 34.

49. Hemphill, "Without Comment," in *Ceremonies*, 76.

50. Hemphill, "Black Beans," in *Ceremonies*, 142.

51. Hemphill, "To Be Real," in *Ceremonies*, 114.

52. Awkward though this phrase "culturally produced as white" might be, it is my attempt to remind the reader that whiteness is not "natural" but produced through culturally specific discursive practices. For example, although an ethnic identity such as "Sicilian" is (largely) culturally understood as "white," the ancient Moorish invasion of Sicily reminds us that, in a biologist (racist) discourse that equates Blackness with the presence of any amount of "African" blood, Sicilians could be rendered as Black.

53. I offer this caveat as a rejoinder to those readers who might respond to my reading of this section of the film with the quarrel that they do not read this sequence in the same way that I do. Both times that I have publicly presented an earlier draft of this chapter, I have been astounded by the hostile responses of a number of women academics—African American and white—to my reading of the film. "I didn't read the film in this way" does not seem to me to be a sufficient critique of my reading. In fact, it seems exactly to the point. Clearly, some women academic film critics—lesbian and straight, African American and white—are not likely to read *Tongues Untied*'s images of gay male s/m culture from a positioning identical to mine.

54. Riggs, "Tongues Untied," 202.

55. The poem qualifies this "seduction" by saying they never touched or kissed one another ("Tongues Untied," 202).

56. My assumption here is that there are historically specific filmic methods of eroticizing the body, such as panning, tilting, and fragmentation, and that these methods are employed here. In other words, I am assuming that spectators will be positioned within that history of erotic imaging.

57. It is a particularly interesting coincidence that Andrea Dworkin, in her testimony before the Meese commission on pornography, cited a series of photographs similar to one of the drawings represented in *Tongues Untied*. This occurrence suggests a relationship among a "liberal" feminism, Black studies, and gay studies, all of which attempt in various ways to deploy an ontology of the visible, to normalize the Other, and to turn to the state to secure that normalization with recourse to a discourse of "equal rights." As Linda Williams reminds us, Dworkin's testimony before the Meese commission made reference to a series of photographs, published in *Penthouse*, of Asian women bound and hung from trees. See Williams, *Hard Core:*

Power, Pleasure, and the "Frenzy of the Visible" (Berkeley and Los Angeles: University of California Press, 1989), 20-21.

58. In other words, the heavy use of what appears to be autobiography and "confessional" poetry in the film allows the film to abandon a more careful and considered cultural analysis in the name of the presentation of "personal experience." See, for example, Hemphill's contention that the film "is grounded in personal testimony from Riggs about his life," testimony that is "validated and elaborated on" through the other poetry in the film (introduction to *Brother to Brother*, xxvi).

59. See, in this context, Judith Butler's "The Force of Fantasy," which argues how a congruence between the antiporn discourse and Helms's reading is made possible. See also Linda Williams, *Hard Core: Power, Pleasure, and the "Frenzy of the Visible"* (Berkeley and Los Angeles: University of California Press, 1989), 16-23, for a very different kind of analysis of how the Meese commission managed to unite apparently left-leaning antiporn feminists with the religious Right.

60. As Bataille reminds us, spectacle, like so-called "perverse" sexuality, is an instance of nonproductive expenditure. This theme will be taken up at some length in the following chapter.

61. This information is admittedly hearsay, conveyed to me by a member of the audience for an earlier draft of the paper presented at the 1993 meeting of the Marxist Literary Group. Concerning this film's intended audience, Riggs has said, "I knew the film would not be restricted to gay audiences and that eventually it would be seen by mainstream audiences and the mainstream press" (Simmons, "Tongues Untied," 195).

62. When a reviewer asked Riggs what one was to make of the end of the film in light of his having had, for the past ten years, a white lover, Riggs first responded that, by "loving," he did not necessarily mean sexual love, but love in the sense of "friendship, community, family, and fraternity" (Simmons, "Tongues Untied," 194). Given the way the second and third sections of Riggs's poem and the images to which it has been set deal explicitly with interracial sex, this reading seems too monolithic. Riggs then adds that he didn't have the time or financial resources to "continue what would have been easily another fifteen or twenty minutes to explain all the nuances of what it means to be involved in an interracial relationship, while at the same time feeling that the love of black men for black men is of supreme importance." In light of this statement, it is curious that Riggs amended the slogan in his film to read "*the* revolutionary act" instead of "*a* revolutionary act," which seems more in keeping with these latter sentiments. In this interview, Riggs seems to be suggesting that the circumstances of interracial sex between gay men are more complicated than *Tongues Untied*—or Hemphill's reading of Mapplethorpe—can acknowledge.

63. My point here is not that the Black men in the parade demonstrate differently from the white men, but that Riggs's camera organizes these two representations differently.

64. Immanuel Wallerstein, *Historical Capitalism* (London: Verso, 1983), 79. See also Wallerstein, "The Ideological Tensions of Capitalism: Universalism versus Racism and Sexism," in Etienne Balibar and Immanuel Wallerstein, *Race, Nation, Class: Ambiguous Identities* (London: Verso, 1991), 29-36.

65. Wallerstein, *Historical Capitalism*, 78. Interestingly, in Wallerstein's analysis, racism works alongside sexism, which induces women "to work to create surplus-value for the owners of capital, who do not even pay them a little bit," by constructing women's work as nonwork (Wallerstein, "The Ideological Tensions of Capitalism," 34-35). Such (nonworking) work in fact " 'compensates' the lowness of the wage-income" in household structures arranged by racism, acting as "an indirect subsidy to the employers of the wage labourers in these households" (34). It is also important to remember here that Wallerstein is examining racism, sexism, and universalism under the period of historical capitalism in particular. He is not denying that ele-

ments of these ideologies existed prior to capitalism, but is rather attempting to demonstrate how capitalism made use of these historically prior ideologies.

66. Wallerstein, *Historical Capitalism*, 81.

67. Wallerstein, "The Ideological Tensions of Capitalism," 31.

68. Wallerstein, *Historical Capitalism*, 82.

69. As Wallerstein suggests ("The Ideological Tensions of Capitalism," 35), a racism taken too far would eject a certain pool of (underpaid) workers from the work force and thus be counterproductive. A universalism taken too far might suggest the need to implement "a truly egalitarian allocation of work roles and work rewards in which race (or its equivalent) and gender genuinely play no part" (ibid., 35). It is thus the particular historical convergence of racism-universalism that has best served the needs of historical capitalism.

70. Wallerstein, *Historical Capitalism*, 85.

71. John Stoltenberg, "Gays and the Propornography Movement: Having the Hots for Sex Discrimination," in *Men Confront Pornography*, ed. Michael S. Kimmel (New York: Crown, 1990), 261-62.

72. Wallerstein, "The Ideological Tensions of Capitalism," 36.

73. Hemphill, "The Tomb of Sorrow," in *Ceremonies*, 83-84.

74. Hemphill complains that Mapplethorpe "pays special attention to the penis at the expense of showing us the subject's face, and thus, a whole person" ("The Imperfect Moment," 18). What can one make of this simple equivalence between "face" and "person"? A metaphysical humanism seems to be operating here, the desire for self-presence emblematized in the subject's desire to see himself reflected in the face of the image.

75. Hemphill, "American Wedding," in *Ceremonies*, 170.

76. Hemphill, "Le Salon," in *Ceremonies*, 151.

77. Hemphill, "Object Lessons," in *Ceremonies*, 69-70.

78. Hemphill, introduction to *Brother to Brother*, xxvi.

79. Hemphill, "Miss Emily's Grandson Won't Hush His Mouth," in *Ceremonies*, 47-48.

4. "I Just Wanna Be a Rich Somebody"

1. As Donald Morton has argued, "Though local reversals in academic discourses may produce spaces for the elaboration of marginal positions, the formation, scope and duration of such spaces are critically conditioned by the dominant academic culture's discursive processes" ("The Politics of the Margin: Theory, Pleasure, and the Postmodern *Conferance*," *American Journal of Semiotics*, 5, no. 4 [1987]: 96.

2. I would want to speculate here that one of the important things to note about this recent appropriation of *queer* is that such an appropriation is made possible by the fact that the term has in the recent historical past fallen out of popular use. In other words, I would suggest polemically that most of the (largely) young activists and academic scholars who work to appropriate this term were in fact not largely discursively positioned within it. To offer, not unproblematically, as I will at times throughout this chapter, a bit of "experience" in evidence here: Although I was hounded throughout my youth by a number of epithets including "fag," "fairy," and "fem," I cannot remember a single instance of being called "queer." My historical relation as subjected subject to this nomination is thus very different from my relation to the other three. Whereas the first three insults perform a certain kind of discursive work on my body that in certain circumstances we might term pain, "queer" performs no such similar work. This situation suggests, among other things, the necessity of undertaking a genealogy of the word that might help us to understand the conditions of possibility of its recent appropriation.

3. Gayatri Spivak has suggested a metaphor for understanding the relationship between work in the humanities and these broader economic and political concerns, characterizing

scholars in the academic humanities as "disc jockeys of an advanced capitalist ethnocracy" who are responsible for the "playing" of "records" she terms "productions of the most recent technology." According to Spivak, although scholars in the humanities are led to believe that they are "free" to play, this illusion of freedom in fact disguises "the brutal ironies of technocracy" through a number of ruses, including "suggesting either that the system protects the humanist's freedom of spirit, or that 'technology,' that vague evil, is something the humanist must confront by inculcating humanist 'values,' or by drawing generalized philosophical analogues from the latest spatio-temporal discoveries of the magical realms of 'pure science,' or yet by welcoming it as a benign and helpful friend" ("Explanation and Culture: Marginalia," in *In Other Worlds: Essays in Cultural Politics* [New York: Routledge, 1988], 110). The fact that certain privileged native informants are increasingly entrusted with the playing of the latest "records" (ironically, Spivak's metaphor has been "eclipsed" by the technological development of the compact disc) should alert us to some of the ways in which even the "multicultural" academy might collude with the ideals of a disciplinary society, a society in which self-policing "economically" takes the place of more brutal and immediate displays of force and control.

4. As an example of this fetishization, I would direct the reader to the fanzine devoted to the academic persona of Judith Butler. I am obviously not suggesting that Butler herself is responsible for this fanzine. In fact, rumor has it that Butler is, not surprisingly, angered by this apparent trivialization of her work. The 'zine is, however, interestingly symptomatic of the emerging field of gay and lesbian studies.

5. For a discussion of these two meanings of *representation*, see Spivak, "Can the Subaltern Speak?" in *Marxism and the Interpretation of Culture*, ed. Cary Nelson and Lawrence Grossberg (Urbana: University of Illinois Press, 1988), 271-313, as well as "Practical Politics of the Open End," in Spivak, *The Post-Colonial Critic*, ed. Sarah Harasym (New York: Routledge, 1990), 108-9.

6. Or, for that matter, queer, to use a term that increasingly allows for subjects discursively positioned as heterosexual to claim a proximity to gays and lesbians. Claiming queerness in the present academic context conveniently allows one to speak *for* gays and lesbians while simultaneously affording oneself the luxury of refusing to speak *as* gay and lesbian. "Queerness" thus provides certain conditions of possibility for avoiding, for example, the violence that might greet speaking as gay.

7. As I suggest in my first chapter, such a project does not take the place of ideology critique, which must accompany ethical considerations.

8. In other words, given the continued "belief" in experience and experiential narratives, it might be politically efficacious and strategically advantageous to attempt to make a modified and provisional use of this term.

9. This is obviously not to suggest that the traffic between the academy and its "outside" should travel only one way. I am, however, deeply mistrustful of recent attempts by well-situated academics to privilege the world outside of the academy as the exclusive place from which significant political change might be initiated. Evoking a kind of nostalgia for those mythic days when politics happened largely in the streets, such attempts often privilege practice over theory, action over thinking, as if some kind of spontaneous, immediate, and mindless response to pressing social problems was either possible or desirable. These "academic" attempts to negate the power of the academy (re)figure the (universal) academic intellectual as the diagnostician of the world's problems who, having recently perceived some of the limits of his or her own individual abilities to inaugurate substantial change from within the academy, believe that the "outside" will provide him or her with more opportunities to shake the world in some significant way. Such a move by academics to the outside of the academy unfortunately sometimes allows them to leave their own house in a mess.

10. It would take me too far afield of my present topic to discuss at any length the question of the multicultural classroom, but I would suggest polemically that what the teaching of the texts of the Other ought to afford students is not an "appreciation" of difference, but an attempt to confront and contest the conditions of possibility of their own historical positioning as (reading) subjects. The teaching of, say, literatures of the so-called third world is necessarily made possible by, and implicated in, the history of Western imperialism. There are obviously different means of giving in to that history, some of which are more pernicious than others. I can read recent attempts by well-meaning scholars to teach the appreciation of cultural difference only as a continuation of the imperialist's prerogative to make a privileged and productive use of the Other. One of the many problems with the practice of appreciation is that it does not necessarily lead to critique. One can obviously enjoy the delights of an ethnic food fair without seriously questioning its conditions of possibility. For a brief but compelling introduction to some of the problems with multiculturalism, see Kanishka Chowdhury, "Multiculturalism in the Classroom: Celebrating Diversity, Accommodating Difference," *Mediations* 17, no. 1 (December 1992): 99-101.

11. Butler, "The Force of Fantasy: Feminism, Mapplethorpe, and Discursive Excess," *Difference* 2, no. 2 (1990): 105.

12. Michel Foucault, "The Discourse on Language," in *Critical Theory since 1965*, ed. Hazard Adams and Leroy Searle (Tallahassee: University Presses of Florida, 1986), 149.

13. Ibid., 150-51. Additionally, there exist what Foucault terms "internal" rules, rules concerned with such things as "classification, ordering and distribution" (ibid., 152).

14. The original title of Foucault's essay is "L'ordre du discours," the French "ordre" suggesting the rituals and prohibitions operating in a religious order.

15. In this same essay, Foucault takes up specifically the theme of what he terms "originating experience" (157). According to Foucault, the belief in a prediscursive realm called "experience" depends on the suggestion that "even before it could be grasped in the form of a *cogito*, prior significations, in some way already spoken, were circulating in the world, scattering it all about us, and from the outset made possible a sort of primitive recognition" (ibid., 157). This theme of originating experience is for Foucault yet another means of eliding what he terms the reality of discourse, for this theme dispenses with the historical materiality of discourse by positing a prediscursive truth, an "essential secret" that discourse merely serves to disclose. For Foucault, experience is not a prediscursive "unthought, floating about the world, interlacing with all its forms and events" (ibid., 158). What Foucault terms "the reality of discourse" is a necessarily inadequate attempt to name the rift between unthinkable heterogeneity and the sign, a rift that humanism attempts to fill with recourse to concepts such as experience. As I have suggested elsewhere in this text, after Spivak, deconstruction insists that our own discursive involvement with what we seek to critique can never be sufficiently thwarted. It is thus possible to read here in Foucault's discourse traces of the very essentialism that he attempts to critique. Such phrases as "the reality of discourse" are obviously problematic. Although a more deconstructively inflected Foucault might have written "something like the reality of discourse," or even "what we might term the reality of discourse," even this gesture would *necessarily* have been insufficient.

16. Michel Foucault, *The Archaeology of Knowledge and the Discourse on Language* (New York: Pantheon Books, 1982), 95-96.

17. The work following the first volume of *The History of Sexuality* is especially relevant here: Foucault attempts to trace out how it was possible for historical subjects to produce true statements about themselves. See *The Use of Pleasure*, trans. Robert Hurley (New York: Pantheon Books, 1985), and *The Care of the Self*, trans. Robert Hurley (New York: Vintage Books, 1988).

18. Foucault, "Truth and Power," in *Power/Knowledge: Selected Interviews and Other Writings* (New York: Pantheon Books, 1980), 131.

19. Foucault, "The Question of Power," in *Foucault Live*, ed. Sylvère Lotringer (New York: Semiotext[e], 1989), 191.

20. Butler, "The Force of Fantasy," 106. As I have implied at various times in this study, however, both Foucault and Spivak have complicated the metaphor of margins, Spivak working deconstructively to reverse and displace (and not merely reverse) the opposition of margin to center, and Foucault arguing that resistance is not "outside" of power, but rather produced by it. See Spivak, "Explanation and Culture: Marginalia."

21. See, in this context, Foucault's critique of popular courts in "On Popular Justice: A Discussion with Maoists," in *Power/Knowledge*, 1-36. This critique suggests the perils of instituting a "minority" discourse that exists primarily in a relation of specularity to the dominant.

22. Butler, "The Force of Fantasy," 107.

23. Antonio Gramsci, "The Study of Philosophy," in *Selections from the Prison Notebooks*, ed. Quintin Hoare and Geoffrey Nowell Smith (New York: International Publishers, 1971), 348.

24. Gramsci, "The Intellectuals," in *Selections from the Prison Notebooks*, 5.

25. Gramsci, "The Study of Philosophy," 333.

26. Gramsci, "Problems of Marxism," in *Selections from the Prison Notebooks*, ed. Hoare and Nowell Smith, 419.

27. Gramsci, "The Study of Philosophy," 326n.

28. Gramsci, "Problems of Marxism," 419.

29. Gramsci, "The Study of Philosophy," 328.

30. Gramsci, "The Study of Philosophy," 330-31. The editors' introduction to Gramsci's prison notebooks suggests that the phrase "philosophy of praxis" was utilized by Gramsci partly as a euphemism for Marxism, employed to deceive the censor, and partly for its own sake (*Selections from the Prison Notebooks*, ed. Hoare and Nowell Smith, xxi).

31. Gilles Deleuze, "Intellectuals and Power: A Conversation between Michel Foucault and Gilles Deleuze," in *Language, Counter-Memory, Practice*, ed. Donald F. Bouchard (Ithaca, N.Y.: Cornell University Press, 1977), 209.

32. In other words, in order for Riggs's video to be read as anything more than a purely idiosyncratic and personal response to the problem of interracial sex, it must evoke Black desire for white men as a collective dilemma.

33. As I have suggested, *Tongues Untied* secures the validity of its version of experience by deploying both poetry and the experimental avant-garde film, both of which are traditionally cast in modernist criticism as highly "personal" forms of expression that paradoxically privilege the individual life story, talent, and vision of the artist while arguing for that vision as "universally" valid. The artist is thus the spokesperson for himself, his community, and all humanity simultaneously. That the video partakes of this modernist ideology of "the universal in the concrete" is evidenced in *Tongues Untied*'s moving back and forth, as it were, between Riggs's "highly personal" vision and universalist claims such as "Black Men Loving Black Men Is *the* Revolutionary Act." Interestingly, when I presented an earlier draft of chapter 4 of this study at a meeting of the Society for Cinema Studies, one of the objections that greeted my argument was that in the video Riggs was speaking merely of his own personal experience and not asking the audience to conclude anything about the cultural problem of interracial gay sex. Such a reading depends on a kind of multiculturalist faith in the desire of the audience to appreciate difference, implying that the value of the film is simply its making visible an "alternative" vision, that of Marlon Riggs. This kind of reading not only reinscribes the autonomy of the artist, but paradoxically undercuts the very "personal is political" mentality on which such

phrases as "Black Men Loving Black Men is *the* Revolutionary Act" depend for their rhetorical force.

34. Leo Bersani, "Is the Rectum a Grave?" in *AIDS: Cultural Analysis, Cultural Activism*, ed. Douglas Crimp (Cambridge, Mass.: MIT Press, 1988), 206.

35. Ibid., 205. Gay activist rhetoric has, perhaps as a result of a perceived failure of a politics rooted exclusively in identity, also managed to produce scathing critiques of its own forgetting that radical sexuality does not equal radical politics. Bersani's observation is perhaps a more sophisticated version of the common activist complaint that many gay men are content to limit their expression of gay pride to participation in a carnival/parade occurring one day a year, as if an annual nose-thumbing at certain forms of power that produce them as (outlawed) gay subjects were equivalent to, and substitutable for, other forms of political protest.

36. Ibid., 207. Bersani is quoting here from Jeffrey Weeks's approving citation of Dyer in *Sexuality and Its Discontents* (London: Routledge & Kegan Paul, 1985), 191.

37. Cornel West, "The New Cultural Politics of Difference," in *Out There: Marginalization and Contemporary Cultures*, ed. Russell Ferguson, Martha Gever, Trinh T. Minh-ha, and Cornel West (New York: New Museum of Contemporary Art, and Cambridge: MIT Press, 1990), 30.

38. Foucault, "The Subject and Power," in Hubert L. Dreyfus and Paul Rabinow, *Michel Foucault: Beyond Structuralism and Hermeneutics* (Chicago: University of Chicago Press, 1983), 212.

39. Marcia Landy, "Cultural Politics and Common Sense," *Critical Studies* 3, no. 1 (1991): 105-34.

40. Gramsci, "The Study of Philosophy," 349.

41. "Ethico-political" is used by Gramsci in the *Prison Notebooks*. See, in particular, "The Study of Philosophy," 366-67. For an extended discussion of the term, see,Sue Golding, *Gramsci's Democratic Theory: Contributions to a Post-Liberal Democracy* (Toronto: University of Toronto Press, 1992).

42. Golding, *Gramsci's Democratic Theory*, 68-87.

43. Gramsci, "The Study of Philosophy," 345.

44. Some of the competitors pursue sex changes; others dress as women in their everyday lives; still others dress only occasionally in women's clothes.

45. bell hooks, "Is Paris Burning?" *Z Magazine*, June 1991, 62.

46. In other words, in reading this necessarily flawed representation of the subaltern, I will be arguing that in this critical moment a valorization rather than a critique of the film will most serve my purposes as a critic. Such a decision necessarily relies on ethics, if we understand ethics as that realm in which "choice," rewritten through the poststructuralist critique of the intentional subject and/in ideology, operates. Clearly, my ethical choices are different from those available to bell hooks, who feels it is imperative to critique this representation of the subaltern. One way of accounting for some of those different choices is to refer to what might be called our differing positionings in relation to this text—my whiteness, hooks's Blackness, my maleness, hooks's femaleness, my homosexuality, hooks's heterosexuality, to name only the most obvious, with the understanding that these terms inadequately name competing historical discursive positionings and not essential qualities. But at least one of the things hooks and I share, though obviously share unevenly, is a certain disciplinary training, and a certain status as colleagues (though of course hooks is by far the more accomplished critic). In my reading of hooks, I will want to focus on the grounds of her critique of the film, and some of the ethical choices on which such grounds rely and depend.

47. Gramsci, "The Study of Philosophy," 330-31.

48. Compare this account of the balls with the following passage from Baudrillard, which describes what Baudrillard terms the recent "satellitization of the real": "What was projected

psychologically and mentally, what used to be lived on earth as metaphor, as mental or meta-phoric scene, is henceforth projected into reality without any metaphor at all, into an absolute space which is also that of simulation" (Jean Baudrillard, "The Ecstasy of Communication," in *The Anti-Aesthetic,* ed. Hal Foster [Port Townsend, Wash.: Bay Press, 1983], 128).

49. For an account of pastiche, see, for example, Fredric Jameson, "Postmodernism and Consumer Society," *The Anti-Aesthetic,* ed. Foster, 111-25.

50. Foucault, "The History of Sexuality," in *Power/Knowledge,* 188.

51. hooks, "Is Paris Burning?" 63.

52. I want to reemphasize here that my critique of Riggs in the previous chapter does not ask that his video move "beyond" its conditions of possibility, but that it attempt to work through them more fully.

53. hooks, "Is Paris Burning?" 62.

54. hooks is also pointing out that had a Black woman "traveled" in a similar fashion to white gay culture to make a film, such questions would undoubtedly be asked of her. Interest-ingly, hooks herself argues that when Livingston is asked directly in an interview about her role as a white lesbian traveling to a world of Black drag queens, her response is completely inad-equate: she suggests that her good will has allowed her to overcome racism and sexism (hooks, "Is Paris Burning?" 63). By drawing attention to the very inadequacy of such confessional mo-ments, hooks's analysis inadvertently highlights here the inadequacy of the very project her theoretical position seems to desire.

55. "Distorted" and "perverted" are hooks's terms ("Is Paris Burning?" 63). hooks's analy-sis seems to depend on one of the old standbys of (white) Western literary criticism, the attrib-uting of the shape of a text to its historical author. hooks's analysis thus reinvigorates the artist as autonomous, intentional subject. Additionally, hooks's extensive focus on the role of Living-ston necessarily involves an essentializing of the subject, an essentializing that also occurs at other moments in her text. hooks in fact ends her essay by implying that "we can confront and accept ourselves as we really are" (64) if we are willing to give up the kind of star identity pursued by the men in the film. This gesture is an instance in which hooks's theoretical project seems to be at cross purposes with itself (not to mention the film and its account of "realness"), for, near the beginning of the essay, hooks insists that drag, one of the obvious themes of Liv-ingston's film, "emerge[s] in a context where the notion of subjectivity is challenged, where identity is always perceived as capable of construction, invention, change" (60). A struggle seems to be occurring in hooks's text between a liberal humanism that fails to problematize the category of the intentional subject, and a more poststructuralist critique of identity.

56. Ibid., 61. Early in her essay, hooks argues that "the film's politics of race, gender, and class are played out in ways that are both progressive and reactionary" ("Is Paris Burning?" 61). Although the theoretical framework from which I read the film would suggest that this state of things is inevitable, hooks appears, in mentioning it, to be criticizing the film. In fact, hooks's essay is structured to withhold its analysis of the "progressive" aspects of the film until its final page, where it discusses the film's representation of Dorian Corey (or, rather, Corey himself). The implication here is that Corey's "experiential" discourse manages to "overcome" Livingston's weaknesses as a filmmaker. This is precisely what the remainder of hooks's analy-sis seeks to deny: the ways in which the film, because of rather than despite its hybrid weave of discursive practices, may produce a multiplicity of readings, some of which might intervene in struggles against racial and class inequity.

57. Before being "discovered" by audiences such as the one described by hooks, the film found its initial success at gay and lesbian film festivals in cities like San Francisco, Los Angeles, and Pittsburgh.

58. hooks, "Is Paris Burning?" 64; my emphasis.

59. This judgment seems in conflict with hooks's initial reading of her own experience of drag as a child, in which she recognizes in the "sites" of cross-dressing and transsexualism "subversive places where gender norms were questioned and challenged" ("Is Paris Burning?" 60).

60. This admittedly idiosyncratic list is culled from my own experience of watching drag shows in gay bars.

61. hooks argues her case that drag privileges white beauty by citing Dorian Corey's contention that "no black drag queen of his day wanted to be Lena Horne" ("Is Paris Burning?" 61). But Corey's testimony here is in fact a statement on how standards of drag glamour have changed. While Corey tells us that in his day everyone wanted to look like Marilyn Monroe, both he and Pepper LaBeija insist that many of the "children" today model themselves not after showgirls or movie stars, but after models, some of whom are Black.

62. See, for example, Judith Butler, *Gender Trouble: Feminism and the Subversion of Identity* (New York: Routledge, 1990). See also, in this context, the more recent work by Marjorie Garber, *Vested Interests: Cross-Dressing and Cultural Anxiety* (New York: Routledge, 1992).

63. hooks, "Is Paris Burning?" 61, quoting Marilyn Frye, "Lesbian Feminism and Gay Rights," in *The Politics of Reality* (Trumansburg, N.Y.: Crossing Press, 1983), 137.

64. Not insignificantly, this aspect of the film suggests that masculinity is as much a masquerade as femininity.

65. For example, the "commonsense" assertion that one must have been "born" gay often arises from the experiential recognition that despite one's best efforts to the contrary, one continues to be positioned within the feminine—the assumption being that only biology can adequately account for this situation in which the subject's intentions are (seemingly) thwarted by his body. Television talk shows seem currently to be one of the discursive arenas in which this "commonsense" formulation circulates, the so-called debates concerning the origin of sexuality always being cast as a matter of either choice or biology, as if it were literally impossible to think of alternatives to these. On more than one occasion, I have seen Oprah Winfrey assert that because the conception of choice makes no sense in this context, one must have been born gay.

66. Drag performances often feature a burlesquing of both male and female bodies through such things as overly large false breasts and grotesque dildos. Though these kinds of "acts" are often separated from the more serious and glamorous numbers, they often occur on the same stage and within the same show.

67. See, for example, Joan Nestle, "The Fem Question," in *Pleasure and Danger*, 232-41.

68. hooks, "Is Paris Burning?" 61.

69. Georges Bataille, "The Notion of Expenditure," in *Visions of Excess: Selected Writings, 1927-1939*, ed. and trans. Alan Stoekl (Minneapolis: University of Minnesota Press, 1985), 118.

70. Bataille, "The Psychological Structure of Fascism," in *Visions of Excess*, ed. and trans. Stoekl, 142.

71. According to Bataille, "Heterogeneous fascist action belongs to the entire set" of imperative forms ("The Psychological Structure of Fascism," 145).

72. Although Bataille might characterize the kind of ostentatious conspicuous consumption detailed in such fantasies as *Dynasty* as privileged instances of nonproductive expenditure, he might also warn that the "fantastic" appeal of *Dynasty*—its appeal as compensatory fantasy—in fact contains, for a middle-class audience at least, its argument in favor of excessive, nonproductive consumption. According to Bataille, there is a tremendous difference between the expenditure of the rich and that of the middle class: "The representatives of the bourgeoisie have adopted an effaced manner; wealth is now displayed behind closed doors, in accordance with depressing and boring conventions. In addition, people in the middle class— employees and small shopkeepers—having attained mediocre or minute fortunes, have man-

aged to debase and subdivide ostentatious expenditure, of which nothing remains but vain efforts tied to tiresome rancor" ("The Notion of Expenditure," 124). Perhaps what helps to render the denizens of *Paris Is Burning* as models for Bataille's ostentatious consumer is that they actually "believe" the "lie" of such fantasies as *Dynasty*. Is it merely a coincidence that the show enjoyed a tremendous gay, as well as minority, following?

73. hooks, "Is Paris Burning?" 61.

74. The instability of representations around Madonna render it difficult to name her form of heterogeneity as definitively elevated or profane. Like the figure of Christ, she seems in the current moment to be slipping back and forth between the two. As I write this draft, her new book, *Sex*, threatens once again either to plunge or elevate her, depending on who is reading her, how she is being read, and where and how those readings circulate.

75. For a more extended discussion of Madonna's relationship to gay and lesbian culture in particular, see my "Stabat Madonna" in *Madonnarama*, ed. Paul Smith and Lisa Frank (Pittsburgh: Cleis Press, 1993), 111-38, as well as several other essays in this collection.

76. Butler, *Gender Trouble*, 142.

77. Kaja Silverman, *Male Subjectivity at the Margins* (New York: Routledge, 1992), 339-88. See pages 342-44 in particular.

78. Butler, *Gender Trouble*, 149.

5. Conclusion

1. Friedrich Nietzsche, "On the Uses and Disadvantages of History for Life," *Untimely Meditations*, trans. R. J. Hollingdale (Cambridge: Cambridge University Press, 1983), 94.

2. An admittedly idiosyncratic list of such work might include: Michel de Certeau, *The Writing of History*, trans. Tom Conley (New York: Columbia University Press, 1988); Dominick LaCapra, *History and Criticism* (New York: Cornell University Press, 1985); Paul Ricoeur, *The Contribution of French Historiography to the Theory of History* (Oxford: Clarendon Press, 1980); and Ranajit Guha and Gayatri Spivak, eds., *Selected Subaltern Studies* (New York: Oxford University Press, 1988).

3. "Rumour evokes comradeship because it belongs to every 'reader' or 'transmitter.' No one is ever its origin or source. Thus rumour is not error but primordially (originarily) errant, always in circulation with no assignable source. This illegitimacy makes it accessible to insurgency" (Gayatri Spivak, "Subaltern Studies: Deconstructing Historiography," in *Selected Subaltern Studies*, ed. Guha and Spivak, 23).

4. Spivak argues, "The problem is that determination, as a critique of causality, has been transformed into determinism as the fixing of causes disguised as the final instance. . . . we are being operated upon by a cultural politics of the transformation of a critique of causality into something that is the most iron-clad philosophy of causality" ("The Problem of Cultural Self-Representation," in *The Post-Colonial Critic*).

5. LaCapra, *History and Criticism*, 17. The first chapter of LaCapra's text is an admittedly brief examination of the continued use by historians of what he terms a documentary model of knowledge.

6. About his course in lesbian and gay history, Michael S. Sherry writes, in the American Historical Association's newsletter, "While I try to experiment in courses on a conventional subject, I try to be conventional in a course whose subject is novel and charged" ("Teaching Lesbian and Gay History," *Perspectives* 31, no. 8 [November 1993]: 8).

7. Nietzsche, "On the Uses and Disadvantages of History for Life," 70.

8. These examples are culled from my own experience of teaching a course in world film history, a course that sought to introduce students to a variety of national cinemas while calling into crisis the unitary status of such terms as "world," "film," and "history."

9. Nietzsche, "On the Uses and Disadvantages of History for Life," 67.

10. Ibid., 116.

11. Walter Benjamin, "Theses on the Philosophy of History," in *Illuminations* (New York: Harcourt, Brace & World, 1968), 256.

12. Nietzsche, "On the Uses and Disadvantages of History for Life," 70. Nietzsche suggests here that such "elevated" effects in themselves might produce effects in future generations. This remark in turn suggests one of the limits of causal thinking: that what we understand as a cause might itself be an effect of an effect (See Spivak's discussion of the term *metalepsis* in "The Post-modern Condition," in *The Post-Colonial Critic*, ed. Sarah Harasym [New York: Routledge, 1990], 23). According to Nietzsche, these effects in themselves are celebrated and fetishized during "popular festivals" and "religious or military anniversaries." Such diverse cultural forms of spectacle as the Fourth of July, the Olympics, and fascist displays of military power all rely to some extent on this privileging of effects in themselves.

13. Michael Denneney, cited in Dennis Altman, *The Homosexualization of America: The Americanization of the Homosexual* (New York: St. Martin's Press, 1982), 73-74.

14. Nietzsche, "On the Uses and Disadvantages of History for Life," 72-74.

15. As Nietzsche warns, "The antiquarian sense of a man, a community, a whole people, always possess an extremely restricted field of vision; most of what exists it does not perceive at all, and the little it does see it sees much too close up and isolated" (74).

16. Ibid., 75. As Nietzsche warns, when history ignores the life of the present, "the habit of scholarliness continues without it and rotates in egoistic self-satisfaction around its own axis. Then there appears the repulsive spectacle of a blind rage for collecting, a reckless raking together of everything that has ever existed. Man is encased in the stench of must and mould" (75). But even when the antiquarian sense does not degenerate into a mindless gathering of obscure and esoteric "facts" and paraphernalia, it still must not rule over the other two modes of historical inquiry. For the antiquarian sense of history "knows only how to preserve life, not how to engender it"; it treats the fact that something has grown old as sufficient cause for preserving it, and hinders the novelty of youth, which necessarily offends some piety or other (75).

17. Paul Monette, *Borrowed Time* (New York: Avon Books, 1988), 21-22. The relationship between a certain image of ancient Greek culture and a contemporary gay identity is explored at length in this memoir, which bears an epigraph from Pindar, "Unsung the noblest deed will die."

18. Nietzsche, "On the Uses and Disadvantages of History for Life," 75-76.

19. These phrases are ransacked from the Benjamin of the "Theses."

20. Nietzsche, "On the Uses and Disadvantages of History for Life," 76.

21. The care of this critique is emblematized nicely in the subtleties of these phrases "new instinct" and "second nature." A careful reading would note that these phrases are oxymorons. Instincts cannot by definition be "new," nor can natures be "second." They are by definition always "old," always historically prior to that which is designated as culture. They attempt to hold the place of that which in the human is not culture. Thus, neither instincts nor natures can literally be implanted by the human. They can't in any sense be new. Nietzsche's deployment of these oxymorons thus interrupts the ease with which we might claim to be capable of escaping our historical placement into a present free from constraints.

22. Gayatri Spivak, "Subaltern Studies: Deconstructing Historiography," in *In Other Worlds* (New York: Routledge, 1988), 201. Spivak explicitly names this here as "the greatest gift of deconstruction."

23. See Michel Foucault, *The Use of Pleasure*, trans. Robert Hurley (New York: Pantheon Books, 1985), and *The Care of the Self*, trans. Robert Hurley (New York: Vintage Books, 1988).

24. "I am well aware that I have never written anything but fictions. I do not mean to say, however, that truth is therefore absent. It seems to me that the possibility exists for fiction to

function in truth, for a fictional discourse to induce effects of truth, and for bringing it about that a true discourse engenders or 'manufactures' something that does not as yet exist, that is, 'fictions' it" (Foucault, "The History of Sexuality," in *Power/Knowledge*, ed. Colin Gordon [New York: Pantheon Books, 1980], 193).

25. Michel Foucault, "Friendship as a Way of Life," in *Foucault Live*, ed. Sylvère Lotringer, trans. John Johnson (New York: Semiotext[e], 1989), 207. This reading of Foucault is defended at length in my "Interrupted Pleasure: A Foucauldian Reading of Hard Core, A *Hard Core* (Mis)reading of Foucault," *boundary* 2, 18, no. 2 (Summer 1991): 181-206.

26. Foucault, "Friendship as a Way of Life," 203-4.

27. Foucault, quoted in Gilles Barbadette, "The Social Triumph of the Sexual Will: A Conversation with Michel Foucault," trans. Brandon Lemon, *Christopher Street* 64 (May 1982): 37.

28. This idea comes from Foucault, cited in Bob Gallagher and Alexander Wilson, "Michel Foucault, An Interview: Sex, Power and the Politics of Identity," *The Advocate*, no. 400 (7 August 1984), 27.

29. As I will be arguing shortly, *Urinal* suggests at a number of different points what Foucault has termed a "reverse" discourse made possible by power. I read this portrayal of the police as pornography as a reminder that, as I have already suggested, pornography represents both an extension of the logic of the visible *and* a counter to that logic.

30. At least one of the conditions of possibility of this hybrid ontological status of film is what Peter Wollen has characterized, after Charles Sanders Peirce, as its deployment of iconic, indexical, and symbolic signs (Wollen, *Signs and Meaning in the Cinema* [Bloomington: Indiana University Press, 1972], 116-54).

31. See, for example, Rudolf Arnheim, "From *Film as Art*," in *Film Theory and Criticism*, ed. Gerald Mast and Marshall Cohen (New York: Oxford University Press, 1985), 246-54; André Bazin, "The Evolution of the Language of Cinema," in *What Is Cinema?* trans. Hugh Gray (Berkeley and Los Angeles: University of California Press, 1967), 23-40; and Jean-Louis Baudry, "Ideological Effects of the Basic Cinematographic Apparatus," in *Movies and Methods II*, ed. Bill Nichols (Berkeley and Los Angeles: University of California Press, 1985), 531-42.

32. I am grateful to Marcia Landy for suggesting the relationship, in a British context, between history, melodrama, and Nietzsche's three modes of historical sense (Landy, "On the Use and Abuse of History in Melodrama," manuscript). Landy in fact discusses a number of British melodramas in relation to Nietzsche's three categories.

33. One man who discusses some of the pleasures and drawbacks of washroom sex appears repeatedly in *Urinal* in a variety of outlandish and campy disguises that parody the kind of disguises worn by guests on such tabloid talk shows as *Geraldo*. The man explains that he is appearing in disguise to prevent what he is saying from being used against him in the future by some court of law or a relative who does not know he is gay. Here, as is often the case in the film, an extremely serious point is made through the use of humor.

34. The difficulty of finding a vocabulary in which to describe a film like *Urinal* adequately highlights some of the ways in which much of the vocabulary of traditional formal film analysis depends on the Hollywood industry. Although film theory of the past twenty years has been interested in attempting to chart the "ideological effects" of the apparatus through a variety of theorists such as Baudry, Mulvey, and Bertolt Brecht, there has been less interest in examining the ideological implications of an analytical vocabulary culled from the industry—as if such a vocabulary were somehow ideologically "neutral." A history of humanist attempts to claim the film analyst as "disinterested" makes possible this continued noninterrogation of such a vocabulary. See, for example, David Bordwell and Kristin Thompson, *Film Art: An Introduction*, 3d ed. (New York: McGraw-Hill, 1990).

35. This image of *Urinal*'s surface as flatbed was suggested to me by Leo Steinberg's discussion of the postmodern canvas surface. See "Other Criteria," *Other Criteria* (London: Ox-

ford University Press, 1976), 84. Steinberg writes, "The flatbed picture plane makes its symbolic allusion to hard surfaces such as tabletops, studio floors, charts, bulletin boards—any receptor surface on which objects are scattered, on which data is entered, on which information may be received, printed, impressed—whether coherently or in confusion" ("Other Criteria," in *Other Criteria* [London: Oxford University Press, 1976], 84).

36. Walter Benjamin, "The Work of Art in the Age of Mechanical Reproduction," in *Film Theory and Criticism*, ed. Gerald Mast and Marshall Cohen (New York: Oxford University Press, 1985), 675-94.

37. Benjamin, "Theses on the Philosophy of History," 255.

38. Nietzsche, "On the Uses and Disadvantages of History for Life," 75, 76.

39. Benjamin, "Theses on the Philosophy of History," 257.

40. Benjamin, "The Work of Art," 694. In our own historical context, it is difficult to read Benjamin's words without being reminded of, for example, the intense spectatorial pleasure unleashed through the media coverage of the Persian Gulf War.

41. Thus, I think it would be a mistake to read Benjamin's account of art in the age of mechanical reproducibility as evidencing primarily or predominantly a nostalgia for the lost aura of the artwork. Such a nostalgia infuses, for example, the first part of John Berger's television series *Ways of Seeing*. One of the difficulties of Benjamin's essay is its rigorous commitment to dialectical thinking. Such thinking appears both in the accounts of historical causality Benjamin provides and in his refusal to assign a clearly negative or positive value to such phenomena as the withering of the artwork's aura.

42. Benjamin, "The Work of Art," 679.

43. Benjamin, "The Author as Producer," in *Reflections*, ed. Peter Demetz (New York: Harcourt Brace Jovanovich, 1978), 220-38.

44. Benjamin's work is clearly in dialogue with that of a variety of his contemporaries. See, for example, *Aesthetics and Politics*, ed. Fredric Jameson (London: Verso, 1980), 120-26, for a brief response by Adorno, in a letter, to Benjamin's essay on art in the age of mechanical reproduction. Adorno suggests that Benjamin's essay is not dialectical enough, in that it overvalorizes the effects of mechanically reproduced art and undervalues the autonomy of high modernist works.

45. Interestingly, Loring's report details how, in 1980, surveillance cameras were deployed by the management of the Puretex factory against women organizers. The management would install cameras over the women's washroom door in order to monitor rest room traffic, as well as the length and frequency of visits. It is thus not merely men's bodies who are subject to such rest room scrutiny.

46. There is also a moment in the film when the police's gaze is directed toward women—in this case, Kahlo and Wyle's tryst in the upstairs washroom, where the police have installed a camera. This moment suggests the commonplace that (presumably) heterosexual men find "lesbian" images arousing.

47. The question of whether gay culture's eroticization of the police also involves an aestheticization is complicated by questions of camp and aesthetics, as well as the question of the relationship between camp and the erotic. I am obliged to read *Urinal*'s eroticization as campy, given such things as the stupidity of the police depicted, and Gray's knowing glance as he dons the police cap. While some theorists have argued that camp is not a turn-on, I would suggest instead that it is a practice so multivalent as not to be antithetical to eroticization. Commonsense examples might include Cher, *The Young Cadets*, and Madonna's "Justify My Love" video.

48. Eisenstein's instructions are as follows: "The Cubicle. (1) Choose one next to an occupied one. (2) After two minutes, flush your toilet, but don't leave. They may do the same. (3) Tap your foot. They may tap theirs. (4) Pass notes back and forth discussing what sort of sex

... (5) Assuming the washroom is empty, you now have several choices: (a) you can both stand on the toilets and watch each other jerk off; (b) you can blow each other under the divider; (c) you can crowd into one cubicle, or (d) have sex with the cubicle doors open, ready to retreat if anyone enters the washroom."

49. Ethics is always an incomplete project, given the fact that the will—always necessarily involved in the production of ethics—can never be absolutely certain of the good grounds for the actions and judgments it directs. Thus there is a continuing need for an understanding of ethics not as a fixed moral code but as a practice of the self subject to transformation.

50. *Urinal* in fact argues against this particular reading of tearoom sex by attempting to deconstruct these binaries. The deconstruction is allegorized in the film's use of the Scrabble board, which spells the two words "public" and "private" out together, joined by the single *P* with which they both begin.

51. Victor Zonana, "Kramer vs. the World," *The Advocate*, 617 (December 1, 1992), 46.

52. Benjamin, "The Author as Producer," 236.

53. See Andreas Huyssen, *After the Great Divide* (Bloomington: Indiana University Press, 1986), 211, and Fredric Jameson, "Postmodernism; or, The Cultural Logic of Late Capitalism," *New Left Review*, no. 146 (July-August 1984), 56.

54. Hal Foster, ed., *The Anti-Aesthetic* (Port Townsend, Wash.: Bay Press, 1983), xi-xii.

55. Benjamin's dialectical understanding of history requires him to note that such concepts as "the long-since-counterfeit wealth of creative personality" are not obliterated in modernity, but rather threaten to be renewed through fascism ("The Author as Producer," 232). Similarly, Benjamin describes not the end of the aura of the work of art but rather its withering. Foster's positing of a "postmodern" break seems thus antidialectical, at least in Benjamin's sense of the term.

56. Huyssen, *After the Great Divide*, 203.

57. Jameson, "Postmodernism and Consumer Society," in *The Anti-Aesthetic*, ed. Foster, 112; emphasis in original.

58. Duchamp is quoted in Edward Lucie-Smith, *Late Modern: The Visual Arts since 1945* (New York: Praeger, 1969), 11.

59. Joan Copjec provides this useful theoretical summary of the theory of the *dispositif* usually translated as "apparatus": "*Dispositif* can be used to signal an adherence to a philosophical tradition which includes, among others, Bachelard, Canguilhem, Foucault, which sets itself against the empiricist position that facts exist outside of the science that discovers them. According to this theory . . . truths are internal to the signifying practices that construct them." According to Copjec, one of the implications of this theory is that "the forms that discourses take are not *expressions* of a last instance, a sovereignty which maintains and reproduces itself through these discourses" (Joan Copjec, "The Anxiety of the Influencing Machine," *October*, no. 23 [Winter 1982], 57-58).

60. *Funk & Wagnalls Standard Dictionary* (New York: New American Library, 1980), s.v. "relative."

61. Interestingly, in an attempt to name the play of effects and countereffects operating in the sexual practices of San Francisco's s/m ghetto, Foucault states: "I dare not use the word *dialectics*—but this comes rather close to it" (Bob Gallagher and Alexander Wilson, "Michel Foucault: An Interview: Sex, Power and the Politics of Identity," 28).

62. Foucault, *The History of Sexuality*, vol. 1, *An Introduction*, trans. Robert Hurley (New York: Vintage Books, 1990), 103. Foucault suggests that sexuality "is not the most intractable element in power relations, but rather one of those endowed with the greatest instrumentality: useful for the greatest number of maneuvers and capable of serving as a point of support, as a linchpin, for the most varied strategies."

Bibliography

Books

Althusser, Louis. *For Marx*. Translated by Ben Brewster. London: Allen Lane, The Penguin Press, 1969.

_____. *Lenin and Philosophy*. Translated by Ben Brewster. New York: Monthly Review Press, 1971.

Altman, Dennis. *The Homosexualization of America: The Americanization of the Homosexual*. New York: St. Martin's Press, 1982.

Ashcroft, Bill, Gareth Griffiths, and Helen Tiffin, eds. *The Empire Writes Back*. London: Routledge: 1989.

Atkins, G. Douglas, and Michael L. Johnson, eds. *Writing and Reading Differently*. Lawrence: University of Kansas Press, 1985.

Bataille, Georges. *Visions of Excess*. Edited and translated by Alan Stoekl. Minneapolis: University of Minnesota Press, 1985.

Bazin, André. *What Is Cinema?* Translated by Hugh Gray. Berkeley and Los Angeles: University of California Press, 1967.

Benjamin, Walter. *Illuminations*. New York: Harcourt, Brace & World, 1968.

_____. *Reflections*. Edited by Peter Demetz. New York: Harcourt Brace Jovanovich, 1978.

Bennett, Tony. *Outside Literature*. London: Routledge, 1990.

Bordwell, David, and Kristin Thompson. *Film Art: An Introduction*. 3d ed. New York: McGraw-Hill, 1990.

Bové, Paul. *In the Wake of Theory*. Hanover, N.H.: University of New England Press, 1992.

Bright, Susie. *Susie Sexpert's Lesbian Sex World*. Pittsburgh: Cleis Press, 1990.

Butler, Judith. *Gender Trouble: Feminism and the Subversion of Identity*. New York: Routledge, 1990.

Butler, Judith, and Joan W. Scott, eds. *Feminists Theorize the Political*. New York: Routledge, 1992.

Certeau, Michel de. *The Writing of History*. Translated by Tom Conley. New York: Columbia University Press, 1988.

Bibliography

Crimp, Douglas, ed. *AIDS: Cultural Analysis / Cultural Activism*. Cambridge: MIT Press, 1988.

de Lauretis, Teresa. *Technologies of Gender*. Bloomington: Indiana University Press, 1987.

Deleuze, Gilles, and Félix Guattari. *A Thousand Plateaus*. Translated by Brian Massumi. Minneapolis: University of Minnesota Press, 1987.

Derrida, Jacques. *Of Grammatology*. Translated, with an introduction, by Gayatri Spivak. Baltimore: The Johns Hopkins University Press, 1976.

Dollimore, Jonathan. *Sexual Dissidence*. Oxford: Clarendon Press, 1991.

Dresher, Melvin. *Games of Strategy*. Englewood Cliffs, N.J.: Prentice-Hall, 1961.

Dreyfus, Hubert L., and Paul Rabinow. *Michel Foucault: Beyond Structuralism and Hermeneutics*. Second edition with an afterword and an interview with Michel Foucault. Chicago: University of Chicago Press, 1983.

Ferguson, Russell, Martha Gever, Trinh T. Minh-ha, and Cornel West, eds. *Out There: Marginalization and Contemporary Cultures*. New York: New Museum of Contemporary Art, and Cambridge: MIT Press, 1990.

Foucault, Michel. *The Archaeology of Knowledge and the Discourse on Language*. Translated by A. M. Sheridan Smith. New York: Pantheon Books, 1982.

_____. *Discipline and Punish*. Translated by Alan Sheridan. New York: Vintage Books, 1979.

_____. *The Final Foucault*. Edited by James Bernauer and David Rasmussen. Cambridge: MIT Press, 1988.

_____. *The History of Sexuality*. Vol. 1, *An Introduction*. Translated by Robert Hurley. New York: Vintage Books, 1990.

_____. *The History of Sexuality*. Vol. 2, *The Use of Pleasure*. Translated by Robert Hurley. New York: Pantheon Books, 1985.

_____. *The History of Sexuality*, Vol. 3, *The Care of the Self*. Translated by Robert Hurley. New York: Vintage Books, 1988.

_____. *Language, Counter-Memory, Practice: Selected Essays and Interview by Michel Foucault*. Translated by Donald F. Bouchard and Sherry Simon. Ithaca, N.Y.: Cornell University Press, 1977.

Gallop, Jane. *Reading Lacan*. Ithaca, N.Y.: Cornell University Press, 1985.

Genette, Gérard. *Palimpsestes: La littérature au second degré*. Paris: Editions du Seuil, 1982.

Gilbert, Sandra. *No Man's Land: The Place of the Woman Writer in the Twentieth Century*. New Haven: Yale University Press, 1988.

Golding, Sue. *Gramsci's Democratic Theory*. Toronto: University of Toronto Press, 1992.

Gramsci, Antonio. *Selections from the Prison Notebooks*. Edited by Quintin Hoare and Geoffrey Nowell Smith. New York: International Publishers, 1971.

Greenberg, David. *The Construction of Homosexuality*. Chicago: University of Chicago Press, 1988.

Griffin, Susan. *Woman and Nature: The Roaring inside Her*. New York: Harper and Row, 1978.

Guha, Ranajit, and Gayatri Spivak, eds. *Selected Subaltern Studies*. New York: Oxford University Press, 1988.

Hart, Jack. *Gay Sex: A Manual for Men Who Love Men*. Boston: Alyson, 1991.

Hemphill, Essex. *Ceremonies: Prose and Poetry*. New York: Plume, 1992.

_____, ed. *Brother to Brother: New Writings by Black Gay Men*. Boston: Alyson Publications, 1991.

hooks, bell. *Feminist Theory from Margin to Center*. Boston: South End Press, 1984.

Huyssen, Andreas. *After the Great Divide*. Bloomington: Indiana University Press, 1986.

Irigaray, Luce. *This Sex Which Is Not One*. Ithaca, N.Y.: Cornell University Press, 1985.

Jameson, Fredric, ed. *Aesthetics and Politics*. London: Verso, 1980.

Bibliography

LaCapra, Dominick. *History and Criticism.* Ithaca, N.Y.: Cornell University Press, 1985.

Lorde, Audre. *Sister Outsider: Essays and Speeches.* Trumansburg, N.Y.: Crossing Press, 1984.

Lucy-Smith, Edward. *Late Modern: Visual Arts since 1945.* New York: Praeger, 1969.

Marx, Karl, and Friedrich Engels. *Basic Writings on Politics and Philosophy.* Edited by Lewis S. Feuer. New York: Anchor Books, 1959.

Mast, Gerald, and Marshall Cohen, eds. *Film Theory and Criticism.* New York: Oxford University Press, 1985.

Monette, Paul. *Borrowed Time.* New York: Avon, 1988.

Morton, Donald, and Zvarzadeh, Mas'ud. *Theory/(Post)Modernity/Opposition.* Washington, D.C.: Maisonneuve Press, 1991.

Nichols, Bill, ed. *Movies and Methods II.* Berkeley and Los Angeles: University of California Press, 1985.

Patton, Cindy. *Inventing AIDS.* New York: Routledge, 1990.

Plummer, Kenneth, ed. *The Making of the Modern Homosexual.* London: Hutchinson, 1981.

Resch, Robert Paul. *Althusser and the Renewal of Marxist Social Theory.* Berkeley and Los Angeles: University of California Press, 1992.

Ricoeur, Paul. *The Contributions of French Historiography to the Theory of History.* Oxford: Clarendon Press, 1980.

Rose, Jacqueline. *Sexuality in the Field of Vision.* London: Verso, 1986.

Said, Edward W. *Orientalism.* New York: Vintage Books, 1978.

_____. *The World, the Text, the Critic.* Cambridge: Harvard University Press, 1983.

Sassoon, Anne Showstack. *Gramsci's Politics.* New York: St. Martin's Press, 1980.

Sedgwick, Eve Kosofsky. *Epistemology of the Closet.* Berkeley and Los Angeles: University of California Press, 1990.

Silverman, Kaja. *Male Subjectivity at the Margins.* New York: Routledge, 1992.

Smith, Barbara Herrnstein. *On the Margins of Discourse.* Chicago: University of Chicago Press, 1978.

Snitow, Ann, Christine Stansell, and Sharon Thomas, eds. *Powers of Desire: The Politics of Sexuality.* New York: Monthly Review Press, 1983.

Spinoza, Benedict de. *The Ethics.* New York: Hafner, 1966.

Spivak, Gayatri. *In Other Worlds: Essays in Cultural Politics.* New York: Routledge, 1988.

Steinberg, Leo. *Other Criteria.* London: Oxford University Press, 1976.

Vance, Carole S., ed. *Pleasure and Danger: Exploring Female Sexuality.* Boston: Routledge, 1984.

Volosinov, V. N. *Marxism and the Philosophy of Language.* Translated by Ladislav Matejka and I. R. Titunik. Cambridge: Harvard University Press, 1986.

Wallerstein, Immanuel. *Historical Capitalism.* London: Verso, 1983.

Weeks, Jeffrey. *Sex, Politics, and Society.* London: Longman, 1981.

_____. *Sexuality and Its Discontents.* London: Routledge & Kegan Paul, 1985.

Williams, Linda. *Hard Core: Power, Pleasure, and the "Frenzy of the Visible."* Berkeley and Los Angeles: University of California Press, 1989.

Wollen, Peter. *Signs and Meaning in the Cinema.* Bloomington: Indiana University Press, 1972.

Wood, Robin. *Hollywood from Vietnam to Reagan.* New York: Columbia University Press, 1986.

Yingling, Thomas E. *Hart Crane and the Homosexual Text.* Chicago: University of Chicago Press, 1990.

Young, Robert. *White Mythologies.* London: Routledge, 1990.

Book-Length Collections of Interviews

Foucault, Michel. *Foucault Live.* Edited by Sylvère Lotringer. New York: Semiotext(e), 1989.

_____. *Power/Knowledge.* Edited by Colin Gordon. New York: Pantheon Books, 1980.

Spivak, Gayatri. *The Post-Colonial Critic.* Edited by Sarah Harasym. New York: Routledge, 1990.

Bibliography

Articles and Essays in Periodicals

Butler, Judith. "The Force of Fantasy: Feminism, Mapplethorpe, and Discursive Excess." *Difference* 2, no. 2 (1990): 105-25.

Champagne, John. "Interrupted Pleasure: A Foucauldian Reading of Hard Core, A *Hard Core* (Mis)Reading of Foucault." *boundary 2* 18, no. 2 (Summer 1991): 181-206.

Chowdhury, Kanishka. "Multiculturalism in the Classroom: Celebrating Diversity, Accommodating Difference." *Mediations* 17, no. 1 (December 1992): 99-101.

Cohen, Ed. "Foucauldian Necrologies: 'Gay' 'Politics'? Politically Gay." *Textual Practices* 2, no. 1 (Spring 1988): 87-101.

Copjec, Joan. "The Anxiety of the Influencing Machine." *October*, no. 23 (Winter 1982): 43-59.

_____. "Response to the Question of the Female Spectator." *Camera Obscura*, no. 20/21 (May-September 1989): 122-23.

Derrida, Jacques. "The Supplement of the Copula." Translated by James Creech and Josue Harari. *Georgia Review* 30 (Fall 1976): 527-64.

Edelman, Lee. "Homographesis." *Yale Journal of Criticism* 3, no. 1 (1989): 189-207.

Flynn, Thomas R. "Truth and Subjectivation in the Later Foucault." *Journal of Philosophy* 82 (October 1985): 531-40.

Gledhill, Christine. "Recent Developments in Feminist Criticism." In *Film Theory and Criticism*, edited by Gerald Mast and Marshall Cohen. New York: Oxford University Press, 1985, 817-45.

Hemphill, Essex. "The Imperfect Moment." *High Performance* 13, no. 50 (Summer 1990): 18-19.

hooks, bell. "Is Paris Burning?" *Z Magazine*, June 1991, 60-64.

Jameson, Fredric. "Postmodernism; or, The Cultural Logic of Late Capitalism." *New Left Review*, no. 146 (July-August 1984): 53-92.

Landy, Marcia. "Cultural Politics and Common Sense." *Critical Studies* 3, no. 1 (1991): 105-34.

Morton, Donald. "The Politics of the Margin: Theory, Pleasure, and the Postmodern Conference." *American Journal of Semiotics* 5, no. 4 (1987): 95-114.

Parker, Andrew. " 'Taking Sides' (On History): Derrida Re-Marx." *Diacritics* 11, no. 4 (Fall 1981): 57-73.

Sherry, Michael S. "Teaching Lesbian and Gay History." *Perspectives* 31, no. 8 (November 1993): 1, 6-9.

Smart, Barry. "On the Subjects of Sexuality, Ethics, and Politics in the Work of Foucault." *boundary 2* 18, no. 1 (Spring 1991): 201-25.

Turetzky, Philip. "Immanent Critique." *Philosophy Today* 33 (Summer 1989): 144-58.

Veyne, Paul. "The Final Foucault and His Ethics." Translated by Catherine Porter and Arnold I. Davidson. *Critical Inquiry* 20 (Autumn 1993): 1-9.

Winders, James A. "Foucault and Marx: A Critical Articulation of Two Theoretical Traditions." *New Orleans Review* 11 (Fall 1984): 134-48.

Zonana, Victor. "Kramer vs. the World." *The Advocate*, no. 617 (1 December 1992): 40-48.

Essays in Anthologies

Baudrillard, Jean. "The Ecstacy of Communication." In *The Anti-Aesthetic*, edited by Hal Foster. Port Townsend, Wash.: Bay Press, 1983. 126-34.

Baudry, Jean Louis. "Ideological Effects of the Basic Cinematographic Apparatus." In *Narrative, Apparatus, Ideology*, edited by Phillip Rosen. New York: Columbia University Press, 1986. 287-98.

Benjamin, Walter. "The Work of Art in the Age of Mechanical Reproduction." In *Film Theory and Criticism*, edited by Gerald Mast and Marshall Cohen. New York: Oxford University Press, 1985. 675-94.

Bibliography

Bersani, Leo. "Is the Rectum a Grave?" In *AIDS: Cultural Analysis/Cultural Activism*, edited by Douglas Crimp. Cambridge: MIT Press, 1988. 197-222.

Cixous, Hélène. "The Laugh of the Medusa." In *Critical Theory since 1965*, edited by Hazard Adams and Leroy Searle. Tallahassee: University Presses of Florida, 1986. 309-20.

Crosby, Christina. "Dealing with Differences." In *Feminists Theorize the Political*, edited by Judith Butler and Joan W. Scott. New York: Routledge, 1992. 130-43.

Derrida, Jacques. "Structure, Sign, and Play in the Discourse of the Human Sciences." In *The Structuralist Controversy*, edited by Richard Macksey and Eugenio Donato. Baltimore: The Johns Hopkins University Press, 1972. 247-72.

Dyer, Richard. "Coming to Terms." In *Out There: Marginalization and Contemporary Culture*, edited by Russell Ferguson, Martha Gever, Trinh T. Minh-ha, and Cornel West. New York: New Museum of Contemporary Art, and Cambridge: MIT Press, 1990. 289-98.

_____. "Resistance through Charisma: Rita Hayworth and *Gilda*." In *Women in Film Noir*, edited by E. Ann Kaplan. London: British Film Institute, 1980. 91-99.

Foucault, Michel. "The Discourse on Language." In *Critical Theory since 1965*, edited by Hazard Adams and Leroy Searle. Tallahassee: University Presses of Florida, 1986. 148-62.

_____. "The Subject and Power." In Hubert L. Dreyfus and Paul Rabinow, *Michel Foucault: Beyond Structuralism and Hermeneutics*. Second Edition with an afterword and an interview with Michel Foucault. Chicago: University of Chicago Press, 1983. 208-26.

_____. "Technologies of the Self." In *Technologies of the Self*, edited by Luther H. Martin, Huck Gutman, and Patrick H. Hutton. Amherst: University of Massachusetts Press, 1988. 16-49.

hooks, bell. "Marginality as Site of Resistance." In *Out There: Marginalization and Contemporary Culture*, edited by Russell Ferguson, Martha Gever, Trinh T. Minh-ha, and Cornel West. New York: New Museum of Contemporary Art, and Cambridge: MIT Press, 1990. 341-43.

Kauffer, David, and Gary Waller. "To Write Is to Read Is to Write, Right?" In *Writing and Reading Differently*, edited by Douglas Atkins and Michael L. Johnson. Lawrence: University Press of Kansas, 1985. 66-92.

Kelly, Dennis D. "Sexual Differentiation of the Nervous System." In *Principles of Neural Science*, edited by Eric Candel and J. Schwartz. New York: Elsevier/North-Holland, 1981. 533-46.

Kipnis, Laura. "(Male) Desire and (Female) Disgust: Reading *Hustler*." In *Cultural Studies*, edited by Lawrence Grossberg, Cary Nelson, and Paula A. Treichler. New York: Routledge, 1992. 373-91.

Luttwak, Edward N. "The Impact of Vietnam on Strategic Thinking in the United States." In *Vietnam: Four American Perspectives*, edited by Patrick J. Hearden. West Lafayette, Ind.: Purdue University Press, 1990. 61-80.

Mercer, Kobena. "Skin Head Sex Thing: Racial Difference and the Homoerotic Imaginary." In *How Do I Look?* edited by Bad Object-Choices. Seattle: Bay Press, 1991. 169-210.

Mulvey, Laura. "Visual Pleasure and Narrative Cinema." In *Movies and Methods II*, edited by Bill Nichols. Berkeley and Los Angeles: University of California Press, 1985. 303-15.

Nietzsche, Friedrich. "On the Uses and Disadvantages of History for Life." In *Untimely Meditations*, translated by R. I. Hollingdale. Cambridge: Cambridge University Press, 1983. 59-123.

Radhakrishnan, R. "Toward an Effective Intellectual: Foucault or Gramsci?" In *Intellectuals: Aesthetics, Politics, Academics*, edited by Bruce Robbins. Minneapolis: University of Minnesota Press, 1990. 57-99.

Scott, Joan W. "Experience." In *Feminists Theorize the Political*, edited by Judith Butler and Joan W. Scott. New York: Routledge, 1992. 22-40.

Bibliography

Spivak, Gayatri. "Can the Subaltern Speak?" In *Marxism and the Interpretation of Culture*, edited by Cary Nelson and Lawrence Grossberg. Urbana: University of Illinois Press, 1988. 271-313.

——. "Reading the World: Literary Studies in the 1980s." In *Writing and Reading Differently*, edited by Douglas Atkins and Michael L. Johnson. Lawrence: University Press of Kansas, 1985. 27-37.

Steinem, Gloria. "Erotica vs. Pornography." In *Outrageous Acts and Everyday Rebellions*. New York: Signet Books, 1983. 247-60.

Stoltenberg, John. "Gays and the Propornography Movement: Having the Hots for Sex Discrimination." In *Men Confront Pornography*, edited by Michael S. Kimmel. New York: Crown, 1990. 248-62.

Studlar, Gaylyn. "Masochism and the Perverse Pleasure of the Cinema." In *Movies and Methods II*, edited by Bill Nichols. Berkeley and Los Angeles: University of California Press, 1985. 602-21.

Wallerstein, Immanuel. "The Ideological Tensions of Capitalism: Universalism versus Racism and Sexism." In Etienne Balibar and Immanuel Wallerstein, *Race, Nation, Class: Ambiguous Identities*. London: Verso, 1991. 29-36.

West, Cornel. "The New Cultural Politics of Difference." In *Out There*. 19-36.

Interviews in Periodicals

Barbadette, Gilles. "The Social Triumph of the Sexual Will: A Conversation with Michel Foucault." Translated by Brendan Lemon. *Christopher Street* 64 (May 1982): 36-41.

Gallagher, Bob, and Alexander Wilson. "Michel Foucault: An Interview: Sex, Power, and the Politics of Identity." *The Advocate*, no. 400 (7 August 1984): 26-30, 58.

Le Bitoux, Jean. "Michel Foucault, Le gai savoir." *Mec* 5 (June 1988): 32-36.

Index

Index

cross dressing, 101, 105-7, 109-12, 116-27, 201 n. 55, 202 nn. 59, 61, 66

deconstruction, 36-37, 39, 65, 91, 173-74 n. 36, 181-82 n. 101, 184 n. 18, 192-93 n. 33, 207 n. 50; American appropriation of, 19; definition of, xxviii-xxix, xxxi, 34-35, 70, 72; and the logic of the supplement, xxvi, xxxviii, xli-xliii, 31, 49; of the real, 93, 109, 116; Spivak on, 141, 171 n. 19, 184-85 n. 32, 198 n. 15, 199 n. 20; West's critique of, 101. *See also* Derrida, Jacques
de Lauretis, Teresa, xl-xliv, 65, 173 n. 36, 174 nn. 37, 42. *See also* Foucault, Michel
Deleuze, Gilles, 8-11, 99, 192 n. 33
Derrida, Jacques, 20, 35-36, 57, 68, 70, 73, 90, 171 n. 19, 173 n. 36, 194 n. 46
Dews, Peter, 176-77 n. 20
Discipline and Punish, xxvii, 29-30, 49, 141, 154
disciplines/disciplinarity, 36-37, 46, 49-50, 56, 140, 156, 165; academic, xxxi-xxxii, xlv, 44-45, 48-49, 60, 87, 194 n. 53, 196 n. 1, 196-97 n. 3, 197 n. 9; Foucault on, xxxi, 4-5, 29-30, 49, 60, 164. *See also* gay and lesbian studies
"Discourse on Language," 14-15, 93-94
dispositif, definition of, 207 n. 59
Dollimore, Jonathan, 176 n. 11, 182 n. 101
drag. *See* cross dressing
Duchamp, Marcel, 147, 159-61
Dworkin, Andrea, 42, 59, 79, 185 n. 48, 194 n. 57
Dyer, Richard, xxx, 32-42, 44-45, 49-50, 56, 100-101, 184 nn. 18, 19, 186 n. 55, 187 n. 63

Edelman, Lee, 181-82 n. 101
ethical criticism, definition of, xxviii-xxxvii, 31-32, 87, 107
ethics, xxxiii-xxxiv, 49, 91, 98-99, 103, 133, 157, 159, 182 n. 101, 200 n. 46, 207 n. 49; Foucault on, xxix-xxx, xxxii, 7, 141, 172 n. 22; Hirsch on, xxviii-xxix; of marginality, definition of, xxxii, 31, 157
"experience," 88-92, 100, 102, 114-15, 195 n. 58, 196 n. 2, 197 n. 8, 199-200 n. 33; as common sense, 98-99, 103-5, 107-8, 110-13, 116-17, 122;

poststructuralist rewriting of, 92-96. *See also* Scott, Joan W.

females/women, xxxvi, 7, 9, 65-66, 154, 195 n. 65. *See also* feminism; gender; homosexuals/homosexuality, female; sexuality, female
feminism, xl-xliv, 7, 69, 93, 115, 132, 174 nn. 2, 42, 43, 177 n. 27, 194 n. 57; and critique of cross dressing, 120-21; and critique of pornography, 33-34, 43, 50, 59, 79; and historicism, 65-66; men in, xxxvi; psychoanalytic, xxvi-xxvii, 43, 186 n. 58
film theory, psychoanalytic, 45-46, 48-49
Foster, Hall, 160
Foucault, Michel, 18, 20, 51, 64, 90, 162, 173-74 n. 36, 176 n. 11, 179 n. 54, 191 n. 28, 199 n. 21, 207 n. 59; on care of the self, xxix-xxx, xxxii, xliii, 52-54, 141-42; on desire, 11, 178-79 n. 48; de Lauretis, Teresa, on, xl-xli, xliii-xliv; on discourse, 93-94, 172 n. 21, 180 n. 84, 198 nn. 13, 14, 15; and Gramsci, 9-10, 99, 178 n. 41, 190-91 n. 16; as a historian, 6, 141-42; on the intellectual, 6, 8-13, 95, 99, 163-64, 190-91 n. 16; on power, xxiii, xxviii, xli, 5-9, 11-13, 21-24, 49, 54-55, 71, 82, 101-2, 113, 162-65, 170-71 n. 12, 176 n. 15, 178 n. 41, 186-87 n. 61, 189 n. 10, 190-91 n. 16, 199 n. 20, 207 n. 62; on struggles, 8, 11-13, 60; on subjugated knowledges, 8-10, 111; on transgression, xxvi-xxvii, xliii, 30; on truth, 23, 95, 181 n. 97, 194 n. 46, 198 n. 17, 204-5 n. 24. *See also* disciplines/disciplinarity; ethics; homosexuals/homosexuality; ideology; politics; subject/subjectivity
Fraser, Nancy, 176-77 n. 20
Freud, Sigmund, 1, 15, 17
Frye, Marilyn, 120-21

Gallop, Jane, 175 n. 4
gay and lesbian studies, xliv-xlvi, 31, 61, 89-91, 127-28, 194 n. 57, 197 nn. 4, 6
gays and lesbians. *See* homosexuality
"Gays and the Propornography Movement." *See* Stoltenberg, John

216

Index

Index

Landy, Marcia, 26-27, 104, 205 n. 32
lang, k. d., 136
"Lesbian Feminism and Gay Rights." *See* Frye, Marilyn
lesbians/lesbianism. *See* homosexuals/ homosexuality, female
Lévi-Strauss, Claude, 2, 35, 70
Livingston, Jennie. *See Paris Is Burning*
Lorde, Audre, 70, 167
Luttwak, Edward N., xxxviii

Madonna, 61, 74, 124-25, 203 n. 74
"(Male) Desire and (Female) Disgust." *See* Kipnis, Laura
Male Subjectivity at the Margins. See Silverman, Kaja
Mapplethorpe, Robert. *See* Hemphill, Essex, reading of
Marx, Karl, 1, 15, 17, 21-23, 26, 172 n. 25, 182 n. 101
Marxism, 1-3, 17-18, 21, 23, 199 n. 30
Meinhold, Keith, 136
"Migrant Identities." *See* Hall, Stuart
Modleski, Tania, xlii, 66
Monette, Paul, 138-39
Morgan, Robin, 59-60
Morton, Donald, 178 n. 43, 196 n. 1
Mulvey, Laura, 187 n. 64

"native informant," figure of, 72-73, 82, 91, 94-95, 106-7, 197 n. 3
Nietzsche, Friedrich, xxxiv, 18, 130, 132, 141-43; on antiquarian history, 133, 137-39, 204 nn. 15, 16; on critical history, 133, 139-40, 147-48, 157; on the greybeards, 129-31, 134-35, 137; on monumental history, 133-35, 139, 204 n. 12. *See also* subject/subjectivity
Ninja, Willi, 74, 106, 112, 124
nonproductive expenditure, 36, 123-25, 134, 166-67, 185 n. 41; Bataille, on, 28-30, 55, 59, 122-24, 129, 140, 143, 187 n. 73, 195 n. 60, 202-3 n. 72. *See also* homosexuals/homosexuality; pornography
"Not a Love Story." *See* Morgan, Robin

Orientalism (Said), xxxv

Paris Is Burning, xxxiv, 74, 88, 104-5, 108-12, 127, 156, 201 n. 57, 203 n. 72; bell

hooks's critique of, 106-7, 113-24, 126, 201 nn. 54, 55, 56, 202 n. 61
Patton, Cindy, 12-13
Peirce, Charles Sanders, 205 n. 30
Pinkerton, James P., xxiii-xxv
politics, xxxii, 8, 51, 91-92, 116, 118; and art, 147-50, 159-62; of explanation, 58, 67, 86, 150, 159; Foucault on, 6, 14-15, 26, 172 n. 24, 177 n. 20; Gramsci's definition of, 17, 104-5; identity, 66, 79, 85-86, 91, 93, 96, 100, 102-3, 116, 125-26, 159; poststructuralist challenge to, xxxviii-xxxix; Spivak on, 172 n. 24; and subjectivity, xxxiii-xxxv, 60-62, 99-103, 120, 122, 126-28, 161, 165-66, 200 n. 35; and visibility, 69-71, 91
pornography, gay, 144-45, 185 n. 36, 194 n. 57, 205 n. 29; as commodity, 32, 44, 47-48; conditions of reception, 34, 37, 39, 45-49, 186 n. 59, 187 n. 63; critique of, 33-34, 41, 44, 50-52, 59-60, 67, 77-79, 83, 195 n. 59; and the gaze, 46-49, 186 nn. 58, 61, 187 nn. 62, 64; and narrative, 33-41; as nonproductive expenditure, xxxiv, 30-32, 42-43, 50-51, 56, 79, 85, 186 n. 55; redundancy of, 38-39, 47-48
postmodernism, 110, 159-60, 205-6 n. 35, 207 n. 55
power, xxx, 32, 44, 68, 105, 112-13, 165-66; and resistance, xlii, 47, 92, 154-57, 161-62, 163, 165-67; as strategic relations, xxv, 32, 107. *See also* Foucault, Michel
Prison Notebooks. See Gramsci, Antonio
privileged marginal, figure of, 31-32, 73, 81-82, 90, 124
psychoanalysis, 1-3, 7, 52, 62, 138, 170-71 n. 12, 174-75 n. 4, 188 n. 77. *See also* feminism, psychoanalytic

QUASH, xxiv-xxv
Queer Nation, xxiii, 139
queer studies/queer theory. *See* gay and lesbian studies

race, 12-13, 57-59, 68, 74-75, 80, 194 n. 52, 195 n. 62
racism, xxvi, 75, 100, 108-9, 114-16, 119; Wallerstein's account of, 80-84, 196 n. 69. *See also* homosexuality and racism

218

John Champagne is currently an assistant professor at Pennsylvania State University, Erie, The Behrend College, where he teaches English. His work has appeared in such journals as *boundary 2, CineAction!* and *PostScript*. He is also a novelist, poet, and essayist. His novels include *The Blue Lady's Hands* and *When the Parrot Boy Sings*, and personal essays have appeared in John Preston's *Hometowns* and *A Member of the Family*.

Donald E. Pease holds the Ted and Helen Geisel Chair in Humanities at Dartmouth College. He is the author of *Visionary Compacts: American Renaissance Writings in Cultural Context*, editor of six volumes on American literature, and general series editor of *New Americanists*.